LIFT UP YOUR eyes

LIFT UP YOUR eyes

DAILY ENCOUNTERS WITH GOD FOR LEADERS

Christopher Shaw

Fort Washington, PA 19034

• Lift Up Your Eyes •

Published by CLC ❖ Publications

U.S.A.
P.O. Box 1449, Fort Washington, PA 19034

GREAT BRITAIN
51 The Dean, Alresford, Hants, SO24 9BJ

AUSTRALIA
P.O. Box 2299, Strathpine, QLD 4500

NEW ZEALAND
10 MacArthur Street, Feilding

ISBN 978-0-87508-989-5

Originally published in Spanish by Desarrollo Cristiano Internacional
as *Alza Tus Ojos*, © 2005

Printed in the United States of America

To my beloved wife, Iris

He who finds a wife finds a good thing,
And obtains favor from the LORD.
(Proverbs 18:22, NAS)

I would like to express my deep appreciation to Audrey Urquhart, who invested six months in producing an excellent English translation of the original Spanish manuscript.

Foreword

Leadership in a society bent on relativism is difficult. Christopher Shaw has written a refreshing devotional for those in today's church called to this responsibility, whatever their positions. Using Scripture, he gently and consistently brings out straightforward truths so easily overlooked in the rush of a pressing culture.

In this challenging book, Christopher points out the limitations and pitfalls of human solutions—including increased programming, overbearing authority structures and exhausting efforts to please individuals. He exhorts leaders to look instead to the Source of help and guidance, Jesus Christ. Warmly and realistically, these daily meditations emphasize that only Christ—living in you—will produce the character necessary for fruitful service.

Luis Palau
World Evangelist

Overcoming Faith

January **1**

Early the next morning Abraham got up and saddled his donkey. He took with him two of his servants and his son Isaac. When he had cut enough wood for the burnt offering, he set out for the place God had told him about. Genesis 22:3

Faith should be a distinguishing quality in the life of a leader. Much confusion exists, however, about the real meaning of faith. For many, faith is little more than a vague desire that things turn out all right or hoping that circumstances may be favorable. We are often told to live with more faith or sing our songs with greater faith—which reveals how often faith is used as another word for enthusiasm.

Abraham's response to the Lord in Genesis 22 gives a clear idea of what faith is all about. God instructed Abraham to take his only son, Isaac, and offer him as a living sacrifice to the Lord. There is no doubt that these words must have precipitated a profound personal crisis for the patriarch. As the long night dragged on, he must have experienced excruciating agony as he fought to reconcile himself with this unbelievable request. How could God ask him to offer up his long-awaited son, his promised heir?

Abraham did not allow his feelings to interfere with his decision. He knew that obedience is absolutely crucial to our relationship with God, even when the Lord's commands make no sense whatsoever. If we walk with Him, our call is that we be "slaves to righteousness" (Rom. 6:18).

Note the abundance of verbs in today's verse: He *got up* early, *saddled* his donkey, *took* two of his servants and *cut* wood and *went* to the place God had told him about. Despite the depth of his anguish, Abraham started very early in the morning to carry out God's instructions, revealing to us the essence of faith. Faith is the certainty that we can only taste God's faithfulness by walking in His Word. It is the assurance that, no matter how difficult our path seems, the Lord will walk with us every step of the way. In this particular situation, "Abraham reasoned that God could raise the dead, and figuratively speaking, he did receive Isaac back from death" (Heb. 11:19).

We live in times in which God's people are constantly faced with trying circumstances. If we expect those we lead to live by faith, we ourselves must show the same steadfast confidence in God that Abraham demonstrated. The most powerful evidence of our trust will be not be found in our efforts to inspire with eloquent words, but rather in the strength of our obedience.

May the Lord grant that the description of our faith contains an abundance of verbs!

Food for Thought

How often do you feel uncomfortable with God's Word? What reaction does His call to absolute obedience produce in you? What steps can you take to make your faith more active?

Living with Injustice

But Joseph said to them, "Don't be afraid. Am I in the place of God? You intended to harm me, but God intended it for good to accomplish what is now being done, the saving of many lives." Genesis 50:19–20

It is easy to make sacrifices and endure trials for worthy causes. But when we are victims of injustice, we struggle with deep feelings of pain and betrayal, especially if the wound is inflicted by someone we love. This agony is expressed by the psalmist: "If an enemy were insulting me, I could endure it; if a foe were raising himself against me, I could hide from him. But it is you, a man like myself, my companion, my close friend, with whom I once enjoyed sweet fellowship as we walked with the throng at the house of God" (Ps. 55:12–14).

Mature leaders must deal with injustice. If they don't, bitterness will slowly steal their joy and peace and eventually end the effectiveness of their ministry. Joseph's brothers provide an example of the poison that can develop from unresolved conflict. Despite the 44 years which had passed since they had mercilessly sold Joseph into slavery, they were still tormented by what they had done, terrified of revenge. They were haunted by something done almost 50 years before!

We don't know exactly when Joseph recovered from the devastating consequences of being sold by his brothers, but today's text contains two principles which helped him get over this crisis. First, Joseph understood that he was not in God's place; therefore, it was not for him to judge his brothers. Our judgment will always be blurred by the limitations of our humanity. Only God can judge according to the truth; that's why this responsibility is not given to men. Even the Son of God abstained from evaluating others, as He pointed out to the Jews: "You judge by human standards; I pass judgment on no one" (John 8:15).

Second, Joseph maintained a profound conviction that God was behind what had happened to him. This is fundamental for God's people. All too often our initial reaction to injustice is to question God's goodness, asking why He has allowed such a thing to happen. Years passed before Joseph was able to see God's purpose in allowing such a tragedy to touch his life. But the conviction that God can transform the worst evil into blessing never left him, and this protected his heart from bitterness and animosity.

Food for Thought

Notice the beauty of the scene presented today. Joseph, who had been so unjustly treated by his brothers, was moved to tears by their anxiety. Then he spoke fondly to them and promised to provide for their future. This is the most convincing evidence that God had been at work in his life: The injured party was able to minister to those who had hurt him. This truly is a gift from on High!

Correction that Restores

And the Lord's servant must not quarrel; instead, he must be kind to everyone, able to teach, not resentful. Those who oppose him he must gently instruct, in the hope that God will grant them repentance leading them to a knowledge of the truth.
2 Timothy 2:24–25

Human beings have a natural tendency to stray from the path of God's choosing. It naturally follows that an aspect of Christian leadership involves turning "many from sin" (Mal. 2:6). The manner in which we do this, however, should be given careful consideration.

Paul reminds Timothy, first of all, that a servant of God should avoid getting involved in pointless heated discussions. This exhortation is repeated several times in the apostle's letters to the young pastor. We tend to believe that truth penetrates peoples' hearts in proportion to the eloquence and vehemence of our arguments. But the intensity with which we make our point frequently reveals impatience and unkindness toward those whose opinions differ from our own.

Second, Paul points out to his spiritual son that he has been called to suffering. And at times suffering can result from having to keep silent. We do have a responsibility to warn others of the consequences of resisting God's truth, but we cannot insist that they take our advice. Sometimes, as when Christ warned Peter that he would later betray Him, we are called to stand by as someone moves ahead in his folly. The Lord twice repeated His warning to the disciple and then said no more. He knew the Word would continue to work in Peter's heart and, in due course, produce the desired result. Knowing we can do nothing to keep someone from the pain of foolish behavior causes us to suffer.

Third, Paul warns that all correction should be carried out in a spirit of tenderness. Correction often comes in the form of heated accusations, filled with anger and censure. God's servants, however, must act with a spirit of affection, clearly understanding that their influence cannot bring about repentance. God is able to speak to every heart; we must maintain a deep conviction that each life is in God's hands. Any correction offered, therefore, should complement what the Lord is already doing in that life. We speak a word from the Lord and then rest—allowing space for the work of the Spirit, part of which is to "convict the world . . . in regard to sin" (John 16:8).

When we know that someone is sinning, we are responsible to speak a timely word into their lives. But the rest of our energy should be spent in speaking to God about the matter. Our help will no doubt be much more effective!

Food for Thought

What is your initial reaction to incorrect attitudes or behavior in others? What does this reveal about you? What adjustments can you make so you can correct others with a more tender attitude?

Swords Always Sharpened

He replied, "This kind can come out only by prayer." Mark 9:29

It is not clear what caused the disciples greater frustration: the fact that they were unable to cure the epileptic or Jesus' explanation as to why they couldn't do it.

We shouldn't be surprised that the disciples felt ashamed. Instead of helping the young man, they got mixed up in an argument with the Pharisees. When Jesus arrived, His simple and authoritative approach toward the boy stood in dramatic contrast to the disciples' insecurity. It was probably embarrassment over their ineffectiveness that made them ask for an explanation!

But the Lord's reply did not seem to shed much light on the situation. Why did He say it was necessary to pray—and to fast, according to some ancient manuscripts—when He in fact neither prayed nor fasted as He delivered the young man? He simply asked His Father something about the situation and then drove out the demon—just like that! So how could He say that prayer and fasting are the keys to success? Did He mean that the disciples should have prayed because they didn't have the same authority He had? I doubt that was His point.

Jesus' comment shows that prayer must be a fundamental component of our armor in the fight against evil. The moment to rely on prayer, however, is not in the heat of battle. We can't stop to sharpen our weapons when the Enemy is upon us. When a situation arises which requires immediate action, the servant of God must be ready as a result of time spent in prayer *before* the battle. Only through time in God's presence can we achieve the wisdom and authority necessary for effective ministry. This is certainly one of the reasons Jesus frequently withdrew alone to pray.

On this occasion Jesus had come from the Mount of Transfiguration where He had experienced a unique encounter with the Father. Spiritually, His senses were sharpened through this time with God; He was already covered in prayer. When the opportunity for ministry arose, He was able to act decisively.

This has been characteristic of fruitful ministry throughout the history of God's people. Those who have led powerfully have always had well-developed prayer lives. This should be true of us today. Leadership constantly brings us face to face with unexpected situations. We often have no advance warning; we must intervene immediately. So how can we fail to utilize times of peace and quiet in order to develop the spiritual vitality needed for moments of action? If we are to defeat the Enemy, we must keep our swords sharpened!

Food for Thought

How much time do you dedicate each day to the development of your spiritual life? Which disciplines do you practice for this purpose? On what aspects of this spiritual exercise do you need to improve?

The Power of Joy

This day is sacred to our Lord. Do not grieve, for the joy of the L*ORD* *is your strength.*
Nehemiah 8:10

While reconstructing the walls of Jerusalem, the Israelites faced many obstacles. They battled rumors, discord, opposition and weariness. More than once they felt overwhelmed and were tempted to quit.

Such a difficult situation invites despair; it is fertile ground for exhaustion to lodge in our souls. Worn out, we carry on with heavy hearts. These are normal reactions to problems that seem endless. Jesus Himself, faced with the imminence of the cross, became sad and downcast. He confessed to His disciples, "My soul is overwhelmed with sorrow to the point of death" (Matt. 26:37).

Wise leaders are under no illusion about their real feelings. Nonetheless, they know these feelings must be dealt with before their spiritual life becomes affected. Jesus didn't hesitate to ask for companionship from His three friends while He prayed. He knew that when this kind of despair becomes a permanent feature of our lives, it deeply affects our perspectives and reactions. We tend to have negative and defeated attitudes; we feel like giving up, believing there is no solution to our problem. This outlook leads invariably to depression, because nobody can live without hope indefinitely. Disheartened individuals are already defeated because they have lost the will to carry on fighting.

Jesus, like Nehemiah, knew it was essential to revive the joy that is the source of our strength. His agony in Gethsemane continued until He had recovered His joy. Thus strengthened, He endured the cross "for the joy set before him" (Heb. 12:2). This kind of joy is not a feeling, but a spiritual conviction. Circumstances may be extremely unfavorable, but joy fills our hearts when we turn our eyes away from visible things and place them firmly on what is unseen (2 Cor. 4:18).

Leaders whose hearts are full of joy are really invincible, because their lives are solidly rooted in things eternal and not in temporary worldly pleasures. They are firmly convinced that a sovereign God reigns over everything, and that He delights to use adversity and even defeat to bless His people.

Do not allow crises to daunt you. In times of need, pour out your soul to God, as Christ did at Gethsemane. Whatever happens, recover the joy of belonging to a people who follow an invincible God. Those you serve need to see a leader unafraid of facing difficulties, a leader who is confident that our heavenly Father has the last word in every situation.

Food for Thought

What is your normal reaction to the difficulties and crises you face? What steps do you take to overcome feelings of defeat and discouragement? What can you do each day to foster joy in your life?

6 January | The Blessing of Being Authentic

Then Saul dressed David in his own tunic. He put a coat of armor on him and a bronze helmet on his head. David fastened on his sword over the tunic and tried walking around, because he was not used to them. "I cannot go in these," he said to Saul, "because I am not used to them." So he took them off. 1 Samuel 17:38–39

Imitation is common throughout the church. A well-known evangelist pounds the Bible and paces the platform, and without a doubt, other evangelists will appear pounding and pacing in the same way. If a renowned musician employs certain phrases to move the public, before long we'll hear the same phrases repeated everywhere. If a television preacher wears a white suit and black shoes, we will soon see others dressed the same way.

This shows our tendency to believe that the *way* we do things, rather than *who* we are, secures God's blessing. We think if we manage to copy someone's style, we will receive the favor bestowed on their ministry.

When David offered to face Goliath, Saul was skeptical, saying, "You are only a boy, and he has been a fighting man from his youth" (1 Sam. 17:33). But Jesse's youngest son decided to follow through. Since David's mind was made up, the king lent him his battle gear. Perhaps out of respect the young shepherd donned the heavy armor and took the sword in his hand, but found them unwieldy. He rejected them, choosing instead the shepherd's crook and sling that he used daily.

Even if Saul's clothes had fit, they would have been no good to David. They were the armor and weapons of another man. David's decision holds an important principle: When the Lord uses people, it is with their own abilities and gifts; they need not reach for the methods of another.

The church does not need imitators of the great leaders of the moment. It needs men and women who are faithful with what they have received. If you try to be something you are not, no one else can fill the space you leave empty. You are the one God prepared for your position. Do not be ashamed of who you are, nor of your weapons. Perhaps they are less impressive than others', but they are the tools which have been useful to you in the past. Don't apologize for what you are. The blessing of the Lord will rest on your life when you genuinely become what God has prepared you to be. No imitation can ever be as good as the original! Hold your head high and walk in confidence. The Lord is with you!

Food for Thought

Do you recognize the tools God has given you for His calling on your life? How can you use them most effectively? What do you think would result if you used someone else's tools in your ministry?

A Two-Edged Sword

January 7

"I tell you the truth," Jesus answered, "this very night, before the rooster crows, you will disown me three times." But Peter declared, "Even if I have to die with you, I will never disown you." And all the other disciples said the same. Matthew 26:34–35

It is wonderful to see someone enthusiastic about their faith, passionately sharing their convictions. We can't help being moved by their fervor and stimulated by their contagious attitudes. It does us good to be around this kind of person.

Peter was a man who lived his life passionately. He was the one who dared to walk on the water. But he didn't realize what he was doing until he noticed the waves surrounding him! He was also the one who enthusiastically suggested building booths on the Mount of Transfiguration, although the Word tells us he didn't know what he was saying (Mark 9:6). When the Lord asked His disciples questions, it was always Peter who answered first.

Enthusiasm is an important quality for a leader to possess. How can we motivate people if our words and behavior show little conviction, or worse still, indifference? There is no question that passion plays an important role in our ministries. We should remember, though, that enthusiasm can also be dangerous. Our passion can be so intense at times that not even the Lord can dissuade us from our goal. Peter loved the Lord greatly! He desperately wanted to express the depth of his commitment. He fervently proclaimed he would never turn his back on Jesus, even if others did. Jesus tried twice to warn him, but his passion was such that he resisted advice from anyone, even the Son of God Himself.

By all means, infuse your ministry with enthusiasm. Celebrate being part of a plan born in the heart of God Himself! But don't forget that passion has more than one source and is not always of the Spirit. There is a passion of the flesh, and it can be our undoing. Paul speaks about the Israelites with sadness saying, "For I can testify about them that they are zealous for God, but their zeal is not based on knowledge" (Rom. 10:2). Who could testify to this better than he? In his youth, out of false passion for God, he had viciously persecuted the church!

Though important, we must be tremendously careful with passion. Do not be bland; let fervor be a characteristic of your leadership. But don't blindly follow the path of emotion. You could end up where you never imagined—denying the Lord.

Food for Thought

Are you a passionate person? How do you demonstrate it? What can you do to ensure that your enthusiasm doesn't lead you astray?

A Mysterious Process

Mourn with those who mourn. Romans 12:15

Tears make us uncomfortable. When we see someone crying, we don't always know how to react. We try to say something helpful, cheer them up or at least get them to stop. This is probably in part because many have been brought up to view tears as unacceptable. In subtle ways it was taught that real winners should not be seen crying.

A leader's tears, however, are a visible manifestation of compassion. Jesus wept. He wept at Lazarus' tomb and again when He saw the spiritual state of Jerusalem. According to Hebrews, He was heard in Gethsemane because "he offered up prayers and petitions with loud cries and tears" (Heb. 5:7).

Jesus' tenderness contrasts strongly with the attitude of Israel's pastors. Ezekiel rebuked them in one of Scripture's toughest passages toward leaders: "You have not strengthened the weak or healed the sick or bound up the injured. You have not brought back the strays or searched for the lost. You have ruled them harshly and brutally" (Ezek. 34:4).

It seems obvious, then, that the subject of compassion is a serious business for those called to leadership. But when we encounter people who have broken down, we find it hard to resist offering advice or quoting Romans 8:28. We are convinced that what they are looking for is an answer to their problems.

Helping *is* important, but Paul directs us to something simpler and much more effective than words. He does not tell us to advise a sorrowing person but rather to weep with those who weep. It's as simple as that.

This doesn't necessarily mean we must shed visible tears. But the intention is that our heart should be deeply affected by the person's suffering. During a crisis advice is not the foremost need. What is essential is the comfort of being understood, of knowing that the pain is felt by those who care. Being able to identify with a troubled person is much more therapeutic than all the wise words we can think of because it opens a channel of God's love from our heart to theirs.

In time opportunities for talking and counseling will undoubtedly arise. But do not lose the chance to become one with those who suffer. God will do great things in healing that life, but He will also touch you deeply. May tears be a distinguishing mark of your leadership!

Food for Thought

What was the attitude to tears in your childhood home? When you see a person crying, what is your first reaction? How can you show compassion for those to whom you minister?

Secure in Him

A furious squall came up, and the waves broke over the boat, so that it was nearly swamped. Jesus was in the stern, sleeping on a cushion. The disciples woke him and said to him, "Teacher, don't you care if we drown?" Mark 4:37–38

It is certainly not difficult to understand the disciples' indignation! Picture the scene. A terrible storm roared all around; the wind howled and the waves smashed fiercely against the boat. The disciples were soaked by the sea foam and by the water collecting in the boat as they fought desperately to stay afloat. And where was Jesus? Asleep in the stern. It's not surprising that they thought He didn't care.

Why was the Lord asleep? He was probably simply exhausted, having spent the day preaching to crowds. His calm, however, came from another source. He had told the disciples to cross the lake—but we can confidently say that these instructions had not just occurred to Him. He taught His disciples, "By myself I can do nothing," (John 5:30) and later in the same Gospel, He stated, "For I have come down from heaven, not to do my will but to do the will of him who sent me" (John 6:38). The order to cross the lake came, first and foremost, from His Father.

This was the key to Jesus' tranquility in the midst of the storm. He was not worried; He knew that His Father, who had told them to cross the lake, would take them safely to the other shore. His peace came from the profound conviction that Someone greater was overseeing their welfare. If God had sent them across the lake, what could stop them?

Leaders need the quiet assurance that comes when one is certain of the destination. Wouldn't it be wonderful if the peace the disciples eventually drew from Jesus was the same peace today's troubled society could draw from the church? For this to happen we need pastors who know not only where they are going, but also why. Like Moses, speaking to the Israelites as they panicked at the Red Sea, we must be able to tell our people, "Do not be afraid. Stand firm and you will see the deliverance the LORD will bring you today. The Egyptians you see today you will never see again. The LORD will fight for you; you need only to be still" (Exod. 14:13–14).

We can have this confident attitude and be filled with peace, if we are absolutely sure of our direction. The only way to obtain that certainty is to seek the will of God, whom we serve. If we walk in "the good works which God prepared in advance" (Eph. 2:10), no storm can possibly block our way! Step out with confidence; God is in control.

Food for Thought

Can we clearly explain our destination? Do we know why we are going this way? What evidence do we have that this direction is from God?

Looking After Our Team

When the apostles returned, they reported to Jesus what they had done. Then he took them with him and they withdrew by themselves to a town called Bethsaida. Luke 9:10

At the end of the disciples' first ministerial journey, they returned to Jesus full of stories of their adventures. They also brought questions concerning situations which had challenged them. The Lord took the necessary time to listen and then led them away to a quiet place.

It is in His last decision that we see another aspect of the Lord's pastoral heart. Jesus knew only too well the cost involved in serving others. Endless demands, intense concentration, energy drain and excitement are all part and parcel of the job we call ministry. All these things affect leaders. Ministers who constantly serve but fail to renew their strength will end up completely exhausted. Their ministry will become ineffective and they will suffer terrible frustration; the work will feel like a continual uphill climb. We need time for rest and recovery in order to continue ministering in the Spirit and not in the flesh. This is why Jesus took the disciples aside by themselves.

As leaders, one of our priorities is to guard the welfare of our team. They may not have the experience we do. Some don't know their limits and can get unwisely involved in too many projects. We, on the other hand, have experienced the demands of ministry and are called to protect our people from over-enthusiasm.

It is sad to see many workers completely worn out by their pastor's constant demands. They have been taught that any sign of weariness reflects spiritual weakness, and that they must always be willing to assume any responsibility given by their church leaders.

Do not follow this example. Do not take for granted the work of those who are serving alongside you. Your workers are one of your most precious assets. A happy worker generates a full and fruitful ministry, while a frustrated worker has only bitterness to share with others.

Therefore, be generous in expressing appreciation to the members of your team. Provide for their emotional and spiritual well-being. Take interest in what they do and encourage them. Offer them support at all times. Each of these workers is helping to lighten your load, and that is no small blessing!

Food for Thought

Are you in danger of overextending yourself in ministry? What can you do to prevent your teammates from facing the same danger? How can you take time today to show them your care and affection?

Dealing with Defeat

The Lord *said to Joshua, "Stand up! What are you doing down on your face?"*
Joshua 7:10

Our defeats must seem much more disastrous to us than to the Lord. It is difficult to accept failure in a culture which constantly demands victory. Accordingly, when we do experience failure in a ministry project or a relationship, we experience a blow to our self-esteem and easily become discouraged and pessimistic.

The Israelites were exhilarated after the great victory God had given them over the stronghold of Jericho. They set off with great confidence to conquer a small town not a tenth its size. As soon as they forgot it was the Lord who had given them victory, they become overconfident. The ecstatic feelings over the fall of Jericho led the Israelites to think the town of Ai, their next military objective, would be a walkover.

We know all about the humiliating defeat they suffered there. Defeat is never so bitter and hard to accept as when we've been absolutely certain about the outcome of our plans. Joshua felt deeply disappointed, even betrayed. He threw himself to the ground, bitterly exclaiming, "If only we had been content to stay on the other side of the Jordan!" (Josh. 7:7).

When we suffer defeat we can waste much time beating ourselves over the head, regretting the decisions we've made. We should certainly learn from our mistakes, but we must also remember that an abundance of recriminations won't change what's done. When we have fallen we need to stand up and identify the source of our failure. This is why the Lord asked Joshua, "What are you doing down on your face?" He commanded him to get up and do what he had to do: lead the people to repentance for their sin.

When you are down, the Enemy wants to keep you there, feeling sorry for yourself or griping about your situation. Our heavenly Father, on the other hand, wants us back on our feet. If we have sin to confess, we should do it. If we have things to put right with people, we must see to that as well. No matter what we do, however, we shouldn't waste time feeling sorry for ourselves or complaining.

Richard Foster, in his excellent book entitled *Prayer: Finding the Heart's True Home*, reminds us: "We make mistakes—lots of them; we sin; we fall down, often—but each time we get up and begin again. We pray again. We seek to follow God again. And again our insolence and self-indulgence defeat us. Never mind. We confess and begin again . . . and again . . . and again."[1]

Food for Thought

When you feel discouraged, how do you deal with it? As a spiritual leader, do you allow defeat to affect your progress toward the Lord's goals for you? What can you do to strengthen yourself in times of failure or difficulty?

Wrestling with God

So Jacob was left alone, and a man wrestled with him till daybreak. When the man saw that he could not overpower him, he touched the socket of Jacob's hip so that his hip was wrenched as he wrestled with the man. Genesis 32:24–25

This is one of those passages we find difficult to understand. God engaged all night in hand-to-hand combat? How is it that we find such an unusual event among the stories of the patriarchs?

To understand the story, we must look at Jacob's prior life. He was born a child of the Promise. He was the grandson of Abraham, who had been chosen by God to be the father of a great nation. For this reason God's blessing had rested on Jacob even when he was in his mother's womb.

A quick glance at his life, however, shows us a person who tried to lay hold of God's blessing by hook or crook. Time and again he shamelessly exploited the weakness of others for his own advantage. He did not hesitate to lie or cheat. In the process he too became the target of deceit. He accumulated great material wealth but made many enemies in the process—including his brother Esau, who pledged to kill him. Jacob's life does not provide the inspiration we expect from a hero of the faith.

Sometimes it takes years before we heed the Lord's voice. He first speaks through a "gentle whisper." However, when we don't listen, He resorts to more direct methods, as in Jacob's case. God reveals to him his life's attitude: an endless struggle to lay hold of God's blessing!

The Lord did not defeat Jacob; this battle was not about physical dominance. Instead, He wanted to show Jacob just how grueling and exhausting was the path he had chosen.

In a very real sense the Lord was saying to the patriarch, "You have been fighting with Me all your life and have not yet understood that I am on *your* side. When will you stop struggling? Be still, and let Me bless you once and for all!" The Lord was more interested in Jacob's prosperity than was Jacob, but He would not give it through the human measures he had been using.

As leaders we are often so desperate to secure God's blessing for our plans that we are willing to grab anything that comes our way. The frenzy with which we often work shows we believe success depends on the strength of our own investments. Sometimes we even achieve our goals, but the way would have been much easier if we had learned to work alongside the Lord.

Food for Thought

Perhaps this is a good time to pause. Take a moment to put things back into correct perspective. You are not working* for *God; You are working* with *God. He doesn't want you to do everything. Learn to rest in Him, and you'll see better results for your efforts.

A True Pastor's Heart

January **13**

The next day Moses said to the people, "You have committed a great sin. But now I will go up to the LORD; perhaps I can make atonement for your sin." So Moses went back to the LORD and said, "Oh, what a great sin these people have committed! They have made themselves gods of gold. But now, please forgive their sin—but if not, then blot me out of the book you have written." Exodus 32:30–32

Who among us would not have despaired of having to endure these people, so hard-hearted and willing to rebel against the Lord? At each stage of their pilgrimage they fell into sin, continually provoking God with their abominations.

Every leader knows what it is to struggle with people who do not respond. We have often dealt with those who, like moths attracted to light, return time and again to the same sinful patterns. We have spent hours counseling those who, despite our best efforts, fall once again into patterns of sinful behavior which binds, weakens and eventually defeats them.

Moses severely rebuked the Israelites for the ugliness of their sin. They had deeply offended God's holiness, and their rebellion had awakened His wrath. Their behavior was completely unacceptable. The prophet did not hesitate to let them know the seriousness of their situation. Despite all this, he offered to enter into God's presence and mediate for them, though skeptical about the outcome.

But note the change in tone as Moses conversed with the Lord. He did not at any moment play down the seriousness of their sin, but Moses asked God to forgive the Israelites. He made it clear that he desired to be counted with God's people—if they were to be punished, he was willing to bear the same punishment. In essence he was saying to the Lord, "Punish them if necessary, but remember that I am one of them."

What an amazing illustration of that mysterious bond which unites us with our people! This is the essence of a pastoral heart. People tire us out. We feel discouraged. We understand Paul's words to the Corinthian Christians: "Besides everything else, I face daily the pressure of my concern for all the churches. Who is weak, and I do not feel weak? Who is led into sin, and I do not inwardly burn?" (2 Cor. 11:28–29). Sometimes we feel like walking away, but God has put a love in our hearts that will not let us go.

They are our people through thick and thin. Their victories are our victories. Their defeats are also our defeats. This is our blessed burden!

Food for Thought

Take a moment now to give thanks to God for the people He has placed in your pastoral care. Ask the great Pastor to revive your passion for them. Cry out to Him, that He would give you the same tenderness of spirit and goodness toward them that He shows to us. Bless your people, whatever they may be like, for that is what your calling is all about!

Blinded by Lies

As they talked and discussed these things with each other, Jesus himself came up and walked along with them; but they were kept from recognizing him. He asked them, "What are you discussing together as you walk along?" Luke 24:15–17

How great the disciples' surprise must have been when Jesus broke bread and they realized who He was! What tremendous joy they must have felt when they recognized that the One who had illuminated the Scriptures was none other than the Messiah!

The glad ending to this encounter, however, was overshadowed by the disciples' previous failure to understand the Word of God. Luke tells us that as they walked, they were discussing recent events. We can easily imagine that their conversation came again and again to the tragedy of the cross, considering it from every angle, trying to find some possible explanation that would relieve the pain of their loss. They were wretched, totally overcome by sadness.

But why were they so sad? It is because they believed Christ was dead. And to add to the tragedy of His death, some of the women now reported that they had seen Him. How could it possibly be true? Everyone had witnessed His crucifixion and subsequent burial.

But the truth, of course, was that Christ was not dead; He was indeed alive! He had told them that on the third day He would be raised again to life. And now some women had seen Him, but the disciples were so despondent they could not see the truth. They were bound by a lie.

The power of that lie was so great that when Jesus began to open the Scriptures, the words did not break the hold of that deceit. Starting with Moses and going through all the prophets, the Son of God explained to them how all that had happened was nothing but the fulfillment of Scripture. But the men were so downhearted they could not receive the Word which had the power to release them from the lie.

Our thoughts have enormous influence over our behavior and emotions. This is why Paul teaches us that "the weapons we fight with are not the weapons of the world. On the contrary, they have divine power to demolish strongholds. We demolish arguments and every pretension that sets itself up against the knowledge of God, and we take captive every thought to make it obedient to Christ" (2 Cor. 10:4–6). A leader must be ruthless with every thought opposed to God's truth. Identify these thoughts, take them prisoner and shackle them in the name of Jesus.

Food for Thought

"Our greatest sins are those of the mind." (Thomas Goodwin) [2]

Building Wisely

See, today I appoint you over nations and kingdoms to uproot and tear down, to destroy and overthrow, to build and to plant. Jeremiah 1:10

Many Christians today believe that the goal of our faith is simply to tidy and improve our messy lives. For this reason many who join the church see little change. Even after years of walking with the Lord, a churchgoer may display very little difference from the average person on the street.

Jeremiah's God-given mission is described vividly in this passage. It leaves us in no doubt that we are called to provoke a deep and dramatic change in the lives of our flock. God is not in the business of patching up lives or carrying out minor repairs so we can get on with the business of Kingdom service. Before He can use us, He must remove all that is needless to His purposes. Thus, there is a "negative" side to rebuilding which involves tearing up, breaking down and destroying. Take note of how radical and uncompromising these words are. We don't tear down and destroy things we expect to use in the future—we demolish only those things which no longer have any usefulness.

I believe the frustration of many pastors stems from attempts to give a "facelift" to situations which, in reality, are beyond redemption. Much work in the church today is related to worldly techniques and methods which are being promoted by church growth experts. Many of these have been imported wholesale from the business world and are entirely unsuited to the task to which we have been called.

These methods encourage Christians to hang on to their comforts and worldly ways, producing a spirituality which is bland and unexciting. Many congregations admit to having more in common with the world than with the kingdom of God. Even if we use the whitest paint to make this lifestyle appear presentable, its substance can never be redeemed. The only way to produce change is to tear down that which is useless.

Surely Jesus was thinking in these terms when He said, "No one tears a patch from a new garment and sews it on an old one. If he does, he will have torn the new garment, and the patch from the new will not match the old" (Luke 5:36). The point He makes is clear: A time will come when the garment is so worn that it is not worth repairing. The solution is to throw the old garment away and keep the new cloth for its intended use.

Food for Thought

The Apostle Paul points out that "we were therefore buried with Him through baptism into death in order that, as Christ was raised from the dead through the glory of the Father, we too may live a new life" (Rom. 6:4). The spiritual destiny of those who come to Christ is not a visit to a beauty salon. It is death. Only through death can something new be born.

16 January | Getting Our Priorities Straight

So the Twelve gathered all the disciples together and said, "It would not be right for us to neglect the ministry of the word of God in order to wait on tables." Acts 6:2

Those who have been in ministry for some time are familiar with the subject of this passage. We are often made responsible for numerous projects at once because there is more work to be done than workers to do it. This is common in most local congregations. Pastors are expected to be multi-talented individuals, able to handle a wide variety of activities.

The apostles quickly found themselves in a similar situation. Because of increasing numbers of people receiving food donations, more and more time was needed for its distribution. The task had to be organized, problems dealt with and new challenges faced. The list of things to be done was simply never ending.

In the midst of it, however, they were able to pause and evaluate what was happening. Although they were caught up in a project which was both laudable and necessary, they were neglecting their true call, which was to dedicate themselves to prayer and to the Word. The apostles' comment may seem a trifle elitist to our ears. I have heard people say the leaders didn't want to dirty their hands with work they considered below their real position within the congregation.

Nothing could be further from the truth. The disciples were not saying they were above waiting on tables. Rather, they knew they were being unfaithful to their calling by getting tied up with things they had *not* been called to do. The decision to choose deacons shows admirable discipline on their part. Despite the hectic pace of ministry, they had not lost their capacity to keep their eyes fixed on the main objective of their calling.

The fact is, God has called us to a specific task. All other activities, however noble and worthy, will serve to distract us from our real vocation. In the newborn church there were many others who could wait on tables. They were probably even able to do it more effectively and graciously than the apostles. But the task of watching over the congregation and teaching them God's Word was one that could not be delegated to others, because it had been entrusted to them.

The incident identifies one of the most common problems faced by pastors: becoming a Jack of all trades, but master of none. Getting involved in too many church activities can lead to a loss of direction in ministry. Incessant activity is not necessarily a sign that someone is making progress toward a specific goal; sometimes all it shows is that they are well and truly disoriented.

Food for Thought

Do you know what your main gifts are? In which area of ministry should you be using them? How much time are you dedicating to this ministry? What practical steps can you take to improve your performance in this area?

Cause for Celebration

January **17**

I tell you that in the same way there will be more rejoicing in heaven over one sinner who repents than over ninety-nine righteous persons who do not need to repent. Luke 15:7

Some time ago I spoke to a pastor who was just concluding an evangelistic crusade. For two weeks his congregation had held nightly meetings in a public park. He had organized the many details and had also preached each evening. He looked spiritually and physically drained. I asked him how things had gone. Unable to conceal his disappointment, he answered, "Only fifteen people made decisions for Christ." The results just didn't seem to justify the enormous investment made: round the clock prayer chains, door-to-door invitations, equipment rental, organization of work teams.

Pastors are under constant pressure to measure success in terms of figures. A new school has emerged in the last thirty years in which the entire focus is on church growth. Its leaders offer seminars, publish articles and produce books that promise "secrets" of unlocking our congregations' potential. We are exposed to "super pastors" who preside over giant-sized congregations filled with apparently ardent and committed Christians.

But these mega churches are not normal. Christian Schwarz, author of *Natural Church Development*, points out that most congregations worldwide number between 80 and 150 people—much like yours or mine.[3] Ministry in these churches has its share of setbacks, tears and frustrations. As leaders we do all we know to do, praying fervently for growth, but we don't always see it as dramatically as we would like.

How good to remember Jesus' parable! In this story the shepherd left ninety-nine sheep to search for just one that was lost. When it was found, he threw a great party, inviting his neighbors and friends to share his joy. The same thing, Jesus said, happens in heaven. The repentance of one sinner is cause for great celebration.

What has happened to us that we are only impressed with crusades in which 45,000 make decisions? Have we lost the Lord's perspective? What are we saying when we lament that "only fifteen" made decisions for Christ? Those fifteen resulted in fifteen heavenly parties. Each of them is indescribably precious to our heavenly Father. Even if only one had repented, He would have said, "It was worth it!"

Rejoice, pastor! You have been given the privilege of sharing in that joyous heavenly celebration. Each new convert sparks new festivities. Don't miss the blessing because your figures don't coincide with those normally associated with success. Success, in the Lord's arithmetic, is one lost sheep found.

Food for Thought

Church growth experts would have labeled John the Baptist a failure. He had hardly any followers by the time his ministry came to an end. The Son of God, however, did not hesitate to call him the greatest prophet of all times. No doubt He saw him through different eyes than our own!

First Things First

He appointed twelve—designating them apostles—that they might be with him and that he might send them out to preach and to have authority to drive out demons. Mark 3:14–15

This verse gives a concise idea of Christ's thinking when He chose His disciples. His "game plan" for the Twelve had three clear objectives: 1) they would spend time with Him, 2) they would be sent out to preach, and 3) they would have authority over the sick and demon-possessed.

In some Scripture passages we can change the order of the components without altering the text's meaning. In this passage, however, each component necessarily builds on the previous one. The established order cannot be altered. We could heal the sick and drive out demons, but this would have little value if we did not nourish people with the Word. Even if we added the proclamation of the Word to our healing ministry but were not rooted in an intimate relationship with Jesus, it would be impossible for us to point others to a true knowledge of Christ.

As leaders we must exercise the greatest care in these directives. The bustle of ministry can lead us to adjust the order of the elements, trapping us in a never-ending flurry of activity. This provides an appearance of godliness, but will rob us of that which is most precious and essential to ministry: our relationship with the Lord.

When I meet with pastors, I look for an opportunity to ask about their spiritual lives. It is easy to assume that, because they are involved in ministry, leaders are naturally enjoying an intimate relationship with the Lord. Unfortunately, this is not always true. I often talk with pastors who have lost their passion for the God they serve with such exertion.

Matthew's Gospel presents a chilling scene. In the Day of Judgment some will try to justify their neglect of relationship with the Lord by pointing to the many works they have done for Him. "Many will say to me on that day, 'Lord, Lord, did we not prophesy in your name, and in your name drive out demons and perform many miracles?'" (Matt. 7:22). The Son of Man responds with this devastating exclamation: "I never knew you. Away from me, you evildoers!" (Matt. 7:23). Notice that Jesus does not hesitate to call them "evildoers." Strong words! They make very clear that all works not sustained by relationship with God—even if done for Him—are, indeed, evil works.

Food for Thought

It has been said that being busy in the King's business is no excuse for neglecting the King. Have you neglected the discipline of spending time with Him, seeking His face and His companionship? Have the church's constant demands worn you out? Why don't you take advantage of this day to put things in order? Approach Him with confidence and renew that relationship designed for your good! The Lord has been waiting for you.

A Question of Perspective

When the angel of the LORD appeared to Gideon, he said, "The LORD is with you, mighty warrior." "But Lord," Gideon asked, "how can I save Israel? My clan is the weakest in Manasseh, and I am the least in my family." Judges 6:12, 15

Gideon was completely downcast when the Lord appeared to him. For years the Midianites had made life impossible for God's people, raiding Israelite lands and stealing the best of their harvest. In fact, at the very moment the angel appeared, Gideon was busy hiding his grain.

Notice the marked contrast between the angel's greeting and Gideon's answer. The angel called him "mighty warrior," but the young Israelite felt neither mighty nor like a warrior! On the contrary, he considered his family to be weak and himself the least among them. As with David, Gideon would not have been the family's first choice for any important undertaking. He was used to being overlooked. Considering his position, his response was quite natural: "What on earth can *I* do?"

We find before us one of the great mysteries of God's workings. To be successful in the plans He sets before us, it doesn't matter in the least how we view or feel about ourselves. What matters is how God sees us!

Sarah perceived herself an elderly, sterile woman with no hope of bearing a child. But the Lord saw her as the mother of a multitude. Moses, who stammered, seemed useful only for looking after sheep. But the Lord deemed him the ideal man to free His people from the Egyptian yoke of slavery. Peter seemed nothing more than a clumsy Galilean fisherman, but Christ perceived him as a rock, a leader with a key role in the foundation of the new church. Ananias viewed Paul as someone entirely dedicated to persecuting the church, but the Lord saw this man as His chosen instrument to bear the gospel to the Gentiles.

So, leader, how do you see yourself? Do you consider yourself a poor unfortunate, having few abilities and even fewer resources? Do you think God sees you in the same light? What would you say to the angel of Jehovah if he appeared before you today?

Food for Thought

It may well be true that you are poor and have scarce resources at your disposal. Gideon* did *belong to a poor family. The real difficulty, however, does not lie in our circumstances—it lies in the belief that our position can limit God's work and purposes. The Lord sees no impediment to His plans for us because* He *does the work, not us. The angel said to Gideon, "Go in the strength you have." He was not asking him to look for more resources, nor to reach for riches he did not possess. He simply wanted him to place his weakness in the hands of an all-powerful God. A useless servant in the hands of God can become an incredibly powerful weapon!

A Radiant Face

When Moses came down from Mount Sinai with the two tablets of the Testimony in his hands, he was not aware that his face was radiant because he had spoken with the LORD.
Exodus 34:29

The person who spends time in the presence of the Lord can't help but be transformed! Can any other passage illustrate this better? The intensity of the encounter Moses had with Jehovah had been so great that his face was shining. We cannot help but think of Christ's transfiguration in which the disciples saw "His clothes became dazzling white, whiter than anyone in the world could bleach them" (Mark 9:3). This radiance refers not merely to His clothing, but rather describes the brilliance of something intensely spiritual.

How many of us would like to experience something similar! Those who walk with Christ long to experience such closeness with the Lord. What must it feel like to experience something like that? Would we be able to stand if faced with such a visitation from God?

Our "righteous envy" of the experience granted to Moses, however, overlooks one small detail: The prophet did not know his face was shining. An unimportant fact, wouldn't you think? But through this detail we recognize part of the mystery at work in such a change. Spiritual transformation, with the experiences accompanying it, is not primarily for our pleasure. Very often we don't even realize God is at work in our lives. The aim of His work is that others may see His glory reflected in us—not that we may show off our spiritual maturity.

For this reason it is important to carefully examine the hidden motives of our hearts. I often see a subtle competitiveness among pastors over who receives greater honor in encounters with other leaders. The Apostle Paul encourages the Philippian church to "do nothing out of selfish ambition or vain conceit" (Phil. 2:3). The term "vain conceit," which the King James translates "vainglory," is a reference to a glory which seems genuine, but really has no value whatsoever. It is based on the recognition and applause of men rather than on our heavenly Father's approval. As such, it is destined to pass away.

As leaders we must live lives of such holiness and intimacy that we shine with glory from above. Our presence alone should testify to the magnificence of the God we serve. But be warned! As soon as we become aware of that radiance, it will disappear. Our good Father knows how quickly we become proud of what is not even ours. That's why Paul was given a thorn in the flesh, so his "greatness" would not be his own, but Christ's.

Food for Thought

Consider the following advice given by Samuel Wilberforce, one of the great saints of the nineteenth century: "Think as little as possible about yourself. Turn your eyes resolutely from any view of your influence, your success, your following. Above all, speak as little as possible about yourself."[4]

The Value of Discipline

Have nothing to do with godless myths and old wives' tales; rather, train yourself to be godly.
1 Timothy 4:7

We have a tendency to speak more about things than to do them. We believe that talking about the importance of a prayer life is almost the same as praying. We think that exhorting and encouraging our brothers to share their faith is just the same as doing it. We believe that praising the virtues of meticulous study of the Word is the same as taking time to meditate on the Word. And who is more exposed to this danger than leaders—we who dedicate ourselves to the teaching and proclamation of God's eternal truths?

Paul recognizes this potential problem for leaders, especially younger ones. That's why he stressed to Timothy that his Christian life should not consist in words. This exhortation, a subject which seems to have seriously concerned the apostle, is repeated seven times in his two letters to the young pastor. His message is evident: "Don't get tied up in endless words because true spirituality does not depend on talk!" The apostle had already indicated in his letter to the Corinthian church that "the kingdom of God is not a matter of talk but of power" (1 Cor. 4:20).

What alternative does he suggest? The way of discipline.

It is interesting to note that the word he uses has the same root as our word "gymnastics." In other words, Paul is encouraging Timothy to "go to the gym" in order to stay in good spiritual shape. The gym he refers to obviously does not involve physical exercise, although he makes it plain that this is also worthwhile. What he has in mind, however, contains that which opens the door to greater intimacy with God: worship, reading, prayer, fasting, solitude, silence, etc.

Many of us do lead disciplined lives. But our discipline can be wrongly directed. We spend much energy on public activities because, in the end, they bring us the most satisfaction. Nevertheless, these do not expose us to the deeper things of God. It is what we do when we are alone which makes a difference to our public behavior.

Excellence in any undertaking requires a price. The musician who wants to be outstanding cannot merely rest on natural talent but must spend hours in practice. The athlete who aims for a coveted prize must dedicate long and grueling hours to training. In the same way, if we want to achieve true depth in our spiritual walk, we must be willing to submit to a vigorous life of spiritual disciplines.

Food for Thought

Scripture tells us that "Jesus often withdrew to lonely places and prayed" (Luke 5:16). Can the same be said of you? If you had to measure your passion for the spiritual life, what score would you receive? What obstacles have most hindered your spiritual exercise at the "gym"? What practical steps can you take to grow in this aspect?

The Learning Process

When he was alone, the Twelve and the others around him asked him about the parables.
Mark 4:10

Have you ever noticed how many times this scene is repeated in the Gospels? Jesus was teaching the crowds. The disciples, among the spectators, also received the Master's teaching, but they did not always understand what they had heard. And so, waiting until they were alone, they would approach Him and ask for clarification or an explanation, or share their thoughts with Him.

From this scene, repeated often in the three years He spent with them, we can draw two important principles for the leader of a teaching ministry. First, teachers should not take for granted that what seems perfectly clear to them—according to their reasoning and their explanations—is also clear to the listeners. Each individual listens and analyzes what is said by way of his own personal culture. In addition, during the communication process something is always lost. So the ideas which seem so easy and simple to a speaker may have reached the listeners in a confusing and garbled way. Do not imagine what you teach or preach is always understood by the listener.

Second, the wise teacher understands that learning is a process. Truth penetrates the lives of those who listen only by degrees. Sometimes the listener's initial reaction could even be hostile, but the Word works slowly, putting down roots in the one who has received it. Recognizing this, it would be correct to say that teaching is more a process than an event. As time passes and the listener meditates on truths heard, conclusions will be reached that open the door to real change.

Wise leaders who understand these principles will provide opportunities for their closest helpers to approach them for clarification or simply to share how they have been touched by the Word. This is a fundamental part of the learning process. The leader who relies only on formal meetings to carry out the ministry of instruction to God's people will find that it is not very effective. What's more, a good teacher understands that those informal moments, where the conversation simply "takes off," are very often the teaching opportunities that will have the biggest impact on others' lives.

Food for Thought

Think for a moment about your own teaching style. Do you place too much emphasis on your public ministry? Would your closest helpers say that you are readily available to others? What can you do to ensure that those you teach really understand what you share with them? How can you create more informal moments in your ministry like those we see illustrated in today's passage?

Teaching that Doesn't Teach

Then Jesus said to the crowds and to his disciples: "The teachers of the law and the Pharisees sit in Moses' seat. So you must obey them and do everything they tell you. But do not do what they do, for they do not practice what they preach."
Matthew 23:1–3

In some congregations it is not unusual to see bitter fights over who should rightfully lead the flock. Accusations fly, each side attempting to prove the other wrong.

There is no doubt that the Pharisees and scribes were not worthy of their influential positions within Jewish society. However, Christ did not attack their positions. He recognized that they sat in Moses' seat and therefore held a place of privilege. Instead of questioning whether they rightfully belonged there, Christ questioned the use they made of their authority.

All teachers will be judged, regardless of whether they deserve their role or not. James warned, "Not many of you should presume to become teachers, my brothers, because you know that we who teach will be judged more strictly" (James 3:1). Jesus' main objection to the Pharisees was that their teaching was contradictory, for they said one thing and lived totally differently.

This is a common problem. Teaching can become theoretical, thus making no impact on others. This ineffectiveness has nothing to do with teaching wrong doctrine; very often what is shared is biblically correct and neatly presented. But the teaching doesn't produce change if it is not backed by a living example of the truth.

When Christ finished preaching His Sermon on the Mount, the crowds marveled because "he taught as one who had authority, and not as their teachers of the law" (Matt. 7:29). The effect of His teaching, no doubt, was due to the fact that there was no difference between what He taught and the way He lived. His testimony completely supported what He said.

This does not mean that teachers must be perfect. We are all in the process of maturing and growing into Christ's likeness. But there must be a serious commitment to live the standards we expect of others. This can remove the harsh edge from teaching, because whoever tries to practice the spiritual disciplines will soon discover the process is more complicated than our words make it out to be. Teachers who struggle to live their message can be tender and compassionate, because they understand that life is not as easy as it appears.

Food for Thought

In his book,* The Seven Laws of the Teacher, *Dr. Howard Hendricks writes: You cannot communicate out of a vacuum. You cannot impart what you do not possess. The effective teacher always teaches from the overflow of a full life."*[5] *The more deeply transformed you are, the more effective you become as a teacher.

The Name of the Father

I have manifested Your name to the men whom You gave Me out of the world; they were Yours and You gave them to Me, and they have kept Your word. John 17:6 (NASB)

In Jesus' wonderful priestly prayer, we find an excellent presentation of the objectives which guided His earthly ministry. He had sought to fulfill two main tasks: The first, to reveal the Father's name, is stated in today's verse. The second was to give them "the words which You gave Me" (John 17:8).

This, in many ways, is a summary of the work that lies before every pastor. We have been called to make disciples, to train the saints for ministry. But how do we achieve this? These verses give a concise idea of God's method. We should impart the *words* of the Father and, at the same time, reveal the *characteristics of His name.*

Imparting the Word has been a central focus of many church leaders in recent times, although there are sectors of the church lacking biblical teaching. In general terms, however, God's people will not perish for want of Scripture knowledge. Much of our lives as children of God revolves around endless meetings in which the truth is shared, taught and preached. Nevertheless, it is true to say that though numbers of Christians know the Word, many do not know the Lord of the Word.

Notice that Christ combined teaching of the Word with the revelation of the Father's name. What does this mean? Simply that Christ not only conferred the *precepts* of the eternal Word of God, but also exposed the *heart* of the Author of that Word.

We can't fail to emphasize how essential is this second part. The Word alone, imparted without a revelation of God's heart, leads to stern, suffocating legalism. There are many exhortations in the Scriptures, and anyone who reads them without knowing the Father may come to the conclusion that this God is no more than a tyrant.

This is why Christ took care to demonstrate to His followers the pastoral heart of the God of the Word. When we perceive the Father's compassion and His desire to do us good, we begin to see the Word in a different light. No longer does it seem full of capricious demands from a severe God, but rich with tender instructions from a Father who longs to bless His children. When people know God's goodness firsthand, obedience becomes easier.

Food for Thought

You can't reveal the name of God through more teaching. You reveal His name when you know Him intimately. The revelation of the nature of God is something that is perceived by people; it is a spiritual reality that can be seen when the Word is imparted. If you are not enjoying the goodness of our heavenly Father daily, your words cannot reveal His name. Don't miss the opportunity today of enjoying time with the Author of the Word.

A Man Just Like Us

Elijah was a man just like us. He prayed earnestly that it would not rain, and it did not rain on the land for three and a half years. Again he prayed, and the heavens gave rain, and the earth produced its crops. James 5:17–18

Many years ago I participated in the first Ibero-American missionary congress, COMIBAN, which took place in Sao Paolo in 1987. One of the most awaited moments in the congress was the arrival, on the final day, of a world-renowned evangelist. When this man stepped up to the platform, hundreds of people crowded around to take photos. Some even got up on the platform to have their picture taken with him. This caused such chaos that the poor man interrupted the meeting to ask the audience to please stop taking photos.

That experience started me thinking about the adulation of prominent figures so often a part of our evangelical culture. Since that meeting I have seen it time and again. We tend to elevate our notable leaders to positions of privilege and admiration that are not good for them or for us.

Why the rush to get close to them, to speak to or touch them? Deep down, perhaps many of us believe that the greatness of their ministries is a direct consequence of who they are. We look on with amazement at their ministries and accomplishments because we feel they belong to another category, having qualities and characteristics we don't have.

James wants to encourage us to be more daring in prayer. To this end he takes the example of Elijah's powerful prayer life. Elijah prayed and the rain stopped; he prayed again and the rain started once more! I don't know what your reaction to this story is, but I suspect most of us would say, "I could never do that."

This is exactly what the apostle is arguing against. Before we can react, he tells us that Elijah was just like we are. He didn't have any special qualities. He became depressed, like us. He got angry, like we do. Sometimes he lacked faith, just like us. However, he prayed and God answered.

What point is James making? Elijah's greatness did not lie in what he was, but in the God in whom he believed. His greatness was not his own, but the Lord's. This is why no Christian should feel intimidated by such an example, because the same God at work in Elijah is also at work in our lives and our ministries.

Food for Thought

As a leader give thanks to God for the example of those who have obtained international recognition in the evangelical world. Thank the Lord for their lives and ministries! But don't be intimidated by what they are. Their greatness is not their own. It belongs to the Lord who works in them. Take that same Lord by the hand and dare to believe that He can also do great things in your life.

Helping the Weak

They tie up heavy loads and put them on men's shoulders, but they themselves are not willing to lift a finger to move them. Matthew 23:4

The well-known Christian intellectual Francis Schaeffer once observed: "Biblical orthodoxy devoid of compassion must be one of the most unpleasant things on the face of the earth." Some commentators tell us the Pharisees had a list of 630 rules they considered necessary for pleasing God. The weight of so many laws, far from encouraging the people to seek God's face, had led most to feel that the spiritual life was for only a handful of select individuals.

The Pharisees' main problem was not, however, the number of rules, although that certainly was a great stumbling block to developing a spiritual life. The basic problem was the style in which they were teaching these precepts. They believed their chief responsibility was to tell the people what to do.

How many pastors work in the same way! We spend inordinate amounts of time haranguing the people to do this, that and the other. Our teaching and preaching is an endless series of exhortations to fulfill various obligations. Under these circumstances, we shouldn't be surprised that people feel worn out and frustrated.

But most members of the church already know their responsibilities. Have you ever met a believer who, after years of attending meetings, hasn't realized we are called to love our neighbor, read the Word, share our faith or dedicate more time to prayer? What's so novel in a sermon that tells us to be generous in service, worship and giving?

The error in this approach is the belief that people are motivated simply by exhortation. But an excess of instruction ends up weighing people down with an unbearable load. The responsibility of pastors is not only to exhort. We must also be willing to accompany our people in their attempts to practice what we have taught them.

This is what Jesus Christ, our own Pastor, did. He taught the disciples to walk in certain truths, but He also walked beside them and showed them how to do it. When He returned to the Father, He summoned the Spirit to continue this work. The Holy Spirit's very name, *paracletos,* indicates that He is called to come alongside others to help them in their weakness.

This is the difference between pulpit pastors and those who "smell" of sheep. The former only exhort, frustrating people who are in need of someone to lead the way. The latter spend time accompanying, showing and correcting their flock so that they may learn to walk with the King.

Food for Thought

Which people have helped you most in your pilgrimage with Christ? How did they do it? How can you achieve a good balance between time invested in exhorting and time invested in helping? What things are preventing you from achieving that equilibrium today?

Life in the Passive Voice

The Lord is my shepherd, I shall not be in want. He makes me lie down in green pastures, he leads me beside quiet waters. Psalm 23:1–2

What blissful images the words of the shepherd-king present in this psalm! This passage has been a source of strength and encouragement for countless generations of believers. It reveals to us, as no other psalm can, intimate details of the Shepherd's love for His people.

Consider for a moment the construction of most of these verbs: He *makes* me lie down in green pastures, He *leads* me beside quiet waters, He *restores* my soul. He *guides* me in paths of righteousness; His rod and staff *comfort* me. He *prepares* a table before me; He *anoints* my head with oil. We don't need a degree in English grammar to see the similar structure of each phrase. The actions are all expressed in passive voice. In every situation the sheep are receivers and not generators. They receive something the Shepherd gives them: provision, rest, direction, restoration, guidance, service or anointing.

These gifts are the product of the Shepherd's work, not the sheep's. It is the Shepherd who loves and cares for His sheep, who continually works to secure their well-being. Theirs is a relationship developed along a simple concept. He gives and they receive.

Why is this important to us today? There are too many sheep in the flock who believe it is their responsibility to secure what the Shepherd wants to give. They run around trying to restore themselves or looking for green pastures and still waters. A sheep's main concern, however, should be one thing: staying close to the Shepherd. He is committed to supplying their every need, but in order to care for them, He requires their willingness to be shepherded.

This principle is what Norman Grubb—a great hero of the modern missionary movement—calls an essential truth of the spiritual life. God always acts according to His eternal nature, and humanity according to theirs, and there can be no variation in the two. God is forever the One who gives, and we are forever the ones who receive.[6] When we forget this, we lose the spirit of dependence which is absolutely essential to a life that pleases God.

How hard it is for leaders to cease being caregivers and to assume the role of sheep! We are accustomed to shepherding others, not being shepherded. But if we do not allow the Shepherd to nurture our souls, we will never be effective in caring for the needs of others.

Food for Thought

Do you allow Jesus to shepherd your soul? You are a leader—but first of all you are a sheep. And as a sheep you too need a shepherd. Why not take a moment, right now, to draw close to the Lord and allow Him to care for your needs? Open your life to the loving ministrations of the Shepherd of Israel!

I Will Be with You

Even though I walk through the valley of the shadow of death, I will fear no evil, for you are with me; your rod and your staff, they comfort me. Psalm 23:4

Note the reason behind the psalmist's confidence. It is not hope that circumstances will change, nor the idea of a life without difficulties or complications. On the contrary, the psalmist realizes he will very possibly be called to walk the valley of death's shadow. The strength to face this comes from a conviction that the Lord will be with him even in the worst of circumstances.

Have you considered how often the Lord repeats the words "I am with you"? Every text stating this phrase has something in common: The main character in the text is in a frightening situation. Jacob, for example, was afraid to return home because his brother had sworn to kill him. The Lord came to him and said, "I will be with you" (Gen. 31:3). Joshua was intimidated by the enormity of leading the people in conquest of the Promised Land. The Lord spoke to him, saying, "Be strong and courageous. Do not be terrified; do not be discouraged, for the LORD your God will be with you wherever you go" (Josh. 1:9). When the angel of the Lord called Gideon to free Israel from the Midianite yoke, he felt insignificant for such a task. But the Lord said, "I will be with you" (Judg. 6:16). The young prophet Jeremiah felt it was useless to proclaim God's Word to the people. There were so many against him! The Lord reminded him, "They will fight against you but will not overcome you, for I am with you and will rescue you" (Jer. 1:19). Even the fearless Apostle Paul felt concerned about the Jewish opposition in Athens. In a vision during the night, the Lord told him, "Do not be afraid; keep on speaking, do not be silent. For I am with you" (Acts 18:9–10).

We are living in difficult times. Economic stability is a growing concern worldwide. In many nations unemployment increases relentlessly day after day. As if that isn't enough, violence is on the rise, leaving many feeling unprotected and vulnerable. In short, these are ideal times for anxiety.

How wonderful it is, then, to remember the psalmist's confident statement: "Even though I walk through the valley of the shadow of death, you are with me." Times of crisis are of inestimable value for those who wish to develop a life of greater dependence on God.

Food for Thought

What time could be better than the present to take the Lord firmly by the hand and say, as Moses did, "If your Presence does not go with us, do not send us up from here" (Exod. 33:15). Very often we can't feel Him; we can never see Him. But He is with us. Let us advance, then, with no fear!

Listening with Discernment

The first to present his case seems right, till another comes forward and questions him.
Proverbs 18:17

One of our ministerial responsibilities is to listen to those around us. It is not uncommon for people to seek help in resolving difficulties in their relationships. The wise leader should act with care in providing spiritual guidance in these situations.

Everything people tell us is seen from their own perspective, of course. But frequently we come upon individuals who are especially able to paint a picture which leaves no doubt as to the other party's guilt. Their words are persuasive, their arguments convincing and their attitude apparently that of a person touched by the Spirit of God. Without realizing it we find ourselves agreeing fully with their opinion. Our comments begin to reveal that we have already decided who is guilty in this situation: the person who is not present!

The author of Proverbs identifies a danger in forming opinions quickly about the situations at hand. Anyone is capable of describing an occurence in which their own actions seem fair and reasonable. But Solomon warns us that we should never take for granted that a person is telling the truth. An astute leader knows that even in the most extreme situation, there are two sides to a story. As well as seeking discernment from the Lord, we are also obliged to examine the situation from every angle, including that of the person who is absent.

In addition, when we as leaders are being consulted, we must realize that we can only deal with the individual who is present. We should therefore be tender in our conversation so that the attitudes and behavior of this individual can be examined. We may agree that the absent party has done wrong, but for the moment we have no access to that person. We can only help the one before us to live according to the eternal parameters of the Word. That is our responsibility.

If we have already formed the opinion that the person who "sinned" is the one absent, it will be very difficult to approach that individual and offer help, since our conclusions will be obvious in our attitude and words. Nobody should be judged by what someone else says about them. Everybody should be heard and examined with the greatest impartiality possible. Only in this way can we be effective instruments in helping resolve conflicts.

Food for Thought

In various situations in the Gospels, Jesus was asked to intervene in claims, as in Luke 10:40, Luke 12:13 and Matthew 20:20–21. Read these passages and meditate on the following: What did each person claim? What solution did the Messiah offer? How did this solution fit in with what the claimants were hoping? What spiritual lesson can be learned from these scenes?

30 January — Words of Encouragement

Since you are precious and honored in my sight, and because I love you, I will give men in exchange for you, and people in exchange for your life. Isaiah 43:4

Henri Nouwen, renowned author of more than twenty books on the spiritual life, gave serious thought to the effect of growing up in a world which curses us. From our childhood, he writes, the world tells us our value as individuals is relative. Its system says our worth does not depend on who we are, but rather on what we do, achieve or have. The devastating effect of this inheritance produces extremely fragile self-esteem, easily damaged by any negative experience.

Being found in Christ should bring dramatic change to our unfortunate human condition. We should discover that we are treasured and valued by the eternal God of the heavens. But our actual experience is often different. Many congregations perpetuate the world's message that our value depends on what we do—the only difference being that now what we do is connected to the many activities going on within the church. The essential message, however, is the same.

As pastors we are charged with the precious work of restoring those who are broken and exhausted. We are called to heal the sick, bind up the injured, bring back the strays and search for the lost (Ezek. 34:4). Our congregations should be therapeutic communities where those in pain are restored to the image of their Creator.

To do this work we must first ensure that we are enjoying the blessedness of the beloved children of God. Our spirit needs the testimony of His Spirit that we are part of His family (Rom. 8:16) and, as such, enjoy favored privileges and treasures. Our value is not in what we do, but in our spiritual identity, which is assured forever by the sacrifice of Christ.

Only when we are sure of our own position can we really bless others. This is one of our choice privileges as priests of the Most High. Nouwen warns us, "That blessing can be given only by those who have heard it themselves." When we hear over and over again that Voice calling us blessed, we receive "words with which to bless others and show them they are not less blessed than we are."[7]

What a precious ministry—to nullify the message of this world (which destroys through cursing) and begin to bless and build up, being the Father's instruments in restoring what the Enemy has tried to destroy! We have been called to administer life to the hurting. It will only be possible if we are enjoying His life ourselves.

Food for Thought

Why not take some time to pray: "Lord, I need You to tell me daily how much You love me. I am vulnerable to wounding, hurtful words. Strengthen my spirit with the blessed testimony that I am Your beloved child, and use me to speak these words of life to others. Amen."

The Measure of Our Strength

If you falter in times of trouble, how small is your strength! Proverbs 24:10

Crisis situations, which we avoid by every possible means in our hedonistic culture, are of enormous value as we seek growth in our spiritual lives. Extremes allow us to evaluate the true state of our spiritual reserves.

We all feel strong and spiritual when life is going well. During these times we proclaim our loyalty to the Lord and affirm our commitment to live according to His Word. When the storm strikes, however, our devotion and commitment can disappear into thin air. In their place rises a question frequently asked in times of trouble: "Why me?"

An essential condition of transformation is becoming aware of areas in our lives that the Lord wants to address. As long as we don't undergo testing, we probably won't have an accurate idea of our spiritual condition. Not only will we be convinced that our development is greater than it is, but we will be unaware of the real nature of our weaknesses. A crisis puts an end to this deception. In the trial we have the chance to see ourselves as we really are. Our imperfections, lack of maturity and failure to be holy—all become very easy to see.

In order to understand this principle, think for a moment about the Apostle Peter. During the Last Supper, profoundly affected by Christ's prediction that His disciples would betray Him, he confidently proclaimed that he was willing to die with Him. He didn't doubt for a moment his own devotion or commitment. Nevertheless, when the test came, he could not even open his mouth to admit loyalty to the Messiah.

Which of the two Peters had more potential for the ministry: the first or the second? The defeated Peter had learned a very important lesson. He had discovered that his own evaluation of his spiritual passion could not be trusted.

As leaders, this truth teaches us two significant things: First of all, we should be careful what we proclaim in times of abundance and blessing. It is easy to feel invincible when everything is going well. And second, we should appreciate more the value of crisis situations in our lives. Nobody enjoys them, but what great fruit they produce in our lives when we don't run from them!

Food for Thought

Reflect on the following observation made by the well-known Christian counselor, Larry Crabb: "Our theology becomes rich only when it survives the onslaught of pain. . . . The pain that opens our hearts to search for God is deep." [8]

A Prophet without Equal

I tell you, among those born of women there is no one greater than John; yet the one who is least in the kingdom of God is greater than he. Luke 7:28

Think about these words of praise by Jesus. The Son of God was declaring John the Baptist the greatest prophet of all times. Bear in mind that John was not being compared to unknown prophets of that period, but rather to great men of God who form Israel's rich prophetic history: Moses, Elijah, Amos, Daniel and Ezekiel, men who had a profound and lasting impact on the nation's life.

Consider John the Baptist's record. Before his birth he was given a unique calling to herald the arrival of the Messiah. He spent most of his life in complete anonymity. When he appeared at the river Jordan, thirty years later, the only detail given is that he came from the desert. We may speculate that he was raised in a community along Israel's borders, but the truth is that John the Baptist was a complete stranger.

The dramatic growth of his ministry is recorded in a few short paragraphs. His preaching attracted huge crowds who flocked to hear his radical call to repentance. Even Jerusalem's most notable religious figures were among the multitudes. He soon developed a group of loyal disciples. The high point of his ministry was the arrival of the Messiah, who also submitted to baptism. Christ's initiation into public ministry, however, spelled the end of John's mission. Shortly after baptizing the Lord, he was arrested. Nine months later Herod had him beheaded. His public ministry had lasted barely one hundred eighty days.

How, then, could Jesus declare John the Baptist the greatest prophet of all times? Isaiah and Jeremiah, two of Israel's great prophets, had ministries that spanned at least forty years. John's ministry was microscopic in comparison!

Our confusion reveals how different our concepts of greatness are from God's. Greatness, in our Christian culture, is typically related to size and extension. In God's kingdom, however, greatness is not measured in terms of numbers, but of faithfulness. Faithfulness refers to the capacity to do precisely what we are asked. Nobody understood this better than John. When his disciples urged him to stop his followers from flocking to Jesus, he stated his mission with striking simplicity: "He must become greater; I must become less" (John 3:30).

Food for Thought

Our utilitarian mindset protests at such wastage of talent. Thirty years to prepare a man for six months of ministry? Surely it makes more sense to pull off thirty years of ministry with only six months' preparation! But what a valuable lesson the son of Zechariah gives. A person shaped by God for a particular ministry, at a precise moment in time, can achieve more in several months than another in many years of well-intentioned service. Let us strive, therefore, to be found involved in that "which God prepared in advance for us to do" (Eph. 2:10).

Praying for Our Own

February 2

Epaphras, who is one of you and a servant of Christ Jesus, sends greetings. He is always wrestling in prayer for you, that you may stand firm in all the will of God, mature and fully assured. Colossians 4:12

We know very little about Epaphras. Many commentators think he is a key person in the establishment of the Colossian church, as well as being Paul's companion in his first imprisonment. To us he is one of thousands of anonymous heroes who played a part in the expansion of the church during the first century.

Today's verse, however, gives us a brief glimpse of Epaphras' character. He was a man of prayer who understood that, even at a distance, he could affect lives through supplication and petition on their behalf. According to Paul's testimony, he carried out this intercession with tremendous fervor and intensity, revealing a passion that is not often seen among Christ's servants.

And this is not all. He also showed great discernment regarding the church. His prayers were not limited to requests concerning the temporary details of this life that so often absorb us. Epaphras asked that that they would be firm, perfect and completely secure in the will of God, conditions that guarantee eternal results.

It is most likely that Epaphras did no more than copy the example of the Apostle Paul. In almost all his letters, we read that the apostle prayed frequently for the churches he had founded or visited. He writes, "constantly I remember you in my prayers" (Rom. 1:9–10) and "I always thank God for you" (1 Cor. 1:4). He shares again, "I have not stopped giving thanks for you, remembering you in my prayers" (Eph. 1:16). His letter to the Philippians begins by saying, "I thank my God every time I remember you. In all my prayers for all of you, I always pray with joy" (Phil. 1:3–4). He tells the Colossians, "we have not stopped praying for you" (Col. 1:9). And again, "we always thank God for all of you, mentioning you in our prayers" (1 Thess. 1:2).

These men understood that prayer is one of the most effective weapons leaders have at their disposal. With prayer we can touch lives in ways that are impossible through activity. I suspect, however, that many of us believe the real work of the ministry is attending meetings, visiting and counseling. Richard Foster, in his book *Prayer*, reminds us that "if we truly love people, we will desire for them far more than it is within our power to give them, and this will lead us to prayer. Intercession is a way of loving others."[1]

Food for Thought

Could it be said of you that you are one who "wrestles in prayer" on behalf of those around you? What stops you from spending more time praying for your congregation? How can you grow in this aspect of your ministry?

Work Which Isn't Really Work

When his father-in-law saw all that Moses was doing for the people, he said, "What is this you are doing for the people? Why do you alone sit as judge, while all these people stand around you from morning till evening?" Moses answered him, "Because the people come to me to seek God's will." Exodus 18:14–15

Moses was so immersed in the mayhem of ministry that he could not see he had lost his stability. From morning till evening crowds of people came before him to obtain wisdom for their diverse problems. Jethro immediately saw the madness of this method and severely questioned his son-in-law.

Moses' answer is very like what I have so often heard from leaders: "If I had my way, I would work differently; but the people seek me out, and I have to see to their needs." In other words, our ministerial priorities are determined by the demands of those around us. Instead of directing our ministry ourselves, we find we are being directed by the crowds and their endless list of concerns.

This situation has been described by Gordon MacDonald in his excellent book, *Ordering Your Private World*. With some humor MacDonald adjusts a well-known spiritual law so that it states: "God loves you and everybody has a marvelous plan for your life!"[2] The fact is that if the leader does not have clear aims and priorities, the congregation will impose theirs. This removes a leader's freedom to be dedicated to the call of God. A similar problem faced the apostles in the sixth chapter of Acts. The need to distribute food among the widows was distracting them from the main task to which they had been called, which was to dedicate themselves to prayer and to the Word.

The wise leader will understand that clear ministerial priorities must be established before God. Once determined, activities can be organized according to this order. When this is done, a congregation will have a clear sense of the direction in which they should go. In addition, the leader will have time to dedicate to important priorities, such as the training of new workers. And this will provide workers for attending to the congregation's individual needs. It will ensure that the priorities are not left to the mercy of those with various needs.

Food for Thought

What are the tasks God has specifically called you to fulfill? How much time are you investing in these priorities? Are there symptoms that might indicate you have wandered away from them? What steps can you take to align your ministry more closely with your calling?

Trusting in His Mercy

For he says to Moses, "I will have mercy on whom I have mercy, and I will have compassion on whom I have compassion." It does not, therefore, depend on man's desire or effort, but on God's mercy. Romans 9:15–16

One of the elements most attractive in religion in general is its means of exercising some control over God's actions. In other words, we believe a set of established rituals should secure His response and obtain blessing. The level of sacrifice required varies from religion to religion, but all—without exception—lead us to believe that our actions can control the deities toward which we direct our efforts.

This idea, to be honest, is a reaction to God's claim of sovereignty in the affairs of our lives. Note, for example, how annoyed the Israelites became when Moses took a long time to come down from the mountain. As with us today, the time factor is what most bothered them. The people went to Aaron and said, "Come, make us gods who will go before us" (Exod. 32:1)—in other words, "We want a god who will do things our way."

Without our noticing, this concept can creep into our congregations. A simple example serves as an illustration: A believer may want something special from God, but they delay asking because their personal lives are not in order. So for a time they try to "behave very well"—and then they make their request, expecting God to listen to them with pleasure.

Today's verse reminds us, in terms that create discomfort, that God is absolutely sovereign. Without beating around the bush, Paul tells us that God's actions do not depend on "man's desire or effort, but on God's mercy" (Rom. 9:16). This makes us uncomfortable because our culture teaches that victory comes from controlling those around us. Our God, however, stands apart from this perverse system. Control is taken out of our hands.

What sustains us, then, in our spiritual lives? It is something much greater than the sad seeking of results through an exchange of favors. Our hearts are encouraged by the profound conviction that God is our heavenly Father and, as such, will always seek our best. We are secure in His love because His love is unconditional. Whoever knows Him understands that He always works for our good. It is this reality that Christ wanted to emphasize to the disciples when He said, "If you, then, though you are evil, know how to give good gifts to your children, how much more will your Father in heaven give good gifts to those who ask Him!" (Matt. 7:11).

Food for Thought

Meditate on the marvelous truth contained in this observation made by Matthew Henry: "God's reasons of mercy are all drawn from himself, not from anything else."[3] We have no option but to kneel at His feet and trust in Him. We are in good hands!

Praying with Vision

"Simon, Simon, Satan has asked to sift you as wheat. But I have prayed for you, Simon, that your faith may not fail. And when you have turned back, strengthen your brothers."
Luke 22:31–32

Jesus' declaration reveals the Son of God's level of commitment to Peter; it shows how profoundly spiritual his earthly pilgrimage was. His words contain at least four important principles for ministry today.

First, we see that Jesus Christ was intensely involved with His disciples. This was evinced by a strong desire to defend them and use every resource at His disposal to ensure that God's will be done in their lives. He was a man who carried His team in His heart at all times and in all places.

Second, His knowledge of the imminent test the disciple would face moved Christ to intercede for him. In our difficulties we often confide in others, and together we bewail how hard our particular situation is. Without realizing it, we fall into a state of despair and defeatism, because talking about problems rarely solves them. Christ did the best He possibly could: He prayed for the life of His disciple.

Third, we see that Christ did not pray for Peter to be freed from the test. Western culture, dedicated to the tireless search for a comfortable and easy life, has twisted our perspective to such a degree that many of our prayers are little more than requests for God to adjust circumstances to our taste. We want to avoid the complications and tests common to most human beings. The Messiah, however, did not pray this way. He asked for Peter to come through the test unhurt, hanging on to that faith without which it is impossible to please God.

And fourth, Christ addressed Peter, reminding him of his life's objective: to strengthen his brothers. When we go through an arduous test, we tend to sink into speculation about how life would have been if we hadn't faced the trial. As a result, we stop advancing toward the objectives God has laid out for our lives. Christ reminded Peter that beyond the test lay a call that should be fulfilled. In this exhortation not only did the Master give a correct perspective on things, but He also expressed a vote of confidence in the apostle. He believed things were going to work out, and He encouraged Peter to go on.

Food for Thought

Amy Carmichael, the great missionary to India, was physically disabled for the last twenty years of her life. Nevertheless, she touched thousands of lives through prayer. Cyril Powell wrote of her faith: "Before we pray the prayer of definite intercession, in faith, we need first to discover what is the Will of God. A listening, responsive heart and mind, steadied by obedience, is trained in discerning this. Hasty assumptions, or self-induced presumptions, will not do. We must be sure about these petitions in the way that the Lord will make us sure. . . . Our praying is then not so much our praying, but the prayer of God in us."[4]

Conditional Support

Moses and Aaron brought together all the elders of the Israelites, and Aaron told them everything the LORD had said to Moses. He also performed the signs before the people, and they believed. And when they heard that the LORD was concerned about them and had seen their misery, they bowed down and worshiped. Exodus 4:29–31

It took some doing for the Lord to convince Moses to return to Egypt for Israel's deliverance. The patriarch had strongly argued his case against accepting the mission. Finally, he gave in, still not really convinced of his calling. So this initial welcome from the people must have encouraged him! When they heard his mission, they received him enthusiastically and gave their heartfelt support.

But the reception given Moses and Aaron by Pharaoh was certainly very different! He threw them out of the palace and doubled the slaves' workload. Notice how quickly the Israelites' enthusiasm and support vanished into thin air. They exclaimed to their would-be deliverer, "May the LORD look upon you and judge you! You have made us a stench to Pharaoh and his officials and have put a sword in their hand to kill us" (Exod. 5:21).

As a leader you have probably experienced similar situations. I remember a construction project I was involved in many years ago with another pastor. The church members received the proposal with eagerness and promised their support. Shortly, however, they lost enthusiasm and only a few of us were left to bear the brunt of the work.

This is a normal reaction in the church. Don't get angry about it. If the people were more persevering, they would be the leaders instead of you. The job of keeping them interested and focused on the work is yours. As pastor you have been called to motivate your people and keep moving ahead steadily, even when they lose hope.

The great example of this pastoral role is Nehemiah. The work of reconstructing the walls was plagued with endless difficulties and tests, and the people very often wanted to "throw in the towel." But Nehemiah, using a variety of strategies, encouraged them to continue until the work was finished.

This kind of encouragement is not given by condemning people for their lack of commitment. Rather, you should provide an example of perseverance in the midst of difficulties, so that they may imitate your faith. With patience and tenderness, encourage them to continue in the work. You will see more people get involved as they see your steady commitment.

Food for Thought

Notice Moses also became discouraged (Exod. 5:22–23). But he had a characteristic that marks the true servant: He took his discouragement to the Lord. And the Lord gave him a word that enabled him to carry on. You need to do the same. Present your despair to the Lord and allow Him to rekindle your hope and faith, then receive the grace you need to continue with the work He has given you.

Moving On to the Goal

Brothers, I do not consider myself yet to have taken hold of it. But one thing I do: Forgetting what is behind and straining toward what is ahead, I press on toward the goal to win the prize for which God has called me heavenward in Christ Jesus. Philippians 3:13–14

In order to fully appreciate the importance of Paul's words, we need to remember that Philippians is one of his last letters, written while he was imprisoned in Rome awaiting a verdict. His declaration is extraordinary when considered in light of at least 20 years of ministry, when he had every right to rest on his laurels.

It is even more surprising that his thinking was so clearly directed toward the future. With the passing of years it is common for us to ruminate increasingly on the past, remembering victories achieved and experiences lived. In particular, however, we repeatedly lament our missed opportunities, the mistakes we have made and our disappointed expectations.

It is undoubtedly meaningful to look back occasionally, if only to acknowledge the path taken and to celebrate God's hand working in our favor. But it is more important to look toward the future. Nobody can walk forward if they are looking elsewhere. This is why Paul says he forgets what lies behind.

This demonstrates that Paul's hope was firmly placed in the future. He was not bound by the past. Former experiences didn't matter; the elderly apostle understood that the best was yet to come. And with this conviction, he proceeded steadily toward the goal put before him by God so many years earlier.

It is needful for a leader to look ahead. We can't let past difficulties and suffering condition our view of the future. Neither can we live off achievements the Lord, in His mercy, allowed us in the past. For those who are in Christ, life always grows toward its fullest expression. The best is still to come.

Even in times of severe crisis, we can look fixedly ahead for encouragement within the storm. When Christ was in Gethsemane, in that agonizing struggle to submit to His Father's will, He managed to lift His eyes and fix them on the joy before Him (Heb. 12:3). Having done this, He could bear the cross and all it implied with a serene and confident spirit. This displays the power of a correct spiritual attitude in our lives.

Food for Thought

The great evangelist Dwight Moody once said, "I am walking towards a bright light, and the closer I get, the brighter it is."[5] With the passing of the years, what seemed far off in our youth can be seen with growing clarity and ever greater beauty. This should encourage us to keep moving forward with renewed strength!

Reducing the Gap

Everything they do is done for men to see: They make their phylacteries wide and the tassels on their garments long; they love the place of honor at banquets and the most important seats in the synagogues; they love to be greeted in the marketplaces and to have men call them "Rabbi." Matthew 23:5–7

A well-known television series for children in Latin America featured a character who always asked to be called by his title. When indulged, he was tremendously gratified. It was really a foolish request. It reflects, however, the keenness of our culture to show off its degrees and achievements.

In this passage Christ identifies similar behavior in the Pharisees. They loved everything that highlighted the difference between them and the rest of the people. They showed off, wearing longer fringes than others, choosing the most visible seats in their meetings and deliberately seeking people who would offer them the pleasure of hearing their title: "Rabbi, Rabbi." Their behavior made it clear that they considered themselves in a higher spiritual dimension. Their conduct, instead of drawing them closer to the people, created the illusion of great distance between them and the man on the street.

The wise leader understands that this kind of distance is an enemy to effective ministry. Nobody transforms lives from a pulpit. A leader's real impact is felt *among* the people. This gives them a chance to examine their shepherd's life closely. Through mixing with them and understanding the reality of their struggles, a leader's ministry will take on a merciful, practical quality based on a realistic perspective of life.

The celebrated educator, Howard Hendricks, names this a foundation of education in his book, *The Seven Laws of the Teacher*. "The word communication," writes Hendricks, "comes from the Latin word *comunis*, meaning common. Before we can communicate we must establish commonness, commonality. The greater the commonality, the greater the potential for communication."[6]

As a leader, get rid of everything that sets you apart from people. Shun titles, places of honor, distinctive clothing and the preferential treatment others want to give you. Our hearts quickly get used to such things, but these distinctions rarely contribute to our authority in the church. Identify everything that can help close the gap between you and your people. This will give you an opening to their lives and allow a much more effective investment.

Food for Thought

Sometimes we hide behind the argument, "I don't want to be treated this way, but the people insist." Christ not only told us to avoid calling others "doctor or professor," but also not to let others call us that. You are responsible to teach your people on this subject. You do not want them to think you are someone special. Your job is to show that only One is special: He who is seated on the throne and reigns sovereign.

Because He First Loved Us

We love because he first loved us. 1 John 4:19

I have frequently come across frustrated Christians. They try everything they can to secure an encounter with God. They exclaim with disillusionment, "I seek Him and try to please Him in every way, but He just doesn't respond! It's as if He is absent." Their frustration is very real, but has nothing to do with a lack of response on the Father's part. It is due to a common error in our thinking.

The problem is that many of us imagine God to be more similar to us than He is revealed in the Bible. We think He is picky about who He chooses to relate to—that He favors a select few with special treatment of extraordinary experiences. We feel that the rest of us have some characteristic that disqualifies us from this kind of experience. So we spend a great deal of our time trying to modify our lives to attract His attention.

In this version of the spiritual life, God is distant and indifferent to us. We look for ways to convince Him to notice us and give importance to our circumstances. Somehow we think He needs to be coaxed to love us.

But God is not the capricious father some of our earthly fathers are. His interest in drawing close to us is greater than all the fervor and passion we can possibly feel for Him. He longs to participate in our lives, to bestow on us blessings He has prepared for His children. It is not necessary to convince Him of this; *He* is the one who took the initiative to seek *us* out. "You did not choose me, but I chose you and appointed you to go and bear fruit—fruit that will last. Then the Father will give you whatever you ask in my name" (John 15:16).

What does this perspective change demand of us? We must merely relax a little and allow Him to love us. When we have forsaken our desperate efforts to reach Him, we will begin to realize we are already touched by His love—that in a thousand ways each day He is seeking us with eternal tenderness.

God cannot be won over by our efforts. We must be like children and let Him captivate us with His incomparable love!

Food for Thought

Thomas Kelly, the author of a small gem called* A Testament of Devotion, *makes the following observation about our relationship with God: "In this humanistic age we suppose man is the initiator and God is the responder. But the living Christ within us is the initiator and we are the responders. God the Lover, the accuser, the revealer of light and darkness presses within us. . . . And all our apparent initiative is already a response, a testimonial to His secret presence and working within us." [7]

The Speck in Another's Eye

Why do you look at the speck of sawdust in your brother's eye and pay no attention to the plank in your own eye? How can you say to your brother, "Let me take the speck out of your eye," when all the time there is a plank in your own eye? Matthew 7:3–4

Many years ago as a young pastor, I had agreed with some men from the church to help a fellow member with construction work on his house. One of the men who had responded most enthusiastically did not turn up on the appointed day, and I could hardly control my anger. My feelings were soon evident in my words. I expected the other person present to at least agree with me. But this brother, mature in Christ, said to me, "I wouldn't dare to say anything about him because my own sins weigh too heavily on my heart." I was so ashamed! And I was the pastor!

Over the years I have learned that criticism says more about the heart of the speaker than about the person under disapproval. Those most lacking in mercy indignantly point out the failure of mercy in others. The most legalistic individuals are the ones who condemn the legalism thay see around them. Those who are never punctual get most irritated when kept waiting.

This is precisely what Christ is highlighting. Criticism comes from those who have not examined their own lives. The speck in their brother's eye offends them because they don't see the enormous log in their own. For this reason their manner of giving advice does not produce positive results. They do not have clear enough vision to carry out the delicate operation of removing a grain of sawdust from another's eye. This showcases our efforts to reform other people before ourselves. As Dallas Willard points out, "We have great confidence in the power of condemnation to straighten out other people's lives."

Truly, we resort to condemnation because the world employs this language. The experienced leader knows that criticism never produces change—even less so if shared publicly from the pulpit. Correction must be carried out with firmness, but in meekness: "But watch yourself, or you also may be tempted" (Gal. 6:1). Criticism is unpleasant to hear, and also dishonors the Lord with its unloving attitude. Since we are part of the Kingdom, shouldn't we speak "only what is helpful for building others up according to their needs, that it may benefit those who listen" (Eph. 4:29)?

Food for Thought

Take a moment to think about the habit of criticism in your own life. What things do you most frequently disparage? What does this reveal about your own heart? How can you deal differently with wrong you see in others' lives? Would you be willing to make this vow to the Lord? "Lord, I want to speak only those words that build up. If I have nothing good to say about others, then I will keep silent. Amen."

11 February

Conflicting Feelings

Peter took him aside and began to rebuke him. "Never, Lord!" he said. "This shall never happen to you!" Jesus turned and said to Peter, "Get behind me, Satan! You are a stumbling block to me; you do not have in mind the things of God, but the things of men."
Mathew 16:22–23

This scene is striking, coming immediately after that most precious moment when Peter acknowledged Jesus as the Christ, the Son of God. Such a revelation, as the Lord pointed out, was the result not of clever deductions, nor of careful observation of the Scriptures. It was revealed to the disciple by the Father Himself.

Soon after, however, we find Peter in a position that shows an incredible lack of discernment and understanding of the Father's purpose for the Son. Peter sought to prevent the fulfillment of Christ's own words: that it was necessary for the Messiah to suffer many things and to be killed at the hands of the scribes and Pharisees.

This scene reveals a truth about spirituality. We may observe in the same person the most extraordinary devotion and, at the same time, the basest expressions of carnality. These two realities coexist within us, and we never lose our propensity to sin. Although there has been much discussion on whether Paul refers to the unredeemed or to the Christian in the seventh chapter of Romans, it is very possible that the apostle spoke of himself. We have all felt within us that terrible struggle between flesh and spirit. "For what I do is not the good I want to do; no, the evil I do not want to do—this I keep on doing. Now if I do what I do not want to do, it is no longer I who do it, but it is sin living in me that does it" (Rom. 7:19–20).

From this observation two points emerge: First, as a leader, we will never be free from stumbling. We must always be on guard against manifestations of the flesh that could cause our downfall. We would do well to remember that more saintly people than us have fallen by the wayside.

Second, we should not become exasperated at displays of the flesh in our own lives. Sometimes, after sublime moments in the Lord's presence, we find horrible thoughts entering our minds. We are not condemned for this. When Christ encouraged His disciples to pray to avoid temptation, He was indicating that the flesh would always disturb those wishing to grow spiritually. We can identify with Paul's cry: "What a wretched man I am! Who will rescue me from this body of death? Thanks be to God—through Jesus Christ our Lord!" (Rom. 7:24–25). It is not the presence of sin in our lives that disqualifies us from ministry, but rather our acceptance of that sin.

Food for Thought

Donald Gray Barnhouse writes, "The greatest struggles that life can know are not within the unsaved, but within the saved."[8]

Ministering According to Need

And we urge you, brothers, warn those who are idle, encourage the timid, help the weak, be patient with everyone. 1 Thessalonians 5:14

With the help of a simple exercise, we can see the importance of a principle in this exhortation of Paul's. If we were to change the order of the words, the verse could be read in the following way: "And we urge you, brothers, encourage those who are idle, warn the timid, be patient with the weak, help everyone."

"Just a minute!" you would say. "This can't be right at all. We would never be asked to encourage the idle, and even less to warn the timid!" You would go on to explain that the idle need to be spoken to firmly. Their laziness is partially a result of our indulging their behavior. And what about the weak? If we admonish them, we will destroy them! What they need is someone to draw alongside them in their weakness to help them gain strength. And the timid also need words of encouragement for gaining confidence and entering into the fullness of Christ's life.

And your response would be right! Your observation is precisely the point made in this series of instructions. Wise leaders need discernment to understand the individual problems of those they are serving. Using the "correct" method with the wrong person will not produce the desired results. On the contrary, it will aggravate a situation instead of contributing to its resolution.

And so the astute leader needs not only various ministerial styles, but also discernment in the application of each one. This challenge is one problem leaders struggle with. Most of us lean toward a particular leadership style, and we use it indiscriminately in all circumstances. But people are not all the same; we have to alter our methods to be as effective as possible in each situation. If you had time to peruse all of Paul's letters, you would notice how he changed his tone according to the particular circumstances of each group. He speaks in strong terms to the Galatian church. When addressing Timothy, he speaks more as a father to a son. In the letters to the Thessalonians, he mentions that he had been "gentle . . . like a mother caring for her little children" (1 Thess. 2:7). In other words, Paul employed a variety of leadership styles, creating effectiveness in the ministry he carried out.

Food for Thought

What style are you most comfortable with? In which situations does this method achieve the best results—or in other cases, poor results? What other styles should you incorporate into your ministry to better serve those God has brought before you?

A Natural Progression

We have much to say about this, but it is hard to explain because you are slow to learn. In fact, though by this time you ought to be teachers, you need someone to teach you the elementary truths of God's word all over again. You need milk, not solid food!
Hebrews 5:11–12

The frustration felt by the author of Hebrews is experienced by many leaders. We have sometimes worked with people who have known the Lord for many years, yet time and again we must go back and remind them the basics of the gospel.

Today's passage contains an important truth. The natural progression of any child of God, through a growing intimacy with Him, is to eventually become a teacher. When the author speaks about being a teacher, he is not saying every Christian should fulfill a ministerial role like that listed in Ephesians four. He is talking about people who, having matured, begin to share their life in Christ with others. This is a natural progression in life. Our biological children grow, mature and eventually form their own families, reproducing life in others.

Within the church, however, many people are unswervingly devoted to nourishing only their own spiritual lives. They spend much time attending conferences, courses and seminars, or reading books to make them better children of God. But they will achieve no great progress until they show more interest in the growth of others than in themselves.

The irony is that all they gather for themselves won't do them much good. They are "slow to hear" and need to return to the basics of the Word again and again, because they are not rightly using what they receive. As with the Israelites' manna, teaching which is not applied goes to waste. Applied truth always involves reaching out to bless others.

How does this affect our pastoral ministries? Well, very often we lose considerable time with these people, because their enthusiasm to learn appears truly spiritual. But they produce no evidence of putting aside the selfishness of considering only themselves. Our responsibility is to dedicate our best resources toward those willing to progress into teachers.

What is your responsibility to people who don't develop? Don't abandon them, nor turn your back on them. But don't expend all your energy on them either. Invest with wisdom so that your investment will bear fruit and your disciples will in turn reproduce life in others.

Food for Thought

Perhaps one reason these people always want more is that we do not sufficiently explain the true nature of God's call. The noted author, Gordon MacDonald, says that Christ took care to clearly explain the cost of discipleship to increasingly large crowds. It is almost as if He felt the size of the crowd indicated that the people had not properly understood the cost of being His disciple.[9]

God's Apprentices

The LORD said to Samuel, "How long will you mourn for Saul, since I have rejected him as king over Israel? Fill your horn with oil and be on your way; I am sending you to Jesse of Bethlehem. I have chosen one of his sons to be king." 1 Samuel 16:1

The Lord could easily have given more precise instructions to His servant Samuel. He could have said, "When you arrive, ask for David, the youngest son of Jesse. He is the one I have chosen as king. Anoint him and bless him in My name." But the Lord, true to His style, gave only the information necessary for the prophet to get started.

When Samuel reached Bethlehem, the process of finding the new king began. God did not intervene. Samuel, using his own criteria, thought he had found him in Jesse's eldest son. But at that moment God gave him additional instructions, expressing the guiding principle of the selection: "The LORD does not look at the things man looks at. Man looks at the outward appearance, but the LORD looks at the heart" (1 Sam. 16:7).

The incomplete instructions given Samuel by the Lord uncover something important about how God relates to His children. In ministry, we sometimes believe we are working for God. If we were only hirelings for His projects, He would give us complete instructions because our role would include nothing more than carrying out an assigned task.

However, this is not our function. In any assignment in which the Lord involves us, He is also interested in furthering the work in our lives. The incomplete instructions God gave Samuel obliged the prophet, first of all, to walk in faith. But during the selection process, having erred by looking at outward appearances, God taught him an important lesson about His standard of choosing servants. This lesson, rendered at the most appropriate moment, was something Samuel would remember for the rest of his life.

So we can affirm that in every task God gives us, He has two important objectives. One is that the work be done according to the instructions He has given us. But the second is that in the process we might continue to grow and learn about how to carry out the work of God.

Never think of yourself merely as God's employee. You are not working *for* God. You are working *with* God as an apprentice. As you work together with Him, your loving Father, He will correct you and teach you some of the "secrets of the trade." My prayer is that your concentration on the task will never be so intense that you miss the precious work He wants to accomplish in you. Each day will bring the promise of new lessons alongside the great Potter.

Food for Thought

Never be discouraged by your mistakes. Some of the most precious and profound lessons in life come about in that period of reflection which automatically follows our slip-ups in ministry.

Perservering in Prayer

Then Jesus told his disciples a parable to show them that they should always pray and not give up. Luke 18:1

Lack of perseverance in prayer is one of the most common problems we face in our walk with the Lord. This is particularly true in these days of instant results. Even though we attempt, time and again, to advance in the practice of this discipline, it would seem that it requires extraordinary effort to make progress in this direction.

According to Jesus' parable, two things can help us persist in prayer. First, we should believe in the validity of our request. The widow was absolutely convinced that her cause was just, so she insisted on a solution. I suspect some of us are not really sold out on the importance of our petition. We ask the Father once or twice for what we want, but when we don't see a result, we soon abandon our efforts—even though previously we had thought the desire essential to our lives.

Second, we should be convinced the answer will come, although we may seem to experience delay along the way. The widow did not give up; she fully believed she would eventually get justice from the unrighteous judge. For a time she had to endure this man's indifference, but she wore him out with her continual coming. Even though Jesus plainly pointed out that our heavenly Father cannot be compared to the unjust judge, we must still overcome the obstacle of God's apparent silence. Only an unshakeable conviction of God's deep desire to bless His children will sustain us when the answer is long in coming.

It is evident, therefore, that to develop the perseverance of continuing prayer, we must overcome the sporadic, lukewarm petitions we often present to God. Dick Eastman, a man who has taught and written much on prayer, shares the following observation on persistence:

> Some think persistent prayer means waiting weeks and years for answers. Although at times this is true, it is not the total picture. A person's prayer may be persistent in a quarter of an hour's time. Lengthy prayers may not qualify as persistent prayers. Most important is how intensely we pray. Prayer must be intense. When one prays with intense feelings of humility—fused with utter dependence on God—he learns the definition of persistent prayer. Persistent prayer is frantic prayer.[10]

Food for Thought

Is it possible that many potential blessings in your church are delayed due to lack of prayer? What do you feel really passionate about? Which of these nourish your prayer life? What stops you from continuing in prayer for the things you need, and how can you develop the perseverance God requires?

Fated Motivations

Then the man who had received the one talent came. "Master," he said, "I knew that you are a hard man, harvesting where you have not sown and gathering where you have not scattered seed. So I was afraid and went out and hid your talent in the ground. See, here is what belongs to you." Matthew 25:24–25

In the third servant's confession, we find one of the reasons many ministries don't prosper. The master did not deny that he was a man who reaped where he hadn't sown, and gathered where he had not scattered. But these characteristics, far from inspiring the servant, filled him with fear because he considered them qualities of a hard man. A flawed vision of his master led to his failure.

Fear does not inspire us, nor move us to take risks. It paralyzes. When fear takes hold of our hearts, we cease to interpret things correctly, and circumstances appear to be unconquerable obstacles. We think that any step we take will result in failure, so we end up doing nothing. This servant, convinced his master was a hard man, was more afraid of potential punishment than of possible failure in his investment attempts.

It seems to me we often try to mobilize people through the use of fear or guilt. We tell them that if they don't take on this or that ministerial responsibility, nobody will. They end up accepting the responsibility without the profound conviction that it is something God wants for their lives. Therefore, their service is destined to failure from the start. The person did not begin with healthy motives, and this will be evident in every step.

The only thing that can really motivate a healthy ministry is the assurance that we are loved by our heavenly Father. When we walk in His love, we can take the risk of "investments" that might fail, because we know we will not be judged on the quality of our achievements. We can work with confidence on the project at hand because we know His love will guide and support us in our undertakings.

Notice how Jesus made the transition from a secret life to a public ministry. When He came out of the water, a Voice from heaven was heard saying, "This is my Son, whom I love; with him I am well pleased" (Matt. 3:17). Before beginning the work He had been sent to do, the Father expressed His unconditional love to the Son. All the controversies, difficulties and even betrayals of the future would not overcome the strength of the relationship between Father and Son. How could He not feel free, then, to go confidently forward on the road marked out for Him!

Food for Thought

What things motivate you to serve the Lord? How do you inspire those working with you—do they know they are loved? What can you do to assure them that, even if they fail, you will continue to love and support them?

17 February | That Which Makes a Difference

But David said to Saul, "Your servant has been keeping his father's sheep. When a lion or a bear came and carried off a sheep from the flock, I went after it, struck it and rescued the sheep from its mouth. When it turned on me, I seized it by its hair, struck it and killed it."
1 Samuel 17:34–35

There's no doubt that David showed exceptional courage when he took on the giant from Gath. The entire Israelite army had been intimidated day after day by the Philistine's humiliating affront. With insults being hurled at the people and their God, the young shepherd was the only one with courage enough to meet the challenge.

Without losing sight of this tremendous display of bravery, let us look for a moment at the explanation David gives Saul. This was not the first time he had faced adverse situations. Tending his father's sheep, he had often been forced to defend them from the attacks of lions or bears. Facing an extremely dangerous situation was not new to David.

This highlights an important principle of leadership. David was going to face Goliath in the sight of an entire army who would be watching his every move. This was, in effect, his first public confrontation. But the preparation for this moment had been carried out entirely in private, with only the sheep for company. David now proposed to do publicly what he had done many times in seclusion.

The leader who wishes to be effective with people must develop the needed qualities through time alone with God. What we are in ministry will impact others' lives only if backed by a secret life of devotion far from the public eye.

This is why many leaders do not get beyond providing entertainment for God's people. Their methods may be attractive, but they lack influence. Their lives do not possess the level of holiness and commitment that can only be developed in private. A passionate experience with God in life's secret places makes the difference in ministry, even though others never witness these intensely personal moments. Spiritual authority, however, will be perceived by any who possess a degree of spiritual sensitivity.

The Holy Spirit, who empowers our efforts and thereby touches others, flows only through those who live in constant communion with God. But He is absent from those who practice piety only when being watched.

Food for Thought

What are you like when nobody is looking? Are you the same as when you are being watched? The real you is not the one that others see, but what you are in secret. What steps can you take to close the gap between what you are in public and what you are in private?

A Man of His Word

February **18**

When Jephthah returned to his home in Mizpah, who should come out to meet him but his daughter, dancing to the sound of tambourines! She was an only child. Except for her he had neither son nor daughter. When he saw her, he tore his clothes and cried, "Oh! My daughter! You have made me miserable and wretched, because I have made a vow to the LORD that I cannot break." Judges 11:34–35

Jephthah, sadly, is well known to us because of his foolish vow to the Lord. Seeking victory over the Ammonites against whom he was fighting, he promised to sacrifice to the Lord whatever he first encountered when he got home. Today's verse relates the dramatic moment of his return and the terrible consequences this had for him.

Without losing sight of how foolish it can be to make such a promise to God, we should value Jephthah's example in one aspect: He was a man of his word. We can't read his story without thinking of the psalmist who said, "LORD, who may dwell in your sanctuary? Who may live on your holy hill? He whose walk is blameless . . . who keeps his oath even when it hurts" (Ps. 15:1, 4). This quality is invaluable in the life of a leader!

Very often in the hustle and bustle of ministry, we commit ourselves to an activity that later proves to be very inconvenient. The ever-present temptation to please others leads us to give our word all too easily. When the moment arrives to carry out our promise, however, we realize we have gotten ourselves in a fix.

It is important that the people we are serving see that we are serious about keeping our word. This means that even when we have committed to something that becomes very complicated, we cannot back out. The effort we make to keep our promise will teach an important lesson about weighing our words, and will also show that we deeply value the people we serve.

Food for Thought

The solution for the problem of inconvenient commitments is not to withdraw our promise; instead, we should think more carefully before giving our word. We are often victims of our own haste. Before obligating yourself, take time to consider whether this is really something you can do. Ask for time to pray before deciding. This not only protects you from commitments you will later regret, but also provides a valuable opportunity to learn not to make decisions alone. Every step should be taken with the approval of our heavenly Father!

19 February | Petitions Which Get No Answer

The weapons we fight with are not the weapons of the world. On the contrary, they have divine power to demolish strongholds. We demolish arguments and every pretension that sets itself up against the knowledge of God, and we take captive every thought to make it obedient to Christ. 2 Corinthians 10:4–5

In a meeting recently I heard someone pray this way: "Lord, we ask You to remove from our minds all thoughts which dishonor You, and to cleanse us of anything that offends You." When they finished praying, today's verse came to mind, and I reflected on the things we sometimes ask of the Lord.

According to this passage, it is not God's responsibility to remove those thoughts which provoke disobedience to Christ. God's commitment is to bring our sin to light through the Holy Spirit (John 16:9). Once revealed, however, it is our responsibility to tame these thoughts and surrender them to Christ. Our heavenly Father will not remove them from our minds because He has called us to do it. Exercising this mental discipline is a fundamental aspect of our transformation in Christ.

On many occasions we misunderstand the nature of our spiritual walk and ask God to do things we should do. Conversely, we also attempt things which we should ask our Father for help with. There is no point, for example, in asking Him to grant us peace; He has told us peace will be ours when we make our needs known to Him (Phil. 4:6–7). In the same way, our efforts to transform our lives will come to nothing, as this is work only the Lord can do (Rom. 8:6–9).

The challenge for us as leaders is to understand spiritual dynamics so our energy is channeled into what we are really called to *do*. At the same time our prayers should be directed toward those things we have really been called to *ask* for. In this way we can be sure our exertion will receive our heavenly Father's blessing, and we will avoid wasting time and energy.

Food for Thought

One of God's saints, W. E. Sangster, sums up today's thoughts in this phrase: "Many people pray for things that can only come about by work, and work for things that can only come by prayer."[11] Think for a moment about your own prayer life. On what are your petitions based? What burdens do you frequently bring before the Lord? Which of these requires more effort on your part, and which can only be worked out by the Lord?

I Beat My Body

Therefore I do not run like a man running aimlessly; I do not fight like a man beating the air. No, I beat my body and make it my slave so that after I have preached to others, I myself will not be disqualified for the prize. 1 Corinthians 9:26–27

There is a rather strong conviction among many in the church that the spiritual life is completely divorced from the physical. This perspective holds that what happens in the physical realm of our lives has little impact on the spiritual realm, and vice versa. Christ, however, defined the great commandment as the need to love the Lord with all our heart, with all our soul, with all our mind and with all our strength. This leads us to understand that a relationship with the Father should be developed with our entire being.

Paul also understood this concept. He knew his body could be a hindrance to his growth if he did not consider it part of his spiritual life. This does not mean his body was wicked; rather, he understood that the Spirit's transformation in us should extend to our body as well. For this reason he sought to discipline his body to bring it under the Lordship of Christ.

Is this principle really important? Think for a moment about the following situations: You plan a time of fasting, but after a while your discomfort becomes so intense that you can't last a minute more without a bite. Or you have determined to get up early to spend time alone with the Lord, but when the alarm rings your body communicates that it needs at least another two hours' sleep. Or perhaps you stand in church to sing praises to God, only to discover your legs are letting you know how desperately you need to sit down. Our bodies very often have the last word in our spiritual activities. They protest, grumble and complain about the way we treat them. The truth is, in this day and age, our bodies have grown unaccustomed to any kind of sacrifice. But if we always listen to our bodies' wants, we will not make much progress in the disciplines of the spiritual life.

As leaders we should naturally be more disciplined and hard-working than our followers. It is precisely this characteristic that sets someone apart as capable of leading others. In order to grow in practicing a disciplined life, we need to teach our bodies that it is *Jesus* who must have the last word on everything. Beating your body and making it your slave will require experiences it may not enjoy, but which are ultimately for its benefit.

Food for Thought

What disciplines do you carry out in order to make your body participate in your spiritual life? How do you teach it that Christ also rules over our physical life? What steps can you take to "beat" your body, lest you should be disqualified?

Commanded to Rest

Six days you shall labor and do all your work, but the seventh day is a Sabbath to the LORD your God. On it you shall not do any work, neither you, nor your son or daughter, nor your manservant or maidservant, nor your animals, nor the alien within your gates.
Exodus 20:9–10

There are two very interesting concepts in the passage we look at today. First of all, we should note the command to rest is precisely that: a command. This surprises us, because in our culture rest is something we enjoy when we have nothing to do. Unfortunately, the day that we have nothing to do never comes, so we rarely take time to slow down. This is exactly why the Lord does not allow us to determine our own needs in this regard. He does not ask us if we want a break, nor whether we have finished our work. He simply orders us to rest.

Our heavenly Father knows well our habit of abusing His gifts. With the invention of electricity and the ability to prolong the day indefinitely, we have increasingly become slaves to our activities. Therefore, our Creator, who fully understands our limitations, commands us to rest for our spiritual, emotional, mental and physical health.

The second thing to note is that the day of rest is for Jehovah. Here we find another concept that contradicts our perspective. In our opinion a day of rest is basically for us. But in the original commandment, the day of rest has a spiritual meaning above all else. It is a day set apart to celebrate the blessing of belonging to God's people. It is for giving thanks for goodness received and for ordering our lives again according to the eternal parameters of the Word.

Leaders who hope to be effective in ministry must incorporate these principles of rest into their lives. Many pastors live in a permanent state of exhaustion which severely depletes their capacity for serving others. Rest is not simply the absence of activity; it is the spiritual renewal a leader needs to maintain a fresh and godly perspective of service. Whenever we neglect these periods of renewal, we do so to the detriment of those in our care.

Food for Thought

Perhaps it would help you to consider rest as another discipline of the spiritual life. Plan it just like any other ministerial activity, and incorporate it into your daily spiritual exercises. Resting is not a waste of time; it is a wise management of time and helps us make the best use of our Kingdom resources.

Deadly Jealousy

As they danced, they sang: "Saul has slain his thousands, and David his tens of thousands." Saul was very angry; this refrain galled him. "They have credited David with tens of thousands," he thought, "but me with only thousands. What more can he get but the kingdom?" And from that time on Saul kept a jealous eye on David. 1 Samuel 18:7–9

There's no sadder figure among God's people than a leader jealous of others' achievements. Such people will always be dominated by fears and suspicions, and their ministries will inevitably suffer the consequences.

Goliath's defeat was a great victory for Israel, and the women's song did no more than proclaim what was obvious to everyone. Paralyzed through indecision and fear, King Saul had not given the clear, decisive instructions his men needed at that time. It was the young shepherd from Bethlehem who displayed a fearless and courageous attitude.

Notice that at no time did David congratulate himself on his prowess; the *people* proclaimed his greatness. But even as they celebrated, the king's heart filled with anger. Scripture informs us of Saul's decision which was born from this experience: "And from that time on Saul kept a jealous eye on David."

The crux of the problem lay in Saul's attitude. Once a leader permits jealousy and envy to enter his heart, it will result in a negative view of others' achievements. Judgment will be permanently blurred from bitterness of heart; the actions of everyone around will appear threatening. Under these conditions, a great deal of time will be spent finding ways to disparage the work of others. In fact, this is an appropriate summary of the remaining years of Saul's life. The king obsessively sought a way to bring about David's death.

The reaction of a leader to another's success is a true measurer of greatness. Mature leaders are not afraid of being "overshadowed" by others' ministries. Instead, they are willing to work so others may progress toward their maximum potential in Christ. Just like a father with his children, they have no greater pleasure than to see people prosper in all they do. With a spirit of generosity, they encourage them and invest in them, even if it makes others greater. Leaders of this caliber know there are greater degrees of excellence yet to be achieved in their own lives.

Food for Thought

Note the wonderful generosity of Christ's words to His disciples: "I tell you the truth, anyone who has faith in me will do what I have been doing. He will do even greater things than these, because I am going to the Father" (John 14:12). The Messiah did not define greatness by the size of the task, but by the faithfulness with which it was carried out. In this sense the disciples' success bore true testimony of Jesus' successful work.

To the Desert

When Pharaoh heard of this, he tried to kill Moses, but Moses fled from Pharaoh and went to live in Midian, where he sat down by a well. Exodus 2:15

It is not difficult to believe that God Himself burdened Moses' heart for the injustice suffered by the Israelite slaves. The spiritual sensitivity gained from his parents had not been lost during his years in Pharaoh's court. Nevertheless, Moses had not yet learned this crucial lesson: God's plans cannot be implemented using human methods. As James pointed out many centuries later, "man's anger does not bring about the righteous life that God desires" (James 1:20).

For Moses to learn this lesson, he needed some time in the "school of the desert." He had too much confidence in his own strength to be useful for God's purposes, and God had to deal with him in a powerful way. And so it was that he spent many years in the wilderness. The passion and jealousy that had led him to kill a man gradually left him, and the peaceful, simple manner of a shepherd took their place. Only when all the dreams and longings had gone did God revive Moses' call, directing him to lead Israel out of Egyptian enslavement.

Think about the strangeness of God's ways. When Moses wanted to serve Him, He did not allow it. And when the prophet didn't want to serve Him, He demanded it! God clearly considers *who* we are a far weightier matter than *what* we actually do.

The great evangelist Dwight Moody once stated: "Moses spent the first forty years of his life thinking he was somebody. He spent the second forty years of his life learning he was nobody. And during the third forty years of his life he saw what God can achieve through a nobody."[12] What an admirable way to sum up God's dealings with this great prophet!

This is a lesson all leaders must learn. God has no need of our plans, our abilities or our efforts. He doesn't even need our passion, as the Apostle Peter discovered. He needs us simply to put ourselves in His hands, so He can direct our lives and show us the attitudes and behavior He desires. This kind of submission is most difficult because of our own ideas about how to please God.

Food for Thought

In ministry it is terribly tempting to make a plan and then ask God to bless our efforts. It is much more difficult to wait on Him, acting only at His direction. We must never forget, however, that the person who lives in complete submission to God is His most powerful instrument and is able to accomplish that which weighs on the Lord's own heart. Beware of being overly hasty!

Show Yourself an Example

Don't let anyone look down on you because you are young, but set an example for the believers in speech, in life, in love, in faith and in purity. 1 Timothy 4:12

Youth live idealistically. Young people look at the world and passionately denounce the injustice and hypocrisy they observe, believing they can promote change where others have failed. It is frequently the same in the church. Youth insist on a hearing and crave recognition by the congregation. Their demands are often delivered with a lack of tenderness and respect for those around them.

Paul valued the young. He told Timothy, who seems to have been shy by nature, not to let others to look down on him because of his youth. But take careful note of the method proposed by the apostle for Timothy to gain the respect he needed: It was to be by his exemplary behavior.

It is precisely in this that many young people fall short. They have fire and passion to make their opinions known, but may not lead a life that gives weight to their suggestions. They are easily able to list mistakes in the lives of others, but they don't realize that this is the easy part. They have yet to walk life's rough road, thereby gaining the experience needed to offer real, practical solutions for peoples' difficulties.

Paul encouraged young Timothy to avoid debates and arguments. Six times in his two letters he warns that God's plans do not advance by an abundance of words. He advised him instead to develop a life that would win him the right to be heard.

For young leaders this is a daily challenge. They must learn that identifying the mistakes of the congregation or its leaders contributes very little to bringing about deep, lasting change in the church. The real challenge is to show with one's behavior that there are other alternatives to handling these problems. When I was still single, I found it very easy to point out mistakes my parents had made. When I got married and had children of my own, I quickly saw that my theory of "how to be a good father" was not so easy to practice! I also found myself committing the very errors I had labeled unacceptable as a youngster.

The young person who accepts the challenge of developing a pure and godly life will be acknowledged without looking for recognition. The reason is simple: Theories abound, but life speaks more loudly than words!

Food for Thought

The English poet and author, Oscar Wilde, once wryly observed, "In America, the young are always ready to give to those older than themselves the full benefit of their inexperience."[13] There is obviously a note of sarcasm in his words, but the statement holds a grain of truth. If you are young, let your life speak louder than your words!

On Loan

They came to John and said to him, "Rabbi, that man who was with you on the other side of the Jordan—the one you testified about—well, he is baptizing, and everyone is going to him." To this John replied, "A man can receive only what is given him from heaven."
John 3:26–27

It had been 400 years since Israel had seen a prophet like John the Baptist. His appearance on the shores of the river Jordan quickly attracted people from all around. As the days and weeks passed, huge crowds accompanied the prophet.

All this changed when Jesus came on the scene. With His arrival John's mission was complete, and soon the crowds were following the One who had been baptized by the prophet. John's most loyal followers watched sadly as the people left him for Another, and suggested he do something about it. Behind these disciples' request was the implicit allegation that Jesus was stealing people the prophet had won through his own ministry.

In John's reply we see one reason Christ praised him so highly. John understood that none of us obtains anything through our own merit or strength. All that he had received had come from the Father, whose heart is immensely merciful. He knew the crowds had been on loan to him, and that the Father could take them away at any time. They did not belong to the prophet, but to God. This is why he did not resist or become bitter when the crowds began to gather around Christ.

As pastors we often act as if people's lives belong to us. We consider it our right to impose our plans and wishes on them, and we make decisions affecting them as if we were their masters. People, however, resist this kind of treatment and soon show their dissatisfaction!

John's attitude was very different. Far from becoming bitter, the prophet acted with that unselfishness and generosity which has the best interests of others at heart. How could he oppose the people's decision to leave if they were going to be a thousand times better off with Christ than with him?!

Mature leaders always seeks what is best for their people, even when it takes prestige from their own ministries. Just as children are lent to their parents for certain years, so are your people lent to you for a time. They have freedom to make decisions and act according to their understanding of God's will for their own lives. Even when they make mistakes, their leaders will respect this freedom which God has also given to them.

Food for Thought

How do you behave when you give instructions to people in your care? What are your reactions when they reject your advice or choose to follow a different path? Is there evidence in your ministry that your people have absolute freedom to do as they choose? What can you do to encourage more of this in them?

The Voice of God

February 26

Again the LORD called, "Samuel!" And Samuel got up and went to Eli and said, "Here I am; you called me." "My son," Eli said, "I did not call; go back and lie down." Now Samuel did not yet know the LORD: The word of the LORD had not yet been revealed to him.
1 Samuel 3:6–7

There are two interesting observations to be made from this incident in the life of young Samuel. First, we can affirm that the voice God used was so like Eli's that Samuel mistook one for the other. Only in movies does God speak with a voice that booms and resounds in the air! In real life God's voice to us is easily confused with those of others, or even with our own.

Second, we should stop for a moment to consider the phrase, "Samuel did not yet know the LORD: The word of the LORD had not yet been revealed to him." What we have here is the description of a novice, someone just beginning the learning process which would finally produce a great prophet and judge of Israel.

It is important to understand this. There is a feeling among God's people that spirituality is something you inherit or can acquire through the laying on of hands. Many believers go from meeting to meeting looking for that special "anointing" that will automatically convert them into great men and women of God. They are convinced that the greatness of those illustrious biblical figures was brought on by a special visitation or some extraordinary gift setting them apart from others.

The truth is that spiritual life is developed through a process of discipline. Just like the development of the physical body, much of our spiritual growth depends on elements beyond our control. Sometimes we don't understand the mysterious procedures leading to the transformation of our hearts. What is clear is that we are called to walk in faithfulness with our Lord, allowing Him to lead and guide us to maturity.

By this method there are no great leaps or moments of dramatic progress. We are occasionally blessed with extraordinary visitations of His presence, but most usually spiritual growth is the product of a slow, deliberate process. This is what the author of Hebrews was referring to when he said, "But solid food is for the mature, who by constant use have trained themselves to distinguish good from evil" (Heb. 5:14). Take note of the phrase "by constant use." This points to a learning process that even includes making mistakes, as did young Samuel.

Food for Thought

Matthew Henry once observed: "Spiritual growth consists most in the growth of the root, which is out of sight." [14]

27 February

The Power of Weakness

But he said to me, "My grace is sufficient for you, for my power is made perfect in weakness." Therefore I will boast all the more gladly about my weaknesses, so that Christ's power may rest on me. 2 Corinthians 12:9

It is a universal human tendency to hide one's weaknesses. When we are sad, we attempt to put on a happy face. When we feel like crying, we try to contain our tears. We feel overloaded, but put on a show of having everything under control. We struggle with depression, but try to convince everyone we are fine.

All this demonstrates how much we value others' high opinions of us. We want them to see us triumphant, people who walk with a firm step toward clear objectives for our lives. This is why we do everything possible to conceal those things that show our true condition of fragility and imperfection.

Paul declared, "I will boast all the more gladly about my weaknesses." Have you ever stopped to think how outlandish this declaration is? Not only would he do nothing to hide his weaknesses, but he would boast about them! Far from causing him shame, they would instead be the proof of his absolute dependence on Christ. Frankly, it is hard for us to understand the apostle's attitude. But we cannot stop ourselves from feeling, deep down, profound admiration for his style of leadership.

Take a moment to think back over the history of God's people. Can you remember any who were used because of their strength and virtue? Abraham was an old man, unable to have children. Joseph was a slave, long forgotten in an Egyptian dungeon. Moses was a stammering shepherd. Gideon was the youngest in his family and poor to boot. David was a simple shepherd. Nehemiah was no more than the king's cupbearer. Jeremiah was young and inexperienced. John the Baptist was completely unknown and lived in the desert. The disciples were simple fishermen, illiterate and uneducated. Paul, the fiery persecutor of the church, was deliberately weakened by the Lord, who sent him a thorn in the flesh to torment him.

And those are just the heroes of Scripture! What can we say about Augustine, Luther, Wesley, Hudson Taylor, Moody, Spurgeon or so many others who have deeply influenced the history of God's people? All of them, without exception, were used because they allowed their deficiencies to be the means for God to express His glory.

Food for Thought

Don't cover up your frailties, and don't waste time justifying them. When you conceal them, trying to look strong, Christ loses power in your life. Make friends with your weaknesses—they are the gate through which the fullness of God can be demonstrated in you!

Places of Refuge

O God, you are my God, earnestly I seek you; my soul thirsts for you, my body longs for you, in a dry and weary land where there is no water. Psalm 63:1

This psalm profoundly reveals David's heart, showing the insatiable longing he had for God. Most interesting, however, is the commentary below the title: "A psalm of David. When he was in the Desert of Judah." This places the passage in context and gives greater meaning to the marvelous sentiments it expresses.

David was in the Desert of Judah on two occasions. The first time he was fleeing from King Saul, who openly sought to kill him. The storyteller relates that at that time "David stayed in the desert strongholds and in the hills of the Desert of Ziph. Day after day Saul searched for him, but God did not give David into his hands" (1 Sam. 23:14). David's second time in the desert was when he had to abandon Jerusalem because of his son Absalom's rebellion. We are told that the king "continued up the Mount of Olives, weeping as he went; his head was covered and he was barefoot. All the people with him covered their heads too and were weeping as they went up" (2 Sam. 15:30).

Both scenes reveal a man caught in situations of intense personal anguish. How amazing, therefore, that in the midst of devastating circumstances he should exclaim, "Oh God, you are my God . . . my soul thirsts for you, my body longs for you."

What principle can we take from this psalm? Leaders should possess the ability, in times of crisis, to distance their lives from the circumstances surrounding them. In this way they can enter the presence of God and find in Him the relief they seek. With this help comes divine perspective, bringing heaven's viewpoint to their experience. Their priorities will once more coincide with God's, and they will passionately declare, "You alone are God, oh Lord!"

If you look at God's greatest servants, you will discover that in times of crisis each retired to a secret place of fellowship with Almighty God. Consider Christ in the Garden of Gethsemane, Paul and Silas in prison, Moses upon discovery of the golden calf or Nehemiah when he heard about the deplorable situation in Jerusalem. They went to a hidden refuge where they poured out their hearts to Him who lives and reigns forever. There they found the comfort and strength they needed to go on.

Food for Thought

The psalmist tells us, "God is our refuge and strength, an ever-present help in trouble. Therefore we will not fear, though the earth give way and the mountains fall into the heart of the sea" (Ps. 46:1–2). It is not simply our knowledge of this truth that brings solace. Comfort comes when we run to the One who is our refuge and hide in His arms. You should be a leader accustomed to sharing your difficulties with the Lord.

The Whole Gospel

That which was from the beginning, which we have heard, which we have seen with our eyes, which we have looked at and our hands have touched—this we proclaim concerning the Word of life. 1 John 1:1

We will not appreciate the full impact of John's words if we do not first consider the characteristics of the age in which we live. At no other time in history have we reached such alarming levels of information overload as today. The colossal amount of data now available through the Internet adds to the vast resources made available through recent technological advances. We now have access to the contents of newspapers, magazines, journals, encyclopedias and many other types of publications which were formerly only found in libraries.

Problematically, we don't have even a fraction of the time needed to process the material which comes our way each day. The only way to survive, we find, is by using a spirit of ruthless pragmatism when deciding what to read or listen to. We quickly scan messages in search of the "bottom line," hoping to save time and effort in accumulating information we have little use for.

This utilitarian spirit has also crept into the church. We have boiled down the gospel to a few concentrated truths. We offer others, or search ourselves, for the three secrets to answered prayer, the five principles to effective ministry or the seven steps to developing a good team. In all this we hope to somehow gain the upper hand as we flounder about in an endless sea of facts.

Notice the refreshing lack of "precision" in the words of the Apostle John. He doesn't want to give us the "bottom line." He is not interested in boiling down his experience to four spiritual principles that we absolutely must know. Instead, he attempts the impossible: to harness the message incarnate to a few words, helping his readers understand what the disciples experienced with Christ as they walked together. He does not draw exclusively from his mind to share these observations, but rather wants to pull together what they *heard* with their ears, what they *saw* with their eyes, what they *looked on* and *touched* with their hands.

John's approach reminds us that the gospel is about more than truth; it is about a relationship. And like any relationship, it has many wonderful features which are only savored through the full engagement of all our senses. Some will defy description, too intimate and profound to be captured by mere words. All, however, will point to the same mysterious truth: the eternal God clothed in human garments.

Food for Thought

As we go about the task of serving others in ministry, we too are called to make the gospel known by the way we live. Those around us should be able to see, feel and touch Jesus as they draw close to our lives, because the gospel is much deeper than anything our senses can perceive.

Running as a Team

March 1

Therefore, since we are surrounded by such a great cloud of witnesses, let us throw off everything that hinders and the sin that so easily entangles, and let us run with perseverance the race marked out for us. Hebrews 12:1

The author of Hebrews, like many of the great masters of the Word, chooses an analogy to illustrate the struggles we encounter as we walk with Christ. This analogy, probably familiar to many readers, is that of a race—specifically, a marathon. This kind of race, inspired by the heroic feat of a Greek warrior, involves running a great distance—more than 26 miles—without a break. The author uses the various challenges of a marathon to identify needed principles for our journey toward heaven.

The first element expressed is that "we are surrounded by such a great cloud of witnesses." This is a reference to the previous chapter which details a long list of heroes who have run the race: Abel, Enoch, Abraham, Sarah, Isaac, Jacob, Joseph, Moses, Rahab, Gideon, Barak, Samson, Jephthah and David. Space does not permit the author to mention countless other victors "whose weakness was turned to strength" (Heb. 11:34).

Through these examples the author seeks to encourage our hearts. The road ahead holds many difficulties and endless setbacks. We may sometimes even believe it is impossible to progress, struggling with the temptation to give up. But he reminds us that a great cloud of witnesses have run the race ahead of us—and what's more, they finished successfully!

The author also implies that the race should not be run alone. In present day marathons all good athletes run in a team. Sharing the discipline of leading the pack, they take turns setting the grueling pace that is crucial for success. At the same time they encourage and motivate each other, because there is always greater strength in numbers.

There is no doubt that a pastor walks a path which inevitably includes times of intense loneliness. But it is also true that the solitude of many leaders is self-imposed. They do not allow themselves to develop the kind of deep relationships which encourage and inspire our spiritual lives. Without this essential support they are easy prey to discouragement; they can begin to see themselves as victims misunderstood by others. Wise leaders, however, understand that all Christians need companions running beside them.

Food for Thought

Who are your fellow runners? If you have to pause to consider who they are, it is because you are running alone. Our teammates should be part of our inner circle of friends. Why not begin by asking God to provide you with these kinds of friends? Part of the richness of your spiritual life is in their hands, and you will not enjoy it to the fullest until you share the race with them.

Running Light

Therefore, since we are surrounded by such a great cloud of witnesses, let us throw off everything that hinders and the sin that so easily entangles, and let us run with perseverance the race marked out for us. Hebrews 12:1

The author of Hebrews has chosen the marathon, the longest race in the world, as an analogy to help us understand some of the dynamics of the Christian life. He gives various recommendations about the best way to run this race. One of those is the exhortation to "throw off everything that hinders," or as expressed in the American Standard Version, to "lay aside every weight."

If you have run or even observed a marathon, you will know that professional runners carry as little weight as possible. Their clothing is ultra light. Their footwear is specially designed for the race and weighs no more than about nine ounces. Some runners go barefoot to reduce even this minor weight. Few professional athletes carry anything extra during the race. The reason for this radical attitude is clear: If you intend to run such a distance, you don't want to carry anything not absolutely essential to the goal. Any additional weight will grow heavier by the mile, especially toward the end when your reserves of strength are sharply decreased.

When Christ instructed His disciples before sending them out to preach in pairs, He urged them to travel light: "Do not take along any gold or silver or copper in your belts; take no bag for the journey, or extra tunic, or sandals or a staff; for the worker is worth his keep" (Matt. 10:9–10). He discouraged them from ensuring their own well-being by the excessive accumulation of goods. Instead, He told them to take as little as possible on the journey and trust their good heavenly Father to provide all they needed along the way.

The word "weight" in today's verse is the same as the word used for a pregnant woman. When in the most advanced stages of pregnancy, a woman moves slowly and uncomfortably. Her size prevents agility and speed. The image speaks for itself. We are encouraged to get rid of excess baggage, all those things that might interfere in our walk with Christ. Even some legitimate things can bring complications into our lives.

The wise laborer knows how to distinguish between what is necessary for ministry and things that, although interesting, will eventually interfere with the work. Discipline is needed in order to say no to things which others may consider indispensable. With an eye on the finish line, you will be disciplined enough to keep free of things that unnecessarily tie you down.

Food for Thought

The challenge is not to choose between good and bad, but between necessary and unnecessary. Something good can be unnecessary for the fulfillment of our vocation and may eventually become an unbearable burden, slowing us down or even disqualifying us from the race.

Free from Sin

Therefore, since we are surrounded by such a great cloud of witnesses, let us throw off everything that hinders and the sin that so easily entangles, and let us run with perseverance the race marked out for us. Hebrews 12:1

In using the analogy of a marathon to help us understand the Christian life, the author of Hebrews exhorts us to "throw off . . . the sin that so easily entangles."

There are two key concepts in the author's admonition. The first lies in the word "easily." Sin, in its essence, is based on subtle distortions of the Word of God, not on gross differences that openly contradict the truth. Remember the subtlety the Enemy used in dialogue with Eve, first confusing her and then sowing the seed of doubt concerning God's goodness. Remember too his cleverness when challenging Jesus in the desert, even to the extent of quoting Scripture in an attempt to trap Him. It is because of this characteristic of sin that we are so often caught in attitudes and thoughts that dishonor the God we love.

The second concept is found in the phrase "entangles us." The Greek word conveys the idea of an obstacle that offers resistance and slows the runner. Imagine trying to run while wrapped in a sheet. Any kind of activity would be difficult in that condition because every part of the body would be limited in its movements.

This is an apt description of the effect of sin on our lives. When we are beset by sin, it hinders movement in all areas of our lives. Our emotions become bitter or sad, and our thoughts become full of condemnation and criticism. Our perspective is tinged with pessimism. Vision becomes clouded and everything is viewed as a potential problem. Our words become instruments of pain and destruction. Above all else, our relationship with God is severely affected. Hear the psalmist's confession: "When I kept silent, my bones wasted away through my groaning all day long. For day and night your hand was heavy upon me; my strength was sapped" (Ps. 32:3–4).

As ministers we cannot neglect for one instant the permanent inclination of humanity to be seduced by sin. In this regard we must always be alert to the wiles of the Enemy. Peter was right on target when he said, "Your enemy the devil prowls around like a roaring lion looking for someone to devour" (1 Pet. 5:8).

Food for Thought

Martin Luther once exclaimed, "I am more afraid of my own heart than of the pope and all his cardinals."[1] Experience and maturity had shown him that our biggest problems are not found in our circumstances, but in the deceit of our own hearts. For this reason the great reformer paid special attention to his inner cleanliness.

Running with Perseverance

Therefore, since we are surrounded by such a great cloud of witnesses, let us throw off everything that hinders and the sin that so easily entangles, and let us run with perseverance the race marked out for us. Hebrews 12:1

Today we continue our study of this passage in which the Christian life is likened to a marathon. Among other things, we are urged to "run with perseverance the race marked out for us."

The Apostle James encourages us to be joyful in difficulty, knowing that an important result of our trials is patience. And what an important virtue this is! Lack of patience led Abraham to seek a son through Hagar. Lack of patience led Joseph to seek a way out of jail by appealing to the cupbearer for assistance. Lack of patience led Moses to murder the Egyptian and flee to the desert, and lack of patience was probably one of the reasons Paul rejected young Mark.

The marathon is one of the few athletic events where youth is not a definite advantage. The world's greatest runners are not 18 or 20 year-olds; rather, the average age of marathon winners is closer to 35. Why is this? The young often lack that indispensable quality needed for a long distance race: knowing how to pace oneself in order to reach the finish line. I have run in marathons where young enthusiasts set off as if they were going to the corner to buy bread. The race lasts several hours, however, and nobody can complete it without establishing a careful stride.

There are many people who begin their spiritual experience with great fire and passion. In a short time they make unusual progress and apparently surpass others who have greater experience. They dazzle with the rate of speed they maintain. But few are able to maintain this pace for long. Most drop out in the same spectacular fashion in which they emerged.

The mature leader knows the race is long and isn't intimidated by those who seem to progress much faster in the Christian life. The prize is not for those who expend great bursts of energy, but rather for those who with a deliberate, constant pace, manage to cross the finish line.

Set a steady pace for the work of the ministry, wisely managing your resources. At the moment of greatest weariness, you will need the reserves you saved when you had abundant energy. This is the secret of great runners. When their bodies tell them to run faster, they apply the brakes. They know that the energy they save will be the key to crossing the finish line.

Food for Thought

St. Augustine once observed, "Patience is the companion of wisdom."[2] Those who are always rushing rarely have time to learn the lessons needful for success. What things make you feel impatient? In situations where you run out of patience, how do you react? What can you do to grow in patience?

Eyes Fixed on the Goal

Let us fix our eyes on Jesus, the author and perfecter of our faith, who for the joy set before him endured the cross, scorning its shame, and sat down at the right hand of the throne of God.
Hebrews 12:2

We have been considering the exhortations in Hebrews in which the analogy of a marathon is used to explain aspects of the Christian life. The author now prompts us to examine the runner's motivation.

The marathon originated with a young Greek soldier who ran a great distance after the Battle of Marathon to bring news of its outcome. The winner of a marathon gains enormous prestige, not just for demonstration of physical prowess, but also in identification with the Greek hero who first ran this distance.

In modern-day races the start and finish lines are often the same. Before running, the athletes glance at the podium. For a few seconds each one dreams of standing on its highest point, surrounded by applause and venerated as the best of all runners. Such a dream, though a fleeting thought, acts as a powerful stimulant for the athletes. Even those who have no chance of medaling cannot help but think of the finish line, that sublime moment in which all the training, discipline and physical agony pay off.

During the race there will be many moments when the marathoners will be tempted to quit. At these times the best runners will again entertain that glorious moment in which they will cross the goal. They will dig deep into their souls for strength to carry on, anticipating the glory to come.

Jesus excellently illustrates this. His greatest crisis came in Gethsemane. He confessed to His disciples His intense struggle with the temptation to quit His race. "My soul is overwhelmed with sorrow to the point of death," He told them (Matt. 26:38). He knelt to pray and concentrated on the intense struggle taking place in His heart, a battle between His Father's will and His own. Finally, He secured what was necessary in order to continue the race. He took His eyes off the imminent agony of death on the cross and fixed them on something which wonderfully inspired Him: the joy of reconciliation with His heavenly Father.

As a leader you need to fix your eyes on something more inspiring than your present situation. Perhaps it is the fulfillment of a word given you by the Lord or the realization of a vision you have received. Perhaps it will be the completion of a project that will glorify His name. Whatever it is, it will inspire and encourage you to carry on when your energy seems depleted.

Food for Thought

Where do you fix your eyes most of the time? What things tend to discourage you? What do you find inspiring? What steps should you take to fix your eyes more often on those things which lift your spirits?

6 March

The Battle No One Sees

Consider him who endured such opposition from sinful men, so that you will not grow weary and lose heart. Hebrews 12:3

The author of Hebrews brings out truths of the Christian life using the marathon as an analogy. One recommendation he makes for running this race is a secret that will keep us from growing weary and losing heart.

The author encourages us to fix our eyes on the example of Jesus Christ. The race was not easy for the Messiah. He had to face questioning, opposition, misunderstanding, ridicule, aggression and, finally, betrayal and abandonment. These would have been more than enough to derail even the strongest of us. But Christ, far from becoming discouraged, proceeded toward His goal with that strength and singleness of purpose characteristic of the truly great. Jesus triumphed because He understood that victories are first won in the heart.

Good athletes know that at least half the ability to win depends on a positive attitude. For this reason they devote as much attention to mental preparation as to physical fitness. They may possess enviable physical stamina, allowing for great achievements in their field. But if in their heart they feel there is no chance of winning, they will almost certainly lose even if possessing superior abilities. The battle is often won or lost in the hidden places of the inner self.

As leaders we must be absolutely clear about the real battle we are facing. The well-known Christian author, Charles Swindoll, has observed, "I am convinced that life is 10% what happens to me and 90% of how I react to it."[3] The key decisions in this life are made in the heart, where the flesh is always ready and willing to offer seductive alternatives to God's truth. Our greatest enemies are the ones hidden in the recesses of our own souls. "For out of the heart come evil thoughts, murder, adultery, sexual immorality, theft, false testimony, slander. These are what make a man 'unclean'" (Matt.15:19–20).

Food for Thought

Paul said that one of the crucial elements for a victorious life was a renewed mind. "Do not conform any longer to the pattern of this world, but be transformed by the renewing of your mind. Then you will be able to test and approve what God's will is—his good, pleasing and perfect will," he wrote (Rom. 12:2). What kinds of thoughts occupy your mind during the day? Which ones cause discouragement? Which motivate you to continue in the good fight? What can you do to bring greater discipline into this area of your life?

Finding Meaning in Circumstances

I went past the field of the sluggard, past the vineyard of the man who lacks judgment; thorns had come up everywhere, the ground was covered with weeds, and the stone wall was in ruins. I applied my heart to what I observed and learned a lesson from what I saw.
Proverbs 24:30–32

The situation described in this verse was surely not uncommon along the roadsides of Israel. Many people would pass by these places and see the state of neglect into which the fields had fallen. They may have been surprised by the level of negligence, but would continue on their way.

The author of this verse instead took time to reflect on the scene before him, trying to discover the reason for what he saw. He attempted to look beyond the obvious to understand what principles the overgrown field would reveal to those with discernment. Such lessons are not evident to people who go through life in a hurry, thinking only about their own affairs. These truths can only be discerned by those who add the rigorous exercise of reflection to the process of observation. For the author of Proverbs, this reflection bore fruit, and he learned a lesson.

All that surrounds us can offer valuable teaching for our own lives; this is why it pays to be observant. The discipline of reflection frees us from simply shaking our heads at our neighbor's lack of responsibility, or from speaking criticisms which do nothing to resolve the situation. Sadly, however, our observations very often produce only meager results.

A well-directed reflection can be tremendously useful when we are seeking to learn from the varied situations we come across. Without doubt this is a recurring theme in Proverbs. In the first chapter the author points out that "wisdom calls aloud in the street, she raises her voice in the public squares; at the head of the noisy streets she cries out, in the gateways of the city she makes her speech" (Prov. 1:20–21). The four places mentioned—the streets, the squares, the street corners and the gateways of the city—are places where the activities of daily life were carried out. In the midst of these activities, a person could learn many useful lessons for life. This is the essence of gaining wisdom. It is wrong to believe that one only learns within the framework of a classroom or at an event specializing in a certain subject. Wisdom is available to all who have eyes to see and hearts ready to meditate on what is going on around them.

Food for Thought

In his famous commentary Matthew Henry states: "It is better to get wisdom than gold. Gold is another's, wisdom is our own; gold is for the body and time, wisdom for the soul and eternity."[4]

Faith in the Disciples

I have revealed you to those whom you gave me out of the world. They were yours; you gave them to me and they have obeyed your word. . . . While I was with them, I protected them and kept them safe by that name you gave me. None has been lost except the one doomed to destruction so that Scripture would be fulfilled. John 17:6, 12

A disciple is, by definition, someone in the process of formation. In this status spiritual maturity will be in a state of flux. There will be moments when a disciple displays great wisdom; at other times immaturity will lead to mistakes, some of which may be serious.

Such was the case with Jesus' disciples. At times they brought profound happiness to the Lord, as at the return of the seventy. Jesus was "full of joy through the Holy Spirit" (Luke 10:21); He was beginning to see the fruit of His ministry to the disciples. On other occasions, however, the same Twelve were the source of great disappointment. When Christ came down from the Mount of Transfiguration, for example, He found His followers caught up in a pointless debate with the Pharisees concerning the healing of an epileptic boy. At this point He exclaimed, "O unbelieving generation . . . how long shall I stay with you? How long shall I put up with you?" (Mark 9:19).

So how do we avoid growing discouraged with the people we are discipling? Our text reveals the secret of Jesus' patience with the Twelve, men who would have had us at our wits' end. Christ did not base His evaluation of the disciples on their behavior. Surely on more than one occasion He would have felt like ditching them. But take note of the Messiah's prayer at the end of His ministry: "I am not praying for the world, but for those you have given me, for they are yours" (John 17:9). Here we find the key. Jesus hadn't chosen these men alone; He had received them from the Father. He could trust that His Father had made no mistake in His choice. This conviction kept Christ steady in the midst of much adversity.

As a leader you need this same conviction about the people you disciple. To persevere in the task, you must be certain God has given you these lives, for there will be many disheartening occasions due to peoples' lack of maturity. A leader who focuses on these disappointments will soon give up! I know a pastor who does not have the same ministerial team for more than six months. Each time someone fails he puts him aside and chooses another. The result is that after many years of ministry, he hasn't formed a single disciple. Only a strong spiritual conviction can keep us firm in the disappointments and frustrations that our disciples bring us at times.

Food for Thought

"The will to persevere is very often the difference between failure and success." (David Sarnoff) [5]

Encouraging Change

That same day Pharaoh gave this order to the slave drivers and foremen in charge of the people: "You are no longer to supply the people with straw for making bricks; let them go and gather their own straw. But require them to make the same number of bricks as before; don't reduce the quota. They are lazy; that is why they are crying out, 'Let us go and sacrifice to our God.'" Exodus 5:6–8

Pharaoh's reply to Moses and Aaron's request was not at all encouraging. Quite the contrary! He first threw them out of the palace. He then increased the Israelites' already difficult workload to a level that was absolutely unbearable. Their brick production was to remain the same, but now the Egyptians would not provide the raw materials with which to make them. Predictably, the people's reaction toward Moses and Aaron took the form of an angry rebuke. Things had already been bad before these two had arrived to intercede for them; but now they were in a situation ten times worse. Faced with unanimous condemnation, the two leaders were completely without support.

If you have studied this time in Israel's history, as well as their unfortunate wandering in the desert, you can't help noticing how often they believed they would have been better off in Egypt. When faced with any obstacle, the people looked back and remembered how "good" things had been in the land of their slavery.

If we take into account their disposition, we can understand why the Lord allowed their situation to deteriorate to such an extent after Moses and Aaron's intervention. God was preparing His people for change.

We often find ourselves in very negative situations. But a stubborn inclination in human beings leads us to accept our circumstances with resignation. A popular saying aptly expresses this propensity: "Better the devil you know than the devil you don't." We stop fighting for or even dreaming of better things to come. We abandon ourselves to fate. We renounce even the hope of change—and when hope is lost, everything is lost.

But amazingly, even when we lose hope, our God goes on fighting for us! The enormous challenge of mobilizing those who have lost all interest in their deliverance rests with Him. So how does He do it? He intervenes in our circumstances, allowing deterioration to provoke discomfort. Finally, out of desperation, we begin to consider the possibility of change. Sometimes this is the only way to move those sunk deep in the pit of resignation!

Food for Thought

I have heard it said that "adversity is frequently an unrecognized opportunity." How do you react when faced with difficulties? What can you do to look for the opportunities they bring? Make the decision to grow and progress in the midst of crisis situations. It may well be that God Himself has provoked the crisis!

10 March | On the Lookout for Hidden Dangers

Who can discern his errors? Forgive my hidden faults. Keep your servant also from willful sins; may they not rule over me. Then will I be blameless, innocent of great transgression.
Psalm19:12–13

The question asked in this verse is rhetorical. It requires no response, the answer being implicit in the question itself. And in this verse the answer is nobody! Not a single person has the capacity to discern his own mistakes.

Despite this, most of us seem quite confident when it comes to defending our innocence. The psalmist understood a fundamental principle of the spiritual life: Human beings can never see clearly when looking into their own souls. This truth was repeated by the prophet Jeremiah: "The heart is deceitful above all things and beyond cure" (Jer. 17:9). Even when we search and examine our lives with great care, we can't discern our own mistakes, because the very essence of sin rests in deceit. What is hidden can't be dealt with, obviously, and therefore has great capacity to derail our lives. This is why the psalmist exclaimed, "Forgive my hidden faults."

It is no coincidence either that the theme of arrogance came to mind while he meditated on the subject of hidden sin. Of all sins, the most difficult to detect is pride. As a wise commentator observed, "Nobody is so close to falling as he who is confident of standing firm."[6] We all have a tremendous ability to recognize the sin of pride in our neighbor, but we are notably lacking in discernment when it comes to examining our own lives.

The psalmist knew that unconfessed arrogance eventually becomes a hard master which drives one's life and leads to perdition. It takes control of a person's behavior. Arrogance, the master, will be the one to decide in each situation which is the "best" way to behave. Nobody will be able to offer suggestions, correction or advice to someone controlled by pride, or even draw close to them; arrogance will not tolerate interference from anyone, lest evil is recognized and the person repents.

A proud leader can bring much pain to a congregation. Therefore, it is good to remember that our own opinion of our spiritual purity is often inaccurate. Wise leaders know there is some information about themselves known only to God. For this reason they do not trust their own heart evaluation, but will want the Lord to examine them, to bring to light that which is hidden so they may obtain true inner purity.

Food for Thought

Saint Augustine once said, "When a man uncovers his sin, God covers it. When a man covers his sin, God uncovers it. When a man confesses his sin, God forgives it."[7]

Friends We Can Count On

And Jonathan made a covenant with David because he loved him as himself. Jonathan took off the robe he was wearing and gave it to David, along with his tunic, and even his sword, his bow and his belt. 1 Samuel 18:3–4

A leader is often in a lonely place. Many problems must be faced alone, and pressures are suffered that others don't understand, often because of a congregation's expectations. A leader treasures a vision that others have not yet glimpsed and has knowledge of facts that most people are unaware of. Because of all this—and much more—a leader's path inevitably contains a certain amount of solitude.

For this reason all leaders need two or three people who are close friends, people with whom they can discuss realities impossible to share with others.

Jonathan and David developed this kind of relationship. They both held important positions within the kingdom, and both had responsibilities among the people. This did not prevent them from establishing a deep friendship which often brought relief and comfort in the midst of pressures they faced daily.

Notice, in addition, that these men took their friendship a step further than normal. Most of us enjoy good moments with our friends, but our relationship is not the result of a deliberate commitment. We simply experience these moments as they arise. David and Jonathan not only shared a close friendship, but they took it to the level of a mutual pact. They made a promise to look after and love each other even in the face of the most adverse circumstances. Together they made the decision to grow as friends and to seek each others' best. Few relationships reach this level of commitment.

In this scene we see one aspect that differentiates a great leader from a common one. Most of us wait for life to send us opportunities and people who will be a blessing to us. Mature leaders do not wait for perfect situations in which to grow. They create them, taking the initiative to work and progress under those conditions which show promise of future blessing.

Friendship constructed on a pact, like that which underlies marriage, is the strongest that can exist between two people. This is a relationship which stands the test of every setback and all adversity. Its point of reference is not the daily ups and downs of life; rather, it is anchored in a promise of eternal dimensions. Thus, it lasts a lifetime, even when the circumstances which birthed it are removed. This is the kind of commitment our heavenly Father has with us.

Food for Thought

Do you have friends? What kind of relationship do you have with them? With which of them can you share the burdens and pressures of ministry? How can you introduce necessary ingredients to your friendships to lead them toward sustained growth?

12 March

When a Crisis Strikes

David was greatly distressed because the men were talking of stoning him; each one was bitter in spirit because of his sons and daughters. But David found strength in the LORD his God. Then David said to Abiathar the priest, the son of Ahimelech, "Bring me the ephod." Abiathar brought it to him, and David inquired of the LORD, "Shall I pursue this raiding party? Will I overtake them?" "Pursue them," he answered. "You will certainly overtake them and succeed in the rescue." 1 Samuel 30:6–8

David had gone out to fight alongside the Philistines, with whom he was obliged to live after suffering years of persecution from Saul. While David and his men were far from home, their city was sacked and their women and children taken prisoner. When the warriors returned, they discovered their homes in ruins. Their profound anguish quickly turned to bitter reproach.

Whoever has taken responsibility for others will occasionally face severe crises with potentially devastating consequences. This is part of leadership. Followers may question their leader and consider drastic retaliatory measures. David's men wanted to kill him.

In extremity our most carnal reactions always surface. We grieve over losses, question the steps that led to the trouble and get angry with those closest to us, looking for someone to blame. We make hasty, rash decisions. We worry about possible consequences. None of these generally helps toward a solution.

We can learn much from observing David's behavior in this critical moment. First, notice the instinctive reaction of a man accustomed to walking with God: "David found strength in the LORD his God." In times of crisis, a mature person should immediately approach the only One who can correct our perspective, restore balance and bring peace in our storm. David, as he had always done, wasted no time in seeking from the Lord the strength he didn't possess.

Second, having calmed his emotions and strengthened his spirit, David did not set about studying the situation to find a resolution. He had the priest seek a specific word from the Lord concerning this grave problem. He knew that at the end of the day, his own opinion and those of his men were worthless. What was vital was to receive direction from the One truly in control of the situation. As a result, David was not only strengthened, but was able to take appropriate steps to recover all they had lost and thus win an important victory for everyone.

Although difficult to live through, we must never forget that our crises provide some of the most striking and powerful lessons in the lives of our followers as they observe our responses. That is when the best—or the worst—in our hearts comes to the surface.

Food for Thought

How do you behave in a dilemma? Which of your reactions actually increases the magnitude of your problem? What can you do to manage crisis situations with greater wisdom?

Making the Most of What We Are Given

The Spirit of the LORD will come upon you in power, and you will prophesy with them; and you will be changed into a different person. Once these signs are fulfilled, do whatever your hand finds to do, for God is with you. 1 Samuel 10:6–7

Which of us would not like to hear such words spoken about us? Who would dare oppose someone to whom such a declaration had been made? The word includes the promise of a powerful visitation of the Spirit of God, a prophetic ministry and a changed heart. Armed with a blessing of this magnitude, this person could confront any challenge in his path, having the backing of God Almighty at all times. What a gift! Is there any obstacle in the way of such a person's ministry?

If we had been present, all of us would have imagined the incredible things God would accomplish through the life of this servant. We would have been thoroughly surprised if someone had said, "The main obstacle to the fulfilling of this word will be *the man himself*!"

And so it was. The person to whom these words were spoken was King Saul. There was such promise in the declaration Samuel made to him. The life of the king, however, illustrates an important spiritual principle: One can receive all the gifts and all the anointing necessary for an extraordinary ministry; but if what we receive is not accompanied by our complete submission to God, all that awaits us is ruin.

I recently read an article by Dr. J. Robert Clinton, a man who has given concentrated study to the great leaders in the history of God's people.[8] Clinton points out that many leaders who failed did so in the latter part of their lives. In other words, they started out with terrific passion in ministries which promised great advance in extending the Kingdom. But on the way many of them fell into adultery, were derailed by other passions or were simply trapped by the apparent "greatness" of their own ministries, obsessed with themselves.

Saul provides us with a sad illustration of this truth. He started out with an enormous advantage over his peers. But he ended up abandoned on the battlefield, without the support of God or his people. He didn't know how to complement his calling with a life of devotion and submission to Him who had given him all these things.

Food for Thought

If you had to evaluate your spiritual life at the moment, how would you describe it? Have you lost your passion for the Lord? Are you more interested in your ministry than in God? Why don't you take a moment now to express your unconditional commitment to God? No achievement is so important that it is worth losing Him.

True Freedom

At daybreak Jesus went out to a solitary place. The people were looking for him and when they came to where he was, they tried to keep him from leaving them. Luke 4:42

The scene described in today's text takes place after an intense period of ministry during which Christ healed many sick and expelled many demons from those who came to see Him. As was His custom, the Son of God had withdrawn to a lonely place, seeking greater intimacy with the Father. The crowds, however, were quick to find Him and tried to keep Him from leaving.

Their reaction reveals humanity's intense desire to "hold on to God" in order to guarantee His blessing over our life plans. But this desire is not a product of the sovereign work of the Spirit. It comes instead from our inclination to control the Most High for our own benefit. The same perverse creativity we display in attempting to secure relationships with others also blurs our spiritual experience with the Lord. We don't hesitate to use any means necessary to achieve our end: to secure for ourselves the Lord's cooperation in the blessing of our personal lives.

Born again believers should understand that freedom forms the only basis for a deep relationship with the Lord. To mature we must understand Christ's words to Nicodemus: "The wind blows wherever it pleases. You hear its sound, but you cannot tell where it comes from or where it is going. So it is with everyone born of the Spirit" (John 3:8). Just as we have no power to generate or control the wind, so it is with our Lord. We cannot stop Him, hold onto Him or redirect Him. We can't impose any condition or project our expectations on Him. Rather, He offers a relationship in which He can enjoy the same freedom He has granted us as human beings.

This way of freedom often causes us difficulty for one simple reason: We live in a world full of pain and suffering. On more than one occasion, we have been hurt in relationships. Because of this we seek to avoid further disappointment by exercising control over circumstances and people. Our objective is to organize life in such a way as to reap the maximum benefit from that which surrounds us. But despite these efforts we continue to suffer anguish and sadness. The truth is that even our most elaborate control strategies cannot prosper, because authority over these things has not been given to us.

Food for Thought

Christ invites us to walk a road in which we abandon our attempts to organize the world—and God—as we please. It is a path that requires an attitude of surrender which seems risky to us. When we cease our efforts, God finds room in us to begin working. He can then produce a transformation which puts us at peace with a world different from the one we would like.

A Servant's Vocation

It was just before the Passover Feast. Jesus knew that the time had come for him to leave this world and go to the Father. Having loved his own who were in the world, he now showed them the full extent of his love. John 13:1

Have you ever met someone who is going through tremendous personal problems? Very few people possess the ability to think about something other than their own issues. We find it difficult to resist introducing our woes into every conversation or wrapping ourselves in a mantle of complete indifference toward others. The Son of Man was not like this.

The agony of crucifixion was not unknown to Christ, though He had not yet experienced it Himself. The Romans had introduced this cruel method of execution many years before the Savior walked this earth. We can imagine that Jesus had more than once seen criminals hanging on wooden crosses outside Israel's cities. But the enormity of His impending trial seems to have been felt in all its intensity in the agonizing struggle He experienced in Gethsemane. It was there that Jesus confessed to those closest to Him that He felt anguish to the point of death. It would have seemed understandable for Him to dedicate the preceding hours and days to strengthening His soul and focusing His spiritual resources. If anyone had the right to withdraw into himself before a crisis, that person was Jesus. Faced with such an unspeakable trial, we would have understood if He had been self-absorbed or melancholic.

In the face of approaching suffering, Christ was fully aware that His hour had come to pass from this world to the Father. And this step would inevitably be taken by way of the cross. At this crucial moment of His life, however, Christ continued to think of His disciples and did not allow His personal struggles to distract Him from loving them at every moment and in all circumstances.

The lesson we learn from His example is clear: True love does not consider difficulties sufficient reason to stop caring for others. Many of us have gone to comfort a terminal patient in the hospital only to be blessed by the very one we went to encourage. Their example reminds us that true love does not take days off, go on vacation or come to an end.

This vocation is not the same as slavery to service, as shown by Martha when the Messiah visited her house (Luke 10:38–42). This is something entirely different. He who truly loves does so in all circumstances, even in the midst of deep personal trials.

Food for Thought

"Love never fails. But where there are prophecies, they will cease; where there are tongues, they will be stilled; where there is knowledge, it will pass away" (1 Cor. 13:8).

Lasting Love

It was just before the Passover Feast. Jesus knew that the time had come for him to leave this world and go to the Father. Having loved his own who were in the world, he now showed them the full extent of his love. John 13:1

Have you ever felt tired of loving someone? Very often in situations of pastoral counseling, I hear people say, "I loved that person too much." Is it possible to love someone too much? Is there some measure which, once reached, allows us to say we have satisfied the demands of love required of a believer? Who sets that level?

When we make a statement like this, we really mean that we have done a lot for the other person but have received very little in return for our investment. Of course, it is possible that the other person could be thinking that *they* have loved much, as well, and received very little in exchange for their effort.

John tells us that Christ, having loved His own, "loved them to the end" (ASV). How conclusive that statement sounds! Jesus didn't receive even a tenth part of the fruit possible in relation to the investment He had made. Under this reasoning He certainly could have said He had loved His own too much. Nevertheless, a few hours before He died, we find Him dedicated to blessing His disciples with the same consideration always characteristic of Him.

The Messiah never measured His level of investment according to the return He would receive. His parameters were different and did not depend on comparing His own effort with that of the disciples. The measure of His love was determined by the pact He had made with His Father. This covenant was based on the distance He was willing to go for others—a distance that went as far as death itself. His commitment, therefore, did not depend on recognition or reward from those around Him. It was a unilateral commitment, the level of which had been agreed on with the Father Himself.

Here we have, then, the true dimension of love. It is not a feeling, but a commitment—a commitment that goes further than the behavior of others or the circumstances in which we find ourselves. It is a covenant that depends entirely on our relationship to God, and should lead us to a love that never ends. Christ Himself illustrated this truth dramatically when, hanging on the cross, He interceded for those who had persecuted Him and asked for their forgiveness.

Food for Thought

As a leader you need to establish this kind of commitment to your own. If you don't, you will cease to love them each time they disappoint, hurt or betray you. The determination to do this does not depend on their behavior, but on the God to whom you have declared your loyalty. He alone can keep you steady in your commitment!

Unselfish Service

The evening meal was being served, and the devil had already prompted Judas Iscariot, son of Simon, to betray Jesus. Jesus knew that the Father had put all things under his power, and that he had come from God and was returning to God; so he got up from the meal, took off his outer clothing, and wrapped a towel around his waist. John 13:2–4

Something that regularly hinders our desire to serve others is our natural desire for personal benefit in what we do. None of us, of course, would openly admit to this tendency. We would like to believe that our service is completely unselfish. However, if we allow the Spirit to scrutinize our hearts with the utmost care, it is likely that some surprising personal interests will come to light.

In his telling of this unique experience, John had already brought out some of the spiritual lessons surrounding Jesus' washing of the disciples' feet. Then he added that Christ knew "that the Father had put all things under his power, and that he had come from God and was returning to God" (John 3:3). This declaration is of singular importance in understanding Christ's actions.

Jesus was about to perform an act of service having distinctly domestic connotations. From a personal perspective, He would receive no benefit at all by performing this task. And Christ was aware of the true dimensions of His spiritual authority: The Father had given all things into His hands! His origin was heavenly, and His destiny was heavenly too. So He was lacking nothing, in need of nothing.

Knowing that this act would not change His personal situation in any way or bring any dramatic benefit to His ministry, Christ took upon Himself a responsibility that was normally the work of a servant.

In this decision we find the most genuine expression of what it means to serve. We often serve those who will be grateful to us or who can help us, or who will perhaps add a bit of prestige to our lives. Rarely, though, do we "lower ourselves" to serve those who have absolutely nothing to offer in return. Christ chose this path, and in His example we see part of the secret of His greatness. Service that makes an impact is found in laying aside the prestige and authority of our position, serving simply for the joy of serving.

Food for Thought

Oswald Chambers writes: "Service is the overflow of superabounding devotion." [9] ***We can offer true service only when it is an expression of an intense relationship with God.***

Everyday Opportunities

The evening meal was being served, and the devil had already prompted Judas Iscariot, son of Simon, to betray Jesus. Jesus knew that the Father had put all things under his power, and that he had come from God and was returning to God; so he got up from the meal, took off his outer clothing, and wrapped a towel around his waist. John 13:2–4

I believe we all have a measure of heroism within. In emergencies or in extreme need, we do not hesitate to step out and serve our neighbor. I remember a personal situation in which I had to go out in an awful storm to get urgently needed medicine for someone. I pedaled my bicycle several miles through torrential rain to get the required medication. In situations of this kind we may even see a hint of romance!

Our vocation as servants is less dramatic, however, when involved with an entirely domestic scene. In that setting we receive no applause for our acts of service. What we do simply forms part of our everyday chores. It is precisely because there is no expectation of reward that we find it so hard to serve others.

Christ rose during the Passover meal. It is likely the disciples had noticed that nobody had washed their feet on arrival at the house. Perhaps they were uncomfortable with their feet dusty and unwashed. The Son of God, however, was the only One who did something about it.

In Latin American culture, the moments when the family sits down to eat are tremendously important. Once everyone is settled at the table, nobody wants to get up for anything else that might be needed. The family would rather eat without salt than get up to retrieve the salt shaker!

But the home offers the best occasions for service, since opportunities abound. It is also the place where we can learn most about the meaning of servanthood. Within the home nobody is going to give us a medal for serving our family. We must learn to serve in situations where we would frankly prefer to be doing something else. Service at home teaches us to see the needs of others before they ask for our help.

The benefits of serving in these situations are countless, and our personal growth will be notable to the extent that we take advantage of these opportunities. In the process of discipling others, our example will also serve to model the path they must walk in their own lives. Many will surely be watching us in these situations that seem so unrelated to real "spirituality." The most incredible lessons, however, can be taught here.

Food for Thought

"The measure of a man is not in the number of his servants, but in the number of people he serves." (Paul Moody) [10]

The Practice of Service

The evening meal was being served, and the devil had already prompted Judas Iscariot, son of Simon, to betray Jesus. Jesus knew that the Father had put all things under his power, and that he had come from God and was returning to God; so he got up from the meal, took off his outer clothing, and wrapped a towel around his waist. John 13:2–4

We have been examining details in the context of Christ's washing of the disciples' feet. Some additional observations may be gained from further study of this passage.

Notice the level of maturity shown in Christ's gesture. An essential step before performing an act of service is to identify the need. When we were children, it was necessary for our elders not only to indicate a need for service but also to compel us to do the job—our perspective of life did not include an interest in the needs of others. Some people never get beyond that stage and, even as adults, do not serve unless they are pressured into doing so. Then there are those who have progressed to a higher level of maturity. They respond with joy when asked to serve their neighbor because they understand that it is a privilege granted those who belong to Christ.

But there is a third level of maturity. At this level it is not necessary for others to draw attention to opportunities for us to serve. Instead, we see the need for service before anyone says anything. As we go about the activities in our daily routine, we are attentive to opportunities that present themselves. Christ saw the need for His disciples' feet to be washed and did something about it.

It is Christ's *action* I want to underscore. Nobody can serve his neighbor from the comfort of an armchair. Neither is it possible to experience the joy of service if one does not move beyond the theory of being willing to care for other's needs. Service is not worth anything until it is converted into concrete action. For this reason Christ rose from the table, laid aside His garments, girded Himself with a towel and, taking water, began to wash the disciples' feet. It was this series of concrete actions which expressed His real desire to serve.

Service is an important part of our role as leaders. To develop this side of our lives, we need to ask our heavenly Father to open our eyes to the opportunities around us and then motivate us to do something about them.

Food for Thought

What are the signs that indicate someone needs your service? How can you teach your followers to be sensitive to these signs? What attitudes are important if you are to be a good example of service?

Service without Favoritism

After that, he poured water into a basin and began to wash his disciples' feet, drying them with the towel that was wrapped around him. John 13:5

Perhaps you have had moments of embarrassment because of some act of service done for you, feeling you did not deserve what you were receiving. If so, you will understand how the disciples must have felt when Jesus bent down to wash their feet, one by one. Imagine how uncomfortable they surely were on seeing the Master fulfilling a service normally rendered by the lowest slave of the household. Once again, Christ shocked them with behavior that was completely different from anything they had ever seen.

It is not on this that I want to focus, however. Today's reflection revolves around something implicit in the text.

Jesus already knew who was going to betray Him. Nevertheless, when washing the disciples' feet, John does not say that Christ skipped Judas. With the same affection and tenderness, He washed the feet of each disciple, including the one who would betray Him.

It is in this gesture that we see the deepest expression of the love of the Son of God. It is difficult enough for us to love and serve people we like. But in Christ we are to show consideration not only to those we appreciate but also to those who would do us wrong. This image offers one of the most sublime evidences of the power of God's grace to melt away rancor and bitterness toward our enemies.

With this action Christ illustrates the parameters of the Word of God for all demonstrations of love. He Himself had taught His disciples: "Love your enemies and pray for those who persecute you, that you may be sons of your Father in heaven. He causes his sun to rise on the evil and the good, and sends rain on the righteous and the unrighteous" (Matt. 5:44–45). The washing of the disciple's feet reveals the dimensions of His commitment to the people He was developing.

We find in this scene, therefore, an important principle for us as leaders. In many congregations there is a group that does not respond to our ministry. One of the best ways to prevent bitterness is to love them with expressions of service. It is possible that this will not change their attitudes. But one thing is certain: It will be impossible for us to continue harboring anger in our hearts toward these people. Our service to them will gradually purify our spirits so the love of God can dwell fully within us. Bless those who do wrong and watch the grace of God work powerfully in your own life.

Food for Thought

"If your enemy is hungry, feed him; if he is thirsty, give him something to drink. In doing this, you will heap burning coals on his head" (Rom. 12:20).

Grace to Receive

He came to Simon Peter, who said to him, "Lord, are you going to wash my feet?" Jesus replied, "You do not realize now what I am doing, but later you will understand." "No," said Peter, "you shall never wash my feet." Jesus answered, "Unless I wash you, you have no part with me." John 13:6–8

True humility is difficult to describe. It has to do with an accurate concept of one's self. There is more to it than this, however, because it is the result of God's Spirit working in our hearts and, as such, retains a certain element of mystery.

Perhaps this is the reason the great writer Robert Murray M'Cheyne exclaimed, "Oh for true, unfeigned humility! I know I have cause to be humble; and yet I do not know one half of that cause. I know I am proud; and yet I do not know the half of that pride."[11]

There is no doubt the disciples were completely baffled by Christ's washing of their feet. This job was normally done by a household servant. How had it not occurred to one of them to undertake this task before the Lord did it? Surely some of them felt ashamed at their lack of sensitivity.

Only Peter, however, dared to say, "You shall never wash my feet!" It seems there is a genuine note of humility in his exclamation. But let's take a closer look. What kind of humility presumes it can forbid the Son of God? The disciple's words reveal his lack of discernment, so the Master tenderly corrects him. But once he understands, Peter goes to the other extreme: "Lord, not just my feet but my hands and my head as well!" (John 13:9).

Do we realize what has just happened? Once again Peter is giving Jesus instructions as to His task. This is nothing but pride! And yet at first glance he seemed truly submissive and humble.

The subtlety of this situation should serve as a warning. Humility is more difficult to put into practice than we expect. Our own efforts to be humble are constantly undermined by the deceit of our hearts. Even apparently spiritual attitudes can have a good dose of pride. This is why we need God to work within us, so that real humility can take root in our lives.

Today's scene leaves us with a simple but distinct message: We desperately need the Lord to work in the deepest parts of our being, to bring to light all that dishonors Him. We must be convinced that pride is an enemy permanently stalking us. Thus, we need to call out for mercy each and every day of our lives.

Food for Thought

Meditate on the wisdom of this observation made by Phillips Brooks: "The true way to be humble is not to stoop until you are smaller than yourself, but to stand at your real height against some higher nature that will show you what the real smallness of your greatness is." [12]

An Unforgettable Lesson

Now that I, your Lord and Teacher, have washed your feet, you also should wash one another's feet. I have set you an example that you should do as I have done for you.
John 13:14–15

Imagine for a moment that Jesus had taught this lesson by today's methods. He would first have announced, with sufficient advance notice, the date of a "Seminar on Service" so the disciples could plan ahead and perhaps invite interested friends. In private Christ would have dedicated long hours to studying biblical texts on the subject, carefully planning His arguments to make a good case on the importance of service. On the established date He would have met with His students and shared His results, highlighting the importance of service and pointing out ways we can learn to serve. He would not have finished His lesson without exhorting the disciples to look for opportunities to practice what they had heard in class.

You will already have realized the enormous distance between our efforts to equip the saints for ministry and the lessons Christ taught His disciples. Take note of His strategy. He did not announce anything or prepare the disciples with a speech. He gave them no explanation. At the least expected moment, when everyone was relaxed over the supper, He rose and began preparing to wash their feet.

Can you imagine the looks that passed among the disciples? What was their unconventional Master up to now? When He was ready, He began His task, not speaking a word. The disciples looked on, torn between embarrassment and curiosity. When He got to Peter, the "spokesman" of the group dared to question Jesus' actions. Only then did the Master offer an explanation, but it was brief and did not clarify His unusual behavior.

When He returned to the table, Jesus was ready to conclude the lesson they had experienced. Except for the dialogue with Peter, He had not uttered a single word. Nevertheless, what He had just taught them was one of the most dramatic lessons they had learned in the three years they had shared with Him.

There is no need to belabor this point. As a leader the most effective lessons can be taught without resorting to words. However, we have developed an almost abnormal dependence on words as the only tool for teaching others. Words abound in our churches; our people are exposed to a never ending succession of classes and sermons.

How much of this remains? Very little, I'm afraid.

Christ did add words to His example; He did not leave the disciples to work out an interpretation. But His words were the perfect conclusion to a lesson already engraved in fire on their hearts. He simply helped them understand what they had seen.

Food for Thought

Howard Hendricks shares this observation on the art of teaching: "Good teaching—and true education—consists simply of a series of teachable moments." [13] ***Take full advantage of these moments!***

Ministers of Consolation

Praise be to the God and Father of our Lord Jesus Christ, the Father of compassion and the God of all comfort, who comforts us in all our troubles, so that we can comfort those in any trouble with the comfort we ourselves have received from God. 2 Corinthians 1:3–4

It is no coincidence that Paul opens this letter with such a declaration. More than any other of his writings, the second letter to the Corinthians contains horrifying details of his many trials. In chapter 11, a list of these experiences includes work, prisons, whippings, beatings, shipwrecks, exhaustion, hunger, thirst, cold and nakedness. So it's not surprising that he speaks with authority on the subject of consolation.

In these verses he mentions at least two things important for us. The first is that God is the Father of compassion and of all comfort. These two features of His personality reveal the goodness of God's heart. Even though He loves all people equally, it seems He has special compassion for those suffering anguish, injustice, oppression or abandonment. In the Old Testament He is often described as the God who heals the brokenhearted (Ps. 147:3). In a supernatural way, He ministers to those in crisis and binds their wounds to restore them to health. He has done this for countless saints throughout history, visiting them in their moments of heartache and bringing upon their lives a powerful manifestation of His grace.

And second, Paul affirms that he can comfort others with this same consolation. It is at this statement I would like you to pause a moment. In ministry you will most certainly be called to walk with people going through terrible seasons of personal anguish. You have probably been on this path yourself more than once. Notice the apostle says he consoled "with the comfort we ourselves have received from God."

In painful situations there are always people who offer comfort, but not divine comfort. Their attempts to help include reciting verses, recounting their own experiences or trying to identify the spiritual angle on the trial the person is going through. None of this helps, and often produces only irritation. The results show how limited the flesh is to undertake truly spiritual works.

The consolation that heals is born of a supernatural work of God. In order to practice it, you must first have experienced it yourself. It is not enough that you have gone through trials; this does not enable you to console. But if you have been consoled by the Lord Himself, then you are intimately acquainted with the tender kindness of Christ. When you draw near to someone in anguish, you will do so with the same sensitivity, tenderness and care.

Food for Thought

You can only comfort others if you undertake the task through Him who has consoled you, God Himself. Do not be hasty and say the first thing that comes to mind. Allow the Lord to guide you, and you will participate in a moment of supernatural healing.

Called to Bless

For God so loved the world that he gave his one and only Son, that whoever believes in him shall not perish but have eternal life. John 3:16

I want to invite you to try a small exercise with me. We are going to take the liberty, for a moment, to cut this verse short so it reads: "For God so loved the world that He gave." Read this phrase two or three times and notice how the word "gave" takes on strength.

If you let this thought penetrate your mind and heart, you will begin to notice that it goes against our normal understanding of love. In the modern definition of love, the concept of giving is not prominent. On the contrary, we spend much of our lives thinking almost exclusively about what others can give us. The word "love" is now almost a synonym for "feelings." This explains why, when feelings have faded, we say that love is gone.

We bring this same concept to our walk with the Lord. Thus, experiencing God's love means no more to us than expecting Him to say nice things and affirm how much He cares. With this goes the presenting of endless requests to Him which, if granted, will be almost exclusively for our own benefit. In other words, we think almost exactly as we did before our conversion.

The depth of our selfishness came clear to me in a testimony I once heard. A lady shared how burglars had broken into her neighbor's house and taken everything the poor folk had. "Even though they lost everything," she joyfully explained, "the burglars took absolutely nothing from our house, praise the Lord!" What kind of faith leads us to this perspective? This woman did not see her neighbor's misfortune as a chance to extend Christ's compassion and love. Her only thought was that she had been spared.

Read our adapted version of John 3:16 again. "For God so loved the world that He gave." Is the difference coming into focus? The emphasis is on giving. We are presented with a picture in which love is translated into action for others. This kind of love does not wait; it takes the initiative. It does not make demands; it offers. It does not focus on benefits, but on sacrifice. What a difference from our own concepts of love!

If we follow such a God, how can we keep from becoming infused with His attitude? The true manifestation of the Spirit in our lives will be an uncontrollable desire to bless others. True spirituality leads us to take our eyes off ourselves and see multitudes around us who desperately need a visitation of the love of God.

Food for Thought

The great evangelist D.L. Moody once said: "A man may be a good doctor without loving his patients; a good lawyer without loving his clients; a good geologist without loving science; but he cannot be a good Christian without love."[14]

Witnessing that Makes a Difference

Jesus did not let him, but said, "Go home to your family and tell them how much the Lord has done for you, and how He has had mercy on you." So the man went away and began to tell in the Decapolis how much Jesus had done for him. And all the people were amazed.
Mark 5:19–20

The Gerasene demoniac had never been treated well. Many times he had been bound with chains and shackles because he was violent and unpredictable. But when Jesus arrived he experienced for the first time the transforming power of God's love. And he was changed into another man! We can easily understand, then, why he did not want to stay where he had lived so many years in torment, isolated from human affection. As Jesus withdrew with His disciples, he begged the Master to take him too.

This is a tendency we all struggle with; we want to hold onto our gratifying experiences as long as we can. I'm sure this is one reason Peter exclaimed on the Mount of Transfiguration, "Rabbi, it is good for us to be here. Let us put up three shelters—one for you, one for Moses and one for Elijah" (Mark 9:5). We simply don't want the good times to end!

Christ knew that the best way to maintain a blessing is to share it. In the Kingdom what is not shared wastes away. This is why, in part, our call includes blessing others with the blessings we have received. The Lord therefore told the man to return to his family and share what had taken place in his life.

Stop and think for a moment about this man's evangelistic skills. He had not been a disciple for a single day. He probably didn't know the most basic Scripture texts or how to defend his beliefs. He had never been trained in sharing his faith and had almost no understanding of ministry. But this new disciple was an expert on one topic: how God can transform a life tormented by demons! And it is precisely this that the Lord sent him to share. "Go home to your family and tell them how much the Lord has done for you." Do you doubt for a moment people didn't find his testimony convincing? This man spoke with conviction born of a powerful and dramatic experience with Christ, and "all the people were amazed."

Many of our attempts to witness fail because they lack our own life changing experience with the risen Lord. If we cannot enthusiastically witness to wonderful things God is doing in us, we will probably not convince many that Christ is worth knowing.

Food for Thought

How, then, will we resolve our lack of credibility? Only one solution presents itself: We must experience His transforming power in us. For this to happen we can't afford to miss a single day in the wonderful adventure of walking with Jesus.

26 March | Measurements of No Value

We do not dare to classify or compare ourselves with some who commend themselves. When they measure themselves by themselves and compare themselves with themselves, they are not wise. 2 Corinthians 10:12

Jesus once told a parable which, according to the evangelist, was directed at those "who were confident of their own righteousness" (Luke 18:9). In the story a Pharisee stood up and spoke, praying in this way: "God, I thank you that I am not like all other men" (Luke 18:11). Without reading further we can spot something wrong in the Pharisee's approach.

From his own perspective, he was set apart from others by his excessively pious behavior. There were two fatal errors in his analysis, however. The first is that the evaluation of his life was carried out by himself. He didn't know the principle that no one is capable of accurately identifying his own faults. The psalmist exclaims, "Who can discern his errors?" (Ps. 19:12). The answer is implicit in the question—nobody can!

The second mistake was the comparison of his life with others. This is very common in our culture, a habit which has been taught to us since we were small. We come into the world competing with our siblings; we are then introduced into an educational structure which perpetuates a competitive system and later launched into the employment market where competition appears a prerequisite for survival. In order to progress in every stage, we believe it is necessary to compare our life with those around us.

The main problem with comparisons is that we choose whom we will compare ourselves with. And inevitably, we choose to compare ourselves with people who will confirm the image we want others to have of us. To show ourselves as generous, we compare ourselves with those who never give. To present ourselves as hard working, we compare ourselves with the laziest. Thus, our comparisons never give a true picture of who we really are.

Paul affirms that those who have fallen into the habit of making comparisons are lacking in understanding. The work of each person must be evaluated alone, with no point of reference but the parameters established by God Himself. At the moment we present ourselves before His throne, we will not be able to point to others' weaknesses to make our own flaws appear less significant than they really are.

It is important, therefore, that we lay aside the responsibility to approve our own lives and instead allow God to make a more accurate evaluation.

Food for Thought

Paul ends this passage with words which should lead us to reflection: "For it is not the one who commends himself who is approved, but the one whom the Lord commends" (2 Cor. 10:18).

A Good Reputation

March 27

As dead flies give perfume a bad smell, so a little folly outweighs wisdom and honor.
Ecclesiastes 10:1

When the apostles named deacons for the early church, they instructed the congregation to choose seven men who had, among other qualities, good reputations.

A reputation has two important characteristics. Like the radiance on Moses' face, a good reputation is something visible to those around us. And even though it is determined by others' observation of our lives, it cannot be perceived in a single encounter, but is the sum of many moments. Reputation is developed gradually over many years and is the most trustworthy reflection of what is really in our hearts. It involves such precious things as responsibility, loyalty, trustworthiness, integrity and wisdom—qualities that cannot be purchased or copied. Reputation is what others say about their leaders when they are not present.

And what is the value of reputation? The respect given a leader by a group of followers depends on it. When leaders have good reputations, their people trust them and are willing to follow them even in the most difficult circumstances. The most eloquent speakers do not inspire profound respect in their followers if their lives have not proven trustworthy.

As we see, this quality is difficult to build into our lives because it is the result of numerous elements adding up over time. It is difficult for young people to have good reputations simply because they have only advanced a short distance along the path of the life.

The author of Ecclesiastes knew the value of a good reputation. He compares it with perfume, which is pleasant to all who smell it. But Solomon also knew that a good reputation can be destroyed in a flash. It only takes one moment of foolishness to reduce our honor to ruins. A hasty decision, an inappropriate relationship, a moment of anger—any of these can instantly erase the good work of years. Sadly, once respectability is lost, it is very difficult for a leader to recover it. Many years after the incident people will remember that moment of foolishness more than all the years of faithful work which went before it.

For this reason wise leaders must be cautious in every decision. They should take the necessary time to evaluate the consequences of their actions and consider carefully the road they will choose. A discerning leader understands that there are many legitimate choices to avoid because they could have an adverse effect on a godly reputation.

Food for Thought

Do you know what opinion others have of you as a leader? What things are taken into account concerning your reputation? Have you dedicated enough time to them? How can you make up for the things that do not speak well of you in your role as leader?

The Power of Decision

Be happy, young man, while you are young, and let your heart give you joy in the days of your youth. Follow the ways of your heart and whatever your eyes see, but know that for all these things God will bring you to judgment. . . . Remember your Creator in the days of your youth, before the days of trouble come and the years approach when you will say, "I find no pleasure in them." Ecclesiastes 11:9, 12:1

When I read this passage, it reminds me of a certain young fellow who longed for a fuller life, filled with fun and all those things that make us feel "alive." Tired of working on his father's farm, he arranged an interview and asked his father for an advance on his part of the inheritance. Life was too short to wait around until he could really begin to live. Assured of his share, he left home in search of the wonderful things for which he had been longing (Luke 15:11–32).

We can recognize this young man's foolishness at once. But how much of our discernment is due to our knowledge of the story's ending? The truth is, many of us lack the inheritance, but we share the philosophy of this youngster. We have no long-term plan for our lives, and our existence revolves exclusively around things that are important to us. For example, a husband spends little time with his wife because his work matters more to him. A son does not study because he has more fun with his friends. A mother has no time to listen to her children because she must have the house spic-and-span.

Few of us can see the long-term consequences of our lifestyles. Always in search of experiences that make us feel good, we do not build into our daily lives that which is essential to the future. In time, however, we begin to realize that things which once seemed important were really of little value. As we come to understand this, we may experience profound remorse for not having correctly ordered our youthful priorities. For many it will be too late to change things.

The author of Ecclesiastes tries to protect us from this painful process of discovery. He tells us that today's decisions have consequences tomorrow. Not only that, but the day will come when we will give an account to our Creator for these choices. Why not, then, make decisions today that will produce fruit we will not be ashamed of? Many of these choices will involve things which perhaps interest us little—but in the future they will reap results which will bring us much joy.

Food for Thought

As a leader, what are you investing your time in? How can you be sure that these things have eternal value? Are there important things—your spouse, your children or your relationship with God—which are being neglected because you are too busy with personal interests?

Walk in a Worthy Manner

For this reason, since the day we heard about you, we have not stopped praying for you and asking God to fill you with the knowledge of his will through all spiritual wisdom and understanding. And we pray this in order that you may live a life worthy of the Lord and may please him in every way: bearing fruit in every good work, growing in the knowledge of God. Colossians 1:9–10

Our struggle to discover the will of God normally occurs during those critical moments in which we are at a crossroads: making the choice of a life partner or a career, facing a job change, selling our house or moving to another state. In these challenges we call out to the Lord, wanting to do what is right in His eyes.

Paul's prayer for the church at Colosse can teach us much in this respect. Paul could have asked many things on their behalf, but he prayed that they would be filled with the knowledge of God's will. Such a prayer takes for granted that knowing God's will is fundamental to the Christian life. In fact, in his letter to the Romans, Paul describes us as slaves to obedience (Rom. 6:16). This condition makes the Lord's instructions for our lives of central importance, for no slave can be obedient if he hasn't received instructions.

But take note of this: Paul asked that they be filled with the knowledge of God's will, but not because they were facing enormous decisions that would affect the church's future. The apostle's desire was that they "live a life worthy of the Lord," so he introduced a more practical element to the subject than we normally consider. He was not thinking of those dramatic dilemmas which occur in life, but of routine events which are part of our everyday existence.

The implications are plain. The Lord seeks to be Ruler in those circumstances we do not really consider "spiritual," like the time we spend relaxing with our family, doing our job or driving our car. It is precisely in these situations that we don't pay too much attention to the spiritual side of life. The Lord's desire, however, is that we please Him in all things, bearing fruit in all good works and growing continuously in our knowledge of Him.

Paul's prayer, then, calls us not only to understand God's will, but also to be alert to the guidance of His Spirit, which will reveal His will to us at each step of our lives. Our search for His guidance should not be limited to those definitive moments of life, but should also include those small moments which we often consider insignificant.

Food for Thought

In which areas of your life are you accustomed to living on "autopilot" without considering the Lord's will? How do you normally discern God's will? In what ways can you become more sensitive to His instructions?

30 March

Seeing What Others Don't See

Jesse had seven of his sons pass before Samuel, but Samuel said to him, "The Lord *has not chosen these." So he asked Jesse, "Are these all the sons you have?" "There is still the youngest," Jesse answered, "but he is tending the sheep." Samuel said, "Send for him; we will not sit down until he arrives."* 1 Samuel 16:10–11

God's instructions to Samuel were clear: "Fill your horn with oil and be on your way; I am sending you to Jesse of Bethlehem. I have chosen one of his sons to be king" (1 Sam. 16:1). The Lord had already seen in David the qualities needed to become the king He wanted for Israel: a passionate love for his Creator and a humble, obedient heart. He was also unbelievably courageous when circumstances required it!

The basic traits which would one day make David the greatest king of all times were already within him as a young shepherd. But consider this important detail. When Jesse consecrated his sons and invited them to participate in Samuel's sacrifice, he didn't bother to call David. Neither do we find any evidence to indicate his brothers noticed his absence.

If David possessed such extraordinary leadership potential, why had his family missed it? I can think of at least two answers to this question. In the first place, the qualities which God finds attractive in a potential leader are rarely those which appeal to us as human beings. This is a main reason many of the popular leadership models in the church today have been imported wholesale from the business world. Scripture, however, reminds us that "God chose the foolish things of the world to shame the wise; God chose the weak things of the world to shame the strong" (1Cor. 1:27).

A second point has to do with the lack of vision that results from living in close proximity with others. When we are often with the same people, the mundane seems to overshadow those qualities others find attractive. Sometimes they must be removed from our midst before we suddenly recognize the excellent traits they had always possessed.

When investing in new leaders, we run the risk of not recognizing potential in those closest to us. Their gifts may go unnoticed, or we may just think they will never be more than what they are today. The people of Nazareth could not see Jesus as anything but a simple carpenter, even when many others were marveling at the scope and depth of His ministry.

Food for Thought

Is it possible that a "future king" is in our midst and we haven't realized it? We need to see those around us through the Lord's eyes, seeing them as He sees them. Don't be fooled by the ordinary setting around them! Somebody extraordinary may be lurking behind that person you consider least important. Ask the Lord to give you eyes to see the ones He has set aside for great service in the Kingdom.

A Never-ending Party

All the days of the oppressed are wretched, but the cheerful heart has a continual feast.
Proverbs 15:15

If you have ever been around someone with a negative attitude, you will know how wearing it is. No matter the circumstances, people like this always find something to complain about. Their remarks are full of criticism and depressing comments about the future. One is tempted to avoid such a person because their attitude gradually extinguishes all cheerfulness and hope in those closest to them.

It is important to identify the source of this problem, because a seed of discontent is present in each of our hearts. This shouldn't surprise us. We are immersed in a culture that tries to convince us that happiness depends on the abundance of our belongings, the size of our salary, the attractiveness of our surroundings and the length of our list of friends. Since life isn't usually a bed of roses, we can easily spend our time moaning that these conditions have been denied us.

With keen wisdom the author of Proverbs maintains that joy has nothing to do with our possessions or circumstances. The ability to see the world around us with gratefulness and joy comes from a reality rooted deep in our hearts—and no conditions are able to budge it. That's why those with cheerful hearts will always find reason to celebrate even in the most adverse circumstances. Negative people, in contrast, can be in enviably fortunate situations and will still concentrate on that which makes them unhappy.

How can we develop this positive attitude? We are talking here about a willingness to celebrate constantly. This celebratory attitude has its origin in the certainty that God is present always, working in every circumstance and procuring the best for our lives. The person with a joyful heart sees God's goodness in everything, and this stimulates a continual expression of thanks and joy. No opportunity to include others in this constant rejoicing is missed. In other words, blessing others is a result of being blessed.

Do we, then, need to *feel* blessed in order to break into this life of celebration? Not at all! For we are already blessed with every spiritual blessing in heavenly places in Christ (Eph. 1:3). Even if we don't feel the blessing, it has been poured out abundantly. What we need instead is to recover a heavenly perspective of life. This is possible if we make a discipline of celebration which will work against the spirit of complaint and criticism so prevalent in our times. "Rejoice in the Lord always. I will say it again: Rejoice!" (Phil. 4:4).

Food for Thought

***Author Richard Foster writes in* Celebration of Discipline*, "Freedom from anxiety and care forms the basis for celebration. Because we know He cares for us we can cast all our care upon Him. God has turned our mourning into dancing."*[15]**

1 April We Wouldn't Have Danced

So David went down and brought up the ark of God from the house of Obed-Edom to the City of David with rejoicing. . . . David, wearing a linen ephod, danced before the LORD with all his might while he and the entire house of Israel brought up the ark of the LORD with shouts and the sound of trumpets. As the ark of the LORD was entering the City of David, Michal daughter of Saul watched from a window. And when she saw . . . she despised him in her heart. 2 Samuel 6:12–16

Imagine for a moment the unbridled spirit of festivity in this scene. Allow your heart to throb with the sheer exuberance of David's celebration. The Scriptures tell us he "danced before the LORD with all his might . . . leaping and dancing." Can you see the king? His joy is out of control! He jumps and shouts, he dances and sings, he claps his hands and sheds tears and bursts into laughter.

Such high-spirited manifestations are so far removed from our Christian experience that it may have been difficult to envision this scene. Our spirituality is very demure. We stand together and we sit together. We sing the same songs and use the same spiritual language. Our celebrations have become so tame and predictable that we can't relate to the unbridled spirit that is impelled to leap and dance before the Lord.

One reason we have trouble rejoicing freely is that we have become overly preoccupied with others' opinions of our behavior. These opinions carry great weight—we would not want anyone to think "badly" of us. This motivates how we dress, speak and act.

We have also heard repeatedly that all things must be done "in a fitting and orderly way" (1 Cor. 14:40). But our commitment to correctness has squeezed the spontaneity out of our meetings. Everything is done according to a set pattern. First, we have a word of welcome; next, a couple of worship songs. Then follow the announcements and the offering. The sermon comes next, then a prayer—and we are ready to go home. These repetitious meetings dull our senses and lull our spirits to sleep.

Despite this I suspect that most of us secretly feel attracted to the dancing king. If only we could lay hold of his passion, how different our walk with Christ would be! If we were to dare, even for a moment, to reveal a more genuine and unrehearsed face to those around us and to give the Lord greater freedom to lead us, how alive our meetings could become!

I wonder if this is one reason David is called a man after God's own heart. What extraordinary delight he found in the One who had called him to be king!

Food for Thought

Take a moment to pray: "Lord, free me from that which is predictable and boring; lead me along the path of David. Awaken in me the same wild spirit of celebration. May the very thought of You always be for me the cause of joyous festivity!"

Second Chances

So I went down to the potter's house, and I saw him working at the wheel. But the pot he was shaping from the clay was marred in his hands; so the potter formed it into another pot, shaping it as seemed best to him. Then the word of the LORD came to me: "O house of Israel, can I not do with you as this potter does?" declares the LORD. "Like clay in the hand of the potter, so are you in my hand, O house of Israel." Jeremiah 18:3–6

When truth is presented using real, visual illustrations from everyday life, it is easily understood. When the Lord wished to make a statement concerning His dealings with Israel, He sent the prophet down to the potter's house to watch him work. Jeremiah obeyed and began to watch the craftsman. With the natural dexterity common to those familiar with their work, he took a lump of clay, placed it on the wheel and spun it quickly. Rinsing his hands in water continually, he gradually worked the clay until a vessel began to emerge. Having formed the outer shape, he began to empty the inside. Suddenly, however, one side of the vessel caved in. The potter patiently took what was left, heaped the clay together and started again.

At this moment the Lord spoke to the prophet: "Like clay in the hand of the potter, so are you in my hand, O house of Israel." In an instant Jeremiah understood the essence of the Lord's persevering spirit: He does not give up when things go wrong. On the contrary, He will not be derailed from His intention of making something useful from the clay. He begins again until He obtains His desired result.

This sublime principle must have deep significance for those of us serving among God's people. First of all, we dare to believe that even when we make the most horrendous mistakes, we always have the chance to start again. The fact that Moses murdered an Egyptian did not alter God's plan. The fact that Elijah fled to the desert seeking death did not lead God to abandon him for another prophet. The fact that Peter denied Christ three times did not mean that the Lord withdrew the apostle's calling. In every case the divine Potter simply took what was left of His original work and began to form it again. So it is with our lives; He can redeem even our worst mistakes.

This should also encourage us concerning those we are discipling. They will often choose the wrong path. We will feel tempted to "throw in the towel" and give up on them. But the Lord reminds us that He doesn't give up on anyone. We should therefore gird ourselves with His patience and goodness to finish the work He has given us.

Food for Thought

When God has chosen someone, nothing and nobody can derail His purpose for them, even though there may be many setbacks along the way.

3 April

Unsettled by the Word

The word of the LORD came to Jonah son of Amittai: "Go to the great city of Nineveh and preach against it, because its wickedness has come up before me." But Jonah ran away from the LORD and headed for Tarshish. He went down to Joppa, where he found a ship bound for that port. After paying the fare, he went aboard and sailed for Tarshish to flee from the LORD. Jonah 1:1–3

How can we know when God is speaking to us? This question is important because a life of obedience to Him will be impossible if we can't discern His voice. We need some way of evaluating the word we receive to determine whether or not it is from God.

We are incredibly able to convince ourselves that what we hear has come from God. But our conviction is no guarantee that we have really heard His voice. When Saul was persecuting David and the Spirit of God had already left Him, some people told him where the shepherd from Bethlehem was hiding. The king exclaimed, "The LORD bless you for your concern for me" (1 Sam. 23:21). We know, however, that this was not from the hand of the Lord. Neither was it true when David was urged to kill Saul: "God has delivered your enemy into your hands" (1 Sam. 26:8). The truth is, if we wish anything passionately enough, we can easily be persuaded that God Himself is behind our plans.

One characteristic of the Lord's truth is that His words unsettle the person who receives them. What God says may even seem scandalous or ridiculous. Remember how Moses argued with God in front of the burning bush. Think about Sarah laughing at the idea of having a baby at her age. Think of Jeremiah, confused by the call of God. Consider Jonah who, as today's verse reminds us, attempted to flee from God's presence. Remember Zechariah's reaction when told he would have a son and the rich young ruler who departed sadly because he had a lot of money. Or consider those who quit following Jesus because they considered His words too harsh.

The list is endless, but these people share one thing in common: When God spoke, they felt uncomfortable, indignant, challenged, scandalized—but never enthusiastic! The reason is simple. We are in the process of being transformed, and His Word will always clash with those aspects of our lives which remain unchanged. When we hear His word to us, the flesh will always be ready to protest.

Food for Thought

If the only words you hear the Father say are words that make you feel good or that agree with your desires, you can be sure it is not the Lord talking. When He speaks, it is likely you will find many reasons to convince yourself that the message is not from God!

But...

But Jonah ran away from the Lord *and headed for Tarshish. He went down to Joppa, where he found a ship bound for that port. After paying the fare, he went aboard and sailed for Tarshish to flee from the* Lord*.* Jonah 1:3

From the comfort of our favorite armchair, it is easy to read Jonah's response and put on our judge's hat, condemning the prophet for his lack of faith. However, we must understand the nature of the task he had been called to. The Assyrians were not peaceful neighbors of the Israelites. They were a fiercely warring people who had defeated nation after nation. Their extreme cruelty to prisoners was well known throughout the region. So when God asked Jonah to go and proclaim judgment on them, the proposal was not the least bit attractive for the young prophet.

Even so, we may still feel some disappointment when we see the small word "but" at the beginning of today's verse. It takes us by surprise because it speaks of a young man who deliberately did the opposite of God's command. It is a word that marks a rebellious attitude and reminds us of debates and arguments. It bothers us because it sounds just like the multitude of "buts" which have been part of our own spiritual pilgrimage.

Have you ever reflected on all the times this word appears in Scripture? The Lord had told Saul not to pardon Agag, the Amalekite king. "*But* Saul and the army spared Agag and the best of the sheep and cattle" (1 Sam. 15:9). God had told the Israelites not to intermarry with other nations. "*But* King Solomon loved many foreign women, as well as the daughter of Pharaoh" (1 Kings 11:1, NKJV). The Lord had instructed Israel not to oppress the widow or the orphan, the stranger or the poor. "*But* they refused to pay attention; stubbornly they turned their backs and stopped up their ears" (Zech. 7:11). Jesus told the leper not to tell anyone about his healing. "*But* he went out and began to proclaim it freely and to spread the news around" (Mark 1:45, NASB). In each of these examples, and many others, the people did exactly what God had told them not to do.

In yesterday's devotional we saw how God's words make us uncomfortable because they challenge us with difficult things. We need to know that when the Lord charges us with something, it will unsettle us. This is always the case. And it is precisely this uneasiness that provokes us to intervene with our "buts"—those myriad reasons why this particular word is not actually for us.

Food for Thought

Are you willing to pray this prayer? "Lord, my 'buts' reveal the seed of rebellion in my heart. It is a manifestation of the flesh that rises up to oppose the Spirit. I want to submit every pretension and argument to the Lordship of Christ. May my 'buts' be transformed into 'Yes, Lord, I will!' Amen."

Fleeing from His Presence

But Jonah ran away from the LORD and headed for Tarshish. He went down to Joppa, where he found a ship bound for that port. After paying the fare, he went aboard and sailed for Tarshish to flee from the LORD. Then the LORD sent a great wind on the sea, and such a violent storm arose that the ship threatened to break up. Jonah 1:3–4

Have you ever been tempted to run away from God? Of course you wouldn't take a boat or a plane to flee the Lord's presence. Like the psalmist we must exclaim, "Where can I go from your Spirit? Where can I flee from your presence?" (Ps. 139:7). We all know it's impossible to flee from Him because He is everywhere.

Nevertheless, let's consider some situations: A church meeting is missed for fear of confrontation for past wrongs. The street where a brother lives is avoided because of the need to ask him for forgiveness. Attendance at a mission meeting is postponed because there will be a call for volunteers. Or an invitation to be part of a discipling process is refused because of the accountability to others it would require.

In each case people are avoiding a situation because they do not want to do what God wants them to. But they won't be able to continue their walk with Him if they refuse to obey. In fact, each one of them is, in their own way, fleeing from the presence of God.

The desire to run away comes when we struggle between our wishes and the declared will of God. Not even the Son of God was free of this battle. In Gethsemane He opened His heart to the Father and prayed with absolute frankness, "Father, if there is any way I can be freed from this test, please show Me." This kind of inner conflict is part of the price we pay to follow Him. It is a normal experience for the Christian.

What is *not* acceptable is to allow our will to impose its desires on the path we are to take. It is not acceptable, first, because it caters to the rebellious seed each of us has inherited from Adam. But second, it is wrong because it is simply not possible to evade God's will, at least if our commitment to Him is real. We may postpone the work God is asking of us for a while. But if the Lord has placed His hand on our lives, He will come to find us no matter where we "hide." Jonah is a perfect example of this truth.

Food for Thought

How many headaches are caused by situations where you delay doing what God has called you to? How can you minimize the time that passes between receiving instructions and carrying them out? In which areas in your life do you struggle most to do what God asks of you?

Reprimanding the Fool

April **6**

All the sailors were afraid and each cried out to his own god. And they threw the cargo into the sea to lighten the ship. But Jonah had gone below deck, where he lay down and fell into a deep sleep. The captain went to him and said, "How can you sleep? Get up and call on your god! Maybe he will take notice of us, and we will not perish." Jonah 1:5–6

Why was Jonah sleeping? When I was young I was called to carry out the obligatory military service in my country. My name was drawn, according to the method at that time, and I was drafted into the navy. After some months we set sail on a warship for some distant naval bases. Three days after leaving, however, we hit a ferocious storm that beat us mercilessly for two interminable days and nights. So violent were the ship's movements that even veteran sailors were suffering from seasickness. On the third day an alarm awakened us at dawn. The ship was at the point of sinking. I don't remember seeing anyone sleep through that storm. On the contrary, desperation and fear were the predominant emotions, and each person tried to cope as best they could. But nobody slept!

So why was Jonah sleeping? I think that the relief of having escaped from his mission was so intense that Jonah felt he deserved a little rest. Why should he be afraid of a storm when he had just escaped the task of preaching repentance to the Assyrians? This was nothing compared with that! His foolishness had lulled him into a false sense of security.

When we choose the path of disobedience, God uses whatever He needs to reprimand us. He has often used pagans, who walk in darkness, as spokespeople for the Most High. Even a donkey might be His instrument, as with Balaam (Num.22:21-31). In this situation the captain of the boat himself came to admonish Jonah, exhorting him to do what he should have done from the beginning: call out to God.

The fact is we can't disobey God in one issue without affecting other circumstances. Disobedience in one area brings consequences in other areas of our lives. When Jonah turned his back on the Lord, he began to walk that dangerous path of trying to follow God in his own way. Sin produces a numbness that makes us insensitive to spiritual things. The psalmist tells us that a person who doesn't confess his sins is like "the horse or the mule, which have no understanding but must be controlled by bit and bridle or they will not come to you" (Ps. 32:9). In a figurative sense, when we turn our backs on God, He must control us with "bit and bridle," because the gentle word no longer affects us.

Food for Thought

"A little sin will add to your trouble, subtract from your energy and multiply your difficulties." (Anonymous)

Contradictions

Then the sailors said to each other, "Come, let us cast lots to find out who is responsible for this calamity." They cast lots and the lot fell on Jonah. So they asked him, "Tell us, who is responsible for making all this trouble for us? What do you do? Where do you come from? What is your country? From what people are you?" He answered, "I am a Hebrew and I worship the Lord, *the God of heaven, who made the sea and the land."* Jonah 1:7–9

When God wishes to speak to us, He can use any means He likes. Even in something as ordinary as casting lots, the Lord can control events so they work out in accordance with His divine will. The sailors, totally without discernment, came to the "conclusion" that their problem was Jonah's fault, and they questioned him closely as to his situation.

I would like to focus for a moment on Jonah's reply: "I am a Hebrew and I worship [or fear] the Lord, the God of heaven, who made the sea and the land." A Bible dictionary defines the word "fear" as an attitude of respect, reverence and adoration. This term is used to describe a posture of submission toward a figure of greater authority. For this reason, fear normally goes hand in hand with obedience. It implies recognition of the fact that when those in authority speak, their words have such weight that they immediately take precedence over personal interests.

We could say many things about Jonah. But one thing we can be sure of: He did not come close to being a man who feared God! In his declaration he not only said he feared the Lord, but also that he recognized God as the Maker of heaven and earth. How could a man, affirming that God is the Creator of all things, be fleeing from Him who made the very sea on which he was sailing? It is absurd!

Jonah's declaration reveals the classic contradiction existing between the words and actions of those who believe only with their heads. The prophet, good Israelite that he was, had all the correct answers memorized. Perhaps he even shared them with his neighbors and workmates and taught them to his children.

We ourselves have often done this very thing, paying lip service to God's eternal truths, but living according to our own personal principles. This incongruence in those who are spiritually sensitive is always accompanied by a certain degree of shame. Along with the Apostle James, we exclaim, "My brothers, this should not be" (James 3:10).

Food for Thought

In which areas of your spiritual experience do you notice that your words do not coincide with your actions? What steps can you take to minimize the distance between what you say and what you do? Take a moment to ask the Lord to work in your life so that what you believe in your mind becomes rooted in your heart.

When the Chips are Down

This terrified them and they asked, "What have you done?" (They knew he was running away from the Lord, *because he had already told them so.) The sea was getting rougher and rougher. So they asked him, "What should we do to you to make the sea calm down for us?" "Pick me up and throw me into the sea," he replied, "and it will become calm. I know that it is my fault that this great storm has come upon you."* Jonah 1:10–12

We can't know what went through Jonah's mind when he told the sailors to throw him into the sea. We can be sure he knew nothing of the great fish the Lord would send to rescue him. What we do see is the conviction of sin which led Jonah to take responsibility for the storm. He was still in possession of sufficient discernment to understand that he had caused it.

Nevertheless, his independence persisted. It would have been appropriate for him to have plead with God for mercy, confessing his sin and declaring his willingness to obey. But Jonah did not understand God's merciful heart and thought that once he had disobeyed, there was no solution. Giving everything up for lost, he decided to throw himself into the sea and face almost certain death.

Have you as a leader found yourself struggling with similar feelings? It seems our sins are more burdensome when we are ministers of the children of God. Perhaps being in the public eye makes us more ashamed. We may have occasionally considered giving everything up because we feel our sin has ended our usefulness to God. Just like Peter we seriously consider returning to our nets.

This thinking is one reason we so seldom practice confession. The Enemy of our souls works to convince us there is no recovery from sins we have committed. He traps us with guilt. We believe God cannot hear us any more because there is no solution to our sin. Convinced this is true, we become desperate and want to end our miserable existence.

The greatest obstacle to relationship with God is not the awful nature of our sin but the requirements we impose on ourselves to regain His favor. Our sin *is* abominable, but it can be pardoned through a simple confession. We, however, like to adorn our confession with unnecessary demonstrations of our repentance. When we are immersed in sin, the best thing to do is draw near to Him in direct repentance, trusting entirely in His unfathomable love.

Food for Thought

"Lose no time in self-recriminations, but breathe a silent prayer for forgiveness and begin again, just where you are. Offer this broken worship up to Him and say: 'This is what I am except Thou aid me.'" (Thomas Kelly) [1]

In Spite of Ourselves

Then they cried to the LORD, "O LORD, please do not let us die for taking this man's life. Do not hold us accountable for killing an innocent man, for you, O LORD, have done as you pleased." Then they took Jonah and threw him overboard, and the raging sea grew calm. At this the men greatly feared the LORD, and they offered a sacrifice to the LORD and made vows to him. Jonah 1:14–16

We have been examining the life of the Lord's reluctant servant, Jonah. His service did not begin in the romantic way we often expect for ministers. He did not like the mission he was assigned. He thought he would be safe running from the Lord; but when all was lost, he decided to throw himself into the sea. We do not see in Jonah a consecrated, inspiring leader who is the perfect example of service for our congregation.

The incredible thing is that God used this man despite his attitudes and behavior. In today's passage we note two results of Jonah's crisis. First, the sailors recognize that Jehovah had done as He wished. This discovery is not insignificant. It implies a declaration that God reigns sovereign over everything, an indispensable discovery if we plan to submit to His designs.

Second, on throwing Jonah into the sea, they saw his words come true: The waters immediately calmed and great tranquility came over the stricken boat. As a result, "the men greatly feared the Lord, and they offered a sacrifice to the Lord and made vows to Him." We are witnesses to the conversions of these pagan men, who had proof that Jehovah's power is superior to that of any other god.

This incident should encourage a leader's heart. The message is clear: The Lord has proposed to bless those He wishes. We are invited to collaborate with Him and very often granted the privilege of being His instruments. What is especially worthy of attention, however, is that the Lord sometimes blesses in spite of our efforts! We make mistakes, are disobedient and sometimes do things reluctantly. Despite this His grace is poured out, and people are blessed in all kinds of ways.

How can we not be thankful to Him for this abundant manifestation of grace? It does not mean we can say, "Really, it doesn't matter how we serve because He is going to do His will anyway." Not at all; this is the poorest display of service. We are called to excellence and that is what we should aim at. Nevertheless, it is a relief to know our weaknesses and shortcomings are covered by His grace. Blessed be His name!

Food for Thought

***"You cannot be too active as regards your own efforts; you cannot be too dependent as regards divine grace. Do everything as if God did nothing; depend upon God as if he did everything." (John A. James)*[2]**

9-1-1 Prayers

But the Lord provided a great fish to swallow Jonah, and Jonah was inside the fish three days and three nights. From inside the fish Jonah prayed to the LORD his God.
Jonah 1:17–2:1

Many of us have a prayer life that could well be accompanied by a sign saying "Use only in case of emergency!" These are prayers we offer in our extremity, when we have no alternative but to look to heaven and cry for help. In His mercy, God often answers, but we don't receive any more than that: a solution to our problem.

To think of prayer on these terms is to have a very limited perspective of this sacred discipline of the spiritual life. It is, however, a common concept among us. The result is that our prayers resemble a shopping list. We raise our petitions to heaven and then go our own sweet way.

"True, whole prayer," said the great St. Augustine, "is nothing but love."[3] Richard Foster wrote on this subject in his book, *Prayer*, saying, "Today, the heart of God is an open wound of love. He aches over our distance and preoccupation. He mourns that we do not draw near to him. He grieves that we have forgotten him. He weeps over our obsession with muchness and manyness. He longs for our presence."[4]

These phrases help us understand the real nature of prayer. Do you think the only reason Jesus often withdrew to isolated places was to ask God for things? Of course not! He sought to enjoy that transforming friendship through moments of prayerful intimacy with the Father. This is probably why the disciples asked that He teach them to pray (Luke 11:1). It's not that they didn't know how to ask God for things; but they had no understanding of the real mystery we call prayer. They realized Christ had a spiritual dimension in His life they were lacking.

It is so easy for us, immersed in the tumult of ministry, to convert prayer into a shopping list because we have so much to do. But the Lord invites us to enter another level of experience. This is why Jesus said that when we pray, we should close ourselves up in our inner room (Matt. 6:6). Nobody closes their door if they intend to leave immediately after arriving. Christ visualized a time of intimacy with the Father in which the main result of prayer would be life transformation. We all need to walk this road!

Food for Thought

Can you make this prayer your own? "Oh my God, adored Trinity, help me to entirely forget myself so I can rest in You, quiet and still, as if my soul dwelt already in eternity. Let nothing disturb my peace or distract me from You, my unchangeable God, and with every minute let me sink deeper into Your Mystery. Amen." (Ignacio Larrañaga)[5]

Desperate Vows

"In my distress I called to the LORD, and he answered me. From the depths of the grave I called for help, and you listened to my cry. I said, 'I have been banished from your sight; yet I will look again toward your holy temple.' Those who cling to worthless idols forfeit the grace that could be theirs. But I, with a song of thanksgiving, will sacrifice to you. What I have vowed I will make good. Salvation comes from the LORD." Jonah 2:2, 4, 8–9

God normally speaks in a gentle whisper. As the prophet Isaiah says, "He will not shout or cry out, or raise his voice in the streets" (Isa. 42:2). The Lord's tender heart leads Him to treat His own with patience and kindness; He desires a response by this personal approach. Sometimes, however, His message is more direct. He tries once, twice or three times and then uses a more dramatic approach. So it was with Jacob, who fought with God till dawn, and with Peter, who took the way of denial before understanding Christ's words.

This happened with Jonah. The prophet was obviously in a state of brokenness due to his disobedience, but this had not led to confession before God. His sorrow was unto death, and he had madly thrown himself into the sea. But the Lord is interested in sorrow unto life: "Godly sorrow brings repentance that leads to salvation and leaves no regret, but wordly sorrow brings death" (2 Cor. 7:10). As soon as he found himself within the great fish, Jonah remembered God and prayed to Him desperately.

Note that his prayer includes vows to the Lord, which is typical of us in desperate circumstances. We are mainly interested in a remedy and, to secure God's help, we make promises we swear to fulfill as soon as we're delivered.

These promises, which display how little we understand God, are rarely kept. As soon as the storm has passed, they are forgotten. We forget them because they do not spring from a devoted heart. Instead, they are simply an agreement between two parties: "You save me, and I'll do this in return." Thus, our Christian life is reduced to nothing but a commercial transaction!

We need to rediscover our Father's loving heart. His love need not be bought; He is always ready to help us. As Christian psychologist Larry Crabb says, "When our strongest passion is to solve our problems, we look for a *plan to follow*, rather than a *person to trust*."[6] Don't allow your relationship with God to sink to this level. Seek daily to nurture your passion, and you won't have need of desperate vows in times of crisis.

Food for Thought

Can you remember a time when you made desperate vows to the Lord? Did you keep your promises? In what kind of situation are you tempted to negotiate with God? How can you move toward a more personal relationship with Him?

A Lesson Repeated

Then the word of the LORD came to Jonah a second time: "Go to the great city of Nineveh and proclaim to it the message I give you." Jonah 3:1–2

During my school days I sometimes skipped class. Perhaps the subject was difficult or boring, or I just didn't feel like going. This was nothing more than a childish prank. My classmates and I always celebrated these silly escapades. What I didn't understand then was that the missed class was part of an annual curriculum, and there would be questions on that subject in the final exam. If I didn't make up what I had missed, I was sure to find myself in deep trouble.

Spiritual life is no different, but the consequences are more serious. We cannot skip stages or avoid lessons God wants to teach us. What we miss today will have to be learned tomorrow. Perhaps the context will have changed, years will have passed and different people will be involved; nevertheless, the lesson will be the same.

It surprises me how often in my life I have wanted to "skip" lessons. Faced with a particularly difficult challenge, I have chosen to change my circumstances, sometimes radically. Years later I find myself struggling with the same problem I earlier failed to resolve spiritually.

The Lord proposes to fashion us into the image of His Son, Jesus Christ. His objectives for us are not optional. All that He wants to achieve in our lives is indispensable to His purpose. Being a patient and careful artisan, He will shape us until He fulfills His goal.

Take note of the phrase "the word of the LORD came to Jonah a second time." Here we see a persistent God who does not give up. We see this again in Paul's affirmation: "He who began a good work in you will carry it on to completion until the day of Christ Jesus" (Phil. 1:6). Note too that the order to Jonah was exactly what it had been at first: "Go to the great city of Nineveh and preach against it, because its wickedness has come up before me" (Jon. 1:2).

When we try to evade divine assignments, we will observe two consequences. First, projects we attempt will not have the spiritual authority we need to fulfill them successfully. They will be built on an incomplete foundation. Second, we will discover that we are faced time and again with the same challenge we had previously avoided. Years may pass, but the call remains. It will not disappear until we meet its demands.

Food for Thought

We do not have to follow this bitter road of repetition. All we have to do is accept that the Lord's proposals are non-negotiable. They may seem unpleasant when we receive them, but the fruit they bear has eternal value. If we are convinced that classes in God's school cannot be skipped, we are on the right path!

A Compassionate Heart

On the first day, Jonah started into the city. He proclaimed: "Forty more days and Nineveh will be overturned." The Ninevites believed God. They declared a fast, and all of them, from the greatest to the least, put on sackcloth. When God saw what they did and how they turned from their evil ways, he had compassion and did not bring upon them the destruction he had threatened. Jonah 3:4–5, 10

The Lord's desire to bless us must be incredibly strong. Even in the most depraved situations, He is willing to reconsider at the slightest sign of repentance! His actions depend not so much on the extent of our brokenness, but rather on the breadth of His compassionate heart. This was also spoken to Jeremiah: "If that nation I warned repents of its evil, then I will relent and not inflict on it the disaster I had planned. And if at another time I announce that a nation or kingdom is to be built up and planted, and if it does evil in my sight and does not obey me, then I will reconsider the good I had intended to do for it" (Jer. 18:8–10).

The purpose behind all God does is restoration, never punishment or destruction. Destruction is an option only when every alternative for reconciliation has failed. But primarily the Lord desires us to return to intimacy with Him, to enjoy His bounteous gifts and share with others what we receive from Him.

Notice how imperfect Jonah's service had been. From the beginning he was in open rebellion against God and stayed distant from Him even when shaken by a violent storm. Only when facing death in the fish's belly did he remember to pray and ask for mercy. So it appears that he completed his mission for fear of further punishment, not out of genuine compassion for the people of Nineveh. In spite of all this, his message was heard, and the people repented.

Have you realized that the real fruits of our labor depend much more on God's compassion and goodness than on our efforts? So often as leaders we believe everything has to be just right in order to see the workings of God's grace. We worry about details and fret over items we deem indispensable to the success of our venture. Usually, however, this does not guarantee the Lord's blessing. As Paul wrote, "'I will have mercy on whom I have mercy, and I will have compassion on whom I have compassion.' It does not, therefore, depend on man's desire or effort, but on God's mercy" (Rom. 9:15–16).

Food for Thought

What should your attitude be? Relax! Don't take everything so seriously. Release yourself from anxiety in your ministry. You are not the one who moves hearts—God is. Do your part, but then rest in the certainty that God will do His. His interest in redeeming the fallen is far greater than yours!

The Dark Side of Success

But Jonah was greatly displeased and became angry. He prayed to the LORD, "O LORD, is this not what I said when I was still at home? That is why I was so quick to flee to Tarshish. I knew that you are a gracious and compassionate God, slow to anger and abounding in love, a God who relents from sending calamity. Now, O LORD, take away my life, for it is better for me to die than to live." Jonah 4:1–3

One of the greatest tests of a leader's heart is success. Many leaders who toil with real holiness and commitment in times of difficulty fall prey to pride when they begin to reap the benefits of their efforts. Their ministries grow, their authority is recognized, their experience is respected—and they start to believe that the Kingdom advances purely and exclusively because of them! The simplicity and humility of their early ministry years disappear like autumn leaves, and in their place emerges an attitude which taints all they do.

This seems to be Jonah's experience. The likelihood that the Assyrians would respond to his message was extremely remote. He probably anticipated certain death—he knew that someone announcing God's destruction on the earth's most powerful nation was unlikely to be warmly welcomed! But contrary to all expectations, the people listened to the unfortunate prophet's message, and it even reached the king's ears. The whole city dressed in sackcloth and ashes, and begged God for mercy. Who would not have felt great after a response like that? Who among us would not have felt more important than we really were? This is exactly what happened to Jonah.

In the middle of this exhilarating response, God pardoned the Assyrians. This was too much for the prophet to take! Now how could he justify his message of Nineveh's imminent destruction? Was not God bringing unnecessary humiliation to Jonah's life? He knew he would lose credibility, and that bothered him terribly.

We surely understand his reaction. More than once we have heard subtle suggestions about our importance to the peoples' response. It's all too easy to be led astray by this vain way of seeing things!

Food for Thought

Are you someone God can trust with success in ministry? To be trustworthy, we need the same deep conviction John the Baptist had. His disciples were indignant about the "sheep stealing" Jesus was carrying out and encouraged John to defend his ministry. The great prophet exclaimed, "A man can receive only what is given him from heaven. You yourselves can testify that I said, 'I am not the Christ but am sent ahead of him.' The bride belongs to the bridegroom. The friend who attends the bridegroom waits and listens for him, and is full of joy when he hears the bridegroom's voice. That joy is mine, and it is now complete. He must become greater; I must become less" (John 3:27–30).

15 April | Worse than Disobedience!

But Jonah was greatly displeased and became angry. He prayed to the LORD, "O LORD, is this not what I said when I was still at home? That is why I was so quick to flee to Tarshish. I knew that you are a gracious and compassionate God, slow to anger and abounding in love, a God who relents from sending calamity. Now, O LORD, take away my life, for it is better for me to die than to live." Jonah 4:1–3

A saint called Henry Smith once said, "A sin is two sins when it is defended."[7] There is a lot of truth in this! There is no doubt that disobedience is hateful to our God. However, to this sin can be added another one even more despicable: our incurable inclination to justify our deeds, whether before men or God Himself. Have you noticed how often this wretched tendency accompanies disobedience? When Adam and Eve were confronted, he said, "The woman you put here with me . . ." and she responded with, "The serpent deceived me" (Gen. 3:12–13). Aaron, faced with creating the golden calf, said, "I threw it [the gold] into the fire, and out came this calf!" (Exod. 32:24). Saul, confronted with rejecting God's instructions, blamed his soldiers (1 Sam. 15:15, 21).

How often have you and I done this? Think of the times we have roundly condemned others for doing things we do ourselves. But in our case we have an elaborate explanation to show that *our* sin is justified.

In spite of this, God is not convinced. The Lord did not punish Adam for Eve's sin nor Eve for the serpent's, the people for Aaron's sin nor the Israelites for Saul's. They each received the just, deserved punishment for their own sins. It is this way for us as well. When we stand before God's throne, all our explanations will be of less value than straw blown away by the wind. "For we must all appear before the judgment seat of Christ, that each one may receive what is due him for the things done while in the body, whether good or bad" (2 Cor. 5:10).

There is a shorter, simpler route to be taken when we have rebelled against His will: the path of humble confession from a contrite, broken heart. Such was the great King David's confession: "For I know my transgressions, and my sin is always before me. Against you, you only, have I sinned and done what is evil in your sight, so that you are proved right when you speak and justified when you judge" (Ps. 51:3–4).

Food for Thought

As a leader you have the challenge of not only walking in simplicity of heart, but also of providing this example for your people. May they know you as one who does not seek to justify that which is clearly unjustifiable. Don't hesitate to choose the way of confession. It will do you good—as well as those you are serving!

Radical Decisions

He prayed to the LORD, "O LORD, is this not what I said when I was still at home? That is why I was so quick to flee to Tarshish. I knew that you are a gracious and compassionate God, slow to anger and abounding in love, a God who relents from sending calamity. Now, O LORD, take away my life, for it is better for me to die than to live." Jonah 4:2–3

How do you react when you don't get your own way? This often marks the difference between those leaders truly submissive to God and those whose main objective is to further their own interests.

Jonah didn't like the Lord's decision regarding the Assyrians one little bit. He got really angry, told God off in no uncertain terms and then asked the Lord to take his life—an extreme reaction to a problem basically caused by his own wounded pride.

This kind of situation reveals a leader's real motives. When I was a young pastor, I used to insist that my vision was the right one for the congregation I led. Other members of the ministerial team did not agree with me.

In my eagerness I presented many arguments to show that my vision and God's were one and the same. Even so, they would not be persuaded. Tired of their arguments and apparent resistance to my ideas, I decided to leave the congregation. This was a radical decision in the face of what was essentially a battle of wills.

This story has been repeated time and again among God's people.

Certain of our rightness, we consider such drastic responses as walking out, abandoning a ministry or even dividing the church. This attitude makes teamwork impossible because everyone is forced to agree with the leader. The beauty and richness of the body's diversity is lost; the chance to learn communication with others and the opportunity to develop the holy character approved by God are wasted.

Take a look at Paul's exhortation: "Do nothing out of selfish ambition or vain conceit, but in humility consider others better than yourselves. Each of you should look not only to your own interests, but also to the interests of others" (Phil. 2:3–4). Vainglory (the King James Version's translation of the word "conceit") is no more than fictitious glory. It has the appearance of being real, but comes from a flawed source. The only One who possesses genuine glory is God Himself; and those in whom His presence is visible reflect this glory. The other "glories" are man-made; they have very little sparkle.

Food for Thought

Think again about the question at the beginning of this devotional: How do you react when you don't get your own way? Do other members of your team regard you as humble? What steps do you take to encourage dialogue with others? In which situations have you backed down because you consider someone else better than you?

17 April — Medicine for the Angry

But the LORD replied, "Have you any right to be angry?" Jonah went out and sat down at a place east of the city. There he made himself a shelter, sat in its shade and waited to see what would happen to the city. Jonah 4:4–5

Among much good advice in the book of Proverbs we find the following: "A gentle answer turns away wrath, but a harsh word stirs up anger" (Prov. 15:1). Angry people are rarely willing to listen to reason; everything said simply adds fuel to the fire of their anger. One should speak with great caution when dealing with an irate individual.

This is just how God deals with Jonah. The prophet's anger is totally selfish and out of proportion to the circumstances, but the Lord knows this is not the right moment to make him listen to reason. Jonah first has to calm down before he can open up and be dealt with. This is why the Lord only asks him a question: "Have you any right to be angry?" He provides Jonah with no answer; He brings no teaching on how to deal with his emotions. Neither does He scold. He simply waits for the question to bring about reflection in Jonah.

This method is similar to the one employed with Elijah in the desert. The tired and discouraged prophet had taken shelter under a juniper tree. He also wished for death. The Lord knew Elijah needed his strength renewed and perspective regained before He could speak with him, so He sent an angel to give very simple instructions: "Get up and eat" (1Kings 19:5). Our response to an angry person can either help them or contribute to the tightening of anger's grip on their lives.

Notice that Jonah didn't even understand the Lord's question. Instead of reflecting on his behavior, which was completely unacceptable for a servant of God, the prophet continued to see everything from his own offended point of view and misinterpreted the question. He thought God was saying, "Don't be impatient: I'm going to destroy them!"

But God is an extraordinary teacher, and He was willing to teach the prophet an important lesson. What amazing patience we see in His dealings with Jonah, a man we would have written off! But we see that even in ministry assignments, the Lord wants to shape His people into all He desires them to be.

In the same way, we should be very patient with the people we serve. We must be wise in our discipline. Correction at the wrong moment adds difficulties, but a gentle word at the right time has power to redeem and transform behavior.

Food for Thought

How do you react to other peoples' anger? Does your response contribute to the problem or provide a solution? What can you do to react more wisely in such situations? Remember—our response to an angry person can either help them or contribute to the tightening of anger's grip on their lives.

Divine Reprimand

But God said to Jonah, "Do you have a right to be angry about the vine?" "I do," he said. "I am angry enough to die." But the LORD said, "You have been concerned about this vine, though you did not tend it or make it grow. It sprang up overnight and died overnight. But Nineveh has more than a hundred and twenty thousand people who cannot tell their right hand from their left, and many cattle as well. Should I not be concerned about that great city?" Jonah 4:9–11

Good teachers know that words are only one of many tools at their disposal. They understand that we learn more through what we see and experience than through what we hear. Therefore, they take every opportunity to present their material in a way that affects the whole person. In this occurrence with Jonah, we see that a non-verbal lesson can be very effective.

God knows how readily we hang on to the gifts we receive, especially when they belong to the material world. The Lord anticipated this instinct and caused a plant to grow beside Jonah. The prophet's reaction was predictable: He had no sooner become comfortable beneath the leafy plant, which provided him with refreshing shade in the scorching desert, than he began to feel it belonged to him. When it withered up and died the next day, the prophet lamented his loss as if it had been a beloved friend.

The contrast God achieves with this excellent illustration reveals the prophet's extreme selfishness. His reaction shows how different our interests are from those of our Father's heart. We worry mostly about things that affect our own well-being. A quick run through the main subjects of our prayer lives will divulge just how centered on ourselves we are.

How can we free ourselves from worrying about the ephemeral and transient? If we can't break away from these things, our ministries will always suffer from a limited, worldly perspective. No human effort will be sufficient to achieve this transformation in us. On the contrary, the flesh can only lead to an increase of fleshly expressions, since "the sinful mind is hostile to God. It does not submit to God's law, nor can it do so. Those controlled by the sinful nature cannot please God" (Rom. 8:7–8).

Food for Thought

Today's message demonstrates one of those biblical scenes in which God allows us to see His heart. He shares His unfathomable compassion with the prophet. This offers us hope for the transformation we desperately need if we are to lose our passion for that which is fleeting and unimportant. Such change occurs as we perceive the heart of God, which is only possible as we draw near to Him and allow Him to share with us His concerns. Compassion is caught more than taught. Let us come to Him so we may understand those things that are naturally seen only from afar.

True to the Word

But Jehoshaphat asked, "Is there not a prophet of the LORD here whom we can inquire of?" The king of Israel answered Jehoshaphat, "There is still one man through whom we can inquire of the LORD, but I hate him because he never prophesies anything good about me, but always bad. He is Micaiah son of Imlah." "The king should not say that," Jehoshaphat replied. 1 Kings 22:7–8

The Word of God frequently confronts. It highlights our rebellious nature and our bent toward disobedience. It sets forth those eternal principles integral to God's kingdom and calls us to make necessary changes, thus aligning our hearts with His manifest will.

This has always been the simplest definition of the prophets' work. They interpreted the meaning of the peoples' experiences and showed them how it differed from the parameters set by the Word of God. Their proclamation of truth always went hand in hand with an exhortation to return to God's plan.

This is where we do not respond well. It is easy to shake our heads and grumble about the lack of spirituality we see in God's people. Almost without trying we can come up with a list of people who would do well to "listen to this message." Our enthusiasm fades, however, when the exhortation is leveled at us. Suddenly we resort to arguments and foolish excuses to justify our lack of commitment.

In today's passage we see an extreme case of resistance to the Word. The king, accustomed to using his power to manipulate those around him, had to deal with a prophet who would not give way to his pressure and insisted on proclaiming prophesies the king didn't care to hear. He had thus earned the king's contempt. The pressure on Micaiah must have been very great, particularly because the other "prophets" were making declarations pleasing to their king's ears!

For those of us involved in the ministry of the Word, the discomfort of resisting pressure from those with "itchy ears" may tempt us to dilute our message. After all, we could argue that popularity will open many doors for us in the future. But this kind of respect from those who want an easy word has a price: It may mean the loss of God's support for our ministry.

Food for Thought

We would do well to note Paul's exhortation to Timothy: "Preach the Word; be prepared in season and out of season; correct, rebuke and encourage—with great patience and careful instruction. For the time will come when men will not put up with sound doctrine. Instead, to suit their own desires, they will gather around them a great number of teachers to say what their itching ears want to hear" (2 Tim. 4:2–3). Do not allow others to impose their desired message on your ministry, and beware of imposing your own words on them. Your words should always be those God has given you to speak. They alone can bear eternal fruit.

Poverty with Potential

When he saw Peter and John about to enter, he asked them for money. Peter looked straight at him, as did John. Then Peter said, "Look at us!" So the man gave them his attention, expecting to get something from them. Then Peter said, "Silver or gold I do not have, but what I have I give you. In the name of Jesus Christ of Nazareth, walk." Acts 3:3–6

How much does a handout cost us? A few cents? Someone begging on the street certainly isn't expecting much—just a few coins to add to those that other merciful souls have given. Certainly we won't go hungry by giving something to those who beg.

Peter and John didn't have even a little to give a needy man they met outside the temple. However, they did have something else. They had a treasure house of experience gleaned from time with the Lord, and their hearts had been transformed by God's compassion. They gave what they had to the beggar, and this man too was remade by the power of God.

Two important lessons can be taken from this incident. First of all, what people ask for is very often not really what they need. Each individual forms petitions according to their own reality and worldview. Thankfully, in His infinite goodness God does not always give us what we ask for, but instead gives us what we need. Also, as servants of the Lord, it is important to analyze what others are asking of us, to determine whether it is a need or a want. Wise leaders will not just give whatever people ask of them, but will seek to give as the Spirit leads.

Second, this passage reveals an important principle: We should work with what we have. This seems too obvious to mention, but the truth is that many congregations do little because they honestly believe they have too few resources. John and Peter could well have had long faces, frustrated at the scarcity of their resources. They could even have returned to their congregation to urge generosity toward the many needs in Jerusalem.

How often I have heard pastors complaining because they don't have the resources they "need" for ministry? God has provided us with everything we need; He has sent no one into ministry without equipping them thoroughly.

Food for Thought

Our resources for ministry do not always match our list of requirements for the job. If God shows us a project, however, then the resources are there too. But, as with all things in the Kingdom, God's support comes into effect once we begin with what we have. As William Plumer once observed, "He who is not liberal with what he has, does but deceive himself when he thinks he would be liberal if he had more." [8]

Overcoming Adversity

Now Joseph had been taken down to Egypt. Potiphar, an Egyptian who was one of Pharaoh's officials, the captain of the guard, bought him from the Ishmaelites who had taken him there. The LORD was with Joseph and he prospered, and he lived in the house of his Egyptian master. . . . His master saw that the LORD was with him and that the LORD gave him success in everything he did. Genesis 39:1–3

It's difficult for us to imagine what a terrible blow it must have been for Joseph to be sold by his brothers. The story of the shameful deed fills only a few verses of the text, but the devastating consequences of such a drastic betrayal are not revealed. In any case, this treachery must have affected the young Israelite to the very depths of his being.

In fact, it couldn't have been otherwise. In the space of a few weeks he lost everything: first his freedom, as he was cast into the pit; then his dignity, when he was sold for a few silver coins. The moment shackles were attached to his ankles, he lost his future, along with any say as to the direction his life would take. On arrival in Egypt, he was bereaved of his culture, his language and the bonds that linked him to his family. And once bought by Potiphar as a slave, Joseph lost any chance of belonging to another family. How could he possibly recover from such a catastrophe? What could stop him from sinking into deep depression and bitterness, harboring heartfelt spite toward his brothers?

In today's passage, nevertheless, we are presented with a successful Joseph.

His prosperity was the result of the presence, company and support of Jehovah in his life. God was with him. As we well know, the Lord doesn't bless those who hold thoughts of hate, resentment and revenge in their hearts. The psalmist asks, "LORD, who may dwell in your sanctuary? Who may live on your holy hill? He whose walk is blameless and who does what is righteous, who speaks the truth from his heart" (Ps. 15:1–2). It is clear Joseph was able to overcome the severe setback he had endured.

This is one quality that distinguishes a leader from others. A leader is not free from difficulties, mishaps and pains; however, these challenges should not be allowed to set the tone for living. Henry Blackaby, author of *Experiencing God*, observes, "Leaders are not people who escape failure, but people who overcome adversity."[9] The history of God's people is replete with examples of men and women who endured intense personal suffering. What is remarkable about them, however, is that they used their pain as a stepping stone to greater things. Through suffering they laid a sturdy foundation on which to build their greatest victories.

Food for Thought

"A mistake is something that happened from which we have not yet reaped the full benefits." (Anonymous)

The Discipline of Gratitude

Shout for joy to the LORD, all the earth. Worship the LORD with gladness; come before him with joyful songs. Know that the LORD is God. It is he who made us, and we are his; we are his people, the sheep of his pasture. Enter his gates with thanksgiving and his courts with praise; give thanks to him and praise his name. For the LORD is good and his love endures forever; his faithfulness continues through all generations. Psalm 100:1–5

Have you ever thought about the verbs in this psalm which invite us to celebrate God's goodness? They are all commands: sing, serve, come, recognize, enter, praise, bless. Rather strange, don't you think?

If we think about our natural disposition, it doesn't seem so strange. Our personalities have been affected by sin. Our culture has nurtured in us a spirit of persistent discontent toward all we have. Consequently, we are dominated by negative thoughts and feelings of melancholy which tend to taint our conversation with criticism and reproach. Since we are convinced our happiness lies in the hands of others, life passes us by while we await the arrival of that person or thing which will make us happy.

The psalmist is inviting us—ordering us—to consider our existence from a perspective which transcends earthly considerations. He encourages us, in the words of Dallas Willard, to "meditate on the greatness of God, revealed in his infinite goodness to us."[10] The psalmist believes that the very act of considering God's gifts will bring forth a festive spirit, expressed in abundant joy, gratitude, praise and declarations of His goodness!

Think for a moment about our reality. God created the skies for us to enjoy. He formed the air we breathe, the food we taste. He gave us families to care for, friends to treasure and dreams to dream. He granted us gifts and entrusted us with ministry. If we allow the Spirit to guide us in this exercise, our list could be endless. Everything, absolutely everything, comes from His generous hand.

How important it is, busy as we are with day to day service, to celebrate the many and varied manifestations of the Lord's goodness to us. Joy and gratitude are the best antidotes to despair! And so the psalmist urges us to join the joyful celebration of His people, declaring that "the Lord is good and his love endures forever."

Food for Thought

When we are feeling low and depression is just around the corner, the moment is ripe to enter God's presence with gratitude. At first only your will enters in; your feelings will shy away from such madness and skulk, offended, in a corner of your soul. If you persist, however, your feelings will not be able to resist the spirit of celebration. In the end, even your body will not want to be left out of the party! Practice the discipline of celebration. You will be amazed at the transformation it brings to your life.

23 April

Partial Obedience

The LORD had said to Abram, "Leave your country, your people and your father's household and go to the land I will show you." . . . So Abram left, as the LORD had told him; and Lot went with him. Genesis 12:1, 4

The instructions God gave Abraham were quite distinct: Leave your country and your relatives. Abraham did exactly that. He arose and left his father's home, along with its customs and contacts, and turned his back on a lifetime in that place. He left for the unknown, a promised land he didn't know how to reach.

The order to leave behind his relatives, however, presented a tremendous challenge. Abraham felt a responsibility toward his brother's son, Lot. It's also possible that he did not want to set out on such an adventure alone and sought the company of the younger man. There could have been dozens of reasons to justify the patriarch's decision.

Here lies the major obstacle to accomplishing God's will. We seem unable to accept that God is not our partner; we are not called to argue the method of fulfilling His assignments. Only with great difficulty do we resist the temptation to make "minor adjustments" to the instructions we receive, to abandon the desire to do things our own way. As a result, although we may obey, our obedience is sometimes incomplete.

Abraham fulfilled most of what he had been sent to do. Perhaps we should recognize that he accomplished a great deal, since the sacrifice he made was not easy—he turned his back on everything that brought him security. But the value of this sacrifice was diminished by the short phrase that follows the main story, almost as an afterthought: "And Lot went with him."

Let's look at the consequences of this decision. No sooner had the patriarch settled in the land than Lot's shepherds began to fight with Abraham's over the grazing pastures. Abraham was forced to intervene and divide the land allotted to each family (Gen. 13). Later on, Abraham had to plead with the Lord to save Lot from the destruction of Sodom, the ill-chosen city to which his nephew had moved (Gen. 18:16–33). Both situations caused unnecessary complications for the patriarch. Worse, however, were the long-term consequences. Lot's descendants, the Moabites and the Ammonites, ended up being a thorn in the flesh to Abraham's descendants.

Unconditional obedience is based on the conviction that God is good and knows what He is doing. As long as we have any doubt on this point, we will always be tempted to tweak the Lord's instructions for our lives. But what we cannot do is measure the consequences of these changes. It is therefore necessary that we cultivate the discipline of absolute obedience. This was the way chosen by the Son, even though He already enjoyed absolute fellowship with the Father.

Food for Thought

Consider these words by Dietrich Bonhoeffer: "Jesus has spoken; to Him belongs the Word, to us belongs obedience." [11]

Keep the Unity

As a prisoner for the Lord, then, I urge you to live a life worthy of the calling you have received. Be completely humble and gentle; be patient, bearing with one another in love. Make every effort to keep the unity of the Spirit through the bond of peace. Ephesians 4:1–3

In religious circles we often hear phrases such as: "We must attain unity; we have to organize activities which encourage unity; we need to approach other congregations in order to foster unity . . ." Such expressions reveal our belief that we can *produce* this quality among the children of God. But today's passage urges us to *keep* the unity. We are being exhorted to preserve something already inherent in the church, not to create something.

"Just a moment!" you say. "How can we speak of church unity already existing when there are so many divisions, differences and fights among its members?" Look at the exhortation preceding the phrase we are concentrating on. It includes such words as "humility," "meekness," "forbearing" and "patience." These expressions don't refer to something under development; rather, they are indispensable attitudes for keeping the unity of the Spirit through the bond of peace.

The fact is that oneness doesn't come naturally to us. It is supernatural. For this reason Paul attributes true unity to the Spirit. We can't produce it or encourage it. We can only enjoy it as evidence of God's presence among us. We can be one because the Father, Son and Holy Spirit are perfectly one. As we are joined to God through the Son, this singleness of heart is transmitted to His people.

So what can we do? We can only break the unity. This we do with attitudes of arrogance, pride, selfishness and impatience. Therefore, the correct road to restoring harmony is not organization of plans to produce it, but rather repentance. Unity will be kept as long as it is not broken by our wrong attitudes. In order for this characteristic to be seen in all its fullness, we must put aside the individualistic tendencies so natural to us and allow the Lord's characteristics of love and meekness to work in our hearts.

It is worth pointing out that unity is a spiritual condition, not a mental one. It is often confused with uniformity, the need for all of us to think and act in exactly the same way. With this in mind we organize massive events and encourage our congregations to participate in order to "demonstrate the unity of the church." It's this kind of "unity" the church in Jerusalem wanted to impose on Paul and Barnabas: everyone working in exactly the same manner. This false oneness does not allow for differences, whereas true unity in the Spirit allows a Father, a Son and a Spirit to live in perfect harmony, despite being different from each other.

Food for Thought

A. W. Tozer's words bear consideration: "Unity in Christ is not something to be achieved; it is something to be recognized." [12]

Spiritual Brokenness

Let your ear be attentive and your eyes open to hear the prayer your servant is praying before you day and night for your servants, the people of Israel. I confess the sins we Israelites, including myself and my father's house, have committed against you. We have acted very wickedly toward you. We have not obeyed the commands, decrees and laws you gave your servant Moses. Nehemiah 1:6–7

Nehemiah's entreaty has to be one of the best examples of prayer in the Bible. It contains many themes essential to an understanding of the spiritual world in which we live, and it serves as a model for our own prayers. Nevertheless, though we can duplicate certain aspects of his prayer, we cannot disguise the fact that its power results from a heart broken by the Spirit of God—something we cannot secure through emulation.

I would like to concentrate on a single aspect of this spiritual brokenness: Nehemiah's confession of sin.

It is common for us to engage in energetic criticism of other people's sins or the sins of the church in general. We often make these accusations in the superior tone of those who naturally believe themselves entirely free of the same evils.

These kinds of allegations do not proceed from the Spirit. Those broken by God don't speak of *their* sin, but rather of *our* sin. Nehemiah had not lived through the times of extreme spiritual difficulty that culminated in the invasion and exile of Israel. Nevertheless, he prayed about the sins "we Israelites . . . have committed against you." The king's cupbearer realized that the seed of rebellion and hard-heartedness possessed by his ancestors was also present in his own heart.

Isaiah experienced this same spiritual awareness of sin when he saw the Lord seated in the holy temple. He did not cry out, "Woe to me! I am ruined! For I live among a people of unclean lips." What he said was, "Woe to me! I am ruined! For I am a man of unclean lips, and I live among a people of unclean lips" (Isa. 6:5). The magnificent revelation he experienced of the greatness and holiness of God allowed him to see that sin had completely tarnished not only the lives of the Israelites, but his own as well.

As a leader you surely know that irate censure of sin in others rarely produces change. On the contrary, those against whom we make our denunciations simply feel assaulted and condemned. When these people can see, however, that we have first been broken by the weight of sin in our own lives, they will be motivated to seek the purifying presence of our Lord. This kind of brokenness is the result of spending time with Him who is light and holiness.

Food for Thought

What is your reaction to the sins of others? What does this say about the kind of person you are? How much time do you dedicate to the confession of your own sins?

Honoring the Bride

Husbands, love your wives, just as Christ loved the church and gave himself up for her to make her holy, cleansing her by the washing with water through the word, and to present her to himself as a radiant church, without stain or wrinkle or any other blemish, but holy and blameless. Ephesians 5:25–27

How wonderful life feels to those in love! No matter how much time the lovers spend together, they never weary of each other. She unhesitatingly declares that "he's everything I ever dreamed of" while he unabashedly states that she is "like no girl I've ever met."

Of course those outside this passionate relationship are often quite aware of shortcomings in these two apparently "perfect" people. Sometimes their relationship causes us pain because we see incompatibilities in them. Before they marry we can predict, with some accuracy, areas in which they will experience tension. In time these traits may become real obstacles to a deeper relationship.

Have you ever tried to point out such faults to someone in love? If there is one person in the world unwilling to listen to censure, it's a person who passionately loves another. People in love tend to be blind to each other's faults. But in a sense, Christ's love for His people is the same!

We daily hear references to the frivolous nature of the church, her lack of spirituality and feeble commitment to things godly. People everywhere indignantly denounce the all too obvious imperfections in the body of Christ. Some are so discouraged they consider leaving the fellowship of believers, for they see other Christians as stumbling blocks to a relationship with the Lord.

And how right they are! The church is all of this and many other things as well. If you are serving the saints in any kind of ministry, you will have undoubtedly experienced despair at the carnality you see in so many. Perhaps you too have indignantly criticized the lack of commitment in God's people. I have often fought these feelings.

But in our desperation Christ speaks to us: "Wait a minute! That's My bride you are talking about." However, our annoyance is so intense that we insist on elaborating her defects. Once again He says: "You're right! But I love her."

If we listen to His words, we will have discovered a great mystery of the Kingdom: God loves His people. It possesses no logic; it defies all explanations; it resists analysis. The Lord *does* know who we are, but He simply refuses to allow that knowledge to dampen His deep passion for us.

Food for Thought

Are you weary of the church? Has serving Christ's bride become somewhat stale? A good way to renew your passion for the bride is by spending time with her Lover. You will almost certainly hear Him say, "If you love Me, you must love My bride as well."

No Place to Turn

When Uriah's wife heard that her husband was dead, she mourned for him. After the time of mourning was over, David had her brought to his house, and she became his wife and bore him a son. But the thing David had done displeased the LORD. 2 Samuel 11:26–27

David had slept with his neighbor's wife and, not surprisingly, she ended up pregnant. The eleventh chapter of Samuel relates the king's desperate efforts to hide his sin. When he found out Bathsheba was expecting a baby, he must have spent hours agonizing over a solution. First, he chose the easiest plan. He brought Uriah back from the battlefront, hoping he would sleep with his wife. How could such a plan fail? But David did not take Uriah's sense of duty into account. The man refused to enjoy his wife while the army was still at war.

Exasperated, David extended Uriah's leave and invited him to a feast where the drinks flowed freely. Surely if he was drunk he would forget his convictions! But the official remained firm in refusing to sleep with his wife.

The king must have been desperate; Bathsheba's pregnancy could not be hidden much longer. Despair eventually led David to consider the unthinkable: He would have the young officer killed. He laid his plans carefully and issued the necessary instructions.

The next weeks must have brought intense anxiety to David. Bathsheba grew day by day, with still no news of Uriah's death. Finally, a report was brought to the king confirming the accomplishment of his despicable goal. The man of principle, who had honored both his fellow soldiers and his king, was dead. The new couple quickly dispensed with the formalities and concluded what the king had begun months before, joining together as man and wife.

If you have ever been as desperate as David, it won't be difficult for you to imagine his relief! This affair had been unexpectedly complicated, but he had now taken care of his catastrophic blunder.

At the end of the story we find this phrase: "But the thing David had done displeased the Lord." Our understanding of the real extent of our sin is so limited! We only consider what is related to this world and throw our energy into rearranging circumstances. We use convoluted and elaborate arguments to convince others we haven't sinned. We forget that the most serious consequences of our sin are not the ones we see, but those we don't see. If we understood the true magnitude of our sin, we would not waste our efforts in meaningless maneuvers which do not solve the real problems at stake.

David found a way to rearrange his circumstances. For a few days he enjoyed relative peace. His troubles, however, had only just begun.

Food for Thought

Sin is serious. Covering it up is more serious still. God is a permanent observer of all we do. Let us choose the shorter, easier route, confessing our sins promptly and laying hold of His forgiveness.

The Eloquence of the Cross

For Christ did not send me to baptize, but to preach the gospel—not with words of human wisdom, lest the cross of Christ be emptied of its power. 1 Corinthians 1:17

At seminary I studied homiletics, the "art of preaching." Spending time with a teacher experienced in preaching was undoubtedly a great benefit. He helped me gain confidence, identify habits that hinder communication and incorporate techniques to make preaching more efficient and attractive.

With these benefits, however, came the inevitable inclination to pay more attention than necessary to eloquence. The careful preparation of the message often led to meticulous concentration on details: the illustrations, the points of my outline, the transitions, the form of delivery, the use of examples, the coherence of my arguments. Without realizing it I became so obsessed with details that I lost sight of the reason for preaching God's Word.

Thankfully, it didn't take me too long to realize I was focused on the wrong things. But when I first completed this class, I could not listen to a message without making a critical analysis of the preacher's style. Had sufficient illustrations been inserted? Were all the points of the presentation clear? Was each point supported by verses? Was the conclusion appealing and precisely presented? These questions and many others hindered my ability to receive the Word of God meekly. I was no longer a disciple seeking the ministry of Scripture, but rather a specialist in communication techniques.

Sadly, after many years of proclaiming God's Word, I have realized that some preachers never get beyond this stage. They have dedicated too much time to perfecting their oratory skills. Their eagerness for polished diction is telling. The wonderful power of God is not producing in them that deep transformation which goes beyond words. They are not convinced that the cross of Christ alone is attractive enough, so they embellish it with unnecessary, elaborate forms of speech.

If you are a preacher of the Word, don't let eloquence go to your head! The Apostle Paul put aside this style because of his tremendous reverence for the cross of Christ. *The Message* translates today's verse this way: "God didn't send me out to collect a following for myself, but to preach the Message of what he has done, collecting a following for him. And he didn't send me to do it with a lot of fancy rhetoric of my own, lest the powerful action at the center—Christ on the Cross—be trivialized into mere words." As preachers we must work to perfect the gift God has given us. But let us not be led astray! It is not our technique which touches hearts; it is the powerful message of the cross. Let us avoid dulling its splendor by keeping free of excessive adornments.

Food for Thought

"For the kingdom of God is not a matter of talk but of power" (1 Cor. 4:20). What a wonderful truth to bear in mind each time we approach the pulpit!

Ministerial Disagreements

Barnabas wanted to take John, also called Mark, with them, but Paul did not think it wise to take him, because he had deserted them in Pamphylia and had not continued with them in the work. They had such a sharp disagreement that they parted company. Barnabas took Mark and sailed for Cyprus, but Paul chose Silas and left, commended by the brothers to the grace of the Lord. Acts 15:37–40

How can we explain this separation? If we are sincere, the apparent vehemence of this incident is hard to grasp. We can't reconcile it with our image of these servants of God. Allow me to share some thoughts on this situation.

Whenever people work together, differences will arise. Sometimes people are discouraged by this. A good team, however, is not one in which everyone agrees with everything said or done. When this happens, it's very likely that the leaders have only surrounded themselves with people who promote their own objectives. But differences in opinion can be wonderful manifestations of diversity in the body of Christ. Ministry is greatly enriched when people totally different from one another interact.

When differences arise, they must be handled spiritually. What hurts the body of Christ is that we believe our differences give us the right to attack others. No matter how right our own perspectives are, God never gives us freedom to humiliate or debase other people. "Get rid of all bitterness, rage and anger, brawling and slander, along with every form of malice. Be kind and compassionate to one another, forgiving each other, just as in Christ God forgave you" (Eph. 4:31–32).

Undoubtedly, parting ways is a radical solution to a serious problem. We should first exhaust all possible means to reach an agreement. We should not cease in our attempts to reconcile diverse perspectives. The Lord commands: "Do nothing out of selfish ambition or vain conceit, but in humility consider others better than yourselves. Each of you should look not only to your own interests, but also to the interests of others" (Phil. 2:3–4). Nevertheless, when all these alternatives have been implemented, separation is sometimes best.

Paul and Barnabas, two spiritual giants, opted for this decision. They both went on to develop highly significant ministries. Since we are of less stature than they were, is it realistic to think we can always reach agreement on things?

Food for Thought

Note the passage does not say they divided, but rather "parted company." Division produces two weaker parts. But parting company allows each group to move forward in their full potential. The difference is found in attitude. When separation is motivated by bitterness, anger and frustration, you can be sure the decision was born of the flesh. In my experience, 95% of separations have not been a parting of ways; they have been divisions.

Grace-filled Leadership

Now Stephen, a man full of God's grace and power, did great wonders and miraculous signs among the people. Acts 6:8

People may think of a number of qualities to describe their leaders. They may speak of their responsibility and dedication to the ministry. Perhaps they talk more about a leader's capacity to persevere in the face of obstacles. Others may praise a leader's virtues as a preacher or a teacher. The qualities and characteristics that distinguish those who serve the church are very diverse, but we do not often hear a congregation say that their leader is "full of grace."

What was the author of Acts thinking when he said Stephen was "full of grace"? He was quoting what the church had said about this extraordinary deacon. But what qualities made them refer to him in this manner? Some verses later Luke writes that when the members of the Sanhedrin "looked intently at Stephen . . . they saw that his face was like the face of an angel" (Acts 6:15).

This phrase may help us analyze the term "full of grace." Apparently it pertains to something supernatural, of a heavenly quality. To tell the truth, this is precisely why we find it difficult to describe; it is a concept far removed from our daily human reality. Our world is filled with people who with gritted teeth push their way ahead in life. Nobody gets far unless they are willing to aggressively compete. Only the most disciplined and determined individuals achieve positions of power and prestige.

Grace is understood from an entirely different concept of life. The ideal environment for grace to thrive is one in which weakness, fragility and insecurity abound. It is most frequently observed among those unable to defend themselves. Grace comes alive when our own resources have been exhausted, when we recognize that we can advance no further on our own.

When the church described Stephen as "full of grace," they were describing a leader who ministered from his weakness, not from his strength.

He was deeply aware of his lack of ability to do the work set before him. Perhaps he was inefficient or lacking in eloquence; perhaps his physical strength was not up to the challenge. We don't know for certain what his weaknesses were. What we can confirm, however, is that the church saw in Stephen a man who was absolutely dependent on the Lord in every area of his life. In other words, he was a man full of the grace of God.

Food for Thought

How would your congregation describe you? Which of your qualities would they choose to highlight? Would they see you as someone who is painfully aware of your lack of qualifications? Wouldn't it be wonderful if they could say of you and me that we are "full of grace"?!

1 May | Prayers that Aren't Really Prayers

The Pharisee stood up and prayed about himself: "God, I thank you that I am not like all other men—robbers, evildoers, adulterers—or even like this tax collector. I fast twice a week and give a tenth of all I get." Luke 18:11–12

Our first reaction to this scene is predictable. We feel immediate indignation at the Pharisee's hypocrisy. How is it possible, we ask ourselves, for a man to be so blind and proud that he dares to speak to God in this way? Certain we have never been guilty of such vulgar spirituality, we are quick to heap scorn on this man. As we read further, the contrast between the tax collector and the Pharisee is just too obvious; it takes no special genius to identify the right posture in prayer exemplified by the contrite tax collector.

Wait a minute—don't go so fast! We missed a deeply troubling phrase. The evangelist says the religious leader "prayed about himself." The New American Standard Bible tells us he "was praying this *to* himself." Forget briefly his obvious selfishness and reflect on this reality: There are prayers which are spoken not to God but to oneself. Does this not frighten you? If we know that our hearts deceive us, it is not so easy to dismiss the idea that we may pray exactly as the Pharisee.

The exercise of prayer lends itself to this distortion because of its innate characteristics. It does not include the capacity to hear the Lord's voice audibly correcting us or gently directing our gaze toward more spiritual themes. We only hear ourselves. We must pay special attention to the Spirit's gentle witness whispered to our spirits, telling us whether our prayers are "on target" or not. Even with His assistance, it's easy to get sidetracked by our own self-centeredness!

There is no easy answer for this; we must be permanently on guard. Just knowing that our prayers may be directed more toward ourselves than to God is an important first step. At the very least we must proceed with great caution.

I would like to add two observations. First, it is always dangerous when we do all the talking. Scripture warns us: "Guard your steps when you go to the house of God. Go near to listen rather than to offer the sacrifice of fools, who do not know that they do wrong. Do not be quick with your mouth, do not be hasty in your heart to utter anything before God. God is in heaven and you are on earth; so let your words be few" (Eccles. 5:1–2). Second, it's very easy to pray completely about ourselves: our desires, our needs, our plans, our confessions. When the words "I" or "my" crop up too often in our prayers, we should become concerned.

Food for Thought

Have you ever analyzed your prayers? How genuine are they? How much empty wordiness is included? What changes should be made so you don't end up "praying to yourself"?

The Downcast Soul

Why are you downcast, O my soul? Why so disturbed within me? Put your hope in God, for I will yet praise him, my Savior and my God. Psalm 42:5–6

This psalm was written by a man completely caught up in an intense, personal struggle. The psalmist describes his condition saying, "My tears have been my food day and night" (Ps. 42:3) and confesses with surprising honesty, "My soul is downcast within me" (Ps. 42:6).

For many of us, depression is inadmissible in those who belong to God. How can someone with access to the unlimited power of Almighty God suffer from depression? Believing this to be sin, we make an enormous effort to put on a brave but empty show to convince others we are living daily in the victory of Christ.

Life frequently leads us into situations in which we experience an entire range of emotions which are part and parcel of our fragile humanity. In the psalmist's honest confession, we find only the sincere expression of feelings with which we have all struggled at one time or another. Not even the Son of God was free of this! Faced with imminent death, He confessed to those closest to Him, "My soul is overwhelmed with sorrow to the point of death" (Matt. 26:38).

The problem does not lie in experiencing these feelings, which are a completely normal reaction to adverse or sad situations. The difficulty lies in our propensity to let feelings take over our lives. This is precisely where many Christians fall. They give way to feelings of dejection, anguish, sadness and discouragement, leading them to abandon prayer, worship and fellowship. This in turn produces greater depression.

Our feelings are changeable and untrustworthy. Think of all the things we have to do each day that can't depend on how we feel. Just getting out of bed each morning produces for some an intense struggle with their emotions! Nevertheless, we pay no attention to the grumbling of our minds and set a foot on the floor.

The psalmist recognizes the danger of allowing feelings to take over the direction of our lives and thus reproves his own heart: "Why are you downcast, O my soul? Why so disturbed within me?" Later he tells his soul with gentle firmness, "Put your hope in God, for I will yet praise him, my Savior and my God," thus imposing eternal principles of the Word on the inconsequential feelings of the moment. As a leader you will often have to give this example of discipline to your people.

Food for Thought

What feelings do you most often struggle with? What kind of behavior brings these about? What must you do in order to prevent these feelings from dominating your life? How can you live a life of greater emotional stability?

3 May An Indisputable Testimony

When he had said this, he knelt down with all of them and prayed. They all wept as they embraced him and kissed him. What grieved them most was his statement that they would never see his face again. Then they accompanied him to the ship. Acts 20:36–38

I have often heard references to Paul's strong character and his rather unyielding heart. A typical illustration of these characteristics, we are told, is the incident with John Mark (Acts 15:36–41). The apostle believed that someone who had abandoned the ministry once should not serve with them on further journeys. But Barnabas thought John Mark should have a second chance. Their disagreement was so intense that the two decided to separate. Some commentators believe that Paul was the cause of this separation, principally due to his lack of compassion toward those weaker than himself.

There is no doubt that over the years God deals with a leader to diminish roughness that can hurt others. Certainly the great apostle was no exception and was also handled this way by the divine Potter. In his second letter to the Corinthians, Paul mentions having experienced lashes, prison, confinement, flogging and numerous lesser sufferings.

The true heart of a leader, however, is known only by those closest to him. They have walked with him through difficulties, have known his weaknesses and have tasted the particular grace poured out on his life. These are the people who have observed him most closely and shared his dreams, victories and defeats. As such, they are well placed to pass a verdict on his life and ministry.

Paul's farewell at Miletus offers one of the best clues as to who he was, since he was surrounded by those who knew him best. Luke tells us they began to cry disconsolately, distressed because Paul had said they would not see him again. Sadly, in many of our congregations, the departure of the leader would be cause for celebration. But the people who were with Paul kissed and hugged him, weeping over the imminent departure of this great teacher and apostle. An onlooker would have had no need to ask how they felt about him; their behavior spoke eloquently of the place he held in their hearts.

Perhaps people won't properly value all that you as their leader have done for them until you are no longer with them. But the farewell they give you will speak volumes about the respect and affection you have won during the years of your ministry. In times of change, their verdict will be more revealing than at any other moment.

Food for Thought

If you had to say goodbye to your congregation today, how would they receive the news? On what do you base your belief that they would behave in this way? How can you make a more personal investment in the lives of those near you? What should you do to make them aware of your unconditional love?

The Secret of the Lord

The Lord *confides in those who fear him; he makes his covenant known to them.*
Psalm 25:14

For many years my ministry included involvement in the academic and theological institutions which serve the church. A great deal of my time and effort was dedicated to identifying, studying and analyzing every conceivable aspect of spiritual experience. Men and women of great intelligence expounded on detailed descriptions of the Lord's ways and His dealings with His people. However, I scarcely remember a member of faculty, or a student for that matter, admitting that there were certain aspects of spirituality they didn't understand. And how could they? It is a commonly held belief that these institutions exist precisely to help students find answers to their most puzzling questions.

When we refer to the person of God, however, we are approaching a Subject unlike any other. He cannot be analyzed, dissected or explained in terms readily comprehensible to men and women. He is essentially different from any created being in heaven or on earth. He does not move according to the laws of creation, nor can He be contained in the abundance of wisdom found among the world's most distinguished scholars. He is, in short, beyond the reach of our intelligence.

The tools of academia which work so well with any other subject have very limited use in explaining God. We are entirely dependent on the Lord's willingness to make Himself known to us. We can know of Him only what He has chosen to reveal. The more we study Him, therefore, the more we should realize how much still remains hidden. The most appropriate response to our inquiries into His nature should be to fall down and worship Him.

Note the irony in the words of the psalmist: "The secret of the Lord is for those who fear Him." A holy fear of the Lord is lacking in the classrooms of many theological institutions. Instead, one can hardly escape the feeling that there is no question too hard to answer. The funny thing is that the Lord reveals His secret to people who are not even pursuing it! A strong sense of God's mystery draws them close to Him in silence and humility to listen rather than explain. To these few the Lord gives an understanding of His person which far transcends things discovered by elaborate intellectual processes.

What is the psalmist saying? The Lord is known primarily through walking with Him. That experience is given to those whose passion is not the *study* of God, but simply God Himself.

Food for Thought

"'But let him who boasts boast about this: that he understands and knows me, that I am the **Lord*****, who exercises kindness, justice and righteousness on earth, for in these I delight,' declares the*** **Lord*****" (Jer. 9:24).***

Fatal Ignorance

You say, "I am rich; I have acquired wealth and do not need a thing." But you do not realize that you are wretched, pitiful, poor, blind and naked. Revelation 3:17

When studying this passage with my students, I often asked for their thoughts about the problem of the Laodicean church. Over the years I received a wide variety of replies as to why this congregation was so harshly judged by the Lord. Some believe they were not committed enough, others think their main problem was pride, while others hold that the church had turned its back on the unity of Christ's body.

Each answer offers a possible explanation for the Lord's strong reprimand, and we can imagine many other spiritual problems that likely burdened them. But none of these address the fundamental difficulty plaguing this congregation. The source of their problem is expressed in the phrase "you do not realize."

The truth is that our spiritual growth is governed by a myriad of factors. But whatever these are, the real obstacle to transformation lies in our lack of ability to discern them. How can we treat an illness we are not aware of? How can we solve a problem if we don't realize it exists? The real problem facing the church at Laodicea was their blindness to the problem.

This small detail is of tremendous importance to us. The trouble is that human beings cannot diagnose their own spiritual condition. "Who can say, 'I have kept my heart pure; I am clean and without sin'?" (Prov. 20:9). Nobody can say they have cleansed their own heart. This work belongs to the Spirit of God, who scrutinizes and examines all things in the light of eternal truth.

Before we can deal with a problem in our lives, it is necessary to realize it exists! As leaders it is important to allow the Lord to regularly examine our lives and ministries. Only God's verdict counts in the judgment of our true spiritual condition. We must come into His presence, putting aside all preconceived ideas, and wait silently for Him to reveal what He sees in our lives. Not only must we be still, but we should also be prepared for surprises. Remember the dramatic difference between the church's evaluation and that of Christ. They said they were rich, but Christ said they were poor, blind and naked! It's possible this shocking disparity exists in our own lives. Only the Lord can reveal it to us.

Food for Thought

What tools do you use to evaluate your own spiritual condition? How do you know this method is up to the task? What place does God have in this process?

Supernatural Strength

Samson went down to Timnah together with his father and mother. As they approached the vineyards of Timnah, suddenly a young lion came roaring toward him. The Spirit of the LORD came upon him in power so that he tore the lion apart with his bare hands as he might have torn a young goat. Judges 14:5–6

Have you ever seen a Hollywood production on the life of Samson? In the ones I've seen, Samson is always a human colossus who possesses such incredibly muscular arms and legs that he would have easily taken first place in any bodybuilding competition! His mere presence inspires awe and fear. We see something similar in children's illustrated versions of the Bible. Samson is always shown as an imposing giant who inspires terror in the Philistines.

Look closely at today's verse. Samson was on his way to Timnah to choose a wife from among the Philistines. On the road a young lion attacked him. Then we are told that "the Spirit of the LORD came upon him in power so that he tore the lion apart with his bare hands." Samson did not destroy the animal by his brute strength, but because the Spirit of God came upon him in power. The strength was not Samson's; it was the Spirit's.

If that's how it was, then Samson's physical appearance could well have attracted no attention in the street. His stature may not have been different from any other man's and his muscles no bigger than his friends', since his strength came not from himself but from the Spirit.

The way we imagine Israel's judge shows how difficult it is for us to accept that victory belongs entirely to the Lord. Usually we imagine that God bestows His blessing on the abilities we already possess, concluding that seventy percent of the merit is ours and thirty percent the Lord's.

How often in the church do we choose people for their natural talents, then ask the Lord to bless that which is already present in them? In the Kingdom completely different principles are at work. The Lord has chosen "the foolish things of the world to shame the wise; God chose the weak things of the world to shame the strong" (1 Cor. 1:27). Hasn't it always been this way? He chose two sterile retirees as parents of a nation, a slave as prime minister of the most powerful nation on earth, a man who stammered as Israel's spokesman to Pharaoh and several uneducated fishermen as apostles of the future church. It is best for us as leaders to feel incapable of the job we are supposed to do. It is only then we will ever be completely dependent on God!

Food for Thought

How often do you feel unable to do what you have to do? What does this reveal about your ministerial style? How can you fight against becoming overconfident?

Believing Him

No one will be able to stand up against you all the days of your life. As I was with Moses, so I will be with you; I will never leave you nor forsake you. Have I not commanded you? Be strong and courageous. Do not be terrified; do not be discouraged, for the L*ORD your God will be with you wherever you go.* Joshua 1:5, 9

Allow me to ask a question: Would you stake your future on a promise?

The moment had come for Joshua to assume responsibility for leadership of Israel, to take the place of the great prophet Moses. The way ahead would be difficult, and Joshua was under no delusion about this. When God said He had been with Moses, Joshua must have remembered the countless times he had seen His powerful hand at work for him. But certainly he would also have thought of the many obstacles, difficulties and setbacks suffered during forty long years in the desert. By way of encouragement God promised him, "The LORD your God will be with you wherever you go."

A promise can have unbelievable power to motivate us. It brings with it hope which lightens our hearts and feeds our imagination concerning the future. When we receive it, we treasure it, believing against all odds in its eventual fulfillment. But a promise has no power unless we choose to believe it.

For most of us, life contains a long list of unfulfilled promises. In some cases this began in childhood, when our parents or closest relatives repeatedly failed to keep their word. Later on friends and loved ones added their share to our string of broken commitments. As adults we have grown accustomed to never-ending promises from public figures, politicians and governors who try to convince us of their plans to meet our needs. As the years have passed, broken promises have left us skeptical.

This is the root of our dilemma! The life God gives is entirely connected to the promises He makes. Peter declares that God "has given us His very great and precious promises, so that through them you may participate in the divine nature" (2 Pet. 1:4). God's promises are an essential part of His plan.

This is precisely why the Lord tells Joshua, "Be strong and courageous. Do not be terrified; do not be discouraged." When we encounter particularly difficult circumstances, it's all too easy to believe we have been forgotten. If we add to this our frequent disappointments at the hands of others, how can we not live in fear? But fear paralyzes us. It hinders that bold conviction inherent in those who believe God's declarations. If we don't believe them, His promises have no power in our lives.

Food for Thought

The challenge for us is to bravely refuse the lies that are presented in times of trial. To be victorious we must choose to believe the vows God has made to us, and He in turn will fulfill them!

Restoring the Fallen

Brothers, if someone is caught in a sin, you who are spiritual should restore him gently. But watch yourself, or you also may be tempted. Galatians 6:1

The restoration of those fallen by the wayside is an important responsibility within the body of Christ. Sin is a reality in the Christian life, and it constantly produces havoc in the family of God. We should pay particular attention to the Word on this subject so our work of restoration may be fruitful.

In the first place, we have to understand there are two kinds of sin. One is the result of an obstinate and rebellious attitude in which the person knows they are doing wrong. They refuse to listen to advice and persist in wrongdoing. In this passage the Apostle Paul has in mind a second category in which the sin committed is unexpected and not premeditated. The word used indicates that the person is suddenly overtaken by sin. Neither kind of sin is excusable, but there is an important difference in attitude to be taken into account when the time for restoration comes. From our simplistic point of view, we too easily consider all sin as being the result of obstinate rebellion.

Second, restoration is part of a leader's calling. The word "restore" means to take something back to its original state and function, to repair it.

We are aware that very often the so-called "restoration" of someone in the church has exactly the opposite effect. Instead of being brought back to good health, the person is cast into a pit of condemnation. Some people never recover from such an experience. But God calls His servants to the restoration of peoples' lives. Even in the extreme case of handing someone over to Satan, Paul mentions that his objective was for their salvation on the day of judgment (1 Cor. 5:5).

Third, restoration should be carried out in a spirit of meekness. This means that all forms of aggression, violence and anger should be absent in the person doing the work. These attitudes greatly hinder the process of restoration. The fact that sin is by definition based on deceit means that the one needing restoration is likely to put up some resistance. If we want to prevent this resistance from turning into rebellion, our attitude should be tender and meek. This can be achieved without casting aside the firmness needed for confrontation.

What can help us most in this process is to look at our own lives. Nothing makes us quite as ruthless with others as the arrogance of believing we would never have stumbled as they have. We should remember that we are subject to exactly the same weaknesses; this will help us proceed with mercy and will allow the grace of God to work profoundly in the lives of those who have fallen.

Food for Thought

Charles Hodge wrote, "The doctrines of grace humble a man without degrading him, and exalt him without inflating him." [1]

Marvelous Mystery!

When I consider your heavens, the work of your fingers, the moon and the stars, which you have set in place, what is man that you are mindful of him, the son of man that you care for him. Psalm 8:3–4

When I was young, I had the opportunity to make a five-month voyage on the open sea. Before leaving, we undertook the grueling task of stocking the ship with needed provisions. Dozens of trucks lined the quay, waiting to be unburdened of their cargo. Anchored in port, the ship looked imposing in comparison with the small trucks and cranes that worked day and night. I was new to this life and terribly impressed by the ship's sophistication: its navigation instruments, endless passageways and hundreds of pipes, cables and conduits wending their way around the interior.

Finally, the day came. The coast gradually disappeared into the distance, and in a few hours we were completely surrounded by water. As far as the horizon stretched, we could see nothing but a vast, untamable expanse of water. It was not long before I felt a sensation common to all who sail: a realization that we are in fact very small. Our ship, so impressive at the pier, was now just a tiny object in the gigantic ocean. That experience helped me understand the awe David expresses in the eighth psalm.

Raising his eyes to the heavens, he was overcome with a similar awareness of insignificance in the face of God's immeasurable creation. The consciousness of how very small we are led him to ask the Lord: "If You are so great, and what You have created is so vast and majestic, why do You care about us who are so inconsequential?"

Who can possibly understand such a penetrating mystery? The God who created the heavens and the earth, who put the stars in place and knows every secret of the universe, has chosen to fellowship with us though we are miniscule beside the immensity of eternity!

In these days, with experiments in cloning and technology taking great leaps forward, wouldn't it be great if we could recover that sense of insignificance? When we lose it, we cease to wonder at God's eternal mystery, that He wants to draw near and take an interest in our lives. Not only do we lose our wonder, but we also get puffed up with an exaggerated sense of our own importance. We believe things happen because of our involvement. We consider our contribution indispensable for the smooth and efficient operation of circumstances. Our own importance diminishes our sense of need—and if we have no need of our Creator, what hope is there for us?

Food for Thought

Take a moment to meditate on the greatness of God. Allow the Spirit to give you a sense of amazement once again so you too may exclaim, "What is man that you are mindful of him, the son of man that you care for him?" Things look different when considered in the correct perspective!

Knowledge Worth Having

His divine power has given us everything we need for life and godliness through our knowledge of him who called us by his own glory and goodness. 2 Peter 1:3

In an attempt to translate the word "knowledge" as faithfully as possible, the American Standard Version uses the phrase "true knowledge." This really is better because it helps us understand that some knowledge is not really knowledge.

There are two different words in Greek used for the term that we translate "knowledge." The first is the word *gnosis*, which conveys learning obtained by study. This typically refers to an academic process—the disciplined and detailed analysis of a topic in order to gain a complete understanding of it. A person who has gone through this process could be considered an expert in the subject.

The other word is *epignosis*. In the original language there is a marked difference between the meanings of the two words. The second kind of knowledge is not the result of study, but of observation. It's the kind of knowledge a husband has of his wife. Nobody taught him that his wife likes two spoons of sugar in her tea, or that she loves to receive flowers as a gift. He has learned this because he has lived with her for many years. Being close to her, he has collected information about her that other people don't have access to.

This is the kind of knowledge the Apostle Peter writes of. It forms the foundation of the spiritual life to which we have been called. It is not the kind of knowledge acquired through our own study or what we are told by others. It is knowledge obtained by spending time with the Lord. We can speak with a certain amount of confidence about Him because we have developed that kind of relationship typical of two people who love each other.

This knowledge, the apostle tells us, is the key to the spiritual life. It encourages our full confidence in the One who has called us, having learned through personal experience that He will not fail us even when the going gets really rough. We can seek Him when we are in need of grace, because we know with certainty that we will not come back empty handed.

Food for Thought

The Apostle Paul, expounder of the deepest New Testament doctrines and an outstanding student of the Scriptures, considered that he still had much to learn about the person of God. Shortly before his death he declared, "But whatever was to my profit I now consider loss for the sake of Christ. What is more, I consider everything a loss compared to the surpassing greatness of knowing Christ Jesus my Lord, for whose sake I have lost all things. I consider them rubbish, that I may gain Christ" (Phil. 3:7–8).

Walking with Confidence

The man of integrity walks securely, but he who takes crooked paths will be found out.
Proverbs 10:9

Integrity is one of the most precious qualities a leader possesses. It dramatically defines the level of confidence followers will have in their leader's ministry. Once integrity is lost, it is very difficult to rebuild, since the damage it brings to the credibility of a minister is far-reaching. On occasion the consequences are irreversible.

The Merriam-Webster online dictionary defines integrity as a "firm adherence to a code of especially moral or artistic values, an unimpaired condition, the quality or state of being complete or undivided."

This reference to the "state of being complete and undivided" points to coherence between a leader's principles and behavior. A lack of integrity will reveal a difference between what a leader preaches and teaches and the way that same leader lives on a day-to-day basis. Consider these scenarios: A leader preaches love, but is hard and insensitive to family members. A teacher urges obedience, but lives in disobedience to the laws of the country. A pastor cries out for honesty, but has questionable practices in financial matters. This double message sent to listeners seriously undermines authority. Writing on the subject, Kouzes and Posner state, "The ultimate test of leaders' credibility is whether they do what they say."[2]

Integrity is not easy to find in any area of life, but when it is absent among God's people, we are particularly culpable. Somehow the church has divorced its doctrine from the daily business many Christians conduct. We find that members of our congregations behave one way in church and another way during the week. Not only is their witness with co-workers and neighbors poor, but in many cases they represent a real stumbling block for those who may be seeking the truth.

As leaders we cannot ignore this sad situation. Very often our followers only imitate what they see in us; our actions speak much more loudly than our words.

Today's passage describes the confidence possessed by a person of integrity. Such a person will face difficulties, obstacles and setbacks. Nevertheless, the commitment to live a life free of double standards leads to a sense of conviction and composure that can greatly inspire others. As we know, our most difficult battles are not those related to our circumstances, but to the intense heart-struggle to overcome our own sinfulness. Those with integrity maintain strength in adversity, since the same behavior is expected from a Christian at all times, whether good or bad. Moral solidity allows godly men and women to walk with their heads held high in the most diverse circumstances.

Food for Thought

The great Bible commentator Matthew Henry observed: "Good principles fixed in the head will produce good resolutions in the heart and good practices in the life."[3]

Learning from Our Mistakes

After they had eaten, Jesus said to Simon Peter, "Simon, son of John, do you love me more than these?" He said, "Yes, Lord. You know that I like you. I am your friend." Jesus said to him, "Feed my lambs." John 21:15 (WEV)

Unlike most translations, the Worldwide English Version communicates an essential difference in the words exchanged between the Lord and Peter. When Christ asked Peter if he loved Him, He used the word *agape*. Of the three words used for love in the Greek language, this is by far the most sublime expression. Its quality was made manifest by the life of Jesus Christ; it is expressed through self-sacrifice in favor of someone else. The best description of this kind of love is found in Philippians 2:5–11.

In his response to Jesus, Peter does not use the same term, but instead chooses *fileo.* This word for love signifies the relationship existing between brothers and certainly expresses a lesser commitment than that described by *agape*. The Worldwide English Version captures this difference in Peter's response: "You know that I like you."

Perhaps it seems we are wasting time on a detail of little significance. But this difference displays an important principle in Peter's life. On the night Jesus was betrayed, Peter had confidently proclaimed he was willing to follow the Lord wherever He went. Even when the Lord warned him it wouldn't be so, he continued to insist he was even willing to die with Christ. He thought he was equal to the kind of sacrifice demanded by *agape*.

Now, however, he understood his presumption. He was living with the shame of having denied the Lord three times. I firmly believe that through this incident the Lord was restoring Peter, preparing him to fill the key position reserved for him in the new church. Nevertheless, in the process of restoration, it was necessary to be sure Peter had grasped the serious limitations of his own zeal for the Lord.

The disciple's answer shows that Peter had certainly learned from his mistakes. Where he had once confidently declared his unconditional love, he was now reluctant to describe his commitment in such lofty terms.

Our mistakes and defeats can be the seedbed of life's most important lessons. Every blunder can teach us something. In order to benefit from our failure, we must be willing to reflect on our defeat, evaluate where we went wrong and work out the changes necessary to avoid the same mistake again. In this way our failures may become our most effective teachers. It's up to us to take advantage of their potential.

Food for Thought

How do you react when you fail? How much time do you lose on regrets and reproaches? What do your reactions reveal about the kind of person you are? How can you transform your mistakes into growth?

Open Books

Are we beginning to commend ourselves again? Or do we need, like some people, letters of recommendation to you or from you? You yourselves are our letter, written on our hearts, known and read by everybody. You show that you are a letter from Christ, the result of our ministry, written not with ink but with the Spirit of the living God, not on tablets of stone but on tablets of human hearts. 2 Corinthians 3:1–3

Children can reveal much about the kind of people their parents are. In their lives we see miniature versions of the adults, since they tend to imitate the behavior and attitudes they see. The convictions and principles important to their parents become part of their own lives, even when these things are not intentionally taught within the family. Sharing the same home means countless messages are communicated daily, and these gradually become ingrained in each member of the family.

The same principle rules the life of a church. To know what kind of person the leader is, we need go no further than the lives and behavior of the congregation. They will provide the best reflection of a pastor's convictions, commitment and style of leadership. Just as in a family, the convictions held by the members have been passed on to them simply by spending time with the leader.

Many of those in leadership fail to grasp this important truth. When they observe reprehensible attitudes or weak commitments in church members, they habitually judge them harshly while thinking wistfully of all they could do if they had "more reliable" people in their congregation. Generally speaking, the main problem is not the members, but the person leading them.

Howard Hendricks, one of America's most extraordinary seminary professors, tells of an invitation he received to speak to a congregation with hundreds of members. When the service was to begin, there were only a handful of people present. The senior pastor, who had publicized the event extensively, complained about the members' lack of commitment. Hendricks listened to him quietly and then said, "Pastor, I know what your problem is." The man was delighted, for he thought he would hear an answer that would motivate his flock. But Hendricks pointed out unhesitatingly, "*You* are the problem! You should be giving thanks for the twenty people who have come, and not wasting precious time thinking about the 480 who didn't!"

Food for Thought

Your attitudes and convictions will be clearly reflected in your followers. They may accurately repeat all the concepts you have taught them, but the clearest message about your work as a leader will be seen in their behavior. If they are not responding, you need to examine how you are ministering to them.

The Right Measure of Faith

The apostles said to the Lord, "Increase our faith!" He replied, "If you have faith as small as a mustard seed, you can say to this mulberry tree, 'Be uprooted and planted in the sea,' and it will obey you." Luke 17:5–6

We shouldn't be surprised at the disciples' request if we bear in mind that Christ was teaching on the subject of forgiveness. The Lord was asking them to do something that sounded absolutely impossible! If a brother came seven times in a day to ask forgiveness for something and was sincerely sorry for his actions, the disciples had to forgive him. At such a challenge the disciples couldn't help but feel alarmed, and understandably asked for more faith. It's difficult to live with others at the best of times, but to pardon someone seven times in a day without getting bitter or annoyed—this seemed more appropriate for spiritual giants!

The disciples' reaction points to a firmly entrenched belief in God's people: the conviction that faith is distributed in varying quantities to those who follow the Lord. We often hear phrases in church such as "Let's sing this song with more faith" or "Those people have a great deal of faith; that's why God uses them." We think that those whose lives lack God's most dazzling manifestations belong to the category of "people of little faith."

Christ corrected this erroneous concept. When we think the amount of a person's faith is what matters, we automatically misunderstand, because we are placing the stress on the person and not on God. To change this perspective, the Lord used a mustard seed as an illustration. A mustard seed is extremely small, and most people would not realize the incredible potential it has.

The crucial element is where we place the faith we already have. That's why great amounts of faith are not necessary in our spiritual lives, because the greatness of the one in whom we put our faith is what makes all the difference. God is sovereign and all-powerful. Whoever puts their faith in Him will have access to all of His extraordinary attributes.

If the truth be told, the real question is not whether we have faith or not, because everybody has faith of some kind. For many of us, though, our faith is not in God, but in our own judgment, in the opinions of others or in a particular venture in which we are involved. Consequently, we shouldn't be surprised when it produces few results. If we really want to see the Lord work in our lives, we need to direct our faith—even when it is exceedingly small—exclusively toward the person of God. It is then we will be witnesses to extraordinary things, such as trees being uprooted and planted in the sea!

Food for Thought

Consider this anonymous statement: "Some people think they need faith the size of a mountain to move a mustard seed!"

The Essence of Faith

The apostles said to the Lord, "Increase our faith!" He replied, "If you have faith as small as a mustard seed, you can say to this mulberry tree, 'Be uprooted and planted in the sea,' and it will obey you." Luke 17:5–6

The concept of obedience appears three times in this short passage on faith. We find it in the verse we're looking at today as well as in the ninth and tenth verses of this chapter. The fact that obedience is mentioned in a passage on faith gives an important clue regarding the nature of this particular grace.

We commonly think that a person full of faith dares to ask God for things which we would never have courage to ask for. We regard these people with a certain amount of awe because they seem to get spectacular results. Our erroneous thinking is that they have great faith which allows them to dream big dreams.

According to Jesus' teaching, faith is tied to God's plans, not ours. Faith is not a blank check God gives His disciples so they may ask for anything they want. It is not an unconditional commitment to endorse whatever we propose to do. Instead, it is the conviction that God will give His full backing to that which He alone has initiated.

We only need a quick look at faith's great heroes to see that whenever the Lord's hand moved powerfully on their behalf, they had done no more than obey His instructions. Abraham offered Isaac as a sacrifice because he believed God's word to him about an heir. Moses lifted his staff over the waters of the Red Sea because he believed the Lord would deliver the Israelites as He had promised. He also struck the rock to obtain water because God had told him to do so. Joshua saw the destruction of Jericho because he accepted God's instructions regarding that city. Elijah defeated the prophets of Baal because he did everything according to the word of the Lord.

This is the theme of the author of Hebrews. He writes, "Therefore, since the promise of entering his rest still stands, let us be careful that none of you be found to have fallen short of it. For we also have had the gospel preached to us, just as they did; but the message they heard was of no value to them, because those who heard did not combine it with faith" (Heb. 4:1–2). It is impossible to exercise faith in something we have not heard directly from the Lord. Faith is only applicable when God has clearly spoken and invited us to follow through by believing Him. When we obey, it is clear proof of our faith.

Food for Thought

Elisabeth Elliot wrote, "You will never understand why God acts the way He does, but if you believe Him, however, that is all that is necessary. Let us learn to trust Him for who He is." [4]

No More Than Expected

Would he thank the servant because he did what he was told to do? So you also, when you have done everything you were told to do, should say, "We are unworthy servants; we have only done our duty." Luke 17:9–10

We are inclined to think that a person's strong expression of faith is something out of the ordinary. When we give testimony to an act of faith, we often do so with amazement, as if we were describing something supernatural and unheard of. Many within the church believe that some Christians have a special capacity to walk in faith, to live in a different spiritual dimension than others. This serves to highlight how unaccustomed we have grown to the life we should be living in Jesus Christ.

Christ illustrated this truth by speaking of the responsibilities of a hired hand on a farm. Having received instructions in the morning, the servant spent the entire day fulfilling commands. When evening came, would the servant's master await him with a warm meal in recompense for the work he had done during the day? Of course not! There was no reward because he had done nothing more than carry out the tasks he was paid to do.

In the same way, the disciple who lives by faith is not showing any extraordinary commitment to Christ or going any further than required. This is simply what the Master expects. God continuously gives us instructions, and we obey, doing exactly what He tells us to do. There is no merit in this, because it is precisely the life we have been called to. When we treat people who live in this dimension as heroes, it displays the fact that the exercise of faith has become a rare occurrence among God's people.

George Müller, a man who cared for thousands of orphans entirely by faith, spoke in many churches toward the end of his life. He often gave testimony of how the Lord had faithfully provided for the needs of thousands of children. Those who heard him were amazed at this man's great commitment. Yet Müller insisted he had done nothing out of the ordinary. He had simply chosen to believe the Lord's promises every day of his long life. He had done what he believed is asked of everyone who follows Christ, and this has no merit in the kingdom of God. He was, in reality, nothing more than an unworthy servant.

Food for Thought

This anonymous quote is worth pondering: "Faith is to the spiritual world what money is to the financial world."

17 May | I Am Only a Man Myself

As Peter entered the house, Cornelius met him and fell at his feet in reverence. But Peter made him get up. "Stand up," he said, "I am only a man myself." Acts 10:25–26

In ministry we often find ourselves in visible places, since our vocation is to serve people. Many of them are needy, and they come to us seeking guidance for important decisions. When they feel troubled, they come for comfort and understanding, perhaps needing support in the sadness of the moment. In times of confusion, they come to us for help in interpreting the Lord's working in their lives. Others seek us out because they see in us a sincere expression of God's love.

This places us in a position of authority with respect to those we serve. We are treated with respect. Many are profoundly grateful for help we have provided in their times of need.

But this submission and appreciation brings us up against one of the most dangerous pitfalls in ministry: We may begin to think we possess some special quality which sets us apart from others. We can lose sight of the fact that fruit is the result of the Lord's gifts and grace alone. We fall into the trap of overestimating our own value, and this leads to pride, which detracts from the vocation to which we have been called.

I remember with some sadness a pastor whose ministry saw considerable growth. Today he goes everywhere surrounded by bodyguards. From being a pastor to the needy he has turned into a star intoxicated with his own importance. The only place you can see him now is on the platform of a major event. It's so easy to fall prey to our own vanity!

Cornelius was in need of counsel and had been waiting for one of the apostles to visit him. When Peter arrived at his house, Cornelius adopted a posture that was totally unacceptable toward any human being: He fell down and worshipped him. But Peter, with admirable simplicity, raised him to his feet and gently corrected him: "I am only a man myself."

If your ministry is reasonably successful, many people will want to raise you to a position that is not healthy for you or for them. Wise leaders work to enable those around them to have a true picture of who they are. They do not encourage others to believe they are indispensable. They do not expect reverential treatment, but help others understand that they too are pilgrims in the process of transformation. They have been called to an important task, but this does not place them above anyone or give them access to special privileges. If their ministries are characterized by humility, they will have a lasting impact on the lives of those entrusted to them.

Food for Thought

Honest consideration of this statement may reveal your own perspective: "Great men never think of themselves as great; small men never think of themselves as small."

The Goal of Ministry

We proclaim him, admonishing and teaching everyone with all wisdom, so that we may present everyone perfect in Christ. To this end I labor, struggling with all his energy, which so powerfully works in me. Colossians 1:28–29

In these two verses we find an admirable summary of the Apostle Paul's philosophy of ministry. It is well worth a few minutes' meditation.

First, the great apostle affirms that his objective is to present everyone complete in Christ. To understand this we need to know the Greek meaning of the word "complete." Paul is not speaking of a sinless state. His expression of completion has to do with restoring the purpose originally created within a person. In other words, the goal of ministry is to restore the relationship and function of men and women to the state God intended when He created them. That means regenerating all that has been warped by sin—undoubtedly, a task that will last a lifetime.

The apostle then tells us that the method for restoration has two functions: to admonish and to teach. Those who know something about construction are aware that it is impossible to build on a faulty foundation. In the same way, to build up a person, the foundation must be as the Word of God demands: Jesus Christ alone. Admonition is necessary, for it helps to identify false groundwork that is offensive to God. A life cannot be rebuilt on admonitions alone, though; teaching must be added for the growth God desires for His children.

Paul explains that this teaching must be presented with all wisdom. As human beings we cannot be treated like machines, as if we are all created exactly alike. Although each person has characteristics in common with others, it is also true that each individual has unique characteristics. Teaching with wisdom means discerning each person's situation and presenting the truth in a way that can be understood within their particular culture. As teachers we must avoid "pre-packaged" instruction, which offers uniformity to everyone.

Finally, the apostle tells us that discipleship demands much work and effort on our part. This is perhaps the point where we fail most frequently in ministry. We believe that delivering a couple of sermons on a subject is enough to educate people in a certain area of their lives. But to fashion Christ in those entrusted to us demands perseverance and continuity. To impart truth is a minister's easiest job—the real challenge is to guide your followers to make this truth part of their day-to-day living.

Food for Thought

Paul makes it clear that his ministry is a result of the power of Christ "which so powerfully works in me." This is essential for success, because ministry done in human strength puts unbearable strain on a leader.

Wise Advice

Peter replied, "Even if all fall away on account of you, I never will." "I tell you the truth," Jesus answered, "this very night, before the rooster crows, you will disown me three times." But Peter declared, "Even if I have to die with you, I will never disown you." And all the other disciples said the same. Matthew 26:33–35

More often than not, teaching on this passage concentrates on Peter's foolish refusal to really hear the Lord. I would like to invite you to view this scene from the angle of Christ's perspective. Put yourself for a moment in His place, as the leader responsible to shape these twelve men. Have you ever found yourself in a similar situation? You perceive a negative attitude or learn about an ill-advised decision. You try to warn those involved, but they won't listen. What do you do?

How do you think Christ felt at the affable Peter's stubborn insistence? We know for certain that Peter understood Christ's words; the Lord had delivered this message to the whole group as well as personally to Peter, prophesying that his denial would come not once, but three times! Peter, however, was not open to receiving the message. Can you feel Jesus' frustration and pain? He wanted to prevent Peter's suffering, but the disciple didn't want the offered help.

A leader's behavior in these situations is central to future involvement in the lives of those being taught. The kind of obstinate, mistaken passion we see in people like Peter often leads us to anger, which in turns leads to excessive arguments as we attempt to pressure people into changing their minds. Needless to say, this kind of behavior rarely produces change. Even more seriously, a response like this can do irreparable damage to our chance of helping these people in the future—after they have run into difficulties through their own foolishness.

Christ chose silence. He had said what He had to. Now the Spirit would use that word at the needed moment to lead Peter to spiritual brokenness. The Master's silence not only allowed room for the Spirit to work, but left an open door for that precious restoration recounted in the last chapter of John's Gospel. Having chosen not to show hostility in any of its subtle manifestations, Christ left intact Peter's confidence in His love. This gave Him the necessary opening to continue working in the disciple's life later on.

Food for Thought

We are making an investment in eternity. Sometimes we act as though we must at all costs secure an immediate decision, not realizing the sweeping consequences of this attitude. Love takes a long-term perspective of life and knows when to speak and when to keep silent. A mature leader understands this balance.

Convenient Interpretations

He pelted David and all the king's officials with stones, though all the troops and the special guard were on David's right and left. As he cursed, Shimei said, "Get out, get out, you man of blood, you scoundrel! The Lord has repaid you for all the blood you shed in the household of Saul, in whose place you have reigned. The Lord has handed the kingdom over to your son Absalom. You have come to ruin because you are a man of blood!"
2 Samuel 16:6–8

The scene in today's text occurs during Absalom's rebellion against his father David. The king left Jerusalem and fled into the desert, fearful for his own life and those of his followers. On the way, when he was tired and hungry, one of Saul's relatives came out to him hurling stones and insults.

Let's reflect for a moment on Shimei's interpretation of the events in Israel at that time. He was bitter and angry at the loss of the kingdom and no doubt felt a perverse satisfaction at seeing David dethroned. He did not hesitate to declare, "The Lord has repaid you for all the blood you shed in the household of Saul, in whose place you have reigned. The Lord has handed the kingdom over to your son Absalom." Shimei judged these events as payment to David for all that had gone wrong for Saul and his house.

What should instill a certain amount of fear in our hearts is the great ease with which we interpret God's actions to suit our own distorted views of life. We should also fear making these statements with such confident conviction, as if there was absolutely no doubt about the accuracy of our viewpoint. Saul had become deluded after turning from God and had also conveniently perceived circumstances selfishly. When David's hiding place was found, he exclaimed, "God has handed him over to me, for David has imprisoned himself by entering a town with gates and bars" (1 Sam. 23:7). The Spirit of God had long since departed from him, but in his zeal to destroy David, he continued to believe the Lord was helping him.

We know these men's interpretations were mistaken. But we know it because we have the complete account of their lives, as well as historic commentary. When we do not have the full picture, it is easy to convince ourselves that we are correctly discerning God's actions—even though we may be completely wrong. The mistake is easily made, since each of us is directed by our personal interests. We imagine God is practically dedicated to arranging life to suit our own needs.

Food for Thought

This is far from true. If we are honest, we must recognize God's ways are radically different from our ways and His thoughts from our thoughts. For this reason we must take care in spiritually interpreting what goes on around us. Who can really understand the mysteries of God?

Loyalty

"What can I do with you, Ephraim? What can I do with you, Judah? Your love is like the morning mist, like the early dew that disappears. For I desire mercy, not sacrifice, and acknowledgment of God rather than burnt offerings." Hosea 6:4, 6

When I read this passage, I feel ashamed of many of our church meetings. At these gatherings we fervently sing and declare our love for the Lord. Tears and spiritual brokenness often accompany these declarations. On Monday we return to our predictable weekly routine, and those around us have no idea that on the previous day we offered passionate vows of commitment and unconditional love to God.

Obviously there is nothing wrong with publicly expressing our love to the Father. Thank the Lord that we have so many opportunities to gather as His children and declare our loyalty to Him! This should be an important element in the lives of Christ's disciples.

The problem is that our loyalty is exactly like "the morning mist." What a great illustration! The day's early mist is sometimes dense and impenetrable, filling the air. It appears that it will never disperse, covering everything like a heavy, suffocating blanket. But no sooner does the sun rise than it begins to evaporate, and in a short time no trace of it whatsoever remains.

The mist disappears due to the heat of the sun. In the same way, our loyalty often continues until a problem begins to "shine its heat" on our lives. When life presents us with complications, our good intentions and our promises to faithfully love the Lord vanish. In their place arises an obsession with finding a way out of our difficulties.

Real loyalty cannot be proven until it is tested through adversity. Any one of us can make promises to God or to our peers. The difficult part is remaining faithful to them when circumstances demand we abandon them. For many of us, this is precisely where our spiritual lives collapse. Just like the Israelites in the desert, the slightest problem leads us to indignantly ask the Lord why He is allowing this to happen to us.

Food for Thought

Should we stop singing and proclaiming our love for God? Absolutely not! But we could be more prudent in our declarations, aware that our flesh is much weaker than our intentions. Even better than this, real devotion to Him would be a guarantee of our words. This would free us from the passing emotions we often experience among God's people or through the persuasive words of a speaker. If the Lord spoke to us, He might say, "Do you know something, My beloved? I love it when you join others in telling Me how much you love Me. But I am more blessed when you continue praising Me when you are alone and life gets tough. That fills My heart with joy!"

Dangerous Trust

This is what the Lord *says: "Cursed is the one who trusts in man, who depends on flesh for his strength and whose heart turns away from the* Lord*."* Jeremiah 17:5

How are we to understand this dramatic declaration in light of passages in which we are told that love "always protects, always trusts, always hopes, always perseveres" (1 Cor. 13:7)? Is the prophet Jeremiah condemning all feelings of confidence in others? Is he inviting us to maintain an attitude of permanent mistrust toward everyone?

If you have ever been around someone who is suspicious by nature, you will surely know this can't be what the prophet had in mind. Suspicious people believe that others are always trying to get the better of them. When presented with an attractive offer, they immediately look for the "catch." Viewing the world, they say to themselves, "If I don't watch out for my own interests, no one will." They are convinced that without being permanently watchful, others will take advantage of them and do them harm. It's very difficult to get close to these people, because their suspicious attitude contaminates everything. In short, what is at work in their lives is not the grace of God, but the fear of man.

So what does the prophet refer to? The rest of the verse contains the answer: It speaks of a person who has stopped trusting God and instead trusts in people. The Lord invites everyone to have confidence in Him, to acknowledge that He is our God and we are His people (Jer. 31:33). In other words, we are to allow Him to provide for all our needs, guide us in our decision-making and be our comfort in times of sorrow. Those who trust in others and depend on the flesh for their strength have decided to transfer God's attributes to human beings. They suppose mere people can provide what can only come from Him.

Our relationships with others do indeed include this kind of interaction. People often provide for us, give us advice in times of confusion and console us when we mourn. This is the blessing of enjoying intimate relationship with others, and we receive it as a gift. The problem arises when we suppose that others will always fulfill these functions for us. If we transfer this burden to them, we will feel betrayed and disillusioned each time they fail us. The root of the problem is not in having relationship with others, but in expecting to receive from human beings what only God can give. Whoever does this is liable to live in constant disappointment.

Food for Thought

Fight the temptation to seek from people what comes only from God. If men fail you, don't be angry with them. Ask the Lord for forgiveness for the unreal expectations you have placed on your friends and return your loyalty to the only One whose commitment is steadfast.

Share and Share Alike

David replied, "No, my brothers, you must not do that with what the LORD has given us. He has protected us and handed over to us the forces that came against us. Who will listen to what you say? The share of the man who stayed with the supplies is to be the same as that of him who went down to the battle. All will share alike." 1 Samuel 30:23–24

This is one of many stories about the great King David that confirms his outstanding spiritual convictions. On this occasion David and his men had returned to their temporary home in Ziklag to find that the Amalekites had taken advantage of their absence. Their wives and children had been taken captive and their belongings plundered. The Lord blessed their rescue operation, and they not only recovered their belongings but also gained the spoils amassed by the Amalekites from raids on other cities. On their return they met up with two hundred of their men who had been too tired to continue with them. Since they had stayed behind guarding the baggage, David's warriors reasoned that they should not share the spoils.

This reaction demonstrates our deep-seated inclination to construct hierarchical systems that separate people into categories. Our readiness to establish these systems—and thus perpetuate a concealed form of elitism—speaks eloquently of sin's devastating effect on human relationships. When the original fall took place, Adam and Eve experienced the same separation and alienation, the direct result of turning their backs on God.

These stratums are inherent in the most basic values of society. The economic system is founded on the conviction that some people are worth more than others. That's why the president of a large company can earn up to one hundred times more than a lowly employee. This is how our world is structured.

Sadly, this system of preferences has infiltrated the church's operations. We regard some members of the congregation as more important than others, and in some cases our reasoning is connected with the size of peoples' offerings. In other cases it concerns how much they do within the ministry. In many congregations the leaders receive more respect and attention than anyone else. Whatever the situation, we find ourselves marking differences between one member and another.

David believed all his men were equally valuable. It is true that some had risked their lives in battle while others had looked after the baggage. But those who fought were able to do so because they didn't have to guard their possessions. David insisted they should all be treated the same way; despite the men's protests, he shared the spoils equally.

Food for Thought

It is important that as leaders we identify these prejudices and avoid imposing disagreeable hierarchies on the people of God. Each individual entrusted to us is priceless to Christ. We must honor and treasure every one, regarding them as an important part of the body of Christ!

The Risks of Counseling

When Ahithophel saw that his advice had not been followed, he saddled his donkey and set out for his house in his hometown. He put his house in order and then hanged himself. So he died and was buried in his father's tomb. 2 Samuel 17:23

How should we react when others don't accept our advice?

To really understand the dramatic ending of today's story, we need to remember the position Ahithophel held among the king's advisors. We don't have to guess what it was like, because the storyteller says that "the advice Ahithophel gave was like that of one who inquires of God; that was how both David and Absalom regarded all of Ahithophel's advice" (2 Sam. 16:23). This man was a conduit of the grace of God as he gave advice in the most complicated situations. But over many years he had come to expect the most powerful men in the nation to consult him on everything. Both the people and the leaders held him in high esteem.

However, the day arrived when Absalom, usurper of the throne, decided to ignore Ahithophel's advice. He based his decision on the counsel of another man. Hushai's advice seemed better to Absalom, so he rejected the words of the man who had directed David's steps for so many years. The outcome was completely unexpected. Ahithophel went home, set his house in order and took his own life.

For a counselor, being heeded has an intoxicating effect. The more we are listened to, the more likely we are to believe that our contribution has been vitally important in resolving a problem. When our counseling is well-received, and many people have come to hear our words of wisdom, it is not surprising that we begin to consider our involvement in every decision indispensable.

The nature of advice is that of a suggestion, not an order. We are asked to share our perspective about certain situations because others appreciate our viewpoint. Nobody who comes to us is obliged to do what we suggest. Good counseling is based on the premise of respecting the freedom of others to make their own decisions—and letting them live with the consequences.

Is this not the way our heavenly Father treats us? On occasion He can be terribly persuasive! But the mystery of our relationship with God revolves around the fact that He respects our freedom to choose. As Richard Foster says, "God grants us perfect freedom because he desires creatures who freely choose to be in relationship with him. . . . Relationships of this kind can never be manipulated or forced."[5] In the same way, wise counselors offer a precious gift when they give others the liberty to choose or to reject their advice.

Food for Thought

How do you react when others don't listen to you? What do these reactions reveal about the kind of leader you are? What changes should you make in your work as a counselor in order to show more respect for people?

Roots of Bitterness

Make every effort to live in peace with all men and to be holy; without holiness no one will see the Lord. See to it that no one misses the grace of God and that no bitter root grows up to cause trouble and defile many. Hebrews 12:14–15

This passage presents several interesting points regarding a root of bitterness in the Christian's life. Note that the context of this problem is interpersonal relationships: The passage begins by encouraging the Hebrews to manage relationships in an atmosphere of peace and sanctification. This means that our ties with other people must be developed in a dimension totally different from those who are not children of God. They should be characterized by purity and joy that testify to the work of the Holy Spirit at all times. Conflicts and differences are resolved within a framework of harmony and mutual respect.

It is from this perspective, therefore, that the warning against a root of bitterness can be understood. The term "root of bitterness" used by the writer is particularly appropriate. The root of the plant is the part we don't see. It sinks down into areas unknown and invisible to us. But its function is vital to the plant, since it provides daily strength and nourishment. Similarly, the root of bitterness lodges in the darkest, most hidden places of the soul. This is why it is particularly difficult to locate, although its despicable fruit is easily seen. From its hidden spot it feeds and conditions a person's life.

Although detection is difficult, the previous verse indicates in which context it springs up. All those conflicts and injustices suffered in everyday life which are not resolved spiritually are fertile soil for a root of bitterness. Its very name describes the kind of "plant" it is. It is characterized by loathing and sharpness which contaminate everything, which do not allow us to think or speak of anything but the terrible deed we have experienced.

One of the casualties of the root of bitterness is joy! But the solution to its insidious influence is the grace of God. For this reason the Scripture urges that no one come short of the grace of God, that divine ingredient which enables even the most devastating situation to be correctly resolved.

Finally, we should be aware that the root of bitterness first develops in an individual's life, but then goes on to contaminate others. Its influence infects those who were previously healthy. Detection and removal must be energetically pursued!

Food for Thought

"You have heard that it was said, 'Love your neighbor and hate your enemy.' But I tell you: Love your enemies and pray for those who persecute you, that you may be sons of your Father in heaven. He causes his sun to rise on the evil and the good, and sends rain on the righteous and the unrighteous" (Matt. 5:43–45).

Divine Confidences

Then the word of the LORD came to Samuel: "I am grieved that I have made Saul king, because he has turned away from me and has not carried out my instructions." Samuel was troubled, and he cried out to the LORD all that night. 1 Samuel 15:10–11

We hardly notice these verses, lost as they are in the dramatic story of Saul's second round of disobedience. The wise historian puts them here, in the middle of an absolutely carnal tale, and gives us a fleeting glimpse of what was happening on the spiritual plane. If we pause briefly at this scene, we can't help but be touched by the extraordinary intimacy it reveals.

Notice the tone of this exchange between God and His prophet. The words have all the characteristics of a confidential talk between friends accustomed to sharing their most intimate secrets. As if talking to an equal, the Lord opens His heart to Samuel and shares His disappointment with him. Apart from the sadness of the confession, the fact that the Lord shares it with Samuel is truly amazing. This is not the kind of intimacy He would share with just anyone. It is obvious that Samuel enjoyed a closeness with God that allowed for access to His most secret and mysterious thoughts.

Samuel's reaction displays the essence of really knowing the plans of the Lord. We have been called to a mission that depends totally on being able to discern what is important to the Lord. As we draw near to Him, we begin to sense the longings and yearnings of His heart, the things that really move Him. We discover that the goals and objectives we often consider important do not necessarily coincide with our heavenly Father's priorities.

Whoever fails to perceive the desires of God's heart is condemned to improvising projects in the hope of pleasing Him. If we are honest with ourselves, this very often happens in our ministries. With no clear idea as to God's desires regarding the congregation we are pastoring, we constantly invent things to do and hope they are pleasing to Him. In this way the church is active, but not always in the works He has prepared for us.

In the days of His ministry on earth, Christ stated, "I tell you the truth, the Son can do nothing by himself; he can do only what he sees his Father doing, because whatever the Father does the Son also does" (John 5:19). How did He know what the Father was doing? Just like Samuel, He developed moments of intimacy where He could feel the Father's heartbeat and see the things He was doing.

Food for Thought

It is fundamentally important to set aside time to be silent, paying attention to what is burdening our Father's heart. The effectiveness of our ministry depends on this knowledge! Do you have time for the Father to confide some of His longings to you?

Standing Firm

Let us hold unswervingly to the hope we profess, for he who promised is faithful.
Hebrews 10:23

Many of the difficulties we suffer in the Christian life have nothing to do with adverse circumstances. If our well-being depended entirely on pleasant surroundings, for most of us there would be little hope of living a life of fullness! Rather, our pain often results from failing to overcome the obstacles in our path. Today's verse urges us to develop the kind of inner strength that will keep us from rejecting our profession of faith in moments of desperation.

Faith is an essential part of the Christian life. That's why the Apostle Paul prayed for the church at Ephesus, asking that the eyes of their hearts would be enlightened, that they "may know the hope to which he has called you" (Eph. 1:18).

He congratulates the Thessalonian church on their "endurance inspired by hope in our Lord Jesus Christ" (1 Thess. 1:3). Hope lightens our hearts because it brings with it the promise of better things.

Most of us have only a rough idea of what is implied by "hope in our Lord Jesus Christ." We know He has promised us eternal life, but we're not sure exactly what that entails. This kind of blurry hope doesn't inspire or strengthen anyone's heart!

So we shouldn't be surprised when we constantly fluctuate in professing our faith. We easily depend on the circumstances and feelings of different moments. When things are going well, we remain steady. In times of difficulty, we waver between hope and hopelessness.

Notice that the writer of Hebrews pays no attention to circumstances or personal situations. He indicates that the irreproachable and trustworthy character of Him who has given us hope is what should motivate us to remain firm. If He has promised a full and abundant life for those who believe, bringing forth streams of living water in them, then He will be faithful to bring it about.

It is precisely on this point that our faith collapses. During difficult times we tend to question God's goodness and His trustworthiness as our Keeper. Think of the countless times in the desert the Israelites doubted God's good intentions toward them! And those doubts repeatedly caused them to look back longingly at their former life in Egypt.

It is not possible to have an intimate relationship with God if we are not absolutely certain we can trust Him. That's why we are encouraged by the writer of Proverbs to "trust in the LORD with all your heart and lean not on your own understanding" (Prov. 3:5).

Food for Thought

The Enemy's most effective strategy is to tempt us to doubt God's goodness. As for you, don't waver in the conviction you have always held. Like Abraham, we can be "fully persuaded that God had power to do what he had promised" (Rom 4:21).

Time to Withdraw

And Ishbi-Benob, one of the descendants of Rapha, whose bronze spearhead weighed three hundred shekels and who was armed with a new sword, said he would kill David. But Abishai son of Zeruiah came to David's rescue; he struck the Philistine down and killed him. Then David's men swore to him, saying, "Never again will you go out with us to battle, so that the lamp of Israel will not be extinguished." 2 Samuel 21:16–17

When is the right time for a leader to stand aside and make way for someone younger?

We have all experienced situations in which a leader no longer has the vitality or enthusiasm of youth, but despite this insists on continuing to lead as in previous years. This causes real frustration in the younger generation who should have received the baton from the leader's hands.

In today's passage we find a scene very similar to the one in which the young David won his victory over the giant of Gath. On that occasion David was no more than a youth. The Lord conceded him a heroic victory that has been recorded for all time in the annals of God's people. To this victory David had added a long list of extraordinary demonstrations of courage on the battlefield.

But now David was no longer the same person. The courage he had exhibited throughout his life was still outstanding in his character, but he lacked the abilities and strength of earlier years. As a result, this second giant almost took the king's life. One of the good, brave men who had always surrounded David intervened, thus avoiding a tragedy for the people.

No sooner had this terrible moment passed than David's men urged him to retire from battle in order to preserve his life. It was a moment of transition for the great king of Israel—a moment which obliged him to make necessary adjustments because of his failing strength.

David could well have been offended by his men's suggestion. He could have fought for what was slowly slipping away with the passing years. But his characteristic greatness of spirit saw him through the moment. He accepted his limitations and listened humbly to his men. He never went into battle again. The time had come for younger men to assume the responsibility of caring for Israel's security.

Food for Thought

Wouldn't it be great if we could prepare for this moment even from our youth? Would you be willing to make the following prayer yours? "Lord, allow me to grow old with grace. Keep me from holding on to my position; allow me a generous spirit to release my ministry joyfully to those who come after me. Keep me free from bitterness in my old age! Amen."

Imparting Dignity

So the Lord said to Moses, "Take Joshua son of Nun, a man in whom is the spirit, and lay your hand on him. Have him stand before Eleazar the priest and the entire assembly and commission him in their presence. Give him some of your authority so the whole Israelite community will obey him." Numbers 27:18–20

How difficult it is for a young leader to replace a veteran in ministry! This is especially true when the one retiring has deep spiritual experience and is held in high esteem by those in the congregation. The people will make comparisons between the two leaders, the younger one inevitably coming out on the losing end. Few will remember that the mature leader was young once, committing blunders and occasionally mistaking the path to be followed.

The transition period between two leaders is crucial to the continuity of the ministry. In this case Moses had led the people to the gates of the Promised Land. His mission had been accomplished. Joshua, the successor chosen by God, had a complicated job ahead of him. He was to guide a people with little war experience in the difficult task of vanquishing Canaan, then take possession of Jacob's inheritance.

It is during the transition phase that people can become disheartened or rebellious. All change produces insecurity, and leaders need a firm hand to guide the peoples' steps. But what a tremendous demonstration of God's care we see in the precise instructions He gave Moses! He was not expected simply to disappear; a public ceremony was carried out in which he handed the leadership over from one generation to the next.

The fact that everybody had to be present conferred much more importance on the ceremony than a private one would have. The people were to witness the backing Joshua was receiving from Moses; they would see that the new leader had his full support. Note too the emphasis on the laying on of hands. This is a rite of little significance to us, but full of meaning to the Israelites. Jacob blessed his grandchildren with the laying on of hands (Gen. 48:14); hands were laid on blasphemers to transfer to them the guilt of their words (Lev. 24:14); worshippers laid hands on the sacrificial animal to indicate that it took their place as payment for sin (Lev. 1:4). Thus, in the ceremony the Israelites knew a spiritual transfer was taking place.

With this transfer Moses passed on two of the most important elements for ministry: authority and dignity. Authority has to do with offering support to the leader. Dignity is related to the integrity of the minister's character. Both attributes had a clear aim, namely, that the Israelites were to obey their new leader in everything.

Food for Thought

Through this ceremony Joshua obtained part of the spiritual wealth Moses had cultivated during his life. What a beautiful legacy for a young leader!

Enlightened Eyes

I pray also that the eyes of your heart may be enlightened. Ephesians 1:18

What do you include in your prayers for the people you serve? I find I sometimes focus on asking for trivial things that don't carry any weight in the spiritual life. When I realize what I am doing, I go back to studying Paul's prayers for the churches he had founded (Eph. 1:15–23, 3:14–19; Phil. 1:4–6; Col.1:9–12). What depth of perception is revealed in them! The apostle clearly understood the things that are truly essential to the spiritual life.

Part of a longer prayer, today's verse is an excellent example of this reality. Very often the cause of a Christian's weakness is our obsession with the trappings of this brief earthly existence. We look at our circumstances with our physical eyes and consider our relationships from an entirely human perspective. We examine our resources and measure them with the same parameters as any person in the street. The result is that our progress is invariably limited by poor vision. We get depressed, feel afraid, are anxious or angry—and we are prisoners of these negative emotions.

Paul begins his prayer by asking God to enlighten the eyes of the peoples' hearts. This is a simple phrase, but it holds a striking image. Those who are spiritual have two sets of eyes. With the physical eyes we see the natural world. But with the eyes of the heart, which can only be activated by the Spirit, we see things belonging exclusively to the spiritual world. Since spiritual matters are the ones that carry eternal weight, this second kind of vision is much more important than the first.

Reflect for a moment on the person of Jesus and think about all the times He saw things others didn't. Consider His lament for Jerusalem (Luke 19:41–44). When He saw it, He wept. Where others saw buildings, streets and crowds, Christ saw a city that did not recognize the reason for His coming. Think about the return of the seventy disciples. They were enthusiastic about the work they had carried out, but Christ saw Satan fall from heaven like lightning (Luke 10:17–18). And what about the Samaritan woman? The disciples saw a woman they could not speak with; Jesus saw a Spirit-given opportunity to minister (John 4:4–27). The same can be said of the rich young ruler. Those around him saw a pious man, eager to bring his life into line with the Kingdom; the Lord saw a man whose god was money (Luke 18:22–26).

Food for Thought

Being able to see spiritual realities is a fruit of the Spirit. But it is also a consequence of discipline on our part. Paul testifies that amid ongoing trials, we must* decide *to "fix our eyes not on what is seen, but on what is unseen. For what is seen is temporary, but what is unseen is eternal" (2 Cor. 4:18).

Useless Grieving

The LORD said to Samuel, "How long will you mourn for Saul, since I have rejected him as king over Israel? Fill your horn with oil and be on your way; I am sending you to Jesse of Bethlehem. I have chosen one of his sons to be king." 1 Samuel 16:1

Disappointments and defeats are among the most difficult things for us to overcome, especially when they are related to ministry. The responsibility we bear adds extra weight to situations that don't work out well. Perhaps our disappointment comes from people we had great hopes for—we invested a lot in their training, but the results were not what we expected. Perhaps we feel discouraged because of a decision we made, believing it was best for the congregation. Now time has shown it was a mistake, and we are paying a high price for it. Maybe there was a problem in the congregation that we handled badly. Today we clearly see the consequences, with tensions and censure affecting our relationships with others. There could be countless reasons for disenchantment. Life rarely lives up to our expectations. Nothing is as simple as it seems, and frustration is a frequent companion in our service to God. As we mature we discover this is part of reality.

For many people life's disappointments and sorrows can become more difficult to overcome than the problems that actually produced the feelings. Trapped by these strong emotions, life can pass us by as we spend our time lamenting all that has happened to us. In these circumstances it is common to think, *If only I had done that, or said the other* . . . Absorbed by such thoughts, we review past situations and imagine what things would be like if we had behaved differently.

Notice that God asked Samuel, "How long will you mourn . . . ?" Mourning is not a very productive engagement, because the past cannot be changed. We can only learn necessary lessons from it so as not to repeat our mistakes. While Samuel was still grieving, the Lord had gone on to the next stage of His plans: "I have chosen one of his sons to be king." He already had His eye on another man and on what He could do through his life.

In God's instructions we see His desire to get His prophet moving again, freeing him from his melancholy. There is only one road we can follow, and that road goes forward. We shouldn't waste more time than necessary reflecting on past defeats. When we have learned our lesson from the experience, we can leave the past and move ahead firmly into the future. Life is waiting for us.

Food for Thought

"Brothers, I do not consider myself yet to have taken hold of it. But one thing I do: Forgetting what is behind and straining toward what is ahead, I press on toward the goal to win the prize for which God has called me heavenward in Christ Jesus" (Phil. 3:13–14).

The God Who Is Sufficient

I love you, O LORD, my strength. The LORD is my rock, my fortress and my deliverer; my God is my rock, in whom I take refuge. He is my shield and the horn of my salvation, my stronghold. Psalm 18:1–2

The New American Standard Bible renders the heading of this psalm "For the choir director. A Psalm of David the servant of the LORD, who spoke to the LORD the words of this song in the day that the LORD delivered him from the hand of all his enemies and from the hand of Saul." Even without this explanation of the psalm's context, the rapturous praise of the poem itself leaves no doubt that it was written from firsthand experience of the Lord's magnificent preservation.

David mentions at least seven of God's qualities, all related to the specific situation he was going through. For years he had been hiding in the desert. But his time there was nothing like the peaceful existence Moses experienced in Midian. Running from cave to cave, always watching for the enemy's movements, he had found himself in countless situations in which only God's miraculous intervention saved him from certain death. This is precisely the theme of this psalm.

These qualities of God were very real to David because he had experienced them directly. But for some of us, they are no more than attributes we assign to God because we feel it is logical to do so. We know in our minds that He our rock, our fortress and our deliverer. We sing of these things. We know innumerable passages describing Him in this way. Others have testified to experiencing these aspects in their walk with the heavenly Father. But for us these truths have never been more than theory.

How can we prove God's character? He *is* this way, but perhaps not in my life or yours. For His attributes to become real in our lives, we must make room for the demonstration of His faithfulness to those in trouble. In other words, to prove He is strong, we must find ourselves in a position of weakness. To know Him as our rock, we must realize we are on shaky foundations. To feel He is our fortress, we must admit to vulnerability. In order to demonstrate He is our deliverer, we must recognize we are trapped. For Him to be our shield, we need to confess our defenselessness. To know Him as the horn of our salvation, we must admit to being lost. For Him to be our stronghold, we need to recognize that we have sunk into the deepest of pits.

Food for Thought

The reality of God's character can be seen only in those who recognize their need of Him. Let us not be sorry for feeling anxiety and despair. On the contrary, let us rejoice, for this is the best place for His powerful visitation in our hour of need.

When Discipline Overwhelms

The punishment inflicted on him by the majority is sufficient for him. Now instead, you ought to forgive and comfort him, so that he will not be overwhelmed by excessive sorrow. I urge you, therefore, to reaffirm your love for him. 2 Corinthians 2:6–8

Someone in the Corinthian church had fallen into sin. By a decision of the majority, this person had been disciplined, and the Apostle Paul apparently supported this measure. He hadn't been present when the decision was made, although he was with them in spirit (1 Cor. 5:3). Now it was necessary for Paul to correct an excessively severe attitude in the way people were dealing with this person. He had to remind them that the objective of all correction is to restore the fallen, to help them once again walk in holiness with the Lord.

We have a definite tendency to lace our discipline with a good dose of anger or spite. As parents, have we not often been excessively hard on our children because we did not act at the appropriate moment for intervention? Our patience is not really patience, but negligence, and we allow feelings of annoyance and anger to build up. When the moment for correction arrives, we use it to vent our frustration on our child. This makes the discipline ineffective, because it is carried out with an inappropriately harsh spirit.

In the same way, discipline within the church is frequently extended with a spirit of harshness toward the guilty party. Those who have sinned are unnecessarily humiliated, and many choose to have as little contact as possible with them.

Nevertheless, discipline is a tremendously positive experience in the lives of those who seek to grow in their walk with the Lord. Through discipline we receive correction and guidance.

Even so, it is never a pleasant experience. We feel attacked, and our pride begins to seek some kind of compensation. We sink into a state of sorrow and dejection which, if not checked, can have serious consequences in our spiritual life. Aware of this, Paul encouraged church members not to overwhelm the person being disciplined with too much sorrow. He did not want people to be so affected by correction that they could no longer recover, lest the whole exercise became pointless.

Paul encouraged members instead to reaffirm their love for the fallen one. This exhortation highlights one of the great truths of the Kingdom. The power that will most transform peoples' lives comes through love. Discipline can correct, but it is love that reaches deep into the heart and opens the way to the most spiritual experiences. This is why Christ was quick to reaffirm His love for Peter after he had denied the Lord three times. The unconditional love in Jesus' action was crucial in restoring the apostle for the ministry to which he had been called.

Food for Thought

"The loneliest place in the world is the human heart when love is absent." (Anonymous)

Questionable Interpretations

Then Isaiah said to Hezekiah, "Hear the word of the LORD Almighty: The time will surely come when everything in your palace, and all that your fathers have stored up until this day, will be carried off to Babylon. Nothing will be left, says the LORD. And some of your descendants, your own flesh and blood who will be born to you, will be taken away, and they will become eunuchs in the palace of the king of Babylon." "The word of the LORD you have spoken is good," Hezekiah replied. For he thought, "There will be peace and security in my lifetime." Isaiah 39:5–8

There are two challenges in our response to the Word of God. The first involves receiving it. Mentioning this seems redundant, for it is rather obvious to all who seek the Lord in righteousness. Nevertheless, there is a vast difference between understanding that we need His Word and learning to daily apply all we hear from Him.

Receiving the Word challenges us because we are caught up in our daily pursuits. If God is to speak to us, it is necessary that we still the whirlwind of our activities, for it is difficult to speak to someone who is concentrating on something else. Even when we manage to stop our outward motion, there is no guarantee we will hear Him. In our inner world there may still remain incessant thoughts and anxieties that constantly worry our souls. For this reason it is vital that we master the discipline of stilling our souls. Silence and an attentive ear are indispensable requirements for hearing the Lord.

If we manage to quiet our spirits to receive the Word with meekness, we will have won half the battle. But then we come to the next challenge, which is to understand the meaning of what we have heard. Here we often wander from the truth, for we interpret the Word as it suits us. We have a strong desire to hear only that which sounds sweet to our ears. These "convenient" interpretations save us from facing discomfort from God's penetrating Word.

None of us has had a prophet of Isaiah's stature proclaim the Word of God to us. King Hezekiah had this privilege, though. He learned through the prophet that all his possessions and some of his children would be taken to Babylon. He imagined that the manner in which this would take place was one of great blessing and thus confidently exclaimed, "The word of the LORD you have spoken is good."

How wrong his interpretation was! The prophet's message referred to the destruction of Jerusalem and captivity for Israel. The lesson for us is plain: We must exercise great caution when explaining the Word of God.

Food for Thought

The main problem with interpretation is in believing there is only one possible explanation to the Word. Beware of explanations in which everything is arranged for the interpreter's convenience. The Word of God usually takes us outside our comfort zone.

Terrifying Surprises

During the fourth watch of the night Jesus went out to them, walking on the lake. When the disciples saw him walking on the lake, they were terrified. "It's a ghost," they said, and cried out in fear. Matthew 14:25–26

How limited we are in our capacity to accept the supernatural! We are able to convince ourselves that we believe in divine manifestation because we know it is theologically possible. We believe God can show Himself however He wants, wherever He wants, using whatever means He likes. We have no problem with this, believing as we do in a God of unlimited power.

But these thoughts sometimes are only an exercise in probability—a probability we generally consider to be remote. None of us doubts that God is capable of doing anything He wants, but when He does show Himself, we are overwhelmed by the means He uses and discover that it produces an intense personal dilemma for us.

The disciples had been with the Messiah at least two years. They knew His face well. They had walked, worked and ministered alongside Jesus. They had had ample opportunity to study His physical appearance. When He came walking on the water, however, they were filled with terror and called out that it was "a ghost."

It wasn't the physical, flesh-and-bone Jesus they failed to recognize; He was the same person with whom they had shared so many intimate moments. It was the way in which He appeared. It was beyond the acceptable. His actions were not even within the realm of the disciples' imagination. Seeing Jesus in a completely different situation than they had ever known, they failed to realize that the Christ they knew and the figure on the water were one and the same. Their mental structures had no parameters to define this extraordinary, startling scene. They ignored the evidence of their eyes and adjusted what they saw to the best interpretation they could find: They must be seeing a ghost!

Their reaction demonstrates how conditioned we are by our guidelines for understanding the world around us. The people from Jesus' hometown couldn't accept that He was anything but a humble carpenter (Matt. 13:55). Was this because that's all He really was? Not at all! He was the Messiah, but the Nazarenes' strong conditioning did not allow them to adjust their point of view. In the same way, when we have strongly formed ideas, we show great reluctance in modifying or discarding our notion—even when confronted with overwhelming evidence to the contrary.

Food for Thought

Where does this reflection leave us? It can help us understand how much our personal makeup influences our viewpoint. Consequently, it is wise to remember that life is much deeper and more mysterious than we can possibly understand. If we hold our interpretations lightly, it will be much easier for us to be corrected, taught and—above all—surprised.

Heavenly Objectives...

In order that in the coming ages he might show the incomparable riches of his grace, expressed in his kindness to us in Christ Jesus. Ephesians 2:7

The first and second chapters of Ephesians present a most extraordinary description of the Lord's sovereign work in redeeming us from living death. In verse after verse Paul describes the sacrifice Jesus made for us, presenting its many resulting blessings for all who have made Christ their Lord. It is a literal testament that should be carefully studied by His children, since a superficial reading will not suffice for understanding the vastness of all we have obtained in Him. Two specific elements in Paul's declaration are of great interest to us.

First, God's purposes extend far beyond ours. Even in the case of the most spiritual among us, our objectives rarely encompass events outside our own lives. For most of us, the goals for our lives are expressed in terms of months and years. For those few who really possess long-term vision, their objectives may be measured in terms of decades. Paul's declaration strikes us because it states that God's objectives are defined in terms of centuries! Long after Paul died and the details of his journeys were forgotten, the Lord would be harvesting the fruit of the work He had accomplished through the great apostle.

We all hope to contribute something to our own generation. But the Lord's perspective is set on eternity, reminding us that our efforts will be counted only on this greater time scale. Many of the things that seem important to us now will be forgotten by future generations.

Second, we observe again that the Lord desires people of all ages to come to know the "incomparable riches of his grace." In other words, He wants us to look back to past generations and say with all our hearts, "The Lord has been exceedingly good to us!"

A New Testament dictionary defines the word grace as "a special manifestation of the presence, activity, power or divine glory, a favor, a gift, a blessing."[1] In this sense, with the passing years, decades and centuries, God wants to show "the incomparable riches of his grace" by the goodness, mercy and patience with which He has pursued us through the ages. His insistent love has continually sought relationship with people who are stubborn and perverse in their ways. What message does the Father's attitude leave us? There is no place in God's persistent love for the thought of "giving up"!

Food for Thought

Great is Thy faithfulness, O God my Father;
There is no shadow of turning with Thee.
Thou changest not, Thy compassions, they fail not;
As Thou hast been Thou forever wilt be.[2]

6 June

Letting Our Light Shine

In the same way, let your light shine before men, that they may see your good deeds and praise your Father in heaven. Matthew 5:16

I often ask Christians, "If you couldn't verbally tell others that you are a disciple of Christ, would they realize you are one?" Don't be hasty in brushing aside this question until you consider its implications. Most peoples' testimonies rely entirely on the spoken word. Since our behavior often contradicts our verbal witness, people conclude that we are no different from them aside from the fact that we call ourselves Christians.

Christ showed us the path He wanted His disciples to follow to indicate their complete identification with Him. Jesus expected that His followers would dedicate themselves to good works so others would marvel at their radically different lifestyle. The good works were not done in order to generate light, but were rather a manifestation of it. In other words, light has no need to *do* anything in order to be detected. Those who observe its brilliance inherently recognize it as light. And so it was Jesus' will that His followers choose goodness as a lifestyle, so that even when speech was not possible, they would be identified as people from another world.

Those of us in the Protestant church have been strongly conditioned against good works by the legacy of the Reformation. We don't want anyone to think we are trying to earn our way to heaven through good deeds. The result is that we have completely discarded good works from our perspective of discipleship. Consider the following declarations: "For we are God's workmanship, created in Christ Jesus to do good works, which God prepared in advance for us to do" (Eph. 2:10); "In everything set them an example by doing what is good" (Titus 2:7); He "gave himself for us to redeem us from all wickedness and to purify for himself a people that are his very own, eager to do what is good" (Titus 2:14); "Stress these things, so that those who have trusted in God may be careful to devote themselves to doing what is good" (Titus 3:8); "And let us consider how we may spur one another on toward love and good deeds" (Heb. 10:24); "Live such good lives among the pagans that, though they accuse you of doing wrong, they may see your good deeds and glorify God on the day he visits us" (1 Pet. 2:12).

None of these verses say that good works are not important for those who follow Jesus. On the contrary, they affirm that believers in Christ are known for their good deeds! Let us ask the Father to show us where He is working, so that we may join Him in all that He prepared in advance for us to do.

Food for Thought

John Wesley's words echo the Scriptures: "Do all the good you can, in all the ways you can, to all the people you can, as long as ever you can." [3]

Word of Life

Pray also for me, that whenever I open my mouth, words may be given me so that I will fearlessly make known the mystery of the gospel. Ephesians 6:19

This request of Paul's to the Ephesians is really interesting! It would be good if all of us who proclaim the Word would pray this before each opportunity to minister.

The construction of this phrase shows us clearly where we can go wrong in ministering the Scriptures. It's easy to open our mouths, but not so easy to speak a word from on High. In fact, one of the most worrying characteristics of the twenty-first century is the absence of God's Word in much preaching and teaching heard today. An increasing tendency is to take a verse and from it share one's own opinions on what God is doing, and how. As a result, we are exposed to an endless succession of spiritual "interpreters" who are enamored with their own discourse, but hardly provide an opportunity to hear the wholesome Word of God—the Word which alone has power to transform listeners' lives.

When the speaker has been trained in the art of good communication, the danger is even greater. Eloquent words can easily disguise our ignorance with clever speech-making. The result may be entertaining, but won't contribute toward the congregation's maturity in Jesus Christ.

Paul's desire was similar to Christ's. The Son of God said to His disciples, "My teaching is not my own. It comes from him who sent me" (John 7:16). Later He explained, "For I did not speak of my own accord, but the Father who sent me commanded me what to say and how to say it" (John 12:49). In the same way, the apostle—no novice when it came to communication—was terrified of wasting anyone's time with his own opinions and ideas. That's why he asked the believers to pray that when he opened his mouth, people would hear not his words, but God's.

As leaders we should be convinced this is the only word worth sharing. Our speech may inform, entertain and clarify; but it gets mixed up with the thousands of words people hear every week in the media as well as from family, friends, workmates and neighbors. Only "the Word of God is living and active. Sharper than any double-edged sword, it penetrates even to dividing soul and spirit, joints and marrow; it judges the thoughts and attitudes of the heart" (Heb. 4:12–13). Even when proclaimed with great simplicity, the effect of God's Word will be profound and lasting because it is, after all, the Word of life.

Food for Thought

In order to proclaim God's Word, we must be students of the Word. How much time are you dedicating to diligent study of the Scriptures? What effect does this have on your personal life and ministry? What can you do to increase your knowledge of the Word?

Short-lived Enthusiasm

Now while he was in Jerusalem at the Passover Feast, many people saw the miraculous signs he was doing and believed in his name. But Jesus would not entrust himself to them, for he knew all men. He did not need man's testimony about man, for he knew what was in a man. John 2:23–25

This visit to Jerusalem probably took place in Jesus' first year of ministry, a year in which His popularity increased dramatically. Wherever the Son of Man went, His signs and wonders attracted increasing crowds. This visit to Jerusalem was no different, with the predictable result that "many . . . believed in His name." The evangelist adds a short commentary to clarify what was leading them to believe, namely, "the miraculous signs."

Perhaps it is the monotony of our lives that attracts us to things supernatural and sensational. Wherever miracles take place, we find crowds of curious onlookers. Others turn up who want to prolong or perpetuate the miraculous manifestations. Most of these people are motivated by their amazement at unusual occurrences, which has little or no relationship with faith or spirituality.

This same enthusiasm is often present in our own decisions to "believe." We like the eloquence of the preacher, are moved by a particular combination of songs or are touched by an emotional testimony. We shouldn't doubt for a moment that God uses these things to affect our hearts. But it should be pointed out that most of these reactions are not spiritual, but emotional. The resulting conviction has little power to change our lives. Unfortunately, if our sentiment doesn't have power to transform, its eternal value is scant.

Christ didn't trust the crowds because He knew their reactions were not based on genuine spiritual conviction. He knew the reality of our hearts: The evil that lies therein does not submit to decisions made in the elation of a single moment. We surrender when an experience of profound brokenness is brought about by God, creating openness to His purifying work in us.

Consider how many things we believe that don't change our behavior. Few of us doubt the importance of a good diet and moderation in our eating habits, but it is difficult to find people who actually apply these principles. Most of us know how essential rest is to a healthy ministry, but few leaders take the time for the respite they need. Those of us who are teachers know how fundamental good preparation is, but not many of us really dedicate enough time to it. All this shows that our persuasions don't often affect our behavior. We shouldn't be surprised that Jesus was not moved by the excited decisions being made around Him.

Food for Thought

The emphasis in our spiritual life should be placed on experiences that produce genuine change in our lives, even when they are unpleasant. When transformation results, we can be sure that our decisions were spiritually motivated.

A Leader's Resolve

For the third time he spoke to them: "Why? What crime has this man committed? I have found in him no grounds for the death penalty. Therefore I will have him punished and then release him." But with loud shouts they insistently demanded that he be crucified, and their shouts prevailed. Luke 23:22–23

Leaders are often in situations which force them to make decisions, some of which may be tremendously important to those around them. If they are wise, they will have developed a team of colleagues with whom they can carefully study the particulars and listen to others' opinions. In the end, nevertheless, they will take responsibility for the decision and communicate it to their people.

Occasionally a leader will face circumstances in which complex ethical principles come into play. The decision will probably come after an agonizing process of evaluation in which every angle will be weighed repeatedly. The journey toward a conclusion will certainly be intensely lonely.

Whatever the peculiarities of each decision-making process, there is one thing they all have in common: You will always be surrounded by people who attempt to coerce you into choosing their preferred way. The pressure may come from friends or from others in your circle of contacts. People will resort to a wide variety of methods to assert their wills, from the use of Scripture to the use of threats, even forming groups who will work tirelessly to achieve their aim.

Pilate found himself in one of these situations. Overwhelmed by the enormity of Christ's trial, he had asked Herod to help him. Herod had not made any decision, but had sent Jesus back to Jerusalem. Pilate found Christ guilty of nothing, but the angry crowd pressured him to act against his will and condemn the Galilean. He tried to reason with them, even to pacify them with the promise of severe punishment for Jesus. But the crowds sought Christ's death, not His freedom.

"And their shouts prevailed."

What a detestable phrase this is! Pilate could not stand up to the pressure and gave way, clearly choosing against his own evaluation of the situation and his conviction of what was right.

Food for Thought

Leaders must be prepared to stand up to the consequences of their decisions, even when the whole world turns against them. The rightness of a decision is often recognizable only with the passing of time. In addition, in many situations it has been plainly shown that the voice of the majority is the voice of sin. It takes a special show of courage to remain firm to the end. The one who chooses correctly will be vindicated by the Lord in the fullness of time.

Not for Sale!

When Simon saw that the Spirit was given at the laying on of the apostles' hands, he offered them money and said, "Give me also this ability so that everyone on whom I lay my hands may receive the Holy Spirit." Acts 8:18–19

A key element to exercising influence over others is authority. A leader may have authority simply by occupying a position. But it can also come through recognition of a leader's knowledge, or because of outstanding qualities not possessed by others. Whatever its source, without authority a leader cannot impact lives.

This is why God always confers authority on those called to serve His people. Moses' credibility before the people was unmistakable. God gave him three signs to use to convince those who doubted his legitimacy (Exod. 4:1–9). When the Lord named Joshua as Moses' successor, He ordered a public ceremony in which the people could see the transfer of authority to the new leader (Num. 27:18–20).

We see something similar in Christ's appointment of the disciples. When He called the Twelve, He gave them "authority to drive out demons" (Mark 3:15). Sending them out two by two, He conferred authority on them to do the work He was giving them (Luke 9:1). Before ascending into heaven, He gathered His followers and commended them to the work of making disciples of all nations. For this, He told them all authority in heaven and on earth had been given to Him; thus, the work they were entrusted with would be backed by the supreme position of the risen Messiah.

In the book of Acts, we see that the apostles moved freely in this authority. Their confidence in God's support gave them boldness to act in even the most difficult situations, and through their ministry they witnessed the most extraordinary manifestations of the Lord.

It was precisely these signs that led Simon the magician—a man also accustomed to being in the public eye—to ask the apostles to sell him the power they were using. He was severely censured by them. The crass desire of Simon's heart was motivated by something many leaders today want, albeit with greater subtlety: to use God-given authority for their own ends. They hope to attract attention, gain popularity or manipulate others. This is more than reprehensible. The authority we receive can only be used within the framework of our calling. The Lord must receive the glory and benefit of that which belongs exclusively to Him.

Food for Thought

In what ways can we abuse the power we have been given? How can we be on our guard against this? What precautions must we take to ensure we do not abuse our authority?

The Mysteries of the Kingdom

June **11**

He also said, "This is what the kingdom of God is like. A man scatters seed on the ground. Night and day, whether he sleeps or gets up, the seed sprouts and grows, though he does not know how. All by itself the soil produces grain—first the stalk, then the head, then the full kernel in the head. As soon as the grain is ripe, he puts the sickle to it, because the harvest has come." Mark 4:26–29

When I was young, I thought everything could be understood if one studied it with a careful and persevering spirit. To tell the truth, like many other young people, I frequently offered explanations for things I didn't really understand. In my role as a teacher, I often felt obliged to provide students with answers, despite not fully grasping the subject they were interested in.

With the passing years, I have understood more and more clearly that a great deal of what goes on around us is veiled in a cloud of mystery. Life has shown me that many things I gave categorical explanations for are not actually as I had thought. Today I feel more comfortable (and I also think it is more honest) admitting to those under my teaching that there are many things I simply don't understand very well.

This is certainly one truth Christ wanted to communicate to His disciples through this parable. Working the land was an activity as old as Israel itself. Most people had some experience with sowing and reaping. The process by which a tiny seed—to all appearances dry and dead—was converted into a leafy, fruit-bearing plant was a complete mystery to those who cultivated the land. They only knew that a seed thrown into the ground would some months later produce a plant from which they could obtain food.

Within God's kingdom the process of growth is also shrouded in mystery. Who can explain the manner by which a rebellious, irate or depressed person becomes a joyful disciple committed to the person of Christ? Who among us understands how the transformation occurs that allows us to resemble the Lord? At what moment does it take place? What makes it happen? What phenomena are involved? The truth is that most of us can only testify to the results, because we see the fruit after a certain period of time has passed.

Why is it important that we understand this? Because we are disposed to believe that our efforts produce the results, our programs ensure the growth of the church and our eloquence persuades those who hear us. None of this is true. Most of what happens in the spiritual world resists explanation. We simply don't understand. We can only celebrate by giving thanks for the fruit we do enjoy!

Food for Thought

Augustus Strong's words express this mystery succinctly: "Growth is not the product of effort, but of life." [4]

Giving Sacrificially

Araunah said to David, "Let my lord the king take whatever pleases him and offer it up. Here are oxen for the burnt offering, and here are threshing sledges and ox yokes for the wood. O king, Araunah gives all this to the king." Araunah also said to him, "May the LORD your God accept you." But the king replied to Araunah, "No, I insist on paying you for it. I will not sacrifice to the LORD my God burnt offerings that cost me nothing." So David bought the threshing floor and the oxen and paid fifty shekels of silver for them. 2 Samuel 24:22–24

Through the word of the prophet Gad, the Lord had instructed David to go to the threshing floor of Araunah the Jebusite to offer a sacrifice. This offering would halt the plague that had fallen on Israel because of a census the king had carried out. Arriving at Araunah's house, David was given freedom to choose from the Jebusite's belongings whatever he needed for the sacrifice. In David's response we are given two important principles about giving.

The first of these is that as king, he could have helped himself to whatever he wanted. It was one of the "privileges" that went with his position. What's more, Araunah himself had offered all his belongings of his own free will. But David understood that a governor must respect other's rights, setting aside even legitimate privileges to do this. The greater one's authority, the greater care one must take when exercising it. This ensures that people don't feel taken advantage of. Many pastors would do well to remember that their position requires extreme caution in exercising privileges with their people.

The second principle is shown in David's refusal to take what Araunah offered. He understood that sacrifices of no cost have no spiritual value. This principle is especially important, because we often give what costs us very little, what is left over and what we can easily do without. Giving in this way rarely involves sacrifice.

So why is it important that our offering involve a certain amount of personal sacrifice? The answer to this question points to a truth at the very heart of God's kingdom.

The price paid to resolve man's sinful situation was the very life of the Son of God. This enormously high price was demanded because of the great magnitude of the problem it solved. Quick fixes are the predictable result of treating human reality frivolously. Whoever takes the problem of sin lightly is condemned to the torments and bonds of its devastating effects. Only when we are willing to accompany Christ's sacrifice with the devotion of self-denial will we see genuine fruit in our spiritual lives. David understood this, and that's why he made his offering sacrificial.

Food for Thought

Consider the weight of these words by J.C. Ryle: "A religion that costs nothing is worth nothing." [5]

You Know Not What You Ask For

"You don't know what you are asking," Jesus said to them. "Can you drink the cup I am going to drink?" "We can," they answered. Jesus said to them, "You will indeed drink from my cup, but to sit at my right or left is not for me to grant. These places belong to those for whom they have been prepared by my Father." Matthew 20:22–23

In John 14 and 15 Christ tells His disciples several times, "I will do whatever you ask in my name, so that the Son may bring glory to the Father" (John 14:13). Despite the condition it sets, this promise has inspired many generations of God's people to pray at all times and in every circumstance.

In church circles we have not always understood the meaning of praying "in His name." Often, with an innocence bordering on foolishness, we have believed that anything we ask will be given to us provided we add that "magic" phrase to the end of our prayer: "And we ask this in the name of Jesus."

The real meaning of this condition for answered prayer can be better understood through an illustration. Imagine that a father says to his son, "Go tell Mom I need the car keys." The child runs to his mother and delivers the message. The request is not from the boy, but from the father; the boy was only the spokesperson. In the same way, asking something in the name of Jesus is making a request that the Son would make for Himself if He was present. Many of our prayers receive no answer because they do not comply with this fundamental condition.

But the sole objective of prayer is not to secure a response from God. Prayer, that most mysterious of spiritual disciplines, leads us into an activity through which we are transformed by the very process of speaking with the Father. In relation to this, St. Augustine astutely observed, "Those who seek him, have already found him."[6] The answer is found in the process of prayer, not in the reply.

Nevertheless, the formative hand of God is also seen in answers. In His wisdom He sometimes gives us what we ask for, though we don't really know what we are asking. But in our insistence the Lord complies with the request. He gave the Israelites a king, but it wasn't what they really needed. Zebedee's sons were permitted to drink from the same cup as Jesus, but it meant something completely different from what they had in mind. Similarly, sometimes we receive an answer even though we have not prayed wisely. God's response does not imply approval, but rather that there is a lesson to be learned.

Food for Thought

J.A. Motyer wrote, "If it were ever the case that whatever we ask God was pledged to give, then I for one, would never pray again, because I would not have sufficient confidence in my own wisdom to ask God for anything."[7]

The Extent of His Vision

He said to them: "It is not for you to know the times or dates the Father has set by his own authority. But you will receive power when the Holy Spirit comes on you; and you will be my witnesses in Jerusalem, and in all Judea and Samaria, and to the ends of the earth." Acts 1:7–8

In the apostles' last meeting with the Messiah, they were still worried about the restoration of the kingdom in Israel. At their insistence Jesus answered them with the words that form part of our reflection today. He instructed them to be more concerned about His Father's vision than about things strictly related to the world in which they lived.

Breaking away from such worries, however, was no easy matter. When God raised up the Apostle Paul to extend the early church to the remotest parts of the earth, the church leaders in Jerusalem fiercely opposed his work. It was only after an intense debate that the apostles finally agreed to this new initiative, although they chose to stay in Jerusalem (Acts 15:1–35).

In today's church our resistance to evangelizing all nations continues to be very similar to that of Jerusalem's early church leaders. The obsession with local ministry is due partly to a misunderstanding of this passage. An incorrect interpretation would lead one to believe that the work in Jerusalem must be completed before the work in Samaria can begin, and the work in Samaria must then be completed before going on to the ends of the earth. Holding to this point of view, many pastors justify their lack of involvement by saying, "How can we get involved in missions if we haven't even reached our own neighborhood?"

A faithful translation of this command tells us that the original Greek indicates a concurrent undertaking of the work in Jerusalem, Judea, Samaria and the ends of the earth. The church has been called to serve simultaneously in a diversity of regions.

In relation to this, it should also be mentioned that those who serve in the missionary movement—even those doing a very profitable work—have not managed to avoid making this mistake either. They also sometimes emphasize one area of work above others. In their case, the work directed to the remotest parts of the earth is often considered more important than the work in Jerusalem.

Food for Thought

God cares for us in such a personal way that He is interested in the small world of each of His children. But His vision is also so far-reaching that He is concerned with the happenings in Argentina, Alaska and Australia. So it should be with His children. We should care about what takes place in our own neighborhood, but we should also work to extend the Kingdom to the remotest regions of the earth. As such, we will live in the full dimension of the work to which we have been called.

The Value of Patience

Be still, and know that I am God. Psalm 46:10

We live in times in which waiting is considered increasingly unacceptable. In the past waiting was defined in terms of days and months, but today we measure "delay" by the time it takes for our computer to open a program, the microwave to heat our coffee, a person to answer the telephone or a traffic light to turn green. In other words, impatience has become so profoundly ingrained in our lives that we measure the efficient use of time by seconds! Even when the wait is momentary, our restless spirit scurries about in anxious haste—something we have come to accept as normal, the distinguishing mark of people who have important business to do.

Popular wisdom states that patience is "the art of knowing how to wait." The problem with this definition lies in the belief that our principal activity during the moments we can't hurry time along is simply empty waiting. The psalmist adds an important element to the process of calming the spirit and resisting feelings of desperation: "Know that I am God." Our primary aim in life is to move toward God's invitation to walk permanently with Him, to seek fellowship with Him even in our most intensely frustrating moments. Living in this way, we might define patience as "the challenge to enjoy God" when our circumstances are inviting us to anxiety, worry and haste.

Imagine the following situation, typical of our contemporary lifestyles. We are waiting in line to do some paperwork in a government office. We have handed in papers to initiate the procedure, but can't leave until the transaction is complete. At one point a government official comes over and tells everyone in line (all of whom are understandably irritable) that the computer network has crashed. Everyone has to wait for the system to start up again. We immediately think of all the other urgent items awaiting our attention at work. We start to pace, thinking angry thoughts about the government, their employees and the system they represent. The more time passes, the more noticeable our agitation and annoyance become. It would be correct to say that we are waiting, but not that we are enjoying the experience. We have lost an opportunity to commune with Him who, two days previously in church, we proclaimed the most important Being in the universe.

Food for Thought

Our greatest challenge in the annoying, "intolerable" delays we "suffer" is to calm our spirit. Our responsibility is to remove our eyes from the circumstances and set them on God, to see that He reigns sovereign at all times. The next time you find yourself in a situation beyond your control, guide your spirit into the presence of the Shepherd of Israel and allow Him to lead you to a place of still waters.

Seeking His Intervention

If my people, who are called by my name, will humble themselves and pray and seek my face and turn from their wicked ways, then will I hear from heaven and will forgive their sin and will heal their land. 2 Chronicles 7:14

This passage is very familiar to us and is especially appropriate for our troubled world, so severely damaged by the corrupt abuse of power that has decimated our natural resources. It contains a series of steps to take in order to ensure God's intervention in times of crisis.

We should note that it is the combination of these steps that produces a response in the Most High. We often choose one or another of the items, but not the complete set. Done in isolation they have little effect. For example, when God declared that Israel would wander in the desert for forty years, the people repented, but didn't prosper. Although they had repented, they did not seek God's face (Num. 14:40–45). Similarly, we see later that the prophet condemned the people because they had humbled themselves before the Lord, but had not repented of their evil ways (Isa. 58:1–4).

Repentance is a process rather than a momentary experience. This implies that there are specific steps confirming the decision to completely arrange one's ways according to God's truth. Walking along this path ensures the change is not merely a religious exercise.

Four steps in this process are included in today's Scripture: We are to humble ourselves, pray, seek His face and turn from our wicked ways. Humiliation, the first step, involves the recognition that we have been proud and self-sufficient, that we have not walked as the Lord requires. It is an admission of the poor results of our own efforts. Following this, prayer ensures that our humbling is not due simply to momentary depression. We put words to our feelings and express our shame before God for the way we have been living—a process healthy for our spirit. Then, seeking His face develops an attitude of attentiveness, so that He may guide us on a new, correct path. Rather than wanting simply to resolve our problem, we now seek repaired relationship with Him. Finally, if we are sure we are willing to change, turning from wickedness implies we will never again follow our old paths. We discard all we previously considered important because we realize it was the source of many of our problems.

Just like Joseph before his regretful brothers, God cannot resist a humble, contrite heart. When there is a genuine change in us, God hears us from heaven, forgives our sins and heals our lives. What a magnificent gift!

Food for Thought

"Repenting is much more than apologizing to God." (Anonymous)

Sin on the Prowl

Then the LORD said to Cain, "Why are you angry? Why is your face downcast? If you do what is right, will you not be accepted? But if you do not do what is right, sin is crouching at your door; it desires to have you, but you must master it." Genesis 4:6–7

I am always impressed by the incredible simplicity of the Lord's teachings to His children. He chooses a language and context we can easily relate to, ensuring that the truth effectively touches our hearts and brings about the desired change. In this passage the Lord uses a dramatic image from Cain's world to bring home an important spiritual principle.

Both Cain and Abel were men accustomed to life outdoors. One of them was employed as a shepherd while the other worked the land. No doubt they had often seen wild beasts hunting. They may occasionally have had to defend themselves or their flock from the attacks of these predators. The Lord used this image to help Cain understand sin's strength in our lives.

When speaking to Cain, He used the phrase "sin is crouching at your door." The term quickly conjures up the image of a predator intently watching its prey, waiting for the exact moment to pounce. It brings to mind dramatic scenes, often presented in documentaries, of lions hidden behind clumps of grass, slowly creeping up on a creature unaware of their presence. In the same way, the person who has chosen to walk in evil has been identified by sin as a likely victim. Thus, the Lord told Cain that "sin desires to have you."

A target selected by a predatory animal will have certain characteristics that make it particularly attractive to the hunter. But predators do not always succeed in catching the animals they hunt; lions, for example, fail in as many as half their attempts to trap other animals. It is precisely because the chance of success is slim that they take their time selecting a target. The best victims are those which have been weakened by injury or illness, or have momentarily let down their guard. Similarly, those who walk in sin lower their spiritual defenses and open themselves to sudden attack from the Enemy.

The Lord encouraged Cain to master the crouching beast before it pounced. In other words, the best form of defense is to seize the initiative and to attack before being assaulted. A predator relies heavily on the element of surprise; once it is discovered, its chances of success are dramatically reduced. Clearly, God expected Cain to be on the lookout for situations in which sin was crouching in the wings, waiting for an opportunity to strike. Nobody could do this for him. It was his responsibility to be watchful and vigilant, and then take decisive action to stop the intended assault.

Food for Thought

"Watch and pray so that you will not fall into temptation. The spirit is willing, but the body is weak" (Matt. 26:41).

Another Name

Joseph, a Levite from Cyprus, whom the apostles called Barnabas (which means Son of Encouragement). Acts 4:36

The practice of changing peoples' names to more faithfully represent God's work in their lives was common in biblical times. In Genesis God changed Abram's name to Abraham (Gen. 17:5) because He had called him to be the father of nations. Jacob's name was changed to Israel (Gen. 32:28) because he had become one who rules like the Lord. Similarly, in the New Testament the angel instructed Mary to name her son Jesus because this name symbolized the mission entrusted to Him. Jesus changed Simon's name to Peter (Matt. 16:18), thus showing that the Spirit's transforming work would convert the insignificant fisherman into a rock within the church.

There would seem to be a principle behind this custom, namely, that the Lord sees and regards us according to the spiritual designs He has for our lives. These purposes generally differ dramatically from the directions we human beings have chosen to take. Therefore, these "spiritual" names reflect what we really are much more faithfully than the names chosen for us by our parents.

Within this framework it is interesting to note that the first-century church also made changes to some names. The man called Joseph was named Barnabas by the apostles, which means "son of encouragement." From what we can learn in the book of Acts, encouragement was a particularly strong characteristic of this servant's life. He was the one in charge of fetching Paul to present him in Jerusalem, was sent to Antioch to calm the people down and chose John Mark as a ministry partner after Paul had discarded him.

The value of this observation lies not in a call to change our names, although it is worth reflecting on what name God might choose if He were to give us one to reflect His work in us. But aside from this question, we should notice the contrast between this biblical custom and the custom of men, which is to give people nicknames according to characteristics they have little or no control over: Shorty, Freckles, Red, etc. These nicknames rarely flatter the person—most often they are derisive.

Food for Thought

Within the family of God, this should not happen. We should develop the capacity to see the spiritual reality of God's work in the lives of our brothers and sisters in Christ and, as we perceive it, contribute to this work of grace. We are citizens of another Kingdom, and our relationships should reflect this.

Pressing on to Maturity

Therefore let us leave the elementary teachings about Christ and go on to maturity.
Hebrews 6:1

What the author of Hebrews was concerned about—as all members of the church of Jesus Christ should be—was that the Christians had come to a standstill in their growth process. He was sharing some deep concepts of the spiritual life with them, but in the midst of his letter he exclaimed in frustration, "We have much to say about this, but it is hard to explain because you are slow to learn" (Heb. 5:11). Evidence seems to suggest that these people had already walked some years in the spiritual life, but they still needed to be fed food suitable for babies, not for adults.

The concept of pressing on toward maturity is difficult for us to understand. In the physical world growth is a process that happens without our intervention. Except in extreme cases of malnutrition, the body grows and reaches adulthood without our help. Obviously a good diet, exercise and necessary rest contribute to a healthier outcome, but even in cases where people don't care for any of these aspects, the body matures just the same.

In the spiritual world growth is governed by an entirely different process. In this dimension adulthood is not achieved with the mere passing of time; it is instead the result of a deliberate effort to develop a continuous relationship with God who produces the growth. Without this effort—which should be carried out in the grace of God—people will remain in a state where practically no transformation is visible. This is precisely why we find so many in the church who have hardly advanced further than the initial stages of fervor for Christ. In spite of this, it is quite common to find these people in positions of responsibility, based on the years they have been in the congregation, without considering if these years have produced real spiritual growth in their lives.

The author of Hebrews urges his readers to press on to maturity with a deliberate and sustained mindset. We are not referring to fleeting enthusiasm, but to carefully developed discipline. There will be endless opportunities in which circumstances invite us to abandon these practices. But the person who ardently seeks maturity will not be persuaded by arguments or overcome with tiredness in the search for a profound, intimate relationship with God. A goal has been set, and with God's help the objective will be reached.

Food for Thought

What plan do you have in order to achieve sustained growth in your spiritual life? What disciplines are included in this plan? What changes should be made in your routine to help you be more purposeful in your search for growth?

Surprised by Christ

When Jesus reached the spot, he looked up and said to him, "Zacchaeus, come down immediately. I must stay at your house today." Luke 19:5

Of all the despicable characters in society at the time of Christ, none was as hateful to the Jew as a tax collector. There were three reasons they were regarded with particular contempt: They collaborated with the enemy that occupied Israel; they were in continual contact with the Gentiles; and they were conspicuously corrupt in their management of funds. As chief publican, Zaccheus not only collected taxes, but also received a percentage of what his employees obtained.

Imagine his life. When he walked through the streets, few would greet him; many would hurl insults at him. His children would have no right to any kind of education. In a court case he would have no access to legal defense because of his status as a non-citizen. He was denied participation in any activities in the synagogue. His neighbors would certainly ignore him. Wherever he went, there would be abundant evidence of his position as an enemy to the public.

When I picture Zaccheus up that tree, I can't help thinking of the thousands of fans crowding the entrance to the pavilion where the Oscar ceremony is held. They are all hoping for a glimpse of their favorite actor or actress. Their desire is so intense that they will spend hours or even days waiting, enduring the discomfort of being jostled by a crowd who shares their desire. When the idols arrive, they might be seen for the few brief minutes it takes to enter the building.

If we were to speak to these fans, none of them would tell us they expected their heroes to talk to them. The stars of Hollywood hardly acknowledge the crowd's existence! They are not interested in knowing them; they are too intoxicated with their own fame to consider them. And so it was that Zacchaeus, always ignored by everybody, did not expect anything more than a glimpse of Jesus. He never imagined Jesus would notice him. Nobody ever looked at him at ground level, so why would he be noticed in a tree?!

Imagine, then, the impact it made when Jesus stopped and called him by name, choosing to visit his home! Should we be surprised at the dramatic change that took place in his heart? Not in his wildest dreams did it occur to him that Jesus would look at him—never mind visit his house! This is our God, who surpasses our wildest dreams, breaking into our lives in the most incredible and wondrous ways. His ways are unique. What amazement we experience when He surprises us!

Food for Thought

"Now to him who is able to do immeasurably more than all we ask or imagine, according to his power that is at work within us, to him be glory in the church and in Christ Jesus throughout all generations, for ever and ever! Amen" (Eph. 3:20–21).

A Question of Timing

She had a sister called Mary, who sat at the Lord's feet listening to what he said. But Martha was distracted by all the preparations that had to be made. Luke 10:39–40

Studying this passage would reveal little if we concentrated on the relative value of the sisters' activities. The Lord was not stressing the value of passivity over activity. Either posture could be harmful if taken to an extreme.

On the one hand, consider the dangers for those inclined to be restless. These persons must always be doing something and find it hard to stop. Very often their chronic activism is rooted in a lack of affection. They hide their pain or insecurity in a lifestyle that leaves no room for reflection, intimacy or even solitude. It is difficult to live with a person like this because their constant movement prevents them from dedicating time to pursuits which cannot be accomplished through activity. Ministry is especially attractive to them, providing as it does a way of receiving the affection and approval they so desperately crave. A pastor once told me he had not taken a holiday or rested from his work for seven years, offering this as evidence of his "unconditional" dedication to the Lord. This is typical of someone with this personality.

On the other hand, we have people lacking interest in any kind of activity. They do as little as possible, always wanting something for themselves without giving much in exchange. These Christians spiritualize their laziness, saying they are called to "greater things." These people have visions, receive words and prophecies, and are always ready to share their opinions with anyone interested in listening. They are never around, however, when it is time to roll up sleeves and get involved in a project requiring effort and sacrifice.

There is no shortage of these two kinds of people in our churches. But we can see that an excess of activity, or a complete lack of it, are both tremendously damaging for those who desire to walk faithfully with Christ.

What lesson did Christ want to teach Martha in this normal, everyday incident, which could have taken place in any one of our homes? He was not condemning her activity, which in itself was good, but rather the timing she chose for her praiseworthy service. Here we see the difference between a mature person and an immature one. The latter is dedicated at the *wrong* time to things which others do at the *correct* time. There is an appropriate time both for contemplation and for exertion. Someone dedicated to rest and stillness when it is time for work is clearly wrong. Conversely, a person focused on work during a time for quiet reflection is also mistaken.

Food for Thought

Make this prayer your own: "Lord, teach me to recognize the times for each of these two activities, so as to dedicate myself wholeheartedly to each one at the right time."

Complete Transformation

When they came to Jesus, they saw the man who had been possessed by the legion of demons, sitting there, dressed and in his right mind; and they were afraid. Mark 5:15

It is not simply to add color to the story that the evangelist describes the exact condition in which the townspeople found the former demoniac. It was precisely his transformed condition that made such a profound impact on those present.

If we compare Mark's story with Luke's, we have a really pathetic picture of this man who lived in utter torment in the most deplorable conditions. Mark tells us that the Gerasene lived "night and day among the tombs and in the hills he would cry out and cut himself with stones" (Mark 5:5). This behavior must have been a desperate attempt to put an end to the agony of his existence. Luke adds that the man was wearing no clothes and could be seen running naked in the hills (Luke 8:27).

It should not escape our notice that the townspeople's "methods" of solving the man's problem were not notably compassionate. To contain him, they had bound him many times with shackles and chains, with totally unjustifiable violence. These are the ways of this world; it is more important to secure our comfort and tranquility than to free captives from their suffering. Today we don't resort to shackles and chains, but we have institutions for isolating people with these kinds of "mental disorders" to keep them well out of our way.

Jesus clearly stated that He came into the world to heal those who were oppressed (Luke 4:18–19). Far from ignoring the man, He ministered to him and put an end to his tortuous experience, guiding him to a restored and healthy life. Take note of the depth of this change. Before, the man had been naked; now he was clothed. Before, he had run around and cut himself with stones; now he was seated. Before, he had screamed and shouted; but now his mind was healthy and normal. What an incredible transformation! This is the kind of change God wants to produce in every life He touches.

In the church we have not always understood this reality, preferring to attend to the needs of a person's soul. The spiritual side of our existence, however, cannot be divorced from the emotional, mental or physical sides. The redemption God offers affects the entire person. We should be committed to this kind of work, seeking transformation in all aspects of people's lives.

Food for Thought

The Apostle James set forth an incisive challenge to first-century Christians which has not lost its power despite the passing of 2000 years. "Suppose a brother or sister is without clothes and daily food. If one of you says to him, 'Go, I wish you well; keep warm and well fed,' but does nothing about his physical needs, what good is it?" (James 2:15–16). This is a question well worth reflecting on.

The Value of Self-Control

Like a city whose walls are broken down is a man who lacks self-control. Proverbs 25:28

The defense of a city was not simply additional security for its inhabitants. In King Solomon's time it was a matter of life or death. According to the custom of the times, wars between peoples often included subduing the population by sacking their cities, thus destroying the administrative, commercial and food distribution centers of an area.

People living near a city knew they could seek its help and protection when faced with an enemy. These cities were typically surrounded by a wall up to twenty-three feet wide and thirty-three feet in height. At the wall's base was a sloping embankment filled with loose stones, making climbing difficult. In some cases the embankment was surrounded by a pit which made it impossible for armies to gain access to the walls. Cities had few entrances, and these were constructed with elaborate designs to prevent large numbers of people passing through at once. There were openings along the walls from which the defending army could attack intruders with arrows and other missiles. In addition, the walls were built with towers in which a large number of soldiers could be positioned for defending strategic points. Some historians say a city built this way could withstand a siege for many years.

This defensive network would prevent an attacking army from entering the city and destroying everything in its way. Once a city was taken, its buildings were torn down; its inhabitants were taken prisoner and their belongings became the victorious army's war spoils. The city ceased to be of any use.

The author of Proverbs compares such a city to a man who lacks self-control. Think about people who don't know when to stop talking. They are constantly involved in arguments, controversies and difficulties because they don't recognize the moment to keep quiet. Think too of those who cannot say no to the requests of others. They lose control of their own life and spend their time trying to satisfy the demands of everyone who comes their way. Think about people who do not discipline their food intake. Their health is affected and their weight is soon out of proportion with their stature, bringing on all the health complications resulting from excessive weight. Think about those who cannot resist the seductive invitation of sin. They lose their state of holiness and fall into all kinds of practices that weaken them considerably, both emotionally and spiritually.

Food for Thought

Having self-control means taking steps to wisely manage and protect the resources we have received from the Lord. It means possessing discipline to resist the natural impulses of the flesh. A disciplined decision may seem unnecessary at the time, but produces precious fruit in the future. Every leader should be exercising self-control.

Living in Abundance and Need

I can do everything through him who gives me strength. Philippians 4:13

There is no doubt that this verse presents a principle for general spiritual life, but today we will consider its meaning within the context of the passage.

This section of Scripture deals with a Christian's reaction to financial situations. The church in Philippi had sent Paul an offering that gave him great joy. But he immediately clarifies that his joy comes primarily from the opportunity these Christians had to give. The gift did come at a particularly appropriate time, Paul being in prison, but he clarifies, "I am not saying this because I am in need, for I have learned to be content whatever the circumstances. I know what it is to be in need, and I know what it is to have plenty. I have learned the secret of being content in any and every situation, whether well fed or hungry, whether living in plenty or in want" (Phil. 4:11–12). He then adds, "I can do all things through Him who strengthens me."

Many challenges affect Christ's disciples, and special commitment to God is required to overcome them victoriously. Of all of them, however, none puts the Christian in such danger as does the subject of money. In another letter Paul had categorically stated, "For the love of money is a root of all kinds of evil. Some people, eager for money, have wandered from the faith and pierced themselves with many griefs" (1 Tim. 6:10). Neither have I found in my pastoral experience anything with greater power to overtake the hearts of God's children than monetary matters.

What precise dangers is the apostle referring to in today's passage?

He addresses the challenges of living either in abundance or in need. Abundance brings with it the particular difficulty of not giving in to the arrogance produced by wealth, trusting more in this world's treasures than in the Lord. Poverty, on the other hand, challenges our belief that money is not the solution to life's problems. The pauper is hounded by need at every turn and may end up being as obsessed with money as the wealthy, although for different reasons.

The Apostle Paul tells the Philippians he had learned to live in contentment. He had gained a disposition of always giving thanks for what was received, without looking at what was lacking. He had the profound, heartfelt conviction that everything we have, much or little, comes from the hand of a loving God who is not obliged to give us anything. In the end, everything is a gift. This is the source of the apostle's abiding joy.

Food for Thought

"Keep falsehood and lies far from me; give me neither poverty nor riches, but give me only my daily bread. Otherwise, I may have too much and disown you and say, 'Who is the Lord?' Or I may become poor and steal, and so dishonor the name of my God" (Prov. 30:8–9).

The Subtlety of Pride

"Now I will make you small among the nations, despised among men. The terror you inspire and the pride of your heart have deceived you, you who live in the clefts of the rocks, who occupy the heights of the hill. Though you build your nest as high as the eagle's, from there I will bring you down," declares the LORD. Jeremiah 49:15–16

There is no condition that neutralizes a child of God as efficiently as pride. With absolute finality, it puts an end to relationship with the Most High and leaves one exposed to all kinds of spiritual deceit. Left uncorrected, it leads to judgment and punishment. We need only look at King Saul's life to see how irreversible the consequences of arrogance were for him.

When we consider the devastating effect pride has, we should all live in fear and trembling lest this attitude become enthroned in our hearts. The struggle against pride is complicated, however, because we are not facing an easily identifiable problem. Pride is tremendously deceptive. Since it is intimately linked to spirituality, it can easily be confused with real passion and devotion for things of the Lord. By its very essence it is much easier to identify in our neighbors than in our own hearts, because if we try to discover and deal with it, we are deceived.

Even when through the working of the Spirit we discover its presence in our lives, pride does not tamely give way to our attempts to unmask it. There will be much in the way of argument, reasoning and justification to persuade us that it is not really what we think. Pride likes to have the last word and never allows us to feel comfortable when asking forgiveness, recognizing our mistakes or giving another person first place.

Where does the root of our pride lie? The Lord alone should be exalted above others; the rest of us are equals. But pride, caused by Lucifer's fall, seeks a position above our peers and, if at all possible, above God Himself. Whether our problem is not accepting correction, or failure to recognize our mistakes, or judging people, or not relating to those who think differently from us, pride will always put us in a position to consider ourselves superior to others.

We should really tremble at the thought of becoming prisoners to pride. Only the Lord can free us because only He can clearly identify the problem. We can't trust our own life evaluation; knowing how evasive pride is, we must ask God to examine our hearts. Then, with courage, we must be silent so He can tell us what He sees. Even if it is painful, His diagnosis is trustworthy and will bring us freedom.

Food for Thought

"Who can discern his errors? Forgive my hidden faults. Keep your servant also from willful sins; may they not rule over me. Then will I be blameless, innocent of great transgression" (Ps. 19:12–13).

Seeking Reconciliation

"Therefore, if you are offering your gift at the altar and there remember that your brother has something against you, leave your gift there in front of the altar. First go and be reconciled to your brother; then come and offer your gift. Matthew 5:23–24

This teaching goes against the popular course of action in situations of personal conflict. We would normally say that if anyone has been hurt by someone, they should go and speak to the person about it. But Christ reverses the roles; He tells us if we know that our brother has something against us, we should take the initiative to seek him out.

The reason for this probably has to do with the way we behave when offended. Far from looking for a way to resolve the conflict, we get angry and tend to avoid the one who has hurt us. We don't naturally try to talk things over and clear everything up. Instead, we close ourselves up and allow indignant thoughts about the other person to fill our hearts. Perhaps the very intensity of these feelings prevents us from speaking to the offender. Whatever the reason, Christ encourages the person who caused the offence (real or imagined) to take the initiative to speak with the offended party. This ensures that a broken relationship does not remain in that state indefinitely.

The Lord considered reconciliation so fundamental for our spiritual health that He even ordered us to pause in our worship of God to take this step of restoration. In many situations we believe that our relationship with God can carry on normally, despite the fact that relationships with our peers are not as healthy as they should be. But Christ highlighted that broken relationships with our brothers and sisters dramatically affect our relationship with the Father. Even when we try to persuade ourselves that our offering is received with pleasure, the Word reveals that God cannot accept the worship of those not at peace with their peers. In a passage strongly denouncing the religious spirit of Israel, Isaiah condemns the people because they fast, dress in sackcloth and pray to the Lord while at the same time oppressing their workers and living as they please. "Your fasting ends in quarreling and strife, and in striking each other with wicked fists" (Isa. 58:4). He goes on to encourage a style of spirituality that translates into harmonious relationships with God and men.

Because of this Christ indicated that the restoration of relationships is a priority not to be ignored or postponed in His children. The fundamental point in the dispute is not who is right or wrong. The essential question is whether the two parties are prepared to take a step toward the law of love—the first law—which summarizes all the others.

Food for Thought

This anonymous statement points to our Source of reconciliation: "We are like beasts when we murder. We are like men when we judge. We are like God when we forgive."

Shaming the Enemy

In everything set them an example by doing what is good. In your teaching show integrity, seriousness and soundness of speech that cannot be condemned, so that those who oppose you may be ashamed because they have nothing bad to say about us. Titus 2:7–8

In the book of Job we are presented with the vivid account of an encounter between God and Satan. At this meeting Satan tried to convince the Lord that Job's well-known piety was only the predictable result of his abundance and prosperity. He suggested that if all this were taken away, Job would soon cease to walk before the Lord in righteousness. This reveals the desire on Satan's part to find something in Job's life to enable him to carry out his favorite activity: accusing the chosen ones. From what we read in Revelation, he does this without ceasing, for the Word tells us he "accuses them before our God day and night" (Rev. 12:10).

Knowing this can help us understand how profoundly spiritual Paul's exhortation to Titus is. We are not speaking about a simple suggestion here, but rather about refusing the Enemy a foothold, protecting ourselves from involuntary participation in any filthy strategies to disrupt God's work. The way to achieve this, according to the apostle's exhortation, is to live in such a way that the Enemy cannot get hold of something to use against us. In other words, even if he painstakingly examines our lives, he won't be able to find anything of which to accuse us before the Father.

This objective necessarily addresses the issue of how we live, giving no consideration to the popular idea that truth is gained by means of elaborate intellectual exercises. In Paul's view, truth is proclaimed by our lives. The Enemy does not examine our doctrines to see if he can find any theological contradictions or lack of biblical evidence in them. He scrutinizes our daily walk. He watches us when we are with our family or in our place of work; when we are talking to others or quietly alone. His one aim is to find those things in us that dishonor the Lord so he can present himself before the throne with evidence of our unworthy condition.

We should be encouraged that, despite persistent accusations from the Enemy, we have Jesus Christ as our Defense Attorney before the Father (1 John 2:1). He intercedes for us and defends our cause—blessed be His name! Nevertheless, in today's passage we hear a very serious call to live in holiness. Paul urges us to live in such a way that the Enemy will have to resort to shameful lies in order to accuse us, being unable to find evidence to use against us. Our works proclaim that we are committed unreservedly to Him who called us from the darkness into His wonderful light. What a tremendous challenge!

Food for Thought

C.H. Spurgeon stated, "Holiness is the visible side of salvation." [8]

Relationships Which Stretch Us

As iron sharpens iron, so one man sharpens another. Proverbs 27:17

Iron was a metal of relatively little value in biblical times, but it was tremendously useful in everyday life. Many utensils and tools used daily were made from it: knives, swords, ploughs, nails and cooking gear. Metal had to be worked carefully, however, to fashion it into a tool or sharpen the cutting edge of a sword. This was done mainly through a process in which one piece of iron was filed against another.

The author of Proverbs uses this image to help us think about the process of "sharpening" through which people grow decisive and efficient in all they do. We should note that his analogy excludes the possibility of any isolated action carried out through an individual's own efforts. In spite of this, many people are determined to limit their process of growth and maturity to projects of their own making. These people, even if often in a social environment, spend much of their existence in a solitary state and avoid significant contact with others.

Without purposeful contact it is impossible to attain the shape and sharpness that forms us into useful tools in the Lord's hands. Just as in filing iron against iron, our contact with others should be deliberate, sustained and planned. It is not occasional brief encounters that produce opportunity for growth. The encounters that stretch us require not only continuity, but also must not be left to chance. As we all know, it is possible to meet with people and spend a long time chatting about things that never lead to meaningful exchange.

For sharpening to happen it is necessary that two people agree to develop their friendship in a direction they would not normally choose. Each makes room for questions that invite the other to open up, or for comments that oblige them to examine their attitudes or behavior. Within a framework of love and commitment, we allow the relationship to include exhortation, correction, admonition, training and teaching. All of these will help our meetings with others to produce more than just a good time together.

For those who occupy a position of responsibility within the church, this is especially important. Ministry can have an isolating effect. We should develop intimate relationships with a few key people that allow for this kind of exchange. These people should be those with whom we feel challenged so that we continue to grow to our full potential in Christ.

Food for Thought

Can you think of two or three people you could share this kind of relationship with? What elements could help the relationship develop into one of mutual "sharpening"? What things could be included in the relationship to stimulate growth in this aspect?

The Price of Success

Where there are no oxen, the manger is empty, but from the strength of an ox comes an abundant harvest. Proverbs 14:4

This proverb invites us to reflect on two important points. First, all of us are inclined to give priority to things of relatively little importance. In this case the author of Proverbs chooses the subject of cleanliness, expressed in terms of an empty manger. Nobody in their right mind would argue that living in a dirty, unhygienic situation is healthy. But I have known many people for whom cleaning is an obsession. They will fight to defend their stance and impose conditions of extreme hygiene on their surroundings, even when these are unnecessary.

We could transfer these obsessions to other aspects of life. Think for a minute about punctuality. It is undoubtedly important to be punctual and to show respect for others' time. But a person obsessed with watching the clock insists on punctuality even on vacation, when there is no need for a set timetable. Or think of a perfectionist. For this person it is absolutely unthinkable for a project to contain imperfections. We agree we should do everything as well as possible, but the perfectionist cannot be satisfied with anything less than faultlessness, even in details completely lacking in significance.

In all this we see how prone we are to building our lives around values that have little importance in spiritual terms. The challenge is to keep this kind of obsession from dominating and controlling our existence.

The author of Proverbs leads us to a second point. Everything we achieve in this life is accompanied by certain unpleasant aspects. It is not possible to succeed in a difficult project without some sacrifices. Today's verse presents us with a very clear example. The ox is indispensable to the farmer. With the help of this beast, he can do much more than he could on his own. But when he brings the ox to the stable for the night, the animal leaves his waste on the floor. This is the price of having an ox! Similarly, anyone who hopes to achieve certain things in life should be willing to pay the price of that achievement. Do you want the church to grow? You must be willing to fill your building with people lacking the polite manners of regular church-goers. Do you want to help the poor? You must be ready to walk through the mud and drink contaminated water. Do you want to train disciples? You must be willing to put up with immaturity and foolishness. Each project has its unpleasant side. It can't be avoided. We must be willing to pay the necessary price for our success.

Food for Thought

What things in your life may be enjoying a more important place than they should? What is the price you must pay for growth in your current projects? What steps should you take to ensure you continue advancing toward success?

Against Intolerance

"Teacher," said John, "we saw a man driving out demons in your name and we told him to stop, because he was not one of us." "Do not stop him," Jesus said. "No one who does a miracle in my name can in the next moment say anything bad about me." Mark 9:38–39

Notice the details of John's testimony. The disciples had come across someone who was ministering to the demon-possessed. Perhaps it was one of the countless people who had been touched by Christ's ministry. Restored by the grace of God, this man may have been dedicating his time to ministering to those under oppression and torment. When the disciples saw him, they immediately tried to stop him from continuing his work. What criteria did they use in deciding to censure his ministry? Simply that he was not part of the select group of men who followed Christ! They showed no interest in discovering the fruits of his ministry or finding out if he was genuinely working in the power and grace of the Holy Spirit. They disqualified his ministry because he was not with them; they assumed his service could not be of God!

This brief incident reveals one of our most persistent affinities, which is to believe there is only one acceptable way of doing things—our own! This position gives rise to the majority of conflicts within the church. It shows how easily we believe that our way of ministry is the only valid one, the only ministry that really matters.

It is precisely this attitude that causes people in our congregations to be in love with their own goals for ministry. Some are passionate about missions and try to convince people that everyone not involved in this work is outside the will of God. Others are burdened for the Jews; they look for ways to show that ministry to the Israelites should be a priority for God's people. Others feel strongly about evangelism and provoke guilt in those who don't share the good news with at least one person per day. Each one pushes their own vision and subtly looks down on others' service.

Christ taught the disciples that the Kingdom is much larger than we can understand. God is working in many ways through many people in many projects—each one important to His purposes. He desires His children to develop a more generous perspective toward others who are serving, even if they are doing it in a completely different way than us. It is the Lord who determines the validity of their ministry, not us.

Food for Thought

Praise the Lord that not everyone works the way we do, or has the same convictions as ours! This is part of the marvelous experience of being members of the body of Christ with its multifaceted functions and ways of expression. Develop the habit of praying for and praising the ministries of others who are working in areas other than yours.

Pleasing Christ

Am I now trying to win the approval of men, or of God? Or am I trying to please men? If I were still trying to please men, I would not be a servant of Christ.
Galatians 1:10

The church in Galatia had gotten tangled up in a series of conflicts related to Christian living. A group favoring Jewish customs argued the necessity of new converts to incorporate the practices of the Law in order to be saved. One of their accusations against the apostle—who insisted that Gentiles could be converted without this elaborate process—was that he had "watered down" the requirements of the Law in order to win favor with the Gentiles. They argued that many of them would never have been converted if they had known the real "requirements" for following Jesus. They considered Paul guilty of adapting the gospel so as not to offend those who heard it.

Such an accusation should not be taken lightly. We all have a deep desire to be accepted by those around us. Nobody likes to live in isolation, ignored by his peers. In some people this desire is so intense that they will give up their convictions to receive approval from others.

For those of us who serve in teaching and preaching ministries within the church, the danger of adapting the gospel is ever present. Consider the unpopularity of many truths we preach from the Word, like the call to holiness, simplicity, self-denial or the absolute rejection of certain sinful ways. Kingdom principles contradict and confront the world's most popular concepts. Whoever is dedicated to preaching them purely may be called radical, insensitive, old-fashioned or simply out of place. It is much easier to adapt the message to fit our culture, sharing and proclaiming those truths that will be well received by people.

This adaptation is a tendency of the church of Christ in recent times. Paul warns Timothy that in the last days "the time will come when men will not put up with sound doctrine. Instead, to suit their own desires, they will gather around them a great number of teachers to say what their itching ears want to hear. They will turn their ears away from the truth and turn aside to myths" (2 Tim. 4:3–4).

Notice how radical Paul's reply is to the Judaizers' accusations in the Galatian church. He declares, quite simply, that it is not possible to serve Christ if one seeks to please men. One aim is incompatible with the other. Anyone dedicated to proclaiming the truth of God must be willing to live with the reproach and condemnation of those horrified at Christ's teaching. We don't deliberately aim to shock, but it will be an inevitable result of proclaiming the Word. All ministers should evaluate their willingness to pay this price for being faithful to their call.

Food for Thought

Martin Luther's words are worthy of reflection: "Live in peace if possible, but live the Truth whatever the cost."

The Blessing of Being Hungry

Blessed are those who hunger and thirst for righteousness, for they will be filled.
Matthew 5:6

The sensations of hunger and thirst, unpleasant though they are, play an indispensable role in the efficient working of the body. They warn us that our energy reserves are low and should be replenished. They urge us to procure food and drink in order to satisfy our body's basic needs. If we didn't feel hunger, we would run the risk of completely depleting our resources.

We can transfer this observation to the spiritual world. It is through sensations of need that we feel impelled to seek from God the elements necessary for our soul's nourishment. This is why Christ could say that those who hunger and thirst for righteousness are "blessed," for their need opens up the way for the provision of God.

A simple principle can be learned from this observation. The Lord's dealings in our lives frequently produce a sense of need so we will seek His face and request His intervention. The awareness of hunger activates our search for Him. Experiences that reveal our weaknesses may be extremely disagreeable to us. Sometimes they come as failures and bitter personal defeats. But when we correctly analyze our struggle, we then recognize our poverty and raise our eyes to Jesus, so that He may give us what we cannot obtain through our own efforts. Without this feeling of need, we would not initiate a search.

The same principle applies to evangelism. Our efforts to save others will not produce results if they don't first know they are lost. We try to interest them in something which they haven't even realized they need! It is fundamental that they first feel hunger and thirst.

If we look at the school that many of the great servants of God attended, we can see they had to go through times of intense distress. This suffering was often the product of their own efforts to help the plans of God. Such was the case of Abraham, who took Hagar to bear him a child; of Moses, who tried to free his people through violent means; and of Peter, who tried to give his life for Christ. The failure of their personal aims opened the way for God to work in their lives in amazing ways. But it was first necessary for them to experience failure so the Lord could build something durable on the ruins of their errors.

We should, therefore, greatly rejoice in those situations that reveal our need. These sensations of hunger and thirst propel our lives in the direction of all that is good—toward God Himself.

Food for Thought

"Come, let us return to the Lord. He has torn us to pieces but he will heal us; he has injured us but he will bind up our wounds" (Hos. 6:1).

The Discipline of the Lord

Because the Lord disciplines those he loves, and he punishes everyone he accepts as a son.
Hebrews 12:6

The subject of discipline is difficult for us to understand, especially as we are conditioned by the culture in which we live. In many spheres of education, any kind of discipline is frowned upon, since it is considered to cause irreparable emotional damage to those who receive it. Influenced by this humanistic philosophy, many Christian parents have backed down at the responsibility of disciplining their children to bring them up in the fear of God. On the other hand, in some cultures it is not unusual to find parents excessively violent in the chastening of their children, using their authority to vent accumulated frustration and anger. It goes without saying that under these circumstances discipline ceases to have any useful effect on the one receiving it!

In today's meditation we want to consider discipline as the result of committed love for the one in need of training. Discipline and love are not mutually exclusive. On the contrary, the author of Hebrews indicates that one of the ways to recognize God's love toward us is through His correction in our lives.

This apparent contradiction is easier to understand if we don't focus on the process of discipline, but on its outcome. Discipline is not administered with a view to short-term results. It is an investment that will produce fruit over many years. Whoever disciplines with this truth in mind knows that the unpleasant moments are necessary if the correction is to produce positive results in the future. This is the perspective of the exhortation in Proverbs, where we are told not to "withhold discipline from a child; if you punish him with the rod, he will not die. Punish him with the rod and save his soul from death" (Prov. 23:13–14). Discipline—or the lack of it—has eternal consequences!

The corrected individual is not the only one who suffers from the experience. He who disciplines also suffers. If you have chastened a child in love, you will know that a father or mother's heart experiences anguish when the need to take action arises. We also feel disappointment at the unacceptable behavior which has made the discipline necessary.

In this sense we can understand our heavenly Father's pain when it is necessary to discipline us. Surely His heart is full of sadness at the inappropriate actions which have led to our need for correction. However, for our own good He does not give way. In the same way, we who have been called to disciple others should be willing to administer discipline when necessary with a tender but firm spirit. It is an essential part of our pastoral work, and we should not neglect it.

Food for Thought

"No discipline seems pleasant at the time, but painful. Later on, however, it produces a harvest of righteousness and peace for those who have been trained by it" (Heb. 12:11).

Living in Him

So then, just as you received Christ Jesus as Lord, continue to live in him.
Colossians 2:6

Think back a moment to your conversion. What was it like? A series of events helped you arrive at the profound conviction that something was missing in your life, and that this something was Jesus. Perhaps you were tired of the blandness of your existence or depressed because your efforts were not producing the desired results. Perhaps you were at the end of your tether, with no way of improving your personal situation. Whatever your experience, you realized that only God could put your life in order. You submitted unreservedly and unconditionally, confessing your fragility and asking the Most High to intervene in your life. The only thing you had was the deep assurance that Jesus could give you what you lacked.

Paul encourages the Colossians to walk in the same spirit in which they had started their spiritual life—in other words, with the same simplicity and confidence that characterized their conversion. This exhortation is not in vain, for we are all disposed to put aside the simplicity of our first love, getting tangled up in complex religious experiences which consist in endless lists of demands. Life in Christ is a relationship. It should be led with the same passion and absolute trust with which we took our first steps toward the gospel.

To make this point clear, the apostle speaks of four aspects he considers indispensable to our daily walk with Christ. First, he refers to the roots of a plant, which nourish and strengthen. In this way the child of God should also be firmly rooted in the person of Christ, obtaining from Him the nutrients needed for growth. Then the apostle refers to a building, urging that everything we build should be in Christ. In essence, all the plans and enterprises of a disciple should be steeped in the person of Jesus. A third element has to do with the confirmation of our faith. For this, we must give God the opportunity to demonstrate that all actions taken in faith will produce their fruit and reward in Him. Finally, Paul recommends that the experience of walking in Christ should be seasoned at all times with continuous expressions of gratitude for all His goodness.

Food for Thought

The value of our life in Christ is lost when we try to reduce it to a series of continuous activities. Instead, we must seek the Lord's presence in all we live and experience. Some verses later, the apostle explains why this is necessary: "For in Christ all the fullness of the Deity lives in bodily form, and you have been given fullness in Christ, who is the head over every power and authority" (Col. 2:9–10). Christ is all we need. Let's make our spiritual experience a permanent romance with the Son of God!

Slaves to Obedience

Don't you know that when you offer yourselves to someone to obey him as slaves, you are slaves to the one whom you obey—whether you are slaves to sin, which leads to death, or to obedience, which leads to righteousness? Romans 6:16

Something we frequently hear stated in the church is that Christ has set us free. The popular idea is that we are now free to choose the path we want, enjoying the added benefit of God's blessing on our decision. Paul affirms in Galatians, "It is for freedom that Christ has set us free. Stand firm, then, and do not let yourselves be burdened again by a yoke of slavery" (Gal. 5:1). But the freedom referred to in the Scriptures is not given to further our personal interests.

To understand this concept more clearly, it will help to look at today's verse. To illustrate a penetrating spiritual truth, Paul uses the image of slavery, common in the world at that time. As we know, slaves were considered the property of their owner. They were not people, but objects. The owner could do with their lives as desired, including having them killed. If we apply this analogy to the popular concept of freedom in Christ, salvation could be compared to the recovered freedom of a slave who can now direct his own life as other people do.

Today's passage contradicts this idea. It indicates, rather, that we have passed from one state of slavery to another. Before, our master was sin. Even when we wanted to be good, we couldn't, because sin reigned in our lives. Now, according to this passage, we have a new master: obedience. If we go back to the analogy of slaves during the Roman Empire, we see another image. The freedom we have been given is not unconditional. We have been freed from the capricious desires of our old master; but now a new master—Jesus Christ—has bought us, and we owe Him the same service we owed the previous one. In other words, we have passed from one state of servitude to another. It is not our state that has changed, but our Master.

It is also interesting to note that Paul could have declared we are now slaves of *Christ*—this would be true. But the apostle chose to say we are slaves to obedience. We have been transferred to a dimension of life in which the Word of God instructs and guides our daily existence. We don't give our opinion or argue about the Lord's requests, because we are slaves to obedience. Even if we want to do things differently, we can't, because our motto is to obey in every place and at all times!

Food for Thought

"For it is God's will that by doing good you should silence the ignorant talk of foolish men. Live as free men, but do not use your freedom as a cover-up for evil; live as servants of God" (1 Pet. 2:15–16).

Shepherds, Not Lords

Be shepherds of God's flock that is under your care . . . not lording it over those entrusted to you, but being examples to the flock. 1 Peter 5:2–3

Among the problems that frequently hinder a pastor's ministry is the confusing of pastoral responsibility with a call to become master of the members of Christ's body. This posture has probably contributed more than anything to constraining the Kingdom and harming the spiritual development of God's people.

Today's passage contains a call to shepherd the Lord's flock. The word "shepherd" carries the concept of goodness, tenderness and tranquility. Whoever has watched a shepherd will have noticed that of all the jobs involving animal care, this one requires the most meekness and gentleness. Sheep are defenseless creatures that easily startle, which often gets them into trouble. A good shepherd leads with a serene spirit; this is sensed by the flock, which will then wander in a slow and deliberate fashion. But violent and aggressive movements will quickly disperse the sheep in all directions.

The Apostle Peter specifically instructs the elders not to lord it over the flock. One definition of "to lord" is to "control, subject, take possession of, impose oneself on." These definitions reveal an aggressive spirit of competition that seeks a position of supremacy over others. This kind of behavior carries the implicit message that pastors deserve positions of superiority and can do with the sheep whatever they please!

In practice, this attitude results in congregations full of tension. The pastors' word cannot be questioned because they have more authority than everyone else. The pastors have the right to make decisions on behalf of everyone, without allowing them to participate in the process. They may impose changes in the church without consulting anyone, simply because they are the pastors. Everyone else's decisions must be authorized by them. Nobody can move forward with a project unless the pastors have given it the nod of approval.

You will realize by now that this has unhealthy undertones. Nevertheless, it is very sad to see the number of congregations that function this way. Peter offers an alternative: elders who serve as examples. With this focus, the emphasis is on the leaders' *lives*. It obliges them to be more careful about their own conduct than about whether others are taking them into consideration. The reason is simple. The factor that most affects transformation in others is the impact made by saintly lives around them. Pastors should not oblige others; but rather, with their own devotion, they should attract people so that they want to be like Christ.

What a tremendous challenge! It is well worth the trouble to invest in this style of leadership. Those you minister to will flourish in ways you cannot even imagine!

Food for Thought

What kind of leader are you? How would those who know you describe you? What do you need in order to be more of a shepherd and less of a "lord"?

The Hope of the Wretched

What a wretched man I am! Who will rescue me from this body of death? Thanks be to God—through Jesus Christ our Lord! Romans 7:24–25

"I do not understand what I do. For what I want to do I do not do, but what I hate I do. . . . For what I do is not the good I want to do; no, the evil I do not want to do—this I keep on doing" (Rom. 7:15, 19). Who among us cannot identify with Paul's vivid struggle? When we read this passage we cannot help but say, "That's me!" This is our daily existence. Our spirit longs for purity, but our body is governed by a law that sometimes seems unconquerable. With every step we hear the seductive insinuations of sin, inviting us to walk that path we hate so much. What wretches we feel!

The apostle's question, "Who will rescue me from this body of death?" is not so much theological as it is a frustrated exclamation due to constant struggle with the flesh. The question conveys his personal agony.

Give careful attention to the answer expressed in the next verse. The solution is not a program, but a person: Jesus Christ. This contradicts all we have learned, for we are of a people who base their existence on doing. Our philosophy values decisive action above passivity and quietness. When challenged, we quickly identify the best steps to take; then we advance confidently toward a solution. We believe that with sufficient effort and perseverance almost any obstacle will disappear. In many areas of life this is so, but sin is never solved with a program; neither does it give way to persistent bouts of discipline. Sin is a reality we cannot conquer.

So who can free us? Jesus Christ our Lord! How does He do it? We don't know! But He is the solution to our struggle. Christ's agony in Gethsemane comes to mind. His battle is ours. The spirit wishes to submit to the Father's will, but the flesh rebels. How did Jesus solve His dilemma? He sought the face of the Father. We see no physical manifestation of the Spirit; we are not witness to any dramatic action by Christ. All we observe is the sharing of His agony with the Father. When He came back the third time, His struggle was over. Peace reigned in His soul; the flesh had submitted to the Spirit.

Perhaps its very mystery makes it hard for us to accept such a simple solution. But we cannot escape this reality. The Word tells us we must seek Him. We can't place our hope in five easy steps, in a book or a course. Who can free us? Thank God for Jesus Christ our Lord!

Food for Thought

How do you feel when you do what you don't want to? What steps do you take to find a solution? What part does Christ play in this process?

The "Logic" of Failure

Then everyone deserted him and fled. Mark 14:50

The work of training leaders is complex. It demands an unusual level of commitment and perseverance from the person carrying out the task. Training cannot happen through a pre-packaged program; an investment is being made in people's lives, and they are all different from each other. Each one possesses a particular background and personal perspective of life and ministry. Each one is a product of culture, influenced by family, friends and experiences. The trainer must be willing to change and adapt the process to the individual needs of the disciples.

With such a challenge we look naturally to the figure of Jesus for inspiration. If ever there was a person who understood what was necessary to convert diverse people into faithful disciples, Christ was that person. He knew how to take perfect advantage of opportunities that came His way, bringing His disciples into ever closer contact with the truth and reality of the Kingdom. What an amazing privilege to be a member of the chosen group, to walk day after day with the Son of God Himself! They could observe His ministry firsthand, His life of communion with God, His personal habits, His love and compassion for those He ministered to. How could they fail to be influenced by the most complete training "program" the people of God have ever been given? What amazing "products" we could expect from such a model as this!

Nevertheless, in the disciples' first big test, all of them—absolutely all—failed. What good was the effort and dedication if the results were going to be so disappointing? If Jesus' passionate dedication to training the Twelve got these results, what possible hope is there for our own feeble efforts?

There are two lessons we can glean from this situation. First, when it comes to dealing with people, there is absolutely no program that guarantees the outcome. Guarantees can be offered when we are working with inanimate material, which is subject to all we do. But each individual has his own personality and processes, and there is no program in existence that can guarantee a certain type of "product." This is the risk all trainers must assume when they invest in others.

Second, failure in the Kingdom is not measured by specific situations. One incident in a person's life can have a profound effect, but our heavenly Father takes the whole life into consideration and measures the results of the entire earthly pilgrimage. Today's scene shows a setback on a journey full of achievements and victories.

Food for Thought

The investment Christ made was good. Its fruit would be seen throughout the lives of the Eleven, who put this bitter experience behind them and took up their walk with the Lord once more. With time, each of them became faithful ministers for the Kingdom. The Master's work was not in vain!

All Authority

Then Jesus came to them and said, "All authority in heaven and on earth has been given to me." Matthew 28:18

I have often asked my students what the Great Commission is. Most of them answer unhesitatingly, "Go and make disciples of all nations" (Matt. 28:19). This is correct, but only in part. Jesus' words do not begin with verse 19, but in verse 18. Our response gives eloquent testimony of how focused we are on our own activities. Most of us believe that the Commission begins with the part that involves us—going to make disciples!

If we had been among the Twelve that day, I think we would have felt a little intimidated by the magnitude of Christ's call. Make disciples of all nations? They had been outside Israel perhaps once or twice in their lives. How could they embark upon such an undertaking when they were already confused and not a little lost? Where could they start? How would they overcome the obstacles they were sure to face? And what about the hostile atmosphere of these last few weeks?

Christ understood these questions, and many others the disciples didn't know to ask. This is why He began with this declaration of His authority. Otherwise, the immensity of the task would surely have overwhelmed them. It is clear from Jesus' words that He was not charging them with an unbearable burden. He was calling them to proceed in the victory He had won through His death and resurrection. This conquest is precisely why He could be given "all authority in heaven and on earth."

The dictionary offers the following synonyms for the word "authority": privilege, capacity, competence, right, influence, control, power, strength. As we read this list we realize what is meant by Christ's words. The Lord is referring to the freedom He has received to go wherever He will, take whatever He will, when and wherever He will. In other words, the obstacles presented by a hitherto undefeated Enemy have now disappeared. Seated at the right hand of the Father, bearing the Name which is above all names, Christ is now the supreme and absolute authority in heaven and on earth.

The disciples were to walk in that authority. Timidity and fear was no longer to form part of their daily experience. They belonged to the family of Him who had conquered death. As long as they depended absolutely on the King, nobody could challenge them, or offer resistance. For those of us in the business of making disciples, knowing His authority should produce boldness in us—a daring bordering on foolishness. Let us proceed where He has already conquered!

Food for Thought

Christ surely anticipated this when He said to Peter, "On this rock I will build my church, and the gates of Hades will not overcome it" (Matt. 16:18). The church advances, bold in Christ's victory, and storms the city of the Enemy. Not even the gates of Sheol can stall the advance of the people of God!

As You Go

Therefore go and make disciples of all nations, baptizing them in the name of the Father and of the Son and of the Holy Spirit. Matthew 28:19

The word "therefore" gives a clear indication that this commission is intimately related to the declaration just made by Christ: "All authority in heaven and on earth has been given to me" (Matt. 28:18). It is vitally important to the success of this enterprise that the disciples walk and work in this authority.

I would like to draw your attention to the verb "go." In Greek, this word is not in the imperative. In other words, it is not a command, although most Christians believe that the Great Commission directs us to leave the place we live in order to go and make disciples. In fact, many missionary organizations use this verse to motivate Christians to become involved in cross-cultural work. And this interpretation has led the church to consider disciple-making as something to be achieved through programs. If we see it as a special ministry, the logical result is to believe that only some people receive this call. Those of us not led this way feel secure that "going" is not our calling.

But because the Greek is not imperative, this verb could be more accurately translated "as you go." So the "going" is not the result of planned or deliberate action on our part; it is simply the road life takes us along. With the challenges and opportunities life brings us, each of us will pass through different places from which we will perform our daily activities. Even when we plan carefully, these activities are rarely under our control. We adapt to circumstances as they present themselves to us. Therefore, it is within the framework of our daily activities through which we are called to make disciples.

This exhortation coincides with the manner of Christ, for whom making disciples was a part of daily life. We see Him walking among the crowds, responding to situations presented by the Spirit. He did not plan special training activities, but wherever He went, He took advantage of opportunities to introduce men and women to the Kingdom of heaven.

From this perspective we don't need special church programs in order to obey the Great Commission. We do need the commitment of every Christian to make disciples through the life they lead from Monday to Saturday. The sales clerk can present Christ to customers in the store. The business executive shares the good news with co-workers. The taxi driver is ready to share the gospel with passengers. Each of us implements this ministry where God has placed us, making disciples as He opens opportunity in the midst of our daily lives.

Food for Thought

For those of us training saints for the work of ministry, it is fundamental that we communicate this concept. Only in this way will we ever fulfill the Great Commission. Making disciples is the work of the whole church.

Making Disciples

Therefore go and make disciples of all nations, baptizing them in the name of the Father and of the Son and of the Holy Spirit. Matthew 28:19

Yesterday we saw that the word "go" is not an order. But the order that *is* in the Great Commission is to "make disciples." The verse could well be translated this way: "As you go through life, dedicate yourself to making disciples of all the nations."

It is amusing that the church has converted into a commandment something that means otherwise, and converted into an option what is really a commandment. We have ended up with a handful of people working tirelessly to achieve what the whole church should be doing.

It is no coincidence that the word "make" is in the imperative. It shows us that disciples are not made by themselves. New converts are not disciples; they must be formed and trained. For this they need someone with the commitment Paul had, whose training consisted of proclaiming Christ Jesus, "admonishing and teaching everyone with all wisdom, so that we may present everyone perfect in Christ. To this end I labor, struggling with all His energy, which so powerfully works in me" (Col. 1:28). Formation includes a process of proclaiming, admonishing and teaching.

We have only to leaf through the Gospels to see that disciples are not produced in the course of a few weeks. Jesus lived with the Twelve and involved them in most of His experiences. They heard Him preach and saw Him heal. They heard Him debate with the Pharisees and watched Him cast out demons. They accompanied Him as He went and knew His frequent withdrawing for prayer. All this was part of their formation.

This growth is the product of a serious commitment on the part of the disciple. We should be willing to walk together with a disciple, to fight for them, to persevere in the work of forming them until Christ is clearly visible in their lives. This requires obligation and sacrifice on our part. When this commitment is not present, we end up incorporating people into the church whose Christian experience will consist mainly of observing what others do, while they remain limited to attending meetings as a sign of their commitment to Jesus.

God has called them to much more than this! It is our responsibility to work tirelessly so they fulfill their maximum potential in Christ. The work involves effort and sacrifice, but there is no activity in the church that gives a leader such satisfaction as making disciples.

Food for Thought

As leaders we always run the risk of ministering to everyone, but investing in no one. Confident that our work with the whole congregation will bear fruit, we avoid the commitment of working in depth in the lives of a few. This is, however, the most productive investment we can make. All leaders, without much thought, should be able to name five or six people they are personally discipling.

Disciples

Then Jesus came to them and said, "All authority in heaven and on earth has been given to me. Therefore go and make disciples of all nations, baptizing them in the name of the Father and of the Son and of the Holy Spirit, and teaching them to obey everything I have commanded you. And surely I am with you always, to the very end of the age."
Matthew 28:18–20

We have been reflecting on the last assignment Jesus gave His disciples. We have seen that the work is to be done within the framework of our daily life, and that a disciples' formation requires unconditional commitment on the part of the discipler. A disciple, as Walter Hendricksen has pointed out, is not born, but made.[1]

Today we want to consider the objective of our efforts, which is to make disciples. A disciple is not the same as a believer. The word "believer" reflects the emphasis in a person's life: believing. Believing, in our context, is an entirely intellectual activity. This helps us understand why so many who attend our churches lead lives that do not testify to the power of Christ. Their lives are based on recognizing and valuing certain doctrinal truths. But the truths stored in their heads lack power to produce change or create genuine commitment to the Lord. The result is that the church has many adherents to Christianity, but few disciples.

Disciples in the New Testament were immediately recognized for the relationship that existed between a student and a teacher. The life of a disciple was inseparable from the teachers' life. When the crowds identified Christ's disciples, they knew they were with the Master from Galilee. They were seen with Him at all times, for they followed Him wherever He went. So here we have the simplest and clearest definition of a Christian disciple. It is someone who is following Christ.

The word "follow" indicates movement. Our call is to lead people to a life of movement—and that doesn't mean the journey to and from church meetings! This movement is a result of following Jesus in our family relationships, our work and our leisure time as well as among other believers. God is never inactive, and neither can His children be. Making a disciple is, in essence, teaching someone the secret of walking all day with Christ.

Once again, this has nothing to do with a class or a three-week course. It requires establishing a relationship where, above all, the other person can observe our own example. We have been called to this holy, difficult commission. We should note that a believer needs constant attention, because they don't possess in themselves the inner reality that produces real spiritual life; but a disciple will eventually learn to walk alone and to reproduce life in others. Thus, the Kingdom is extended.

Food for Thought

Juan Carlos Ortiz stated, "Discipleship is more than getting to know what the teacher knows. It is getting to be what the teacher is."[2]

Of All Nations

Therefore go and make disciples of all nations, baptizing them in the name of the Father and of the Son and of the Holy Spirit. Matthew 28:19

We have been reflecting on the final instructions Christ gave His disciples; these laid out the objectives for their work in the coming years. In its simplest form the Great Commission challenged the disciples to repeat again and again the pattern they had experienced with Jesus. In this sense the commandment is extremely simple, since the easiest assignments involve repeating what we have personally experienced. In commissioning them for the work, Christ indicated it was to be aimed at "all nations."

As with all Jesus' teaching, this exhortation is perfectly in line with the spirit of the Old Testament. At the beginning, when the Lord spoke with Abraham, He described His plan clearly: "I will make you into a great nation and I will bless you; I will make your name great, and you will be a blessing. I will bless those who bless you, and whoever curses you I will curse; and all peoples on earth will be blessed through you" (Gen. 12:2–3). God raised up a nation for Himself, not only because He wanted to have fellowship with these people, but also because through them He wished to touch all the peoples of the earth. They would be, in the words of the prophet, "a light for the Gentiles" (Isa. 42:6).

One of the tragedies in Israel's history is that they never understood their call to fulfill a mission on earth. Instead, Israel isolated itself and developed an attitude of indifference and even contempt toward other nations. But God's plan still stood, and Jesus reminded His followers that they were to make disciples of all nations.

The word "nations" is derived from the Greek term *ethnia*. Its use shows that Christ was not thinking of political divisions by which we divide human groups into "nations," but rather of those people groups who share a culture, language and history. From this perspective there are many more ethnic groups than nations on earth. Each one of these should have access to the gospel, the "good news of great joy" (Luke 2:10).

It is in the incredible scope of this goal that we most clearly see the extraordinary love of our God. He includes those who share our own culture as well as those most different from us. We simply cannot be limited to people groups that live and think as we do. Our mission is to reach those distant from us, both geographically and culturally. They too should be told they are treasured by the God who made heaven and earth.

Food for Thought

What things are done in your congregation to reach ethnic groups different from your own? How much effort do you put into praying for and promoting outreach in other parts of the world? How can you develop a more global vision of ministry?

Identified with Christ

Therefore go and make disciples of all nations, baptizing them in the name of the Father and of the Son and of the Holy Spirit. Matthew 28:19

We have been reflecting on the implications of the Great Commission, the last assignment Jesus gave His disciples. We have seen the importance of walking in the authority of Christ, living out our commitment to make disciples wherever life takes us. We have also reflected on the effort involved in the process of forming disciples of the Lord.

As Jesus begins to give the means of implementing this call, He tells the Eleven they should baptize the disciples. Today it is not always clear to us why baptism is such an important part of disciple-making. In our congregations it is often seen as nothing more than a religious ceremony. But in New Testament times, baptism indicated a radical conversion and identification with the Kingdom message.

A clear picture of this important step can be seen in the ministry of John the Baptist as we observe the conversion of crowds who flocked to hear his message. Luke tells us that John "went into all the country around the Jordan, preaching a baptism of repentance for the forgiveness of sins" (Luke 3:3). If we examine his message, we can plainly see the intimate link between baptism and repentance. John exhorted each one who approached him, in very practical and personal terms, to choose a different way of living. He did not present the crowd with a list of requirements, but brought the application of life change into each one's personal world. Exhortations to the Pharisees were different from those made to soldiers, which were different again from those made to tax collectors. He was not inviting them to join a religion, but rather asking them to allow the Lord to personally transform them.

It is in this life change that we find the essence of baptism's meaning. By the physical action of being immersed in water, we represent our decision to die to our old lives and become one with Christ. The water, which cleanses our soiled bodies, opens the way for spiritual cleansing—burying our old life so that we are born to a new existence. The Apostle Paul explains its significance: "Or don't you know that all of us who were baptized into Christ Jesus were baptized into his death? We were therefore buried with him through baptism into death in order that, just as Christ was raised from the dead through the glory of the Father, we too may live a new life" (Rom. 6:3–4).

Food for Thought

This radical identification with Christ is the foundation on which we build a new life; it constitutes a decision to turn our back on the old ways. We are not committing ourselves to mend the old life, but to cast it aside and walk a new path. The old is discarded, and God's plan for our life begins to unfold.

Sent in His Name

Therefore go and make disciples of all nations, baptizing them in the name of the Father and of the Son and of the Holy Spirit. Matthew 28:19

We often speak of the Great Commission as instructions Christ gave His disciples. And so they were. But when we speak of Jesus' commands, we often forget that the Son did not act alone. His exhortation is to baptize disciples in the name of the whole "Team," that is, the Father, Son and Holy Spirit.

It is hard for us to understand the unity that exists among the members of the Trinity. Our experience in ministry is most often limited to our own efforts, our vision and our way of doing things. Only on rare occasions have I observed Christian workers who really work as a team. I'm thinking of a group in which each member honors the others; duties are performed while giving careful consideration to the opinion of every member, supported by the profound conviction that each one has received gifts and grace from God to be full participants in Kingdom work. In most "teams" there is usually someone whose opinion carries greater weight than the others'. Often there is even an implicit understanding that agreement with this leader's opinion is a condition of being included. Sadly, many pastors expect their teams to function in this manner.

This is so different from the way the Father, Son and Holy Spirit work! Each seeks honor and glory for the Others. Christ said, "He who speaks on his own does so to gain honor for himself, but he who works for the honor of the one who sent him is a man of truth; there is nothing false about him" (John 7:18). He said of His Father, "If I glorify myself, my glory means nothing. My Father, whom you claim as your God, is the one who glorifies me" (John 8:54). In His last prayer He requested, "Father, the time has come. Glorify your Son, that your Son may glorify you" (John 17:1). Of the Spirit He declared, "He will bring glory to me by taking from what is mine and making it known to you" (John 16:14). These Three delight in exalting the other Two. They work in perfect harmony, and never without being in complete agreement.

The disciples were not only to work with the support of God the Father, Son and Spirit evident in all they did; they were actually called to join this very Team. They were not working alone, but as an extension of and under submission to the God who had sent them. Their walk had to demonstrate this same desire to honor and seek the glory of Another much greater than themselves.

Food for Thought

Meditate on John Wesley's profound statement: "Tell me how it is that in this room there are three candles and but one light, and I will explain to you the mode of the divine existence."

16 July | The "Ministry" of Teaching

"Teaching them to obey everything I have commanded you. And surely I am with you always, to the very end of the age." Matthew 28:20

We have been reflecting on Jesus' instructions to make disciples of all nations. Having analyzed the magnitude and scope of this charge we are now attempting to understand how it can be carried out. The first step requires that those who draw near to Christ identify themselves with Him through baptism. The next step is dealt with in today's verse, and involves teaching the disciple.

To our modern way of thinking, the word "teaching" almost automatically brings classrooms, books and courses to mind. "Teaching" has become almost synonymous with "classroom." We need to put this concept aside if we are to understand Jesus' intention for teaching. Even though none of the disciples had studied pedagogy or teaching techniques, they had clearly seen the methodology they needed in the life and ministry of the Master.

Christ's teaching ministry took various forms. The most formal was His preaching. We find a good example of this in the Sermon on the Mount. It is one of the ways we teach, and the emphasis in this method is on communicating the truth by way of public proclamation. A less formal technique the Messiah used frequently was dialogue. There were endless situations that arose in everyday life where the disciples brought their doubts and questions to Him. Jesus guided them toward the truth through the skillful use of questions, stimulating their reflective processes. Another form of teaching had to do with the disciples' own experience. Christ gave them various ministerial tasks which, in themselves, constituted learning experiences. Afterward, they would dedicate time to sharing and evaluating what they had been through, and this is when valuable lessons were learned concerning the principles which guide effective ministry.

But the most common method Christ used was that of teaching through the example of His own life. For instance, the disciples had observed and heard Him praying, and saw something in the quality of His fellowship with the Father which they lacked. They approached Him, asking Him to teach them to pray (Luke 11:1). On another occasion He washed their feet, saying nothing, thus giving them the clearest lesson on service they had ever received (John 13:1–5).

And so we see that the modes of teaching follow many different paths. The effective teacher will not limit his lesson to a classroom and a forty-five minute lecture. Teaching is something much deeper and more extensive than this. Seen from this perspective, all Christians may exercise a teaching ministry without necessarily having the ability to formally present the truth. This is why the call to teach disciples is a call to all of God's people.

Food for Thought

Howard Hendricks wrote, "God's method is always incarnational. He loves to take His Truth and wrap it in a person." [3]

Keeping His Word

"Teaching them to obey everything I have commanded you. And surely I am with you always, to the very end of the age." Matthew 28:20

Yesterday's reflection, part of a series on the Great Commission, focused on the diverse methods of teaching those who are becoming disciples. In His continuing instruction, Jesus specified that the "students" should be taught to observe everything He had commanded.

If we pause for a moment to look at the phrase "everything I have commanded you," we will quickly understand what the Master meant. A lot of what is taught in the church today is aimed at passing information on to those who attend our meetings. We get drawn in to endless studies on every possible theme related to the Christian life. On examining the Gospels, however, we find that Christ never focused on giving the disciples information. On more than one occasion they pressed Him to this end, such as when they wanted to know when the kingdom of Israel would be restored. Jesus evaded these questions and concentrated on instructing them about their behavior within the Kingdom. His teachings were not a collection of opinions on spiritual life. They were a series of commandments which aimed at producing obedience in those who followed Him.

This is a key point for every disciple. James warns of the danger we are in when we "merely listen" to the Word (James 1:22). The apostle writes that people who do this are deluded, for they understand that the Word is good for their edification, but do nothing about it. The blessed are those who convert the Word into a way of life (James 1:25).

One of the most important objectives of a teaching ministry is to produce transformation in the lives of those who hear the Word. It is no good if the hearers are enthused by our teaching, but carry on living in the same way as before! When many Jews were excited at Jesus' teaching, He faced them and said in no uncertain terms, "If you hold to my teaching, you are really my disciples" (John 8:31).

Dr. Bruce Wilkinson, author of various books on the learning process, calls this application of truth one of the seven laws of the learner. He points out that the lesson which will make the biggest impact on a student is that which first made its mark on the teacher's life.[4] This is why we must be permanently on guard against the temptation to entertain ourselves with details of Scripture, losing sight of the fact that it was written "that you may believe that Jesus is the Christ, the Son of God, and that by believing you may have life in his name" (John 20:31).

Food for Thought

D. L. Moody wrote, "The Scriptures were not given to increase our knowledge, but to change our lives."[5]

All God's Counsel

"Teaching them to obey everything I have commanded you. And surely I am with you always, to the very end of the age." Matthew 28:20

Our meditation on this text has led us to reflect on different implications of the last commandment Christ gave His disciples. We have seen the importance of absolute identification with the death of Christ, and have examined some possible means of teaching others the Word of God. Now we will focus on the exhortation to teach *all* that Christ had commanded His disciples.

There are at least two observations related to this point. First, the instructions are to teach what Christ had *commanded.* He did not say they were to teach what He had taught, but what He had commanded. In other words, they should not simply retell the stories and truths they had heard from the Master. Within our churches much of the teaching revolves around simply repeating what we have heard others say. But Christ was telling them to teach those commands they had come to understand and know through their own obedience.

This makes it clear that the work of teaching others is founded on personal experience. The disciples were not freed from obeying the commands they were communicating to others. On the contrary, their ministries had to be built on the solid basis of personal identification. This ensured that what they taught others would be more than abstract theory—one reason teaching today has so little impact. This kind of teaching is sustained by an intellectual grasp of truth, but it has not been tested in the real world of everyday living. It is personal obedience to God's commands that gives a teacher real spiritual authority.

Second, we notice that the "subject" to be taught should be *all* that the Master had instructed them in. Very often we reduce the whole truth to three or four principles that the new disciple should understand, as if life consisted in nothing more than this. But Christ aimed at complete transformation in His disciples. For this to happen in us, the light of God's Word must be brought to bear on every aspect of our lives. I am not referring to a list of topics to cover, but rather a call to a lifestyle where all aspects of life are touched by the Word of God: the way we dress, our eating habits, our family relationships, our attitude to work, the way we behave in public, the entertainment we choose, our involvement in God's service and countless other aspects. The true transformation of our lives comes precisely when the Word challenges every area of our lives so that we are obliged to enthrone Christ as Lord at every moment, wherever we are.

Food for Thought

John Wesley wrote, "All the knowledge you want is comprised in one book, the Bible."[6]

A Friend for Eternity

"Teaching them to obey everything I have commanded you. And surely I am with you always, to the very end of the age." Matthew 28:20

We began this series of reflections on the Great Commission meditating on the fact that making disciples is rooted in Christ's absolute authority. It is His authority that allows us to advance with confidence in this ministry, grounded in the conviction that in Christ we are more than conquerors (Rom. 8:37).

This conviction, however, will not free us from the difficulties and setbacks typical of ministry. Jesus came up against these problems daily. He faced exhaustion, harassment from crowds, misunderstandings and endless disputes. In addition, He had to endure constant challenges from His own disciples. There were moments when they, like the crowds, questioned or opposed His decisions; at other times, they demonstrated lack of maturity or spiritual vision. On more than one occasion, He was disappointed with their selfish attitudes.

Jesus had warned His disciples that they would live an experience very similar to His. He told them they would be blessed "when people insult you, persecute you and falsely say all kinds of evil against you because of me" (Matt. 5:11). He also said that "a student is not above his teacher, nor a servant above his master. It is enough for the student to be like his teacher, and the servant like his master. If the head of the house has been called Beelzebub, how much more the members of his household!" (Matt. 10:24–25). He explained in graphic terms that discipleship meant taking up a cross to follow Him (Matt. 10:38), a plain indication that persecution and suffering awaited those identified with Him.

Because of this, the disciples knew the road ahead was full of difficulties. But they had been assured that the final victory was already granted them through the risen Messiah. The knowledge that they had been conceded a clear victory gave them an iron-like spirit of perseverance. Now Christ added more: His presence at all times and in every place. When they were persecuted, He would be with them; when they felt alone, He would be with them; when they had to give an account of their faith, He would be with them; when they had to face poverty and sickness, He would be with them. They would never be alone in the work; Jesus would be their constant companion.

For those serving God's people, this truth is priceless. We need not be burdened with the difficulties, setbacks and adversities of ministering alone—although many pastors are. We always have Someone to turn to, Someone we can trust with our most intense struggles. He is heedful of much more than our supplications. He wishes to intervene and lighten our load. Why would we not accept such an incredible opportunity?

Food for Thought

Augustine stated, "God is an infinite circle whose center is everywhere and whose circumference is nowhere." [7]

Christ, Firsthand

And because of his words many more became believers. They said to the woman, "We no longer believe just because of what you said; now we have heard for ourselves, and we know that this man really is the Savior of the world." John 4:41–42

Christ's dialogue with the Samaritan woman at the well has to be one of the most incredible conversations registered in Scripture. Jesus was neither aggressive nor disrespectful, but skillfully guided her to the point of facing her need for profound change.

When we consider the woman's past, we can understand why her testimony to the townspeople was so dramatic. She lacked a solid reputation. She had been married five times and was heading, quite probably, for a sixth failure. After her conversation with Christ, however, something happened that changed her words into a powerful testimony. The whole town came to see the "prophet" who had revealed the truth of God. They ended up begging Christ to stay with them, and the result was that many more believed because of His Word.

The behavior of these people indicates the importance of a personal experience with Christ. They said to the woman, "We no longer believe just because of what you said; now we have heard for ourselves, and we know that this man really is the Savior of the world." Their initial experience, triggered by the woman's words, was rapidly replaced by personal contact with the Messiah. In this their lives were changed forever.

Most of us had a similar conversion experience. We came to Christ because of what others told us or because of what we saw in their lives. Their testimonies awoke in us a desire to know Jesus in person, and this experience established the basis for our first steps in the Christian life.

This is typical in any spiritually transforming situation. But sadly, many Christians never go further than this initial experience. Their "evidence" of effective spiritual life rests entirely on the testimonies of others. They do not nourish their relationship with Christ so that it moves beyond their early enthusiasm. Lacking an everyday relationship with Jesus, these people become resigned to observing in others what they do not possess in their own lives. They know Christ is real, but not through their own experience; they know of Him from others. As time passes, this produces cynicism and the kind of religiosity that causes grace to wither and die.

How important it is to renew our walk with Him daily! We should seek day by day the reality which allows us to share the Samaritans' testimony, "Now we have heard for ourselves, and we know that this man really is the Savior of the world."

Food for Thought

How is your relationship with the Lord? Can you give testimony that He speaks and ministers to you daily? What can you do to develop greater intimacy with Him? What expectations does Christ have of His relationship with you?

Living with Waves

But when he saw the wind, he was afraid and, beginning to sink, cried out, "Lord, save me!" Matthew 14:30

Peter's adventure of walking on the water has a special appeal for us. It is something completely different from all we know. His bold request also touches something within us—we never cease to be surprised at the impulsive, spontaneous replies of this most daring disciple. I would like to make some observations on this particular point in the story, when the wild and furious waves put an end to the apostle's short adventure.

The waves did not appear threatening when Peter first stepped onto the water. The text tells us the disciples had been rowing for some hours, making little headway because the wind was against them and the waves were crashing against the boat (Matt. 14:24). Conditions had been like this all night. But until Jesus appeared, the waves were no more than a vexing nuisance slowing their progress. These men were accustomed to the sea; this was surely a well-known situation for them. Similarly, it is possible for us to be surrounded by difficulties and affliction, but be less affected than we might be under other circumstances.

When Peter stepped out of the boat, the waves were the same ones he had seen from the safety of the boat. But now he was so engrossed in his adventure that he didn't pay attention to the waves. He was completely absorbed by the challenge of walking on the water toward Christ. In the same way, in moments of great spiritual passion, we don't really notice the setbacks and obstacles in our way. Their existence or non-existence makes absolutely no difference to our spiritual experience.

Then Peter took his eyes off Jesus and looked at the water. He saw the waves that had been there all the time—all through the night, in fact. But his personal situation had changed dramatically; it was suddenly extremely precarious and dangerous. The same waves now filled him with paralyzing fear and brought an abrupt end to his walking on the water. He began to sink, and only the rapid intervention of the Master saved him from drowning.

What conclusion can we come to from these observations? We often believe that the cause of our stumbling comes from the particular circumstances in which we find ourselves. Peter's experience suggests something different. It is not the circumstances that affect us, but the way we view them. Our spiritual posture at the moment of the storm's arrival determines the way we will react. The waves didn't change, but Peter did. The disciple's ordeal shows plainly that a person can react entirely differently in two similar situations. The perspective we have makes all the difference in the world!

Food for Thought

How do you react in critical moments? What do these reactions say about you? What should you adjust in order to react in a spiritually healthier fashion?

Peace in Christ

"I have told you these things, so that in me you may have peace. In this world you will have trouble. But take heart! I have overcome the world." John 16:33

Christ's sincerity with His disciples contrasts dramatically with the proclamations of many "prophets" of our times. They offer a life of pure blessing in which everything is a bed of roses. One of the famous groups to appear in recent times even has as its motto, "Suffer no more!" Christ did not beat around the bush or try to hide the truth from His disciples. His declaration is simple and direct: "In this world you will have trouble!"

Further explanation on the subject was unnecessary; the disciples were witnesses to Jesus' suffering on earth. He had faced hunger, weariness and loneliness. Each day He had to deal with the harassment of the crowds, with endless processions of the inquisitive, self-interested and needy. In addition, He bore the disputes, suspicions and accusations of the religious figures of the times. And what can we say about the particular anguish He suffered, more than once, at the hands of the men closest to Him? All these formed part of His experience in this world.

On this occasion Christ added some important principles to this revelation. A great deal of our suffering in times of trouble is not produced by our circumstances, but by our reaction to them. Our response is generally negative because we have been surprised by whatever has happened. Our naive perspective is evident in the question we immediately ask in our suffering: "Why me?"

None of the men could say they hadn't been warned about the consequences of becoming Christ's disciples. In giving them the full picture, He substantially reduced obstacles regarding their ability to handle conflicts.

Jesus told the Twelve these things so that as children of God they might have peace in Him. This is the most outstanding characteristic of those who live according to the Spirit and not the flesh. It is not that they are free of difficulties, setbacks and suffering, but that in the midst of the fiercest storm they have an inner tranquility that has no explanation. They don't shift from their stance, since what happens around them cannot touch this inner reality.

Christ made it clear to them that this peace was available in Him. It was not a product of discipline, or of carrying out a series of religious requirements, or a past decision to follow Christ. This peace was to be found in the person of Christ, and only those close to Him would have access to it. Peace is, after all, a direct result of His victory, not ours.

Food for Thought

God, in His wisdom, doesn't give us peace; He gives us access to the Person who is peace. This places us under obligation to seek Him always, for He is the eternal source of life and fullness.

Private Sins?

But the Israelites acted unfaithfully in regard to the devoted things; Achan son of Carmi, the son of Zimri, the son of Zerah, of the tribe of Judah, took some of them. So the LORD'S anger burned against Israel. Joshua 7:1

This story hits hard, coming as it does immediately after the extraordinary victory the Lord conceded the Israelites over Jericho. The dramatic way the city was taken was a powerful testimony of God's faithfulness to His people when they walked hand in hand with Him. But in the following chapter, we see Israel defeated and humiliated by an insignificant enemy. Today's passage, taken from the chapter that tells the whole sad story, offers an explanation for this defeat. Sin was present among the people, and this halted the working of God in a dramatic way.

The incredible thing about this episode is that only one man had sinned. Achan, of the tribe of Benjamin, saw among the spoils of Jericho "a beautiful robe from Babylonia, two hundred shekels of silver and a wedge of gold weighing fifty shekels," and he coveted them and took them (Josh. 7:21). God, however, had given specific instructions as to the city. "The city and all that is in it are to be devoted to the LORD . . . But keep away from the devoted things, so that you will not bring about your own destruction by taking any of them. Otherwise you will make the camp of Israel liable to destruction and bring trouble on it" (Josh. 6:17–18).

It is amazing that all the people should suffer the consequences of one man's sinful action. Our surprise shows that we perceive sin as something personal, a matter between us and God. This story presents the most decisive and dramatic evidence that there is no such thing as "private sin." All sin is an offense against God and His people and, as such, has results that go beyond our personal lives.

Being one of God's people implies the existence of spiritual bonds beyond us. We do not exist in isolation, whether or not we have active relationship with others. When one of us sins, we don't only sin against God. We also damage our relationship with our brothers, since the work of God among all of us has been interrupted. Secret sin is a serious matter because it affects everyone related to the offender, in the same way that an alcoholic brings misery to everyone in the home. Although we may not see the consequences, the results of our actions cannot be reversed.

Food for Thought

Paul must have had this principle in mind when he wrote, "If one part suffers, every part suffers with it" (1 Cor. 12:26). The concept is not that we **should** ***suffer with our brother, but that the pain of one affects the whole body, even if we choose to ignore it. In the same way, sin has consequences for the community. Knowing this gives extra weight to the call to live in holiness.***

The Road to Humility

In his distress he sought the favor of the LORD his God and humbled himself greatly before the God of his fathers. And when he prayed to him, the LORD was moved by his entreaty and listened to his plea; so he brought him back to Jerusalem and to his kingdom. Then Manasseh knew that the LORD is God. 2 Chronicles 33:12–13

After Israel's defeat due to the insatiable expansionist appetites of the Assyrians, Manasseh took the throne in Judah. He succeeded Hezekiah, the king of reforms, and reigned for fifty-five long years. The Bible chronicler tells us that Manasseh "did evil in the eyes of the LORD, following the detestable practices of the nations the LORD had driven out before the Israelites" (2 Chron. 33:2). In other words, he brought Judah back to all the abominable practices of the Canaanites, even going so far as to set up idols within Solomon's temple. It is also thought that the prophet Isaiah was killed during this time, a result of severe persecution against all who remained faithful to Jehovah.

God judged him, and Manasseh was captured and taken to Babylon. It was the Assyrian custom to lead captured kings by way of a hook that passed through their nose or lips. Then they were put to work as slaves in conditions of extreme cruelty. It was during this period that Manasseh called out to God, as described in today's passage. In anguish, completely broken, he asked the God of his fathers for forgiveness and begged to be freed from his torment. The Lord heard him, and he was brought back to Jerusalem and restored to the throne. Deeply repentant, Manasseh carried out a series of reforms in which he rid the land of the idols and places of sacrifice he had previously established.

This story teaches two clear lessons. First, we must note that no matter how far a person falls from God's grace, the way back is never closed. God is essentially a God of mercy and compassion. The cry of a repentant heart reaches His presence immediately, even when the person has been involved in the worst abominations. His wish is always to restore relationship with His children. No matter how many times we repent and fall, He will always be willing to intervene, to restore that which our sin has destroyed.

Second, we notice the final result of this great suffering was that "Manasseh knew that the LORD is God." Our tendency, when hurt, is to be vengeful and inflict on others the suffering they have caused us; but the Lord's dealings with us always reveal who He really is. His method may be severe and painful, but its result reveals a true and accurate image of His person. This knowledge is priceless, even though gained through tears and anguish.

Food for Thought

As Vance Havner so wisely remind us, "The alternative to discipline is disaster." [8]

The Meditation of the Wise

And all who heard it were amazed at what the shepherds said to them. But Mary treasured up all these things and pondered them in her heart. Luke 2:18–19

How could the shepherds fail to marvel at what they had seen? Bear in mind that these were simple men. Their lives were spent in the peace and solitude of those who live outdoors, leading and caring for their sheep with the unhurried style typical of shepherds. Suddenly their peaceful existence was interrupted by a scene of dramatic, supernatural proportions. An angel of the Lord appeared and the dazzling glory of God surrounded them! The angel calmed their fearful hearts and shared the good news of Christ with them. Even as he was still speaking, a multitude of the heavenly host appeared with him, proclaiming the wonders of the Most High.

With the lack of fuss common to those of humble station, they hurried to the place indicated to them and found the baby Jesus as they had been told. This second encounter must surely have built on the amazement they had felt in the fields. We can imagine many interruptions as perhaps they tripped over each other in attempting to share the details of that night. And all who heard were also filled with wonder.

This is often our reaction when faced with divine manifestations. Perhaps we have been granted a special visitation from the Lord concerning someone's life or seen Him miraculously touch a sick friend; or perhaps someone resisting the gospel has finally accepted the insistent invitation of Christ. Whatever the manifestation, we are left with a feeling of euphoria and enthusiasm.

Then the evangelist adds a brief comment to the shepherds' testimony: "But Mary treasured up all these things and pondered them in her heart." The word "but" helps us understand that Jesus' mother had adopted a posture contrasting with that of the shepherds. Can it be that she didn't experience feelings of wonder? I doubt it, since it is likely she was continually surprised by the way God was working in her life.

The difference in her reaction is that she added an attitude of meditation to the wonder she had experienced. That is, Mary recognized that behind the incredible manifestations of the Most High, there lay a spiritual reality to be understood. This comprehension will be granted to those willing to pause in the midst of events, to wait on the Lord for further revelation as they slowly ponder what has happened.

This is a mature attitude, worthy of imitation. Beyond our temporary enthusiasm, God calls us to meditate on the events and experiences we live through. It is through meditation that we glimpse the full dimension and richness of what we have been through.

Food for Thought

"Truths are concocted and ripened by meditation." (Thomas Manton)[9]

Sowing with Tears

Those who sow in tears will reap with songs of joy. He who goes out weeping, carrying seed to sow, will return with songs of joy, carrying sheaves with him. Psalm 126:5–6

In his book *God Tells the Man Who Cares*, the well known author A.W. Tozer observes, "The Bible was written in tears, and to tears it yields its best treasures. God has nothing to say to the frivolous man." Tozer identifies an important principle concerning spiritual matters: Tears have always been part of sharing deep intimacy with God. Most of us probably don't understand the reason for this; perhaps understanding is not necessary. It is enough to accept it as an unavoidable component of spiritual life.

If we look through the pages of Scripture, we quickly realize that countless heroes of the faith were accustomed to brokenness. Job wept bitterly before God in anguish at his affliction (Job 16:20). Joseph could not hold back tears when he saw his brothers again (Gen. 43:30). Hannah, Samuel's mother, wept disconsolately because of her barrenness (1 Sam. 1:7). When David found his city destroyed by the Amalekites, he cried until he had no strength left (1 Sam. 30:4); he also confessed that tears were frequently his food, day and night (Ps. 42:3). Elijah fled to the desert in such anguish that he sought death (1 Kings 19:4). King Hezekiah wept in great distress when his death was announced, and he was heard because of his tears (Isa. 38:5). Jeremiah has frequently been called the prophet of tears (Jer. 13:17). Jesus wept on various occasions, and the Word testifies that He was heard because of His reverent submission (Heb. 5:7). Paul served the Lord with humility and with many tears and trials (Acts 20:19).

Although we may not understand it very well, we know something happens in our hearts when we weep. An abundance of tears usually softens our soul—and how precious this is, since there is no obstacle that hinders our communion with God as much as a hard heart. When frustration is added to failure, it may be the point at which we abandon our effort to direct our own lives and admit before God our fragility and need. It is the beginning of something new. This is surely why Jesus declared, "Blessed are those who mourn, for they will be comforted" (Matt. 5:4).

Tears are not always the product of frustration; they can also indicate a heart which God has made sensitive to the Spirit's moving. This kind of weeping occurs over the things that break God's heart. Consider Christ's tears for Jerusalem (Luke 19:41) or John's over the unopened seal (Rev. 5:4). They sensed a spiritual reality of such magnitude that they wept before God.

Whatever their reason, for those who walk with the Lord, tears are the gateway to a deeper and more meaningful spiritual experience.

Food for Thought

Watchman Nee courageously said, "To keep our hand on the plough while wiping away our tears—that is Christianity." [10]

Absolute Sovereignty

So he sent men to capture him. But when they saw a group of prophets prophesying, with Samuel standing there as their leader, the Spirit of God came upon Saul's men and they also prophesied. 1 Samuel 19:20

This is one of many peculiar scenes we come across in the Scriptures. It is strange, because we can't quite grasp the real meaning of the events it describes.

Even so, it is worth brief reflection. Saul's hate for David had reached grotesque proportions. On at least two occasions, he had tried to pin him to the wall with his spear. He had given distinct orders to his men to capture the young shepherd from Bethlehem, but David always managed to elude them.

On this occasion Saul had been informed of David's whereabouts, and he immediately sent messengers to bring him back. But God's Spirit came upon them, and they began to prophesy with Samuel and the prophets. This scene was repeated three times; each time the Spirit of God seized the messengers. In the end, Saul decided to apprehend David himself. By this time the king must have been furious with the apparent "incompetence" of his men. When Saul arrived, however, the Spirit of God came also upon him, and he prophesied for a whole day and night. He could do absolutely nothing to prevent the situation; neither could he carry out his evil plans to take the life of the young Israelite who had aroused such jealousy in him.

I will venture to make two simple observations on what took place. First, each of the messengers—and the king himself—prophesied, but this did not make them prophets. This distinction is important, because we are often inclined to confuse the works with the person. We believe that anyone who does God's work has God's approval. But the Lord can use whoever He likes, even a donkey if necessary. The fact that He does this does not convert the donkey into a consecrated servant of the Lord! To be a minister in the house of God, much more is demanded than the ability to do good things for Him.

Second, human plans will not prosper if God does not authorize them—even plans for evil. We often believe that the Enemy is on the loose and does as he pleases, that we have no way of defending ourselves against his strategies. This story clearly reveals that the Enemy advances only as far as he is allowed and not one inch further. God's authority extends even to the lives of those who plan evil day and night.

Food for Thought

"He brings princes to naught and reduces the rulers of this world to nothing. No sooner are they planted, no sooner are they sown, no sooner do they take root in the ground, than he blows on them and they wither, and a whirlwind sweeps them away like chaff" (Isa. 40:23–24).

True Worshipers

Yet a time is coming and has now come when the true worshipers will worship the Father in spirit and truth, for they are the kind of worshipers the Father seeks. John 4:23

This scene holds special value for those who desire to know God better. It is one of the few times Jesus reveals the desires of His Father in such forthright terms. We can't help but feel baffled by His revelation. In the middle of a discussion on the "forms" of worship—something absolutely transitory, but which has nevertheless, kept us bickering all too long—Christ utters a phrase that suddenly reveals the true "essence" of worship.

One aspect of His declaration immediately draws our attention. There are two kinds of worshipers: true and false. It goes without saying that a false worshiper is not really a worshiper at all, but someone who simply plays the role. This obliges us to think about our own worship experience. Do we really worship? Or do we simply pretend to worship during the moments set aside for it in our meetings?

Simply thinking about this highlights the difference between the two kinds of worshippers. False worshipers consider worship an activity. That is, they put aside for the moment whatever they were doing in order to concentrate on the business of worshiping the Father. They are just going through the motions and mouthing the words that fit the activity. Perhaps they have seen others do it and have no difficulty imitating them. In any case, to their minds worship is just one of many activities associated with the practice of piety.

When Christ speaks of the true worshiper, He is not referring to the person's activities; He is talking about what that person *is*. We can describe someone according to their origin, saying they are Greek, Polish or Spanish, and this will be understood not as an activity, but as part of their identity. In the same way, Christ identifies certain people within the Kingdom by the faithful heart they possess. These are real worshipers of the Father.

A worshiper cannot live in the flesh or in sin. Worship is, after all, the result of a dramatic, penetrating encounter with God in which fleshly things have become abominable. The Father longs for true worshipers who will worship in spirit and truth. These are people who combine the spiritual reality produced by the Spirit of God (for nobody can relate to God except through the Spirit) and the purification of the inner man which comes through the cleansing power of the truth. In other words, their entire beings reflect the relationship in which they are profoundly immersed.

Food for Thought

How would you describe yourself as a worshiper? Is your worship limited to activities in public meetings? How can you further develop your identity as a worshiper?

Invisible Blessings

The Queen of the South will rise at the judgment with the men of this generation and condemn them; for she came from the ends of the earth to listen to Solomon's wisdom, and now one greater than Solomon is here. Luke 11:31

Enormous crowds accompanied Jesus. Many were inquisitive, and indicated they might be willing to follow Him. They only lacked a sign from heaven to be sure He was really the Messiah. Jesus told them, "This is a wicked generation. It asks for a miraculous sign, but none will be given it except the sign of Jonah" (Luke 11:29).

Asking for a sign was no more than an excuse. People who disbelieve God will not change their minds even when confronted with the most dramatic and convincing evidence of His intervention in human affairs. Such were the Israelites who came out of Egypt, an obstinate and capricious generation that didn't believe even when they saw what no one had ever seen.

Faith is essentially a spiritual response to the Spirit within us. Despite this, we often convince ourselves that our faith would be stronger if we had more evidence of God's working in our lives. We feel that all the effort to believe falls on us, and it would be great to have "a little help" for our faith.

But the Lord wanted to show these people something different. The signs they were looking for already existed; they just couldn't see them. As He had done many times before, Christ used Gentiles as examples to illustrate a correct attitude toward faith. He mentioned the people of Nineveh who believed Jonah's message, though he had communicated God's word with ill grace. Still, they believed because they possessed the spiritual openness necessary for faith.

In today's passage Jesus also mentioned the Queen of the South, that is, the Queen of Sheba, who visited Solomon (1Kings 10:1–13). This woman was queen of an African nation, accustomed to being served however she wanted. Setting aside her royal privileges, she journeyed a very long way to appreciate for herself the wisdom of the legendary king of Israel. The Ninevites and the Queen of the South had something in common: a spiritual openness noticeably absent in the Israelites. We should observe too that neither the Ninevites nor the Queen of Sheba possessed the rich spiritual heritage the people of God enjoyed. Those surrounding Jesus had access to the most extraordinary sign ever seen by humankind. However, among those who had most we also find the greatest lack of discernment.

This is true of us also. We are often obsessed with finding something we think we really need. Our obstinacy blinds us from perceiving or enjoying those blessings already around us and which are very often greater than what we so desperately seek.

Food for Thought

Augustine wrote, "God does not expect us to submit our faith to him without reason, but the very limits of our reason make faith a necessity." [11]

The Foolishness of a King

The king was distressed, but because of his oaths and his dinner guests, he ordered that her request be granted and had John beheaded in the prison. Matthew 14:9–10

It was God's wish that John should die, but in what a tragic way it took place! His destiny was decided in a moment of partying, when decisions are ruled by emotions. Herod, impelled by the graceful movements of Herodias' daughter, found the perfect way to ingratiate his guests; the proclamation of his generous offer couldn't fail to impress those present. But the exaggerated form of his vow reveals that he said the first thing that came into his head, without measuring the consequences of his words. In this way, then, John died the victim of an unruly, perverse governor influenced during a birthday party.

The desire of people to please and impress others is immensely profound! This need to "look good," to make an impact on people with our behavior in order to win favor and appreciation, springs from the very essence of what we are as human beings. We all hunger for recognition and the value and consideration of those around us. In the case of ministers who have been wounded because of having little or no affection in their homes, this need can become an obsession. There are not enough hours in the day or days in the week to serve their congregations, which in turn show some gratitude and appreciation, thus partly satisfying these pastors' needs.

Herod's story illustrates how entangled we can get if we allow these desires to rule our actions. The king was saddened by what he had said because he suddenly realized it had been a crazy promise to make. His wish to protect his image in front of his guests, however, was stronger than the momentary discomfort caused by his foolish actions. To go back on his oath would have required the kind of courage such men do not possess.

In our enthusiasm to please, we often commit ourselves to things we cannot accomplish. We will probably never get involved in something as serious as the tetrarch's pledge, but promises made this way always bring complications. We end up in unwelcome or even disagreeable situations. This is why keeping our word is often accompanied by complaints and regrets. Even more important than this, over time impulsive words tend to erode our authority as leaders because many of them cannot be fulfilled. We run the risk of becoming known as people whose word carries little weight.

Food for Thought

When Jesus taught that we should give our word without the need to swear by anything (Matt. 5:34), He was referring to simplicity in our speech. This not only includes economy in the use of words, but also more deliberation and thoughtfulness when we communicate with others. In this way we will avoid becoming entangled by the words of our mouths.

A Love Like No Other Love

Who shall separate us from the love of Christ? Shall trouble or hardship or persecution or famine or nakedness or danger or sword? Romans 8:35

I used to have great difficulty understanding this passage because it seemed to contradict my experience as a Christian, as well as what I observed in many others of the faith. How could Paul possibly make this statement when on a day-to-day basis a whole host of factors competes with our love for the Lord? These not only interfere with our desire to follow Him, but often move us in the opposite direction of His desire for our lives.

The trouble was that I was viewing this verse from the wrong angle, trying to understand it as a statement of *my* devotion to God. Such a perspective reveals our deep conviction that we are the center of our own spiritual pilgrimage. Most of us secretly believe it is *our* activity that keeps our life in Christ vigorous and exciting. My confusion with this passage disappeared when I understood that Paul was not declaring our own fragile and fluctuating expressions of devotion, but rather the eternal love of the Father toward His children.

The elements Paul used to describe what could potentially separate us from God share one characteristic in common: They refer to sufferings that sorely test our faith—hardship, persecution, hunger, poverty, danger and death.

Why did Paul choose these particular conditions when talking about God's love? The almost universal response of Christians in the midst of intense pain is to believe that God has abandoned or forgotten them. Consider the response of Gideon to the visiting angel (Judg. 6:13) or the reaction of the Israelites when their escape route was blocked by the Red Sea (Exod. 14:11–12). David speaks for generations of hurting believers when he bluntly asks God, "Why have you forgotten me? Why must I go about mourning, oppressed by the enemy?" (Ps. 42:9). In our anguish we are sorely tempted to question God's love and commitment to us.

The apostle states that not even the most extreme afflictions can extinguish God's love. You and I may occasionally "feel" He has left us, especially when overwhelmed by intense grief. But feelings are notoriously unreliable as a means of gauging reality.

Paul's declaration is foundational to our faith. Those who cease doubting the constancy of God's love, even when in great agony, will experience the greatest degree of spiritual fulfillment. Faith in such a life is built on the unshakeable conviction that the Father's love for us—unwavering, unceasing and unrelenting—is as real as the very ground we walk on.

Food for Thought

"For I am convinced that neither death nor life, neither angels nor demons, neither the present nor the future, nor any powers, neither height nor depth, nor anything else in all creation, will be able to separate us from the love of God that is in Christ Jesus our Lord" (Rom. 8:38–39).

Sadness with Promise

So the king asked me, "Why does your face look so sad when you are not ill? This can be nothing but sadness of heart." I was very much afraid, but I said to the king, "May the king live forever! Why should my face not look sad when the city where my fathers are buried lies in ruins, and its gates have been destroyed by fire?" Nehemiah 2:2–3

The first chapter of this book tells of Nehemiah's meeting with Hanani, who had returned from Jerusalem. Nehemiah, anxious to know the state of things in his homeland, asked for a report on the Jews who had escaped the exile. Hanani told him, "Those who survived the exile and are back in the province are in great trouble and disgrace. The wall of Jerusalem is broken down, and its gates have been burned with fire" (Neh. 1:3). This report provoked great sorrow in Nehemiah, who broke down and wept.

Just like Nehemiah, we live in times when bad news abounds. Around the world violence, poverty and injustice are on the increase. Not a day passes without the consequences of these evils reported on the news. In addition to this, as leaders we are in daily contact with the most anguishing manifestations of evil in human beings. The difficulties we come across daily tend to burden our hearts with a sadness which gives way to discouragement, despair and resignation. How often we have attended meetings where the tragedy and sadness of others served only to feed our morbid habit of dwelling on the details of what we have heard. As long as we feed this "mood" with new horror stories, we can almost visibly see people deflating before our eyes as feelings of despair take over their hearts. In doing this we repeat the model we see constantly around us in which discussing the awfulness of things has almost become a pastime.

What was different about Nehemiah is that he did something with his discouragement. His sadness brought him into God's presence, and he poured out his anguish before the throne of grace. The process of pouring his heart out to the Lord prepared his soul to move as God directed.

We need to incorporate this response into our own lives.

Our sadness can be used as a vehicle for something productive, perhaps providing a means for the Lord's intervention in areas of society where His healing is most needed. What we see and hear can motivate us to seek the face of our good heavenly Father. He has the correct perspective on things and knows what action should be taken. He may also have instructions to give us with respect to the situation. We must stop focusing on the problem and start thinking about the answer. What we desperately need in our world today are people with solutions.

Food for Thought

"Cast your cares on the LORD and he will sustain you; he will never let the righteous fall" (Ps. 55:22).

Living in Tension

Then Moses said, "Now show me your glory." And the LORD said, "I will cause all my goodness to pass in front of you, and I will proclaim my name, the LORD, in your presence. I will have mercy on whom I will have mercy, and I will have compassion on whom I will have compassion. But," he said, "you cannot see my face, for no one may see me and live."
Exodus 33:18–20

The spiritual world is full of opposites which exist in perfect tension. An example is the tension that exists between faith and works. We are clearly called to live by faith. However, as James points out, "faith by itself, if it is not accompanied by action, is dead" (James 2:17). Similarly, works not prompted by a living, effective faith are nothing more than human works.

Another contrast has to do with effort and grace. Consider for a moment the apparent contradictions when Paul exhorts Timothy, "You then, my son, be strong in the grace that is in Christ Jesus" (2 Tim. 2:1). Grace is what God supplies to counteract our weaknesses, while effort speaks of our own disciplined contribution to the work given us by the Lord. If effort exists alone then we obviously think we are the ones who get things done. On the other hand, if grace exists alone we develop an attitude of spiritual indolence. For this Dietrich Bonhoeffer coined the phrase "cheap grace," namely, grace that does not take into account the cost of what has been received.

Today's passage highlights another contrast which lies directly at the heart of our spiritual experience. It refers to experiencing both satisfaction and dissatisfaction at the same time. Moses had experienced moments of great intensity and intimacy with God. We are told, "The LORD would speak to Moses face to face, as a man speaks with his friend" (Exod. 33:11). Not many men can claim the same. In today's passage, however, we find Moses asking God for something even more dramatic: "Show me your glory!"

His request pinpoints a tension we must learn to live with. In one respect, our experience of God satisfies the deepest desires of our hearts, and when we are walking with Him, we feel a spiritual delight impossible to describe with words. But these experiences also awaken in us a hunger for deeper things. We become aware of how much we need Him. The feeling that we are lacking something only increases, which spurs us to continue searching.

Food for Thought

Living with these contradictions is a challenge for us. If we don't accept the reality that our thirst increases alongside our satisfaction, we may think our spiritual experience has been useless, since we never find all we are looking for. But our thirst is from God. This is how He calls us into His presence to drink of the water of life. If we didn't continue longing, we would not continue to know God's working in our lives!

Professional Ministers

Yet I hold this against you: You have forsaken your first love. Revelation 2:4

The letter John wrote to the angel of the church in Ephesus is not by any account condemnatory. He congratulates the church on their work, which they had carried out with great patience and perseverance. They had developed a praiseworthy intolerance to sin. This congregation had faced those who claimed to be apostles, but weren't, and denounced them as false ministers of the gospel. As well as this, the Ephesian Christians had patiently borne the trials that came to them as a result of following Christ. "In everything," stated Christ through His servant John, "you have persevered and have endured hardships for my name, and have not grown weary" (Rev. 2:3). In the midst of all these worthy qualities, however, is inserted this short phrase: "Yet I hold this against you: You have forsaken your first love." Unexpectedly, we discover that this impressive congregation was lacking the most important ingredient: passion for the One they served.

In this the church reflects something common to most human relationships. Consider the path many marriages follow. The couple starts out full of passion and love, so that the relationship is the very focus of all they do and think. There are not enough hours to enjoy each other's company and discover the hidden treasures to be found in any intimate relationship. But as the years pass, the couple loses their passion and falls into ordered routines in which the salient characteristic is habit.

This experience is so common that we might be tempted to believe the church's experience is normal. How can passion be kept alive after 20 or 30 years? Nevertheless, the Lord calls the church to remember the height from which they have fallen and exhorts them to return to their first deeds. In other words, He asks them to recover the passion-filled life they had in their early days with Him.

Recovering this passion is not as complicated as we think. When the continuity of a relationship is affected, the missing ingredient is time. We become so preoccupied and absorbed with our many daily projects that the relationship languishes. In order to keep a relationship alive, it is absolutely essential to make daily investments in it. This dedication is the distinct result of commitment to the other person—a commitment with no exception clauses. Romance and passion can only be maintained if we insist on celebrating our affection daily. We can do this by means of gifts, gestures of service and abundant expressions of appreciation for the One we love.

Food for Thought

Would the Lord say you have lost your first love? What things did you do with Christ when you were first converted that you have stopped doing? Which of these should you reincorporate into your life?

The Road to Repentance

"When he came to his senses, he said, 'How many of my father's hired men have food to spare, and here I am starving to death! I will set out and go back to my father and say to him: Father, I have sinned against heaven and against you. I am no longer worthy to be called your son; make me like one of your hired men.'" Luke 15:17–19

The parable of the prodigal son is one of the most beautiful illustrations of God's merciful love, in this case poured out on two sons who didn't understand their father's compassionate heart. In today's passage we find the younger of these two sitting among pigs, weary, hungry and forgotten by everyone. His partying days are over, and despair looms wherever he looks.

The passage tells us that in this moment the young man "came to his senses." This expression could be applied to someone who was awaking from anesthesia. It helps us understand that during this time he was not really conscious of what had been happening to his life. In fact, this is exactly the effect sin has on us. It deadens our senses so we don't recognize the foolishness of our ways. The first step of repentance comes when we recover this lost consciousness. Suddenly we realize the error of our ways. Light illuminates our darkened understanding and we see things with new eyes. This young man glimpsed the reality of his situation and saw clearly how far he had fallen in abandoning his father's house.

The second step came when the young man understood that his road to recovery inevitably led back home. He came to see his health and well-being would be found in relationship with his father. Repentance is not only recognizing our wrong; it inevitably leads to a new journey that brings communion and intimacy with God. This journey should put an end to the silence and estrangement in our lives.

It is in the third step, however, that we detect an error in the young man's thinking. He worked out a plan to correct his life: "Make me like one of your hired men." It is precisely here that repentance is often derailed. We recognize our wrong, and we draw near to the Father, but we bring with us a plan to fix everything. God has no need of our help in undoing what we have done. He has His own methods that are effective and sure. All we have to do is let Him work. The Father is the solution to our problems. We need to draw close to Him—not to speak, but to listen. If we have to do something, He will show us. If He doesn't say anything, then we should enjoy the hugs and kisses He gives, knowing that in our Father's house we will always be welcome.

Food for Thought

***"Repentance and faith are gifts we have received, not goals we have reached."* (*Anonymous*)**

A Servant's Prayer

"Now, O Lord my God, you have made your servant king in place of my father David. But I am only a little child and do not know how to carry out my duties. Your servant is here among the people you have chosen, a great people, too numerous to count or number. So give your servant a discerning heart to govern your people and to distinguish between right and wrong. For who is able to govern this great people of yours?" 1 Kings 3:7–9

Solomon was still young when God appeared to him in a dream and said, "Ask for whatever you want me to give you" (I Kings 3:5). I am sure he could have asked for anything, and God would have granted it—for unlike us, the Lord is faithful to keep His promises.

What would we have asked for if given a similar offer? Solomon's answer is amazing not only for his depth of vision, but also for the marked contrast with the mean requests of our own prayers. This could well serve as a model for those in positions of responsibility in God's house.

First, Solomon was aware that his position was not due to his own efforts or his qualities as a man. The king knew that God had chosen him and made him king.

Second, Solomon was absolutely certain that he lacked the ability to accomplish the task ahead. He stated plainly, "I am only a little child and do not know how to carry out my duties." It is so refreshing to find someone who honestly confesses his limitations and recognizes his lack of experience to carry out his calling! We should know that our weaknesses are the principal means by which God's grace is expressed in our lives. Nonetheless, we spend a lot of time and effort trying to hide them!

Third, Solomon knew that the people he reigned over were the people of God. They were not a people to be ruled according to his own criteria; they had been bought by the Most High. He must be careful and respectful, as we are with anything that is not ours. How great it would be if we as leaders could remember that the people we are among are not ours, but the Lord's! The day will come when we will have to give account for each of them, down to the very smallest.

Finally, Solomon knew that he could fulfill this responsibility only if God equipped him with the necessary gifts and abilities. He would be unable to do it in his own strength. He needed power from above and asked, "Give your servant a discerning heart to govern your people and to distinguish between right and wrong." He was not looking for fame or recognition. He only sought the abilities necessary to please God.

Food for Thought

Solomon's prayer is truly inspiring. Would you dare to make it your own for the ministry that has been entrusted to you?

The Crisis of the Righteous

When I tried to understand all this, it was oppressive to me till I entered the sanctuary of God; then I understood their final destiny. Psalm 73:16–17

The psalmist had sunk into a deep crisis of faith, something most of us face at some point in our pilgrimage. Perhaps his depression came from a severe personal trial. Or perhaps he was suffering persecution as a result of his desire to honor God. Whatever his circumstances, he looked at the ungodly and saw that things were easier for them than for the righteous.

He observed that the ungodly were not only prosperous, but had no pain in their death. Their vigor knew no bounds, and they didn't have to work hard all their lives as most do. With an ease that smacks of mockery, they laid hold of the comforts and wealth we struggle so hard to obtain. And as if this were not enough, they displayed an intolerably arrogant attitude, showing off their situation and looking with scorn on those who struggled to subsist day after day.

It's no surprise the psalmist was in crisis! The more he reflected, the more indignant he felt. *All my effort and faithfulness— to what end is it? These others achieve comfort without going through all the anguish of trying to be righteous.* His obedient investment was not reflected in their meager results. Completely frustrated, he exclaimed, "Surely in vain have I kept my heart pure; in vain have I washed my hands in innocence" (Ps. 73:13).

It is more than likely we have struggled with such thoughts. It often seems we are achieving nothing with our devotion. We go through storms, suffer weaknesses and make mistakes. Our efforts to honor the Lord seem only to have added complications to our lives. Our honesty is condemned by those around us. Our holiness is ridiculed. Our commitment to service receives reproach and ungratefulness. Who among us has not been tempted at some time to quit?

The answer to our questions is not found in analyzing our surroundings. Like the psalmist, the more we think about them, the more unjust our lives seem to be. But the psalmist shows the way: He entered God's sanctuary. There in the Lord's presence, he understood that his perspective was seriously limited by his humanity. God raised him to a higher level, focused on eternity. Our lives are not limited to our brief time on earth. The psalmist came to understand "their final destiny," and he saw how close he had come to a fatal decision. Thus, he exclaimed with gratitude, "My feet had almost slipped; I had nearly lost my foothold" (Ps. 73:2). But the Lord brought him back from the abyss.

Food for Thought

This psalm teaches an important principle. Quandaries, doubts and worries about this life are more easily resolved in the presence of the Most High. Don't hesitate to seek His face. Make it your first option!

Hunger for God

Then you will call upon me and come and pray to me, and I will listen to you. You will seek me and find me when you seek me with all your heart. Jeremiah 29:12–13

This text is part of a letter from Jeremiah to the Jewish exiles in Babylon. There had arisen among them the inevitable messengers of ease who said that in no time they would be back in Judah. Jeremiah advised the people to "put down roots" in Babylon because their stay there would be long. The prophecy contained, however, the promise that God would be found when the people laid aside their religious habits and sought Him sincerely and wholeheartedly.

Despite the historical context, this is a text which could well be directed at today's church. It is not referring to how wicked God's people are, but rather recognizing humanity's basic inclination toward religiosity. By religiosity we mean the activities we carry out in exchange for God's favor—as opposed to relationship with Him. We fulfill the demands required by religion and the Supreme Being blesses us.

This way of thinking is not characteristic of any particular group, although it is more noticeable in some. Sadly, we have to recognize that many activities in our own congregations are built on this foundation. Our passion lasts only as long as the meeting we are in. Later we go back to our boring routines in which everything carries on as usual.

"You will seek me and find me when you seek me with all your heart." This phrase says it all. It holds the promise of an encounter with God which, we dare to believe, could even contain some of the dramatic elements experienced by great heroes of the faith: Abraham, Moses, David, Isaiah, Peter, Paul or John. Without dwelling on details, the prophecy affirms that the days of imagining we are in touch with God—the days of fishing around for complicated explanations to prove His presence—will come to an end. Life will be different, entirely changed, and our experience of God will pervade all things.

Who will be granted this? It is for those who seek with all their hearts. This phrase rules out that kind of search that lasts hardly a few minutes or which is over as soon as our gatherings disperse. We are speaking here of those consumed with an overwhelming passion for God. These are people who "hunger and thirst for righteousness" (Matt. 5:6). The psalmist calls out, "My soul thirsts for you, my body longs for you, in a dry and weary land where there is no water" (Ps. 63:1). A full experience of God is reserved for these people.

Food for Thought

Where are those who groan after the Lord today? Where are those who find no rest because they are continually calling out for a visitation from God? Could it be that the revival we so long for is delayed because we are not yet sufficiently desperate for the Lord's visitation?

Anointing

"The Spirit of the Lord is on me, because he has anointed me to preach good news to the poor. He has sent me to proclaim freedom for the prisoners and recovery of sight for the blind, to release the oppressed." Luke 4:18

In our culture we hold the firm conviction that how we do things makes the difference between success and failure. When things go wrong, we analyze every detail of what we have done to find our mistake. For those of us in the church, this way of thinking is spread through endless seminars and workshops where we are given steps to more effective leadership, better team relations or greater congregational growth. A typical example of this is our captivation with cell groups. Crowds of teachers have appeared, entirely dedicated to explaining the processes and conditions of starting cells in the local church, promising explosive growth. Countless leaders attend these classes and faithfully go through the steps, but don't see the promised results.

Today's reflection touches on the subject of anointing. The passage Christ read in a Nazarene synagogue mentions a list of works commended to Him: preaching, healing, setting free . . . . All these have to do with the practical implementation of ministry. But the key is not in the activities; it is in the anointing of the Spirit. Two pastors can carry out the same activities in their congregations. In one there is no visible result of the leader's efforts; in the other there is. Where does the difference lie? It is in the anointing of the servant.

What does this anointing consist of? A number of groups in our midst have tried to convince us that they possess God's anointing and can pass it on as they choose. Others, who give the concept a looser meaning, say that anyone in a position to teach or preach is anointed. It seems obvious, however, that anointing is not directed by men, but something granted by God. In biblical times anointing was a rite by which someone or something was set apart for special service. In the case of the kings and prophets, anointing was accompanied by a visitation of the Spirit which equipped the person for the work of God.

This divine equipping is greatly lacking in our ministries. We have methods, but we are lacking the power which comes through the action of the Spirit. As happened when the disciples failed to deliver the epileptic boy, the error is not in the way we minister, but in the lack of prayer and fasting through which we obtain God's enabling.

Food for Thought

This divine authority is visible in the lives of men and women who have great intimacy with God. There are no shortcuts here. The church groans for a new generation of ministers whose credentials are not according to their work, but to their intimate communion with the Father. On such people rests the anointing from on High!

Praying in the Spirit

And pray in the Spirit on all occasions with all kinds of prayers and requests. With this in mind, be alert and always keep on praying for all the saints.' Ephesians 6:18

This verse is obviously talking about much more than speaking in tongues, although that is one manifestation of the Spirit. The words accompanying the apostle's exhortation—"prayers . . . requests . . . be alert and always keep on praying"—speak of an intensity that goes beyond the ordinary experience of most of our prayers. Our method often consists of presenting a list of requests to God, hoping it will please Him to bless us in these things.

Let's reflect for a moment on the phrase "in the Spirit." What is the difference between a prayer delivered with our passion and one offered in the Spirit? Just asking the question may begin to show us the difference. The prayer built on our own passion may be very profound and intense, but it has just that problem—it is ours! But the prayer spoken in the Spirit is one in which the leading role belongs to the Spirit. In other words, the One who mobilizes us to offer up petitions and expressions of praise toward God is the Lord Himself. It is, in the words of Richard Foster, "Christ praying through us."[1]

Consider this in light of Paul's declaration: "In the same way, the Spirit helps us in our weakness. We do not know what we ought to pray for, but the Spirit himself intercedes for us with groans that words cannot express" (Rom. 8:26). Two concepts are clear in this verse. First, our praying should be carried out from a position of weakness, not knowing how we should pray or what to ask for. But in most of our prayers we act as if we know what to say, as if we were completely sure of our requests. Praying in the Spirit, then, means we should be much more cautious about asking for things or even about speaking in His presence. He invites us to listen so the Spirit can lead us as to the petition we should make.

Second, Paul informs us that no matter how well-arranged our prayers are, the Spirit translates them into something intelligible to the Father. Does this mean that the Father can't understand us? Not at all! What we are saying is that the Spirit takes our very human prayers and converts them into something much more in harmony with the Father's desires and burdens. He interprets the feelings in our hearts, although we cannot put them into words or even understand them ourselves.

Just like all activities in the lives of the children of God, prayer should be a fruit of the Spirit's working. Will we be able to control our own impulses sufficiently to make room for Him?

Food for Thought

Henry Blackaby wrote, "A person may be a leader without the working of the Spirit, but He will never be a spiritual leader." [2]

More than Just a Fancy

David longed for water and said, "Oh, that someone would get me a drink of water from the well near the gate of Bethlehem!" 2 Samuel 23:15

David was at war with the Philistines when this event took place. Surrounded by the brave men who always accompanied him, the king simply expressed a desire for fresh water from one of Bethlehem's wells. His wish, however, mobilized three of these men to go down to the city, risking their lives to bring back the water the king was longing for.

The courage of these men was unbelievable! The fact that they were willing to run such a risk to fetch some water offers an eloquent testimony to their loyalty and affection for David. A leader does not earn this kind of respect easily. It is the result of deep commitment to people in which love is valued above plans, in which people know their lives are important to the leader. For a pastor this is achieved when interest in the people who serve in the church supersedes interest in the ministries they are carrying out. But very often people realize that the pastor is only interested in filling "vacancies" in the congregation's ministries—looking for Sunday school teachers, singers for the choir or a leader for the young people's group. Once these areas are covered, this kind of pastor shows little interest in the lives of those serving. David was a leader for whom his men were willing to give their lives.

This incident serves as a warning to those of us in positions of ministry. When those in authority are respected and recognized, they will exercise greater influence in peoples' lives than we sometimes recognize. Their words carry weight that the words of others don't. When they speak, people listen with special attention and interpret what they say differently than what their friends, relatives or acquaintances say.

The wise leader understands that even things spoken lightly are taken seriously by the people. It is the price of being in a position of authority. Of course, this influence on others is open to abuse, but mature leaders will carefully measure all they say. We don't know how our words may be taken by those who admire us!

Food for Thought

A leader is always being observed—even in those moments we don't consider spiritual, or when we are not officially acting in our capacities as leaders.

11 August The Blessing of Counselors

For lack of guidance a nation falls, but many advisers make victory sure. Proverbs 11:14

Today's verse invites us to reflect on two possible outcomes in the history of a people: defeat or victory. The difference between these outcomes lies not in the peoples' leadership, but in the counsel their leaders have received. The presence of counselors indicates openness by those in authority to opinions that may enrich their perspective. This does not free a leader from the need to make decisions; but an abundance of counselors helps a leader make these decisions while in possession of all the relevant information. This will allow every aspect of pertinent matters to be carefully considered.

This is why a good leader is always surrounded by wise counselors. But there is a tendency among those in church leadership to act alone. There is no doubt that this kind of leadership is less complicated than the style which requires listening to and carefully considering others' opinions. However, without the benefit of group counsel, people are exposed to the whims and limitations of a single person, and the end result is that the congregation suffers from the same weaknesses the leader has. This style is vulnerable to the power abuse typical of those who are not required to give account of themselves to anyone.

In order to work well with counselors, certain conditions must be met. First, the leader must have a teachable spirit. When leaders think nobody can teach them anything—believing their very position as leader makes them the authority on any subject related to the church—then they will not value the opinions of others. In their hearts they believe nobody understands things as well as they do, and this will block all productive communication with others.

Second, leaders must surround themselves with people who can offer a variety of opinions and views on church matters. Many leaders have formed a group of counselors to advise them, but they only select people who think exactly as they do. Naturally, in this group there will be unanimity because everyone agrees with the leader! Perhaps there is an unspoken feeling in this group that the only people who will be heard are those who hold the same opinions as the pastor.

Third, in order to take full advantage of the counselors, leaders should listen very carefully and show appreciation for peoples' opinions, even when the ideas go against their own. They will earn the respect of their people when the congregation feels they are part of a team in which ideas can be freely expressed—whether they coincide with the leader's ideas or not. The richness of having diversity in a group of counselors is that the group perspective always offers a more realistic perspective of things.

Food for Thought

"Good leaders never give their leadership away, but they share the visibility and responsibility of leading." (Calvin Miller)[3]

Submission

Submit to one another out of reverence for Christ. Ephesians 5:21

Submission is a matter of great importance for a disciple of Christ. Within the church there is much ignorance about this subject, and it is also true that in the name of submission terrible abuse has occurred. It is good, therefore, to reflect for a moment on this concept.

Today's verse encourages us to practice mutual submission. This is different from the idea of many leaders that submission is a one way street. In other words, it is something that church members do toward those in authority, while they themselves need not submit to anyone. Paul's exhortation is very clear: "Submit to one another."

To give practical examples of this, Paul chose three kinds of human relationship in which reciprocity exists to explain the attitude we should have. These three relationships are within the structures of marriage, family and work. In each case submission takes different forms, but it is equally binding for all involved. And so, transferring these instructions to the church, we can say that a pastor should not insist that submission is the sole responsibility of the members. Leaders must also submit to the people they serve.

It is interesting to note that the worst abuse in terms of submission is perpetrated by leaders who feel they need not give account of their behavior to anyone. These people constantly demand submission from the people they have been called to shepherd. One of the fundamental principles of submission is that it cannot be demanded—it is something to be freely offered as a gift. We cannot force others to submit through angry rebukes, by denouncing rebellious behavior or by constantly reminding them that the Bible demands submission from the people of God. Submission is earned by living in such a way that others are attracted to placing their lives in our care. If we look through the pages of the Gospels, we will not find a single example of Christ reminding His disciples to submit to Him. Nevertheless, they understood that submission was indispensable to a healthy relationship with Him.

The apostle points out a second principle in today's verse. Submission should be done in the fear of God. We often don't yield because we don't see qualities in the other person that we feel merit our submission. Paul clarifies that when it comes to submission, we should not look at the other person, but rather yield in the fear of the Lord. What should motivate us is our desire to please our Father. The Lord has worked intensely in the lives of all His great servants to teach them submission. Without learning this lesson it is impossible to please Him. Even the Son of God submitted absolutely to the will of the Father.

Food for Thought

"Scripture is not attempting to set forth a series of hierarchichal relationships but to communicate to us an inner attitude of mutual subordination." (Richard Foster)[4]

13 August | The Overflow of the Heart

You brood of vipers, how can you who are evil say anything good? For out of the overflow of the heart the mouth speaks. The good man brings good things out of the good stored up in him, and the evil man brings evil things out of the evil stored up in him.
Matthew 12:34–35

Anyone who has been around for a few years knows that words have tremendous potential. On one hand, they can be a means of blessing those around us. The right word spoken at an opportune moment can really encourage someone who is feeling low. With words we can strengthen, confront, exhort and correct—all tasks related to the ministry of shaping lives. But the destructive power of words is also known to us and is no less powerful. We know people who have been systematically humiliated by comments from peers, parents or workmates. Even though the hurt came through nothing more than words, it has left deep wounds in people's lives.

Life has taught us, therefore, to be cautious when we speak—although the tongue is terribly resistant to discipline. But Christ shows us there is a simpler way to sanctify the mouth. The tongue, in a sense, is only the spokesperson for the heart, which is the real source of trouble. Though we must still use care in our speech, the wise person will concentrate effort on the heart more than on the tongue.

When we speak of something we shouldn't, we are simply revealing our heart. People who are critical possess legalistic hearts that habitually measure others' actions. People who always see the negative side of things have ungrateful hearts. Those who always justify their actions have hearts full of insecurity and fear. People whose conversation revolves around money have the god mammon enthroned in their hearts. For those of us who serve in the church, it is important to take note of peoples' words; they will help us know where the real problems lie.

So the challenge for each of us is to fill our hearts with good things. This will season our conversation in such a way that those who listen will be blessed and edified. To do this we must pay close attention to our words, being absolutely honest with ourselves. What does our speech reveal about our hearts? What topics dominate our conversation? How do we behave toward others when we speak to them? The answers will give us valuable clues as to the real content of our heart. Knowing what is inside, we can draw close to the Lord and ask Him to begin in us the work of transformation we so need. As we identify and confess our wrongs, the Lord will have opportunity to begin replacing these with what is good and righteous.

Food for Thought

"Therefore, get rid of all moral filth and the evil that is so prevalent and humbly accept the word planted in you, which can save you" (James 1:21).

Being like Children

And he said: "I tell you the truth, unless you change and become like little children, you will never enter the kingdom of heaven." Matthew 18:3

This declaration made by Christ answered a question from the disciples: "Who is the greatest in the kingdom of heaven?" (Matt. 18:1). This was not the only time they discussed the subject of greatness. At times differences arose among them about their desired positions and responsibilities in the coming kingdom of God.

The Master could have given a detailed description of the kind they expected to hear. But He didn't. He simply took a child—never far from the adults constantly flocking to Him—and placed the little one in their midst. Pointing at the child, He said, "Unless you change and become like little children, you will never enter the kingdom of heaven."

We immediately see an apparent contradiction in Christ's words. With no more than a glance at the child, perhaps a little girl, we see no greatness. She did not carry on her shoulders the responsibility of weighty human decisions. She didn't need to provide for her family each day. She did not participate in discussions related to matters of the nation. Even her size made her easily unnoticeable. Christ, however, didn't see her as others did. He noticed those qualities that adults have lost and which need to be recovered. Bear with me as we reflect on some of these.

The first thing children do in the morning is play. They aren't worried or weary because they haven't slept well; they wake up and simply begin to enjoy the day. Neither do children worry about what they will need that day. They don't spend hours thinking about where lunch will come from or who will prepare it. They play calmly because they know others are looking after their needs.

When they need something, they approach an adult and ask; children don't beat around the bush or mince words. They ask, confident that the adult can meet their needs. When they get hurt, they immediately run to mom or dad to receive the necessary consolation. Sometimes all they need is a hug or a kiss to make the tears disappear, and happiness returns. Children don't remember bad things that have happened to them. They don't bear grudges or look for revenge as adults do. They can be disciplined by their parents, and within a few minutes are back to their play.

Children also have an amazing ability to dream and imagine. Have you ever seen a child who doubted the existence of Santa Claus? If you tell them about him, they simply ask if they can leave him a plate of cookies on Christmas Eve. Only as adults do we acquire the disposition of skepticism about everything.

Food for Thought

For these reasons and many more, children point us in the direction of spiritual maturity. It is the way of simplicity, faith and innocence. The primary objective is to enjoy every moment of every day.

Not Being like Children

Anyone who lives on milk, being still an infant, is not acquainted with the teaching about righteousness. But solid food is for the mature. Hebrews 5:13–14

In this passage the author of Hebrews expresses a certain amount of frustration with the people he is writing to. His subject is not easy to explain, and the difficulty is magnified by the fact that his readers are slow to understand. Instead of progressing to matters of maturity, they have continued to go around in circles regarding matters more appropriate for children. In this context, therefore, the author points out that it is not natural for someone who has been walking with Christ for some years to continue with immature attitudes and behavior.

What attitudes and behavior are we referring to? To begin with, children cannot relate very well to others. They are not experienced enough to understand that the world does not revolve exclusively around them. Similarly, immature Christians have a limited perspective on spiritual life, believing that the church and its leaders are there wholly for their personal needs. They measure all that happens in the church with respect to their own lives and don't manage to relate to a bigger picture of ministry.

Children don't have the experience necessary to distinguish between what is healthy and what is potentially dangerous. A child finds a toy lying on the floor just as attractive as the flame on a stove or the openings of an electrical socket. Children approach everything with the same curiosity, which is why parents have to be alert, watching them all the time. Immature Christians have no discernment about what they should or should not do. This is why they are carried along by "every wind of teaching" and easily fall prey to strange teachings that appear in the church.

Neither are children able to see to their own needs. They can't prepare food, change their clothes or keep themselves clean. They depend on their parents for everything. In the same way, immature Christians need attention all the time. They can't study alone or present the gospel to a friend. They need others to do it for them, and if they don't, then the job just isn't done.

This kind of behavior is understandable in the very young. We know this and expect to assist them in the early stages of life. What we don't consider acceptable, however, is to be giving this kind of care to someone twenty or thirty years old. Spiritually speaking, it is not acceptable for people who have been in the church ten, fifteen or twenty years to continue behaving like children.

Food for Thought

In order to progress toward maturity, it is necessary to set aside childish ways. These selfish, infantile attitudes must be abandoned to make room for behavior and perspectives appropriate to adults.

Newness of Life

You were taught, with regard to your former way of life, to put off your old self, which is being corrupted by its deceitful desires; to be made new in the attitude of your minds; and to put on the new self, created to be like God in true righteousness and holiness.
Ephesians 4:22–24

In my experience there is a problem in the church which is a permanent source of preoccupation. I am referring to the lack of evident moral conversion in God's people. Despite being part of the church and walking with the Lord for years, many Christians continue to behave exactly as they did when they were in the world. I have observed that lying, deceit, dishonesty and lack of transparency are common in the way many congregations function. Even if this is simply a manifestation of what is commonplace in our culture, it is sad that this kind of behavior seems quite natural among God's people as well.

In a lengthy passage dedicated to this subject, Paul exhorts the Christians: "With regard to your former way of life . . . put off your old self." The phrase "put off" means that the old way of life has to be discarded, buried, rejected. There is no future for it. It is absolutely clear that the old self cannot be redeemed; we cannot find a way of improving our former life. Those who walk in Christ must live a new life with entirely new behavior.

This exhortation is so comprehensive that sometimes we believe it is open to interpretation for each believer. To avoid such confusion, the apostle provides distinct examples of what it means to walk in newness of life. It includes laying aside falsehood, anger, stealing, unwholesome words and brawling; in their place the disciple must walk in truth, tenderness and generosity, and speak compassionately with words that edify (Eph. 4:25–31). In the following chapter Paul also exhorts us to lay aside filthiness, foolish talk and coarse joking (Eph. 5:4).

After abandoning old habits, those who belong to the Kingdom must put on the new self. Take note once more that this doesn't mean reforming the old self. It is the "putting on" of something different, just as we do when we change our clothes. The key to this is the transformation of our minds, which is produced by the Spirit of God. This is why the apostle mentions that the new self has been "created to be like God in true righteousness and holiness." It is precisely because of these origins that life is so completely different from the way it was before.

Food for Thought

Although all God's people should put on the new self, the influence of leaders is vital in this process. Those who have more responsibility should be the ones who give an example of morally transformed lives. Honesty, simplicity, truth and transparency should be visible qualities in the lives of all God's ministers.

17 August

Faithfulness in Afflicting

I know, O Lord, that your laws are righteous, and in faithfulness you have afflicted me.
Psalm 119:75

I am sure most of us agree completely that the Lord's laws are righteous. We believe it with all our heart, and so we study His Word diligently in order to better understand the Lord's precepts. The second part of the psalmist's declaration, however, introduces a theme that we have difficulty accepting. Some may even passionately argue that it is impossible to associate God's faithfulness with His willfully afflicting us.

It is easy to believe that affliction is part of life—although some have difficulty accepting even that, preferring a brand of spirituality which completely negates the existence of suffering. But we only have to take a look around to see that pain is an inescapable part of our landscape. Our theology informs us that our heavenly Father allows these afflictions for our good and that we must seek in Him the strength and integrity we need to handle them with faithfulness.

In this passage David adds an observation on the subject of suffering which frankly takes us completely outside our comfort zone. The psalmist declares that affliction is a demonstration of the Lord's love for us! How can we embrace this truth when suffering causes so much grief? Who can really believe that God, in His faithfulness, afflicts us? The phrase itself seems contradictory, since faithfulness as we understand it supposes that God will free us from affliction—not bring it upon us!

If we consider the relationship of a father to his son, in which we normally see the strongest demonstration of faithfulness, we can understand our resistance to David's statement. Anybody who has children tries to prevent, albeit imperfectly, suffering for them. It may be in small things, like doing their homework for them so they avoid trouble at school, or in things as big as securing their future by appealing to people of influence to provide them with a job. The objective is always the same: to save our children from suffering.

Our fallible love, however, has long-term consequences. The easiest result to identify is these children's eventual inability to deal with adversity, which is unavoidable in life. Neither will they acquire the strength of character which can only be developed through pain. By preventing immediate discomfort we harm their future development.

When the Lord invests in us, He does so with eternity in mind. There are aspects of our lives that need to be dealt with. There are lessons we must learn to faithfully walk in His ways. Our character must be polished and refined. This is why He not only permits affliction in our lives, but sometimes produces it.

Food for Thought

David reveals an aspect of God's love that we have great difficulty understanding. Would you be willing, in faith, to thank God that He afflicts us in faithfulness? Your perspective of the Father will change radically when you do this!

A Servant's Struggle

I want you to know how much I am struggling for you and for those at Laodicea, and for all who have not met me personally. My purpose is that they may be encouraged in heart and united in love, so that they may have the full riches of complete understanding, in order that they may know the mystery of God, namely, Christ. Colossians 2:1–2

As in all of Paul's writings, this letter reveals briefly something of his heart toward the Gentiles. Without going into details, the apostle states that he is involved in an intense struggle for the church. We know certainly that this fight included many external trials, some of which are mentioned in his second letter to the Corinthians. These included hunger, prison, lashings and shipwrecks suffered for the gospel. But here Paul is referring to another kind of struggle in the inner self of the servant. This is the pastoral burden God puts on the hearts of those who serve His people. In the same passage Paul writes, "Besides everything else, I face daily the pressure of my concern for all the churches. Who is weak, and I do not feel weak? Who is led into sin, and I do not inwardly burn?" (2 Cor. 11:28–29)

This burden is what distinguishes those pastors with a heavenly vocation from those working for a salary. The main objective of hired laborers is to keep the church's programs running. They don't have much time for people because they are busy supervising all the activities. But those pastors who give of themselves, heart and soul, understand that the programs are simply a means to an end: the formation of Christ in the lives of every believer. They have their eyes fixed firmly on this objective, and know with certainty that it cannot be brought about through good programs. The formation of a disciple is an essentially spiritual process, and the pastor lives this process intensely with prayer, supplication, tears and pleas for each person in the congregation.

The most conclusive evidence that this burden is produced by the Spirit of God is found in what Paul says about his own struggle: It includes those who have never seen his face. What greatness of spirit! Most of us hardly struggle for our own people. In fact, we are not often interested in the work of others, especially if they live elsewhere! Paul worked and suffered for the congregations he had never personally visited, but which were of great interest to his Lord. The burdens of Christ were his burdens. When the interests of others begin to be important to us, we will know that God has freed us from the selfishness that so hinders His work in us.

Food for Thought

As a leader, how much time do you spend interceding for the ministries of others? How much effort do you dedicate to promoting projects not your own? How do you communicate this passion for God's kingdom to your congregation?

19 August

The Gift of Jesus

It was he who gave some to be apostles, some to be prophets, some to be evangelists, and some to be pastors and teachers, to prepare God's people for works of service, so that the body of Christ may be built up. Ephesians 4:11–12

It has been observed that there are three New Testament passages that speak of the gifts granted the church by the Trinity.[5] We find a list of gifts that the Father has given His children (Rom. 12:3–9), further gifts given by the Spirit (1 Cor. 12, 14) and then gifts given by Jesus to the church (Eph. 4:11–12). If the commentator's interpretation is correct, it reveals something very interesting about God's heart for His people, along with the specific role played by each member of the Trinity in our formation.

The gifts given the church by the Father and the Spirit are visible graces such as mercy, service, exhortation, discernment, words of knowledge or healing. Through these graces good works, which are part of our calling, can be accomplished. As Scripture says, the people of God should be "zealous for good deeds" (Titus 2:14, NASB).

When we look at Christ's gifts to the church, however, we notice an important difference. The passage does not say that He gave the church apostolic, prophetic, evangelistic, pastoral and teaching *ministries*. What Christ gave the church were not ministries, but *people*. We should not be surprised at this, since Jesus brought the good news from the Father in person. "The Word became flesh and made his dwelling among us. We have seen his glory, the glory of the One and Only, who came from the Father, full of grace and truth" (John 1:14). By giving the church people who were apostles, prophets, evangelists, pastors and teachers, Jesus was repeating the pattern He himself had modeled by investing in the lives of the disciples.

This observation has important connotations for all those established by Christ in these ministries. The principle value of having apostles, prophets, evangelists, pastors and teachers in the church is not to be found in the service they carry out, even though we tend to value people according to the work they do. The main value of these servants is in the kind of people they are. They teach with their lives, even as Christ did. The call to be a leader within the church demands the very highest level of devotion, commitment and holiness from us.

Food for Thought

In times of sorrow, confusion and persecution, the church should not seek inspiration in doctrines, but in the lives of those who have been called to develop the saints. The contact God's people have with these leaders cannot be limited to formal meetings within the established church program. People need access to their lives because they are, after all, Christ's gift to the body!

The Dimensions of Our Call

It was he who gave some to be apostles, some to be prophets, some to be evangelists, and some to be pastors and teachers, to prepare God's people for works of service, so that the body of Christ may be built up. Ephesians 4:11–12

There are some texts in Scripture we could call job descriptions. In other words, they help us understand what we should be doing in our various positions as we serve in the body of Christ. Today's passage is such a text, and it gives a clear description of leadership roles within the church.

Paul's list includes some roles prominently lacking in today's church. The most common among us, without a doubt, are the roles of pastor and teacher. The church has not really known what to do with the other three ministries of apostle, prophet and evangelist. Some groups, through an inexplicable exegetical leap, claim that they are no longer valid. Others show a certain amount of tolerance toward them, but don't create the necessary opportunities within the church for them to function. This has obliged those who fill these roles to opt for the so-called "para-church ministries," which frequently exist because the local church fails to recognize these callings. In the last few years we have seen the reappearance of the non-traditional ministries of prophet and apostle, but I suspect this has more to do with an insatiable desire for prestige than a genuine understanding of these ministries in the body of Christ.

Paul makes three statements concerning these ministers in the church. First, their purpose—all of them, not just the pastor—is the training of the saints. By this we mean giving the believers what they need to fulfill their role. This task of training has not been delegated to any other group within the body, and it is fundamental that these leaders understand this.

Second, it is the role of the saints to carry out the work of ministry. That is, activities such as visitation, service, restoring the fallen, discipling new converts, personal evangelism and many other activities of extending the Kingdom should be the responsibility of the saints, not the leaders. Here we find one of the most commonly held misconceptions in the church, because the saints think this is the responsibility of the pastor. Our language reflects this idea when we talk about the pastor working "full-time" in ministry. In most cases, this converts the believers into passive observers.

Paul's third statement is that the adequate performance of each individual within the body is what produces its edification. Note that he doesn't say the pastor builds the church, but that Christ builds it as everyone does what they have been called to do.

Food for Thought

This model has fabulous implications and great potential. What an excellent time to rediscover God's brilliant plan to establish the church, the body of Christ, on earth!

Preaching in the Flesh

It is true that some preach Christ out of envy and rivalry, but others out of goodwill. But what does it matter? The important thing is that in every way, whether from false motives or true, Christ is preached. And because of this I rejoice. Philippians 1:15, 18

Paul was a prisoner in Rome when he wrote to the church in Philippi. To the many things he had already suffered for the gospel, he could now add the attacks of people who sought to contest the elderly apostle's work. There are always some of these people in the house of God. They probably saw Paul's imprisonment as punishment for his intransigent teaching and took advantage of the moment to publicize his errors. The text does not give specific details of their activities, but we know the apostle was hurt by them.

Despite this suffering, Paul couldn't hide his joy at these circumstances. Even though their motives were wrong, the gospel of Christ still benefited from these reprehensible ministries. Wanting to hurt Paul, they were yet proclaiming the word of Christ and helping advance the Kingdom.

Today's text reveals the depth of the apostle's spiritual understanding and underlines an important principle respecting ministry. The Lord in His sovereignty uses even the most adverse situations to advance His plans. Even more surprising, He has always called men and women to serve Him who are a mixture of spirituality and carnality. Jacob, one of Israel's patriarchs, was inclined to lie and deceive. Moses was given to violence, and his anger led him to kill an Egyptian. Rahab, a key player in the conquest of Jericho, was nothing but a prostitute. David, one of the most outstanding men in the history of God's people, committed adultery and, to cover his sin, killed the husband of the woman he had slept with. Peter, called to be an apostle, publicly denied Christ three times. Paul, who proclaimed the incomparable greatness of God's love, ditched Mark because he had let him down. We can see that even in the most consecrated individuals there were notable expressions of the flesh. God used them all the same, and His plans were not foiled.

This might lead us to say it really doesn't matter what state we are in when we serve the Lord because God will use us anyway. In a sense, we would be right! But what, then, is the value of a consecrated, holy life? The level of our surrender is proportional to the effectiveness of our work for the Kingdom. It is true that the Lord will always reap some benefit from what we do; but when this service is done by saintly laborers, the fruit is greatly multiplied. Godliness in a minister very definitely does matter!

Food for Thought

"If a man cleanses himself from the latter [ignoble purposes], he will be an instrument for noble purposes, made holy, useful to the Master and prepared to do any good work" (2 Tim. 2:21).

It Makes No Difference

"And you say, 'What a burden!' and you sniff at it contemptuously," says the LORD Almighty. "When you bring injured, crippled or diseased animals and offer them as sacrifices, should I accept them from your hands?" says the LORD. Malachi 1:13

There are some things about people that are difficult to change. We all have a stubborn propensity for doing wrong, even when we have proved beyond a shadow of doubt that it produces sorrow, pain and tribulation. But of all the destructive conditions we may suffer from, none is as difficult to break as an attitude of indifference that has become lodged in our hearts.

Indifference is that condition in which we have lost interest in everything. It is possible that in earlier days we felt passion and commitment for a plan, a dream or a person that overflowed and touched the lives of others. But over time the complications of life, disappointments with people or simply a lack of success caused the fire of our passion to flicker and die. As a result, the only attitude we seem capable of is absolute disinterest in everything. Even if an opportunity suddenly arose to fulfill that long-forgotten dream, it wouldn't produce a flicker of enthusiasm in us. We have entered the worst possible state a person can find himself in: being dead while still alive.

This attitude is often the result of prolonged frustration. As the years have passed, we have discovered that even our best efforts don't produce change or have any effect on people. In the days of our fervor and passion, we were convinced there was nothing we could not achieve if we invested enough enthusiasm and energy. But nothing changed; we saw no results and our dreams didn't come true. We came to the conclusion that no matter what we did, it wouldn't make any difference. Why waste any more time?

Indifference can find its way into the ministry. We believed our passion and devotion were going to be key ingredients to fulfilling God's call. But time did not produce the fruitful ministry or the congregational growth we were expecting. First we became disillusioned, then cynical. Today we continue to serve, but we are only going through the motions. Our heart is no longer in what we do.

Realizing that we are not the ones to make things happen in the Kingdom is a healthy lesson for every minister to learn. It is God's hand that produces life—life in abundance. When we reach the point of really understanding that "unless the LORD builds the house, its builders labor in vain" (Ps. 127:1), we are in the best position to participate in God's plans. Then we will have abandoned reliance on our own abilities, passions and motivation, and have deposited all confidence in our heavenly Father. What a thrilling position to be in!

Food for Thought

"In his heart a man plans his course, but the LORD determines his steps" (Prov. 16:9).

Appealing to Love

Therefore, although in Christ I could be bold and order you to do what you ought to do, yet I appeal to you on the basis of love. I then, as Paul—an old man and now also a prisoner of Christ Jesus—I appeal to you. Philemon 8–10

This is one of those situations in which, living as we do when slave trading is illegal, there would seem to be a simple solution. As Christians, we believe that slavery is unacceptable in any form, whether work-related, economical or racial. Our assurance, however, is mostly related to the fact that slavery is not really a part of the world in which we live. In other subjects—such as divorce, unbridled greed or uncontrollable debt—our convictions waver, since these are very much a part of our culture today.

In the first century slavery was part of everyday reality. People of quite modest economical means would own at least one slave. This is important because it will help us understand how radical Paul's gesture was. Defending a runaway slave—whose offence carried the death penalty—was a position totally incomprehensible to most people. The reaction it would have produced might be similar to our reaction if a Christian today stated that divorce is unacceptable for a believer. But the apostle, moved by a law stronger than that imposed by Rome, appealed to Philemon, asking him to show an attitude of forgiveness toward his lost slave.

I would like to reflect on how the apostle presented this request to Philemon. We don't know when Philemon met Paul, but it seems likely that the apostle had been central to his conversion. Paul's investment in his life must have been profound, and perhaps prolonged. The apostle writes to remind him "that you owe me your very self" (Philem. 19). This is what Paul refers to in today's verse; the position of spiritual authority he held respecting Philemon gave Paul the right to order him to do as he was told. Not only did the apostle believe he held this right, but he also trusted that if he exercised it, Philemon would obey.

But Paul did not choose this option. Instead, he made his request on the basis of love, the love that united the two men's lives. This is an important lesson as to how leaders urge their followers to obedience. Imposed orders must be a pastor's last resort. They tend to produce resentment and resistance, because among adults dialogue is always the best option. Paul wanted to avoid any possible resentment which may later be taken out on Onesimus. He appealed to love, which produces a powerful transformation in our lives. It is always the best road to choose.

Food for Thought

Appealing to love assumes a relationship between leader and follower; no appeal will work if this is nonexistent. The leader's priority should be to develop this relationship. It is an investment for the future which is well worth pursuing.

Course Correction

When they came to the border of Mysia, they tried to enter Bithynia, but the Spirit of Jesus would not allow them to. So they passed by Mysia and went down to Troas. During the night Paul had a vision of a man of Macedonia standing and begging him, "Come over to Macedonia and help us." Acts 16:7–9

From this incident with Paul's missionary team, we can learn something about the relationship between God's workers and His Spirit. It reminds us that we should seek "to do good works, which God prepared in advance for us to do" (Eph. 2:10).

Christ left specific instructions for the disciples when He went to the Father: "You will be my witnesses in Jerusalem, and in all Judea and Samaria, and to the ends of the earth" (Acts 1:8). Having received such instructions, we would think the next step should be to carry them out. In this respect, Paul did nothing but seek ways to extend the Kingdom to the ends of the earth. He had the general instructions, and the implementation of them was in his hands. But this position makes unnecessary the work of the Spirit, who is to guide God's children (Rom. 8:14). It also contradicts the method used in the book of Acts. In this book we find much evidence as to how our Lord works out His plans, with us participating fully at each step. He desires His children to include Him in all they do.

I can't help feeling uncomfortable with evangelistic projects which divide a city, region or even the world into segments and then simply assign these areas to groups—as if moving the Kingdom forward required little more than a mathematical mind! There is nothing wrong with the idea, except it is simply rational and human. God's guidance seems to be entirely different from these plans which rely so heavily on systematic strategies. He knows when the moment is ripe for our collaboration. He doesn't lose sight of the final objective; but our exact steps must be guided by His awareness of countless elements we know nothing about. Knowing His will requires permanent communication with the Lord as well as absolute sensitivity to the ways in which He wants to correct our steps.

The Lord does not reveal His will to those sitting comfortably, waiting to know His wishes before they move. We have enough general instructions to know in which direction we should start. As we go, He will make the necessary corrections so we arrive at the approved destination. This assumes willingness on our part to be guided and to abandon our plans in favor of His. It is not a bad way to work. The church in Acts managed to turn the Roman world upside down with this strategy!

Food for Thought

How do you discover God's will for your ministry? What part does the Lord play in the planning process? What steps do you take so the Lord can modify plans if necessary?

Part of a Larger Story

He said to them, "How foolish you are, and how slow of heart to believe all that the prophets have spoken! Did not the Christ have to suffer these things and then enter his glory?" And beginning with Moses and all the Prophets, he explained to them what was said in all the Scriptures concerning himself. Luke 24:25–27

The disciples walking to Emmaus were totally baffled by events of recent days. In the time they had shared with the Messiah, they had discovered His amazing qualities. They had imagined an incredible, thrilling future with Jesus. But now everything had collapsed. In one fell swoop Christ had been removed from their lives and hung on a cross, and His followers scattered in a state of panic.

The depression and discouragement they felt was due partly to their inability to stop thinking about the tragedy. They weren't able to recollect from among Jesus' many teachings what He had spoken about this very event. The only reality they could see was the present, and this caused them acute sorrow. Caught in this unhappy mindset, they couldn't see to rebuild their shattered world or face the future.

Christ came to them anonymously, and "beginning with Moses and all the Prophets, he explained to them what was said in all the Scriptures concerning himself." In other words, the Messiah lifted them beyond their immediate circumstances and showed them a more accurate picture of the situation, introducing them to the development of events according to the vision of Him who determines man's ways: God Himself.

How important it is to be able to step back from our immediate circumstances, contemplating our reality within the framework of God's working throughout the centuries! We all tend to believe that life begins and ends with ourselves, that our ministry was born because of our own initiative and revolves around us. With this terribly limited perspective, our investments tend to be temporary and our commitment brief. It is important that we picture our existence within the history of a people who have walked with God since ancient times. We do not exist in a vacuum; our lives are part of the march of a holy nation set apart for God's purposes.

When we understand that we play a very small part in something much bigger than ourselves, our feelings of importance decrease considerably. We are not in any way indispensable, and what we are doing is not as vital as we would like to believe. We are granted the grace of participating in God's eternal plans; but long before we were born He was already at work, and long after we disappear He will still be at work. Our part makes sense only when we consider it within the brushstrokes of our eternal God.

Food for Thought

"Any philosophy which deals with the here and now is not adequate for man." (Billy Graham) [6]

A Serious Offense

For whenever you eat this bread and drink this cup, you proclaim the Lord's death until he comes. Therefore, whoever eats the bread or drinks the cup of the Lord in an unworthy manner will be guilty of sinning against the body and blood of the Lord.
1 Corinthians 11:26–27

In all the years I have served within the church, studying and teaching the Word of God, I have never been able to understand the origin of a firmly held concept in most of the congregations I have known. This teaching states that participating in the Lord's Supper in an unworthy manner refers to those who have not been baptized. The more I read today's passage, the less evidence I find to support this argument.

It is true that Paul says we were all baptized into one body by one Spirit (1 Cor. 12:13). This statement, however, gives no indication that this is what he had in mind in exhorting the church with respect to the Lord's Supper. Paul admonished the church because of a matter which had been mentioned elsewhere in the letter—specifically, the divisions existing among them. This is the basis of his exhortation. His sadness is because "as you eat, each of you goes ahead without waiting for anybody else" (1 Cor. 11:21). In their meetings the same selfish, individualistic behavior was seen as in those who did not know Christ. Each of them thought only about their own needs without considering anyone else. This is why the apostle says that in meeting together "your meetings do more harm than good" (1 Cor. 11:17).

In the letter to the church at Ephesus, the apostle declares that "the whole body, joined and held together by every supporting ligament, grows and builds itself up in love, as each part does its work" (Eph. 4:16). The text clearly shows that the body grows when the parts are united and functioning correctly together. When each part of the body thinks only of its own need, it cannot fulfill the function for which it was created, i.e., to bless and complement the other parts of the body.

The Lord's Supper is a time when we remember the death of Christ. Our remembrance, however, does not focus on the physical death of the Messiah, but on the reason His death was necessary: the sin that converted us into beings with no interest in God or others. When we participate in an unworthy manner, we are scorning the sacrifice which sought to reverse this situation, because we insist on behaving in the sinful manner that has characterized humanity since the Fall.

Food for Thought

What attitudes in your life might hinder the edification of the body of Christ? What steps do you take to fight the individualism so common in man? How can you show more appreciation for Christ's sacrifice on the cross?

The Salt of the Earth

"You are the salt of the earth. But if the salt loses its saltiness, how can it be made salty again? It is no longer good for anything, except to be thrown out and trampled by men."
Matthew 5:13

As He did on many other occasions, Jesus chose something very common in the Israelites' everyday lives to illustrate the influence a disciple should have in the world. In ancient Palestine, salt had two principal uses: It gave flavor to food and was a means of preserving meat. It was also included in some religious ceremonies in the temple in which it symbolized purity. The salt the Israelites used came from the shores of the Dead Sea. Since it was mixed with other minerals, it was not of the purest quality, but was easily accessible.

Christ compared the disciples' effectiveness in the world with the use of salt. First, we should note that salt is entirely different from food and maintains its own flavor when added to meals. It does not take on the flavor of the food it has been added to, but rather the food's flavor is enhanced by the salt. In the same way, disciples of Christ should lead lives different from those around them. When they participate in activities which bring them into contact with worldly people, believers should transmit their principles and conduct to others. A disciple should not under any circumstances take on the "flavor" of the world.

Second, when salt is mixed with food, there is no particular reaction that produces the salty flavor. The flavor is due simply to its presence in the food. In the same way, disciples need not dedicate themselves to special activities in order to "salt" their surroundings. The action of "salting" is not programmed; it is the result of lifestyles in which influence is consistent, but not specifically planned.

Third, we should note that salt is most effective when it is used in just the right measure. If we put too much salt on our food, it cannot be eaten. In the same way, the presence of Christ's disciples in the world is more effective when their testimony is produced in a natural, spontaneous way as part of their everyday lives. Some sectors of the church have dedicated their efforts to preaching nothing but condemnation toward those who do not walk with Christ. In general, all this does is turn people against the gospel.

Finally, salt was used to prevent the decomposition of food, especially meat. The presence of the church in society should be a factor that preserves mankind from the natural decay produced by sin. Wherever the children of God are, the redeeming action of the Lord should also be visible.

Food for Thought

Salt is only useful for its intended purposes. If it cannot be employed as it was meant, then there is really no use for it.

Christ, the True Vine

"I am the true vine, and my Father is the gardener. He cuts off every branch in me that bears no fruit, while every branch that does bear fruit he prunes so that it will be even more fruitful." John 15:1–2

Israel had frequently been represented in the Old Testament as a vine. This was usually not complimentary since the prophets almost always criticized the poor quality of its produce. Christ declared to the disciples that He was the true vine. He nourishes all the branches, shoots, leaves, clusters and grapes. The church is not the vine; neither are the pastors or those in charge of ministries within the church; the church is represented in the branches. But the Sustainer of every component of the plant is Christ.

The Father is not the vine. The Father is the Owner and, therefore, the One who works the vine. He is the only One who sees the plant as a whole and knows where it needs to be pruned, where it needs support or where its soil needs to be turned. He knows the vine's needs in a way that the most astute human observers cannot. The work of the Father is to ensure that the vine functions according to its created intention—that it produces grapes in abundance.

To secure this result the Father carries out two basic activities. His first job is to cut off and throw away the branches that don't bear fruit. Concerning this work Christ did not mince words; He made absolutely clear the Father's procedure. The branch exists to carry the vine's fruit. The branch that doesn't generate fruit cannot remain as an ornament. If its infertility persists even after receiving necessary care, it is removed from the plant. This branch is using up resources and energy that could be better employed by the productive branches.

The Father's second activity has to do with the fruit-bearing branches. Christ did not say that the branches would be compared to see which bore the most or the tastiest fruit. Neither did He say that the Father would give them "a pat on the back" for their good work in fruit production. The Lord declared that the Father pruned these branches so they would produce more. Any gardener knows that this process, although painful at the time, strengthens the branch and the plant in general.

Food for Thought

This analogy leads to two conclusions. First, there are not different categories of branches, some with a "call" and others without. Every branch, without exception, should produce fruit; none have been designed for decorative purposes. Second, nobody can be saved from the Lord God's pruning, not even those who are "doing well." Everybody gets pruned! For some it means life, for others death. Read Isaiah 5:1–7 and ask the Lord to reveal to you the passion He has for a robust, productive vine.

A Two-way Street

"Remain in me, and I will remain in you. No branch can bear fruit by itself; it must remain in the vine. Neither can you bear fruit unless you remain in me. I am the vine; you are the branches. If a man remains in me and I in him, he will bear much fruit; apart from me you can do nothing." John 15:4–5

When a branch is removed from a plant, it dries out and dies. It cannot survive alone and certainly can't bear fruit. All the components it needs for life are in the vine. It can't store these or supply its own needs. Its only hope is to be nourished by the vine, and so must abide in it.

Christ called the disciples to abide in Him because without Him they could do nothing. It is important that we realize how categorical this phrase is. It is not that without Him things would be difficult or that their achievements would be insignificant. Christ told them there was not a single thing they could do if they were not united to Him.

So what does it mean, this "abiding," or remaining, in Him? The branch has a continuous relationship with the plant. It doesn't meet with the vine once a day or twice a week. It receives nourishment from the vine constantly. "Abide," in its simplest meaning, implies being open at every step to receiving the life of Christ. It means focusing our lives fully on Him, wishing Him to be everything to us.

But Christ added another condition for the bearing of fruit. He told the disciples it was necessary for *Him* to abide in *them*; the relationship doesn't entirely depend on us. Very often, with our list of spiritual disciplines, we believe we are abiding in Him. But Christ said all of this would be of little value if He did not abide in us.

How does He abide? Jesus' words—"If you remain [or abide] in Me, and My words remain in you" (John 15:7)—indicated it was not only by seeking Him, but by heeding His words. In case they still didn't understand, He added, "If you obey My commands, you will remain in My love" (John 15:10). Our devotion, worship and prayer are all for nothing if not accompanied by obedience. It is by keeping His commandments that we ensure His participation in our lives, and not just our participation in His.

It is clear that our lives cannot prosper if we insist on directing them ourselves. We have not been asked to strive, but to let Him guide us. This implies that our activities are not as important as the activities He performs in us.

Food for Thought

"Whoever has my commands and obeys them, he is the one who loves me. He who loves me will be loved by my Father, and I too will love him and show myself to him" (John 14:21).

Two by Two

After this the Lord appointed seventy-two others and sent them two by two ahead of him to every town and place where he was about to go. Luke 10:1

The Lord Jesus did not believe a laborer should not be trusted with responsibility until fully trained and sufficiently mature to bear the weight of the call. Even as He invested in the disciples' training, He gave them a task to complete. To help them carry out this work, He gave instructions for the journey. The disciples probably didn't notice Christ's love for them expressed in another detail: He sent them in pairs.

What a good strategy! There was great wisdom in that decision, and it leaves a great example for training people for ministry. Let's look at some blessings of this method.

When we take on a project with someone else, the challenges seem less daunting. We can bounce ideas off each other, share doubts and fears, and display greater boldness. Even if the other person doesn't have all the answers, their company and friendship is already part of God's provision for our needs.

Working in pairs enriches our perspective. Instead of depending entirely on our own criteria, we can listen to the other person and consider their point of view. Inevitably, they will see things we have not considered, and this will provide greater stability in everything we do.

Two can accomplish the work better than one. Our gifts and talents complement each other in such a way that better results are achieved. The person accompanying me will certainly contribute special qualities and abilities, demonstrating the incredible diversity with which the Lord has created us.

Working together provides someone at our side to help evaluate our own performance. They can tell us how they perceive what we say and do. They can help us correct mistakes and can offer recognition for our achievements, helping us grow wiser in the way we carry out our tasks.

This person will be a source of consolation and support when things don't go as we expect. During the journey we will probably experience opposition, discouragement and confusion. Having a friend means we can share the sorrow of failure and together bring our frustration before God.

Finally, this companion will bring joy to our lives as we share happy experiences. When we live through moments of intense gladness, there is nothing better than sharing them with someone else. Victories and achievements definitely take on a different flavor when we experience them as a team.

Food for Thought

We still have one small detail to consider. In order to work together with others, we must be absolutely convinced that they really are a gift from God for our lives. We will discover, as soon as we start considering them this way, what a great gift they truly are!

The Value of a Mirror

Do not merely listen to the word, and so deceive yourselves. Do what it says. Anyone who listens to the word but does not do what it says is like a man who looks at his face in a mirror and, after looking at himself, goes away and immediately forgets what he looks like.
James 1:22–24

James identifies a problem with our intake of the Word: our chronic tendency to forget what we have heard. This is very noticeable in our day because we have become increasingly saturated with the Word. We hear it in endless meetings during the week, on the radio, on cassettes, on the Internet, in books and in our quiet time. Imagine what we would be like if we practiced even ten percent of all we hear. We would truly be giants in the Kingdom!

Sadly, most of what we hear is quickly forgotten. But an insistent message throughout Scripture urges us to put God's Word into practice. People who merely listen, the apostle tells us, deceive themselves. What does this delusion consist of? It may be compared to the empty promises of a father who doesn't keep his word to his children. He tells them he will do a certain activity with them; the children naturally get excited and anticipate the special time with their dad. But their enthusiasm is for nothing because the father is not a man of his word. The same thing happens with those who only hear the Word. They recognize its valuable advice for the particular situation they are facing. They may even feel joy because the Lord has spoken so clearly. But a short while later all the enthusiasm has fizzled out because they did nothing with what they had heard.

James, with the simplicity characteristic of great Bible teachers, helps us understand this matter using a very simple analogy. Have you ever considered the function of a mirror? It does not just enable us to look at ourselves; its job is more important than that. It allows us to see parts of ourselves we normally can't see with our own eyes—it gives us access to what is normally hidden from sight. Viewing our image, we can see changes that should be made to make us presentable in public.

The Word carries out this function in our lives. It allows us to see things we can't see for ourselves, things seen only "in the Spirit." These are what you and I should act upon. We don't waste time looking in a natural mirror and then do nothing about what we see. In the same way, we must not waste time with the Word if we have no intention of addressing what we discover. The Word has its function—but it is up to us to take advantage of it.

Food for Thought

Thomas à Kempis wrote, "On the Day of Judgment, you will not be asked 'What did you read?' but 'What did you do?'"

Consider it Pure Joy

Consider it pure joy, my brothers, whenever you face trials of many kinds, because you know that the testing of your faith develops perseverance. Perseverance must finish its work so that you may be mature and complete, not lacking anything. James 1:2–4

This passage is well-known to those who have walked for some time with the Lord. But we should not allow familiarity with the text to deprive us of hearing what God would say to us through it. There are several important points in the Apostle Paul's exhortation.

We should note that the apostle encourages the brethren to maintain an attitude of joy in the midst of difficulties. Joy is a characteristic of those who know Christ, and there should be no situation that deprives us of it. Normally, joy is the result of something good—an event, a word, a pleasant experience. In these times our joy overflows, and we share it with others.

But in this text we discover a challenge. How can we be joyful when we find ourselves in trying situations? Most of us don't feel the least bit glad when immersed in sad or negative circumstances. But James does not say that joy comes from fixing our eyes on the trials or tribulations themselves. Logically, no crisis is going to inspire us to give thanks or feel happiness. On the contrary, the more we analyze the situation, the more discouraged we feel.

Instead, James exhorts us to look not at the trial, but at its outcome. What are its consequences? It will cause us to be perfect and complete, not lacking anything. This expression "not lacking anything" includes the circumstances which at this very moment deprive us of our joy! The word "complete," sometimes translated "perfect," is very important in the New Testament. It doesn't mean we never make mistakes or fall into sin. Not at all! It refers to perfection in God's eyes: the chance to live fully the life the Lord has called us to, fulfilling the purpose for which we were created.

Take note of an important detail in the text. It is not *you* who are being tested, it is your *faith*. Of course, you could point out that it is you who have to suffer the trial anyway. The Lord, however, does not allow our struggles on a whim. He is working to make our faith what it should be. You and I know this is very important, for faith is one of the basic ingredients of spiritual life. "Without faith," Scripture tells us, "it is impossible to please God" (Heb. 11:6). And so we need all the help He can give us, so our faith can be lively, dynamic and sturdy.

Food for Thought

How can this be put into practice? Read Acts 16:22–34 to see how Paul and Silas practiced this truth. There we have a tremendous example of joy in the midst of affliction!

Called to Be in This World

I have given them your word and the world has hated them, for they are not of the world any more than I am of the world. My prayer is not that you take them out of the world but that you protect them from the evil one. John 17:14–15

The Lord's words seem at first sight to be contradictory. On one hand, He states that the world has rejected His disciples because they belong to a different Kingdom; the differences in their lifestyles, values and commitments highlight what is lacking in those who identify with this present evil age. The result for Christ's followers is conflict and persecution.

In the next phrase, however, Jesus asks the Father exactly the opposite of what we would have asked. He prays that we not be taken out of the world. This opposes our own instincts because we believe the best thing, if possible, is to shelter our friends from adversity.

Christ states clearly that the disciples are not of the world. He doesn't expect for a moment that we will feel comfortable here. Despite this, many children of God dedicate their efforts to having the best time they can on earth while making their way to eternity.

Meditate on Jesus' request to the Father: "My prayer is not that you take them out of the world but that you protect them from the evil one." Why does He pray this? We have been called to fulfill a mission—not somewhere else, but right here on earth. God has blessed us to make us a blessing to everyone He puts in our path. "As the Father has sent me, I am sending you" (John 20:21). This is an essential part of every disciple's calling. It is not possible to fulfill this call if we are not among the very people who reject us!

It should make us feel rather sad to see how the church has isolated itself from the world, taking refuge in a variety of programs which continue blessing those who have already been blessed. As pastors we are often guilty of producing this state of affairs, for no sooner is someone part of the body than we begin to cut their links with people from the world. We say it is to protect them from ungodly influences, but what we really do is frustrate Christ's prayer in which He specifically asked the Father not to take us out of the world.

What we should do is pray that while they are living actively in the world, God will protect them from harm. This was Christ's prayer, and we would do well to make it our own. If we leave the world, we will reject our vocation. And without it, we cannot be disciples.

Food for Thought

Do you have friends in the world? How much time do you dedicate to them? Do they feel loved by you? How much time do you spend with other Christians?

Special in Their Own Way

The glory of young men is their strength, gray hair the splendor of the old.
Proverbs 20:29

To share an important observation, the author of Proverbs chooses two groups of people at extreme ends of life. The young are just beginning to plan their futures, working toward the process of integration that will convert them into useful members of society. At the other extreme we find the elderly, finishing up their race and largely having already made their contribution to society. Both of them, this verse tells us, are special in their own way.

We live in a day in which the young are given a privileged position. We pay enormous sums of money to youngsters who dazzle us with their ability to play soccer or basketball. The "super" models of the fashion world are followed madly by crowds of teenagers trying to imitate them. Young people with musical talent, having recording contracts worth millions, are the conveyers of values and preferences to the generation following them. In the business world people with forty years' faithful service under their belts become expendable, replaced by a wave of university graduates who are believed to represent the market's future.

Within this framework old age is a penalty. Anyone who has entered retirement has no challenge ahead but to passively await death. Even in cases where we show some tenderness toward the elderly, few of us consider them valuable members of society.

Today's text corrects the commonly held belief that some stages of life are worth more than others. Each one is special, bringing with it challenges different from those of other periods. It is only when we measure every stage with the same criteria that some appear unattractive. If we take the glory of youth and compare it to old age, we will naturally feel that the senior years are a sad time. The elderly, day by day, lose the vitality and strength they enjoyed abundantly in their youth. If our ideal has to do with physical beauty, a sculptured body and a sparkling face, we will resist the advancement of years with all our might.

But today's passage tells us that the beauty of the elderly is precisely in their years. Behind those wrinkles and gray hair, there is a whole lifetime of experience, adversity and triumph. Their lives tell a story that deserves to be heard. There are many lessons we can learn from their mistakes and achievements. We owe them our respect because they have run the race of life with perseverance. We don't know if we will reach as far as they have. The elderly are valued in God's kingdom because they make a contribution the young are unable to offer.

Food for Thought

"Rise in the presence of the aged, show respect for the elderly and revere your God. I am the LORD" (Lev. 19:32).

Radical Advice

If your hand or your foot causes you to sin, cut it off and throw it away. It is better for you to enter life maimed or crippled than to have two hands or two feet and be thrown into eternal fire. And if your eye causes you to sin, gouge it out and throw it away. It is better for you to enter life with one eye than to have two eyes and be thrown into the fire of hell. Matthew 18:8–9

The Word gives at least two distinct ways of dealing with sin. One method addresses what we might call "occasional sin." These are sins which are common to everybody, which we all commit at times. Paul discusses this in his second letter to the Corinthians. If we are spiritually discerning, we can detect the birth of a thought that may lead to sin. Paul tells us that in order to walk in obedience, these thoughts must be taken captive (2 Cor. 10:5). In other words, we must arrest the emerging thought and lay it at the feet of Jesus, reaffirming His lordship.

Today's text refers to a second category of sin we could call "habitual." These are sins that have already taken deep root in our lives. In these we find ourselves trapped in a vicious cycle which produces no definitive solution to our problem. We fall into sin, we confess, we vow never to commit that sin again—but shortly we are back again where we started.

Christ deals radically with this kind of situation. He tells us that when we can no longer defeat a problem by means of our own will, having grown weak in that area, we must take more ruthless steps. We must expunge from our lives the activity, circumstance or situation that continuously feeds our sinful habit.

Allow me to illustrate this. Imagine a young man passionate about soccer. Every time he plays, however, he loses his temper and behaves shamefully toward other players. He has confessed this sin many times and has asked forgiveness from those involved. But he always loses control again. What is the solution Christ proposes? He should quit the game until he can control himself and play without dishonoring the Lord.

The same principle could apply to someone who watches too much television, is argumentative or is a compulsive spender. Attempts to rein these things in have failed, so a drastic solution is needed. We must avoid the circumstances that lead us to fall repeatedly into the same sinful habits.

Sin is not to be taken lightly. When left uncorrected, it gradually blurs our vision and hardens our heart, and eventually leads to death (James 1:15). The only decisions that help in such situations are those which bring a definitive end to the problem. It is preferable to lose some things on earth if by doing so we secure greater eternal blessings.

Food for Thought

"Better to starve than go to the devil for provender." (Thomas Watson)[1]

Revenge and the Kingdom

If it is possible, as far as it depends on you, live at peace with everyone. Do not take revenge, my friends, but leave room for God's wrath, for it is written: "It is mine to avenge; I will repay," says the Lord. Romans 12:18–19

There are few things that wound us as deeply as a wrong suffered at the hands of others. It is far easier to bear economic trials, unemployment or illness. When people betray us we feel wounded to the core. Overcoming this pain is a tremendous challenge.

In today's text Paul provides some guidance on this matter. He reminds us that peace should be a characteristic of Christ's servants, since we follow a God of peace. The phrase "as far as it depends on you" indicates that being fully at peace with others requires the goodwill of everyone involved. In other words, it requires not only an absence of hostility on our part, but the same commitment from those with whom we interact. Peace is not always complete, because our efforts at conciliation may not be shared by everyone. We are called to exhaust every possible means in developing and maintaining a peaceful relationship with the people who are part of our lives.

But it is hardest for us to carry this out in relationships in which we have been hurt, scorned or unfairly treated. Our desire for peace vanishes because the intensity of our indignation is so severe. This feeling must be corrected, no matter what it takes to achieve.

If our hurt is not laid aside, we begin to struggle with a desire for revenge. Sometimes we consider revenge a form of open aggression toward someone else, but it can in fact wear many disguises. It is conveyed simply by wishing adversity on another person. Revenge may include something as indirect as publicly humiliating someone or criticizing them behind their backs. At the end of the day, it is an attitude that becomes lodged in our hearts. Revenge is no more than an outward expression of the bitter spirit that dwells within us.

Paul urges us to hand this over to God. This is wise, not only because God is the One who defends His children, but also because only He correctly understands all the angles of a situation and discerns the correct action to take. When we leave things in His hands, we affirm that He knows exactly what we need, and He will do nothing but the best for us.

Food for Thought

"To this you were called, because Christ suffered for you, leaving you an example, that you should follow in his steps. 'He committed no sin, and no deceit was found in his mouth.' When they hurled their insults at him, he did not retaliate; when he suffered, he made no threats. Instead, he entrusted himself to him who judges justly" (1 Pet. 2:21–23).

Fair Judgments

And I charged your judges at that time: Hear the disputes between your brothers and judge fairly, whether the case is between brother Israelites or between one of them and an alien. Do not show partiality in judging; hear both small and great alike. Do not be afraid of any man, for judgment belongs to God. Bring me any case too hard for you, and I will hear it. Deuteronomy 1:16–17

One of our responsibilities as leaders is to intervene in quarrels or conflicts between believers. These are normal occurrences in peoples' lives, but very often they require intervention of a third party for correct resolution.

The great challenge for a leader in these problems is to avoid leaning on natural feelings as much as possible. This does not mean it is impossible to reach a fair judgment on a human level; we do retain some degree of understanding of the truth. But in most situations our humanity impairs our judgment of others.

Moses encouraged those in authority under him to judge fairly in the resolution of conflicts; they were not to make exceptions. That is, they were not to give way to the temptation to prefer one person above another. A typical instance of this would be to pay more attention to the rich than the poor, or to favor a national above a foreigner. This might seem unlikely in a church setting, until we remember that we often pay more attention to people who give more substantial offerings or to the families who have been longest in the congregation.

Moses argues that a minister should not fear men, because judgment belongs to God. The Lord judges correctly in all situations because He knows the intentions of the heart. Moses also points out that a leader's authority to judge has been given by the Lord. Paul tells the Romans that "there is no authority except that which God has established. The authorities that exist have been established by God. Consequently, he who rebels against the authority is rebelling against what God has instituted, and those who do so will bring judgment on themselves" (Rom. 13:1–2). This is why we must proclaim our judgments in fear, because we must justify before the God of heaven our use of this responsibility.

Solomon felt unable to carry out this task and asked God for the wisdom he so desperately needed to fulfill his royal obligations. The Lord granted his request, and his fame as a judge spread throughout all the earth. His example is invaluable. The responsibility to judge others' conflict should not be taken lightly.

Perhaps the most important thing to keep in mind is not to rush a decision. This caution will give us time to consider carefully all we have heard, seeking guidance from the Spirit. Then when we speak, our words will coincide with the thoughts of the God we serve.

Food for Thought

"Righteousness exalts a nation, but sin is a disgrace to any people" (Prov. 14:34).

From the Mountainside

Now when he saw the crowds, he went up on a mountainside and sat down. His disciples came to him, and he began to teach them. Matthew 5:1–2

There is a direct connection between the crowds following Christ and His decision to go up the mountainside. This was no improvised teaching thought up on the spur of the moment; Jesus saw that the moment was ripe to give the crowds—and His disciples—a series of lessons to illustrate Kingdom values.

It's not that they lacked spiritual teaching in Israel. The teaching of the scribes and Pharisees, however, focused on blind adherence to the law, especially in areas that affected how others saw them. This is why Christ warned His listeners, "Be careful not to do your 'acts of righteousness' before men, to be seen by them. If you do, you will have no reward from your Father in heaven" (Matt. 6:1). This temptation of being affected by the opinions of others is one we continually have to face. The struggle is especially intense for those in public ministry. How easy it is to use phrases and postures solely for the purpose of impressing others with our apparent devotion!

In the Sermon on the Mount, Christ challenged His listeners to consider the hidden aspect of life that holds eternal importance: the secret place of the spirit known intimately only to the Lord. He carefully directed the people to stop thinking about their actions and instead to evaluate the motives behind them.

When speaking the Beatitudes, Jesus was describing characteristics of a citizen of the Kingdom. He was not handing out a new formula for reaching God, such as the long list of requirements presented by the religious leaders of that day. Rather, He described the qualities present in those who have been led into a spiritual life by the Lord Himself. This work is not the fruit of human effort, but the product of supernatural visitation; this is the origin of all that has an eternal quality.

The word "blessed" does not refer to an emotional state; it describes much more than happiness. It is the fullness of life found by those whose hearts God has touched. The Lord brings life—abundant life. Possessing this means being blessed. When Christ began to proclaim this, He wanted the people to understand that submitting to the life of God was worth the trouble. He described a completely different realm, distinct from the mean, bitter, depressing world they saw every day. All our preaching and teaching should, like this sermon, contain a generous dose of joy, hope and encouragement, for we too are heralds of good news.

Food for Thought

"When Jesus had finished saying these things, the crowds were amazed at his teaching, because he taught as one who had authority, and not as their teachers of the law" (Matt. 7:28–29). What kind of response do you get when you preach about the Kingdom?

Blessed Are the Poor in Spirit

"Blessed are the poor in spirit, for theirs is the kingdom of heaven." Matthew 5:3

The first beatitude identifies the starting point of every genuine spiritual experience: recognition of our needy condition. It is the result of illumination, brought about by the Lord, in which everything that has elevated our pride vanishes into thin air. We see ourselves as He does, recognizing our spiritual bankruptcy.

The best example of this is in the story of the prodigal son. He had days of glory when, thanks to a bulging wallet and an endless stream of admirers, life was one big party. But these days didn't last, and he eventually found himself sitting among pigs with torn and dirty clothes. Tormented by gnawing pangs of hunger, "he came to his senses" (Luke 15:17). The moment came when his eyes were opened to his real condition, and he understood that he was absolutely lost and alone in the world. The poverty of his situation moved him to return to his father's house.

Poverty of spirit does not refer exclusively to the time preceding our initial conversion. Rather, it is a posture that routinely leads us to come before our Lord. As we go through life, time and again we fall into attitudes of arrogance and superiority which oppose the spirit of the Kingdom. The only hope for us is to recognize again the reality of our spiritual need. Such was Peter's experience when he was led astray by his own enthusiasm and proclaimed his willingness even to die with Christ. The brokenness that followed—painful and intense though it was—helped him see his personal condition with absolute clarity.

Christ proclaimed that the blessing of this condition is to possess the kingdom of heaven. We cannot help but note the marked contrast with the world's ideas in which kingdoms are conquered with strength and violence. The aggressive ambitions of those who have reached the highest posts in the political, business or art world confirm this. Our culture has no room for the weak or the humble. And we believed this, until a Mother Teresa appeared in our midst—a tiny, frail figure tirelessly dedicated to serving those who had been completely forgotten by humanity. Right up to the end of her life she rubbed shoulders with the powerful, interviewed presidents and kings, and shared her message with billions of people. She did not achieve this through effort, but through poverty of spirit. In the spiritual realm the Kingdom is given to those who recognize their dearth of those qualities that make for true greatness. They have understood the words of the prophet Isaiah: "In repentance and rest is your salvation, in quietness and trust is your strength" (Isa. 30:15).

Food for Thought

"You say, 'I am rich; I have acquired wealth and do not need a thing.' But you do not realize that you are wretched, pitiful, poor, blind and naked" (Rev. 3:17).

Blessed Are Those Who Mourn

"Blessed are those who mourn, for they will be comforted." Matthew 5:4

The beginning of a significant spiritual experience, according to the first beatitude, is recognizing the poverty of our own hearts. It means taking a spiritual inventory of ourselves and discovering the complete lack of richness in our lives. This discovery could provoke a fresh beginning, but not necessarily so.

Though many of us recognize that there are aspects of our lives in lamentable shape, often our only reaction is a shrug of the shoulders. Our discovery of poverty could even awaken a warped sense of pride in our hearts.

When the revelation is from the Spirit of God, however, it leads to the next step, which is weeping. Recognizing our true condition before God brings profound sadness because we understand the enormity of our offense against Him. In His mercy He allows us to shed tears over our state—an essential part of the healing process.

This truth goes against our culture's perspective, especially if we are men. "Men don't cry," our elders used to tell us, even when we were still too young to understand what a man was. The absence of tears, however, indicates a strange hardness of heart; it is the product of little contact with the emotional side of life. People who don't cry have learned at some point that tears only bring problems. To avoid these difficulties they have repressed an aspect of their personality as natural and necessary as eating.

David, one of the most genuinely spiritual men in the Bible, frequently shed tears. He confessed that he had flooded his bed with weeping (Ps. 6:6) and declared that tears had been his food, day and night (Ps. 42:3). Christ wept on more than one occasion over things we don't even understand. Peter wept disconsolately after denying his Lord (Matt. 26:75). The brethren at Ephesus wept miserably when Paul told them he would not see them again (Acts 20:37). All this suggests a completely natural way of expressing sadness as well as opening our hearts to the working of God.

This is precisely what Christ meant when He said that those who mourn are blessed. Their tears will not leave them empty and alone. Sorrow that is spiritual in origin does not produce regret (2 Cor. 7:10). Tears open a way for the Father's tender hand to minister to us, for He consoles the afflicted and dries their tears, "heals the brokenhearted and binds up their wounds" (Ps. 147:3). Whoever has felt this comforting grace knows that after weeping one feels purified and refreshed, like the earth after a shower of rain.

As leaders we must encourage our people to be genuine in the expression of feelings, even as we must be. There is no shame in crying through the Spirit's working in our lives. Heavenly tears are blessed indeed!

Food for Thought

Woe to those who never cry, for sadness and anguish will follow them all the days of their lives.

Blessed Are the Meek

"Blessed are the meek, for they will inherit the earth." Matthew 5:5

The first two beatitudes reflect the spiritual state produced in our lives by God's intervention. They refer to the action of the Spirit through which we discover our true human condition. All our postures and attitudes, which at one time led us to believe we were something, are laid bare. Our spiritual poverty becomes painfully obvious, and we are broken by this reality, so radically different from what we thought we were.

Today's beatitude builds on the spiritual condition depicted in the first and second. Like the links in a chain, this condition cannot be isolated from spiritual poverty and brokenness. Meekness, however, moves us to the plane of human relationships. Healthy relationships don't depend on the quality of the people involved, but on the existence of an honest spiritual foundation.

Meekness is an attitude of humility. It enables us to see that our awareness of spiritual poverty is the product of God's working, not our own efforts. When we are clothed in meekness, we can accept things that are hurtful, humiliating or difficult with a peaceful, tranquil attitude. When others approach us to point out errors and defects, we don't react in angry indignation, seeking to justify the unjustifiable. It is the Spirit who has brought to light these very conditions, so we can take others' words as confirmation of what has already been revealed to us.

Faced with situations of injustice, we are slow to react. We do not worry about insults or actions that damage our reputation. We hold to the conviction that God protects His own and doesn't need our assistance. Such was Moses' attitude when Miriam and Aaron rose up against him (Num. 12) and when the sons of Korah rebelled (Num. 16); the Word describes Moses as the meekest man on earth (Num. 12:3). Jesus Christ invited all who are burdened and grieving to come to Him, because He was "gentle and humble in heart" (Matt. 11:29). At the most trying moment of His earthly pilgrimage, He showed absolute meekness, for "when they hurled their insults at him, he did not retaliate; when he suffered, he made no threats" (1 Pet. 2:23). I suspect that a great deal of our weariness is due precisely to endless attempts to defend and justify ourselves.

Once again, the reward stands in strong contrast to the popular concepts of our culture. The earth, say today's experts, belongs to those who don't "let the grass grow under their feet." In the Kingdom, the earth belongs to those who cease to struggle and fight for recognition. They rest in the Lord and know that it is He who raises up and tears down, who gives and takes away. He is wonderfully generous in watching over the interests of His children.

Food for Thought

Woe to those who never lower their guard, for they will always have to depend entirely on their own efforts.

Hunger and Thirst for Righteousness

"Blessed are those who hunger and thirst for righteousness, for they will be filled."
Matthew 5:6

We have been meditating on the process God uses to make people aware of their true spiritual condition. As the Holy Spirit exposes our need, it leads to genuine, healing brokenness. We make no attempt to argue or defend ourselves. What others may say about us only confirms what has already been shown by God.

This brokenness, in which we reject our former way of life, could lead to the decision for life transformation—whatever it takes and no matter the cost. But here lies the danger in this revelation. It could impel us to take responsibility for the change we hope takes place in our lives. Aware of where we have failed, we vow never to return there again, and we put all our energy into producing the change we feel is needed. A decision of this kind will only derail the Lord's working in our hearts.

The Beatitudes reveal a different path, namely, yielding to the sovereign action of our Lord. Christ does not offer us a method that with our faithful implementation will guarantee a certain outcome. As soon as we take responsibility for the process of transforming our lives, our spiritual growth halts. As the prodigal son discovered, we cannot dictate to the Father how He should deal with our lives. He knows what is needed and doesn't require suggestions from us. We should heed the warning in Paul's question to the Galatians: "After beginning with the Spirit, are you now trying to attain your goal by human effort?" (Gal. 3:3). Our response should be a definite, "No way!"

The path open before us leads us to come to the Lord with our weaknesses and errors, and call out to Him for that work which only the Spirit can do in us. The blessing is to be found in being hungry and thirsty for righteousness. Righteousness is not something man can bring about, but a reality that is the product of divine intervention. The spiritual life we so long for must be sought in fellowship with Him. "Christ in us" is the answer we are looking for.

The reward, Christ tells us, is that our hunger will be satisfied. The Lord is not indifferent to our pleas, "for we do not have a high priest who is unable to sympathize with our weaknesses, but we have one who has been tempted in every way, just as we are—yet was without sin. Let us then approach the throne of grace with confidence, so that we may receive mercy and find grace to help us in our time of need" (Heb. 4:15–16). He is more interested than we are in producing the transformation we seek!

Food for Thought

Woe to those who have no interest in godliness, for they will live in torment, seeking to satisfy their thirst with that which does not satisfy.

Blessed Are the Merciful

"Blessed are the merciful, for they will be shown mercy." Matthew 5:7

In this beatitude we have some of the clearest evidence that life transformation comes from God and not from us. Mercy, simply defined, is sensitivity to the suffering of others, which in turn produces a desire to bring relief to the afflicted. This quality most reflects the character of God, since mercy has to do with a compassionate, generous heart which doesn't evaluate whether or not the help is deserved, but instead gives unconditionally.

The spiritual progression of the Beatitudes makes mercy the logical outcome of a hunger and thirst for righteousness. Hunger and thirst can only be satisfied by entering into intimacy with God Himself. Closeness to Him satisfies the needs of our soul, which then begins to awaken in our hearts an interest in the concerns of others. We no longer harshly judge those in difficult situations, condemning them through our recognition of sin in their lives. Rather, we begin to see that they are trapped in an evil system, blinded by the darkness of this world and desperately in need of light and life.

The display of mercy often shocks those who are supposedly the true representatives of all that is good and just. The Pharisees, for example, didn't show any mercy toward the woman caught in adultery (John 8:3–5). Far from showing the necessary compassion to free her from her snare, they brought her to Jesus to confirm the condemnation already formed in their own hearts. Jesus did not say at any time that He approved of adultery. Nevertheless, He showed compassion for the woman and refused to condemn her, even though she deserved punishment.

In the same way, Simon the Pharisee was horrified when the Master permitted a sinful woman to touch Him (Luke 7:37–39). A Pharisee would never have made contact with a person like that! But Jesus showed her the generous compassion of God, and she was literally transformed into a new person. When we have been touched by mercy, we can then be merciful to others. For this attitude to be formed in our character, it is necessary to be reminded periodically of how much God has forgiven us, since those who love much have been forgiven much.

At various times during His earthly pilgrimage, Christ reminded the disciples that God would be generous with those who were generous. The principle is clear: We have all received an invitation to be part of the Kingdom—but once we have been admitted, it is totally inadmissible that we should fail to show the mercy to others that has been shown to us. Blessed are the merciful, for they will receive even greater displays of mercy.

Food for Thought

Woe to those with a hard heart, because they will be treated with the same hardness they have shown others.

Pure in Heart

"Blessed are the pure in heart, for they will see God." Matthew 5:8

We have been considering the progressive restoration that occurs when God breaks into our lives. Just like the prodigal son, everything starts in that moment when our eyes are opened and we see our lives as they really are: mired down in the worst kind of misery. This discovery is enough to begin a process that will eventually bring us into the arms of our heavenly Father. In today's text Jesus declares that those who are pure in heart are blessed.

Once again the teachings of Christ move us away from the practice of a religious life with its stress on rites and external appearances. By means of discipline we can make an impact on those around us and give an impression of tremendous piety, but we can't deceive God. He does not look at the visible part of man; He weighs the heart. That which is hidden to most eyes is what really matters when it comes to spiritual life.

The heart is the source of motives and thoughts behind our behavior. This is where true holiness is developed. On this occasion Christ surprised the crowds, taking them to a deeper level than they had ever known. In the case of the physical act of adultery, Christ indicated that the root of the issue was a secret desire of the heart (Matt. 5:28). In the act of murder, Jesus taught that the real problem was the angry name-calling that occurs in the hidden places of our hearts (Matt. 5:22). The lesson is clear. The only life pleasing to the Father is one that is as pure inside as it is outside. This is what holiness is all about, an attitude of sincerity and innocence. The psalmist offers a good description of this condition: "Who may ascend the hill of the LORD? Who may stand in his holy place? He who has clean hands and a pure heart, who does not lift up his soul to an idol or swear by what is false" (Ps. 24:3–4).

The writer of Hebrews exhorts, "Make every effort to live in peace with all men and to be holy; without holiness no one will see the Lord" (Heb. 12:14). This is precisely what Christ is saying. The blessing involved in a life of inner purity is the ability to see God. He is holy, and no impure person can approach Him. But for the pure in heart, the way is always open.

We should note that purity cannot be divorced from personal relationship with others. This is where selfish motives, double intentions and manipulations become evident. The area in which we most need God's purifying process is in our daily dealings with those who share our lives.

Food for Thought

Woe to the hypocrites, for they will have to be satisfied with the pretence of experiencing God.

Peacemakers

"Blessed are the peacemakers, for they will be called sons of God." Matthew 5:9

As we move through the process of transformation by God's working in our lives, we are increasingly better equipped to bless others with spiritual blessings.

Relationships between human beings are plagued by all kinds of conflicts. The simple reality of two people living in the same house leads to tense situations, since the interests of one will surely interfere with those of the other. When we transfer these tensions to society, in which commitments to our neighbors are much weaker, it is easy to understand why conflicts and clashes are so common. God has created us to live together in harmony, but the presence of sin in our lives often makes this difficult to practice.

It is not possible to give these relationships a peace-filled quality—which in the Word means much more than the absence of conflict—except by means of a supernatural intervention. Humanity has tried to impose peace on its own terms, but this always ends up being an act of aggression toward others. This was Peter's mistake when he tried to defend Christ by using his sword (John 18:10) and Moses' when he wanted to bless his Hebrew brothers by murdering an Egyptian (Exod. 2:11–12), "for man's anger does not bring about the righteous life that God desires" (James 1:20). It is important to understand that true peace is the result of profound transformation in the heart, just as Christ describes in the Beatitudes.

It was because of this peace that Christ could ask the Father not to take into account the sin of those who crucified Him (Luke 23:34). Through this same supernatural peace, Stephen prayed for those who were stoning him, even in the midst of an agonizing death (Acts 7:60). People who seek peace want the fullness of God's blessing to extend to those around them, allowing them to enjoy relationships that are not hampered by the persistent fear of offense. Peacemakers are also committed to intervention in any potential conflict, preventing a fight from escalating to a crisis of uncontrollable proportion. They understand that "starting a quarrel is like breaching a dam" (Prov. 17:14).

This attitude results in the blessing of being called children of God—a privilege that bestows a spiritual authority without equal. The children of God are those who enjoy the backing and the special favor of the Father. They are able to advance without fear in all that He asks, for God will accompany them each step of the way.

Food for Thought

Woe to those who "look the other way" in situations of conflict. When they themselves need assistance, they will have to resolve their conflicts alone.

Blessed Are the Persecuted

"Blessed are those who are persecuted because of righteousness, for theirs is the kingdom of heaven. Blessed are you when people insult you, persecute you and falsely say all kinds of evil against you because of me." Matthew 5:10–11

One of the ironies of the Beatitudes is that this aligning of our lives with God's purposes is not well-received by the world. On the contrary, it is inevitable that anyone who goes against the values that regulate a fallen world will be persecuted and rejected by those who walk in sin. The lives of the redeemed expose the weakness and illness of a sinful culture. Anybody whose behavior proclaims that the world is in need of change will suffer persecution.

We should note, however, that this blessing proclaimed by Jesus is conditional: It is for those who receive insults, injustice and opposition as a result of following Christ. Conflicts and misunderstandings are common in everyone's life; most people will experience them at some time or other. But the difference with fleshly conflicts is that they are often the result of one's own foolishness. This kind of opposition obviously has no merit; we are just bearing the consequences of our own sin. This is why the Apostle Peter asks, "But how is it to your credit if you receive a beating for doing wrong and endure it? But if you suffer for doing good and you endure it, this is commendable before God" (1 Pet. 2:20).

As we have seen, persecution has been the mark of all the great prophets and servants of God. Scripture tells us that "some faced jeers and flogging, while still others were chained and put in prison. They were stoned; they were sawed in two; they were put to death by the sword. They went about in sheepskins and goatskins, destitute, persecuted and mistreated—the world was not worthy of them. They wandered in deserts and mountains, and in caves and holes in the ground" (Heb. 11:36–38). Thus, we need not be surprised at worldly opposition, but rather see it as confirmation that we have fully entered into a new dimension of life, one in which Christ establishes the principles.

The reward for this is precisely that mentioned by Christ: "Theirs is the kingdom of heaven." Persecution often places people in situations where they lose everything. In extreme cases like those of Paul, Stephen, Peter and other martyrs, persecution even meant the loss of life. Nevertheless, there is something that can't be taken away from any human being, and that is the full and complete participation in the life God grants His own, even when the body has died. This is not a right of humanity; it is a reward given by God for faithfulness on the part of His people.

Food for Thought

Woe to those who flee from suffering, for they will neither receive approval nor be counted among the heroes of the faith.

Training Workers

"But commission Joshua, and encourage and strengthen him, for he will lead this people across and will cause them to inherit the land that you will see." Deuteronomy 3:28

The challenge awaiting Israel was tremendously complex and arduous. Together with Moses they had conquered much of the territory east of the river Jordan. God had clearly told the patriarch, however, that he would not be entering the Promised Land. This part of the undertaking would be in the hands of Joshua, the successor chosen by Jehovah. This young leader had been affected dramatically by his mission with the twelve spies. When he and Caleb had insisted the land could be taken if Israel was willing to wait on the Lord, the people almost stoned him. Surely now that the time had come for the task, he felt completely inadequate for the magnitude of the challenge ahead.

This is probably one reason the Lord spoke to Moses, giving him clear instructions for preparing his successor. These consisted of three steps: commission, encourage and strengthen.

God did not leave Joshua to guess about his appointment or to invent tasks for the people. Moses was to explain specifically what the Lord expected of Joshua. For each step there were precise instructions. This is an important aspect of a leader's work. We often ask our helpers to take responsibility for a project without explaining what is expected of them. If they don't have clear instructions, they won't know what they should do and will very probably make mistakes.

Next, Moses was instructed to encourage. The original word means to impart power and strength. The principal way of doing this is to help people understand their responsibilities as servants of God, indicating the Source of assistance available to them. Notice that when God called people in the Bible, part of His strategy was to remind them they would not be alone, that the Lord Himself would go with them. Sadly, many leaders abandon workers to the task and don't take the trouble to ensure they have strong and healthy relations with God. The work of inspiring and encouraging workers is vital if they are to be effective.

Moses' third responsibility was to strengthen. The word used in the Hebrew text refers to the task of identifying workers' weaknesses and taking necessary steps to build them up. This also is important. Joshua was apparently a fearful and timid man, qualities that could potentially derail his ministry. The solution was not to condemn him for these characteristics, but to help him overcome them. Properly strengthened, he could face any challenge. As leaders we have to be aware of our workers' weaknesses—not to denounce them, but to find a way to overcome them.

Food for Thought

Many leaders try to produce change through constant criticism of their peoples' mistakes. The only thing this achieves is frustration and ill feeling. Make sure you are somebody who encourages and builds up your workers!

Never Early or Late

But the boat was already a considerable distance from land, buffeted by the waves because the wind was against it. During the fourth watch of the night Jesus went out to them, walking on the lake. Matthew 14:24–25

Having received instructions from the Lord to cross to the other side of the sea, the disciples probably set off at dusk. The passage clearly tells us that Jesus was alone when night fell. The Messiah reached them at some time during the fourth watch, which lasted from three to six in the morning. We can estimate, therefore, that they had been at least nine hours on the water, trying to make a crossing that usually took no more than an hour.

Imagine the state of the disciples by this time. They would have been physically exhausted from struggling with the fierce winds impeding their progress, beside the fact that they wouldn't have slept at all that night. And this came after a day of intense ministry involving strong, conflicting emotions.

How would they have been feeling? How would you have felt in this situation? They were accustomed to Christ giving them instructions and guiding them through situations of crisis. But Jesus was not with them. Some of them must have wondered why the Master had sent them on alone. Had He not realized strong winds were coming? Did He not care what happened to them? And where was He, anyway? How was He going to reach them now?

Meanwhile, the Word tells us that Jesus had gone up the mountain to pray. There was only one mountain in that area, and from the summit the whole Sea of Galilee could be seen. It is most likely, speaking from a human point of view, that for most of the night the disciples' boat was visible to Him. We can also be sure that in the Spirit, Christ knew what they were going through. Nevertheless, He allowed time to pass without intervening or moving from where He was. To an observer Jesus' attitude would appear indifferent, showing questionable commitment to the men He said He loved.

It is so true that God's ways are not our ways! The Lord undoubtedly wanted to teach them something and so was slow to intervene. Our intervention to help others in times of trouble, albeit well-meaning, is not always best for them. Sometimes the crisis is necessary for our strengthening. At other times it is good for us to realize how limited our resources are. Whatever the situation, God comes to us at just the right moment, in perfect time for us to get the most out of the circumstances we are living through.

Food for Thought

Sometimes it seems as though He has forgotten us, but God sees everything from a place that allows Him a better perspective than ours. Don't despair. When the time is right, He will come to you in the manner and moment you least expect.

The Pilgrim's Prayer

I am a stranger on earth; do not hide your commands from me. Psalm 119:19

I never cease to be surprised by the concepts presented in the Word. Some of these, like today's verse, are incredibly simple, but hold penetrating truth.

On coming before God, the psalmist recognizes that his true situation on earth is that of a pilgrim, or a stranger. A dictionary of synonyms offers alternatives for this word such as migrant, nomad, wanderer, traveler and wayfarer. In other words, pilgrims are people who are in a place temporarily. They are not where they normally live; circumstances have led them away from their home. They have no intention of staying permanently.

In this simple description we can discern the essence of Christ's call to those who walk with Him. They do not intend to stay long on this earth, so they travel light and quickly, like the Israelites in the desert, so they don't get attached to anything which could become an unnecessary burden. But this situation contradicts the perspective of most Christians. Anyone looking at us from a distance would not easily conclude we were just passing through. On the contrary, they would believe we are settling down for a long stay, gathering all kinds of belongings in order to be as comfortable as possible.

The other characteristic of pilgrims is that they are not familiar with the customs and culture of the place they are in. As anyone who has been in a strange country knows, we feel extremely insecure and alone in the culture. We need someone to accompany us, to explain the customs, the places to visit and the behavior that is appropriate on each occasion. If the pilgrim does not know the language, he will be like a child who needs help with even the smallest details.

This total dependence led the psalmist to call out to God in prayer, "Do not hide your commands from me." If the guide does not provide a map and necessary instructions, the pilgrim will be completely lost in the unfamiliar land. This is a good picture of our relationship with Christ. As Christians we should be convinced that it is not possible to take even a step forward without precise instructions from the One who knows the way. Such a conviction should lead to deep dependence on Him. Like Moses we should exclaim each day, "If your Presence does not go with us, do not send us up from here" (Exod. 33:15).

Finally, we should deduce from David's prayer that he cannot obtain the instructions by himself. By asking God not to hide His Word, he is recognizing that all revelation of His will is an act of pure grace toward us. This affirms our dependence on the kindness of Him who is our guide in this strange and lonely land.

Food for Thought

"If we loved the world as God loves it, we would not love it the way we do." (Anonymous)

Good, but Not Right

Jesus turned and said to Peter, "Out of my sight, Satan! You are a stumbling block to me; you do not have in mind the things of God, but the things of men." Matthew 16:23

Can you imagine how you would feel if someone rebuked you this way? Peter must have been terribly surprised to find his good wishes toward Christ had provoked such a violent reply! There is no doubt that Jesus had the authority to reprimand Peter and was justified in doing so. But the scene still shocks us, since Christ does not call Peter by name, but refers to him as Satan.

Our confusion is probably due to a failure to understand clearly the kingdom of God and the kingdom of darkness. Our spiritual walk can be described as a confused combination of right and wrong rather than a confident demonstration of the call of God. Things that seem trivial to us are weighty matters to Christ. Above all, we don't understand that our call consists of something essentially different from just being good people. Good intentions are very often a powerful tool in the Enemy's hands to sidetrack us from the path God has set before us.

Beyond this, there is a lesson for us in this incident. The Enemy can use us to develop attitudes and behavior contrary to God's purposes. The fact that we are "in Christ" is no guarantee we will not occasionally do some efficient work for the Enemy.

For this to happen we don't have to be an ally of Satan, or even close to it. He helps himself to all he can use for the spreading of darkness. The substance of sin is what Christ identifies in Peter: "You do not have in mind the things of God, but the things of men." In other words, to do the work of the Enemy is to encourage, in yourself and in others, a perspective of life not rooted in the eternal principles of God, but conforming to the wisdom of this present evil time. This is why it is easy to confuse what is good with what is right. Not all that we consider good is consistent with the righteousness of God.

Abraham and Sarah considered it a "good" idea for him to have a child with Hagar. The Israelites, repenting of their lack of faith, believed God would approve of their "good" attempts to take the land by their own means. David's men thought God had delivered Saul into their leader's hands to kill him and bring about "good." We can think of dozens of examples. In each case good intentions were not correct when it came to doing the will of God.

Food for Thought

"Do not conform any longer to the pattern of this world, but be transformed by the renewing of your mind. Then you will be able to test and approve what God's will is—his good, pleasing and perfect will" (Rom. 12:2).

Facing Opposition

"Now, Lord, consider their threats and enable your servants to speak your word with great boldness. Stretch out your hand to heal and perform miraculous signs and wonders through the name of your holy servant Jesus." Acts 4:29–30

Everyone who has clearly identified with Christ to obey Him in everything is sure to face some kind of persecution. This is as predictable as the rising of the sun. A great cloud of witnesses from history testifies that persecution is part of the price we pay for following the Son of God. In numerous Scripture passages, especially in the New Testament, we are told we will suffer for the gospel. The fact is that we are not part of this world's system, nor do we conform to its parameters. As happens with a foreign substance in our bodies, the world seeks to expel all that does not belong to it.

The key question for us, then, is not whether or not we will suffer, but what our attitude will be to suffering. The apostles in the early church preached that Christ had risen from the dead and was now seated at the Father's right hand, reigning with all authority. Signs and wonders were done among those who believed, and their numbers grew daily. For those who had killed Jesus, this was obviously a new threat, and they reacted swiftly by arresting the apostles. On the apostles' release they were threatened and forbidden to preach in the name of Jesus.

Their reaction to this setback teaches a clear lesson about the way a leader should behave in times of opposition. In most cases that I have seen personally, when people come up against these kinds of difficulties, they become obsessed with eliminating the problem. Their prayers go in one direction: "Lord, I pray that You would remove me from this situation or eliminate the difficulty from my path."

The apostles did not pray this way—they understood that opposition was part of their call. Instead, they asked God to keep them faithful in the midst of the storm. In other words, their concern was that persecution would cause them to be unfaithful to Christ. They had a vocation to proclaim the good news of the Kingdom; the Sanhedrin's threats put their mission in danger. But they wanted to continue in their calling, even when things got difficult.

As they determined to carry on, whatever the circumstances, they asked God not only to give them courage, but that He would confirm the work with signs and wonders. This prayer was clearly to God's liking, for they had no sooner finished than the whole place shook, and they were all filled with the Spirit. They received what they needed, and the work continued according to the will of the Most High.

Food for Thought

How do you react to difficult times? What do your reactions reveal about your relationship with God? What would others think of your management of crisis situations?

Reason's Unreason

But the men who had gone up with him said, "We can't attack those people; they are stronger than we are." Numbers 13:31

This serious concern facing the Israelites originated in their failure to heed God's instructions to them. He had clearly directed Moses, "Send some men to explore the land of Canaan, which I am giving to the Israelites" (Num. 13:2). These men were not at any time to evaluate the feasibility of conquering the land. They were only to inspect it, since God had already said He would give it to them. I can imagine the Lord wanted to encourage the people with the wonders of this land promised to their fathers, just as we would be excited to see a video or a website of someplace we planned to visit.

Because they misunderstood the nature of their mission, these men believed they had authority to decide whether conquest was viable or not. The result of this mistake? A whole generation lost the opportunity to enter the land reserved for them.

It is of great interest to look at the arguments the men presented to justify their report. In their explanations we see evidence of a common strategy used by the Enemy against the children of God. He appeals to the human mind, presenting logical, carefully reasoned arguments to derail us from obedience to God. We need do no more than observe the lives of various Bible heroes to see that this is very common.

Consider Moses' calling. He presented at least three arguments to the Lord to try convincing Him that He had made a mistake: The people wouldn't believe him, he had a stutter and he was insignificant—all accurate observations. When God called Gideon, he argued that he was the youngest of a poor family, which was also true. When Saul saw David's willingness to face Goliath, he pointed out that the young shepherd had no experience in war. Again, this was true. In each case reason was definitely on the side of the person who argued with God.

The point is that spiritual life is not based on reason. On the contrary, reason is almost always a hindrance to those who seek to grow in faith. God laughs at our logic. He does not choose people we would choose nor do things as we would. There is nothing wrong with reason. But when it comes to following the Lord, it is not our arguments that should guide our steps. We must be led by the absolute conviction that God knows what He is doing, even if His proposals seem completely unreasonable to us. And so, armed with faith built upon the Word, we move ahead in the Lord's plans.

Food for Thought

"The supreme achievement of reason is to bring us to see that there is a limit to reason." (Blaise Pascal)[2]

Willingness to Listen

As a dream comes when there are many cares, so the speech of a fool when there are many words. Ecclesiastes 5:3

Recently I had an opportunity to meet the pastor of a large congregation in an important Latin American city. I approached him to introduce myself. When we had exchanged greetings, he began to talk about all he was doing in his ministry. Since the meeting at which he had been invited to speak was about to start, he apologized and went to share the Word with other pastors. The meeting lasted three hours, during which this leader spoke without a break! Afterward, he sat with the other pastors to share a meal. I watched him and saw, to my amazement, that he continued to speak about himself and his work. At no time did he show interest in the others, not even to find out who they were. He was too puffed up with his own importance to think that there might be something more important to discuss than his own experiences.

How can we be pastors if we are not willing to listen to others? The only alternative is to become a "pulpit" pastor, the kind that speaks to people, but not with them! In fact, this leader was no more than a program director. He did not have the qualities of a true shepherd.

For someone called to work with peoples' lives, it is absolutely essential to have the capacity to listen. How can we find out about the burdens, struggles and achievements of our people if we don't listen to them? How can we bring the right Word for their circumstances if we don't know what they live through and struggle with each day? The only way is to open our eyes and ears to their reality.

Being ready to listen, however, involves a price. We must love others more than we love ourselves. Too many pastors are in love with themselves; they like to hear the sound of their own voices, especially with a microphone in their hands! But those pastors who are shepherds delight in being with the flock. When they are with the people, they take the initiative to draw near and ask them how they are. It is not mere formality, but genuine interest in knowing what God is doing in their lives. These shepherds make time to listen not only with their ears, but with their hearts, for the heart perceives the real meaning behind the words. They do not rush or get distracted. Their whole posture says, "I am interested in your life! I want to hear what you have to say."

This requires discipline, for it is invariably easier to talk than to listen. But, as wise Solomon said, in many words there is foolishness. People will not trust a pastor who only knows how to talk.

Food for Thought

"Though silence sometimes involves the absence of speech it always involves the act of listening." (Richard Foster)[3]

Life on the Way

Walk in all the way that the Lord *your God has commanded you, so that you may live and prosper and prolong your days in the land that you will possess.* Deuteronomy 5:33

The Bible often uses the word "way" to describe the life of a person—some 595 times, according to my concordance. These references include allusions to the good way, the way laid out by Jehovah, the twisted way, the evil way that leads to perdition and the person who leaves the way. In the New Testament Christ Himself is presented as the way (John 14:6), revealing that the road to the Father is through the Son.

For the purpose of this meditation, the analogy of the way, or path, will reflect our spiritual pilgrimage through life. It will help us to recognize that there is only one road of life. The key is not in identifying the path, but in determining the direction we are moving on it. There are only two possible directions, since a path forces us to choose one way or the other. And so we can imagine all of humanity at different points along this way.

Depending on the direction in which we move, there are two possible destinations. One of these is Jesus Christ. The Word describes this destination as becoming like Him (Rom. 8:29), until we all reach "the whole measure of the fullness of Christ" (Eph. 4:13). In the opposite direction we have the other destination, which is perdition. This means the loss of divine likeness—becoming as abominable as Satan, the father of deceit.

How do we move along this path, regardless of the way we are facing? It is by definite actions, the result of decisions made as we walk along the way. Each action produces movement leading to one of the two possible outcomes. Our choices take us toward Christ or away from Him. Our existence is the sum of the decisions we make, each of which has spiritual consequence.

We are, then, constantly moving along the path of life, though often unaware of it. Most of our decisions are unconscious and automatic. Yet each of them has eternal weight and, in the analogy of the way, moves us in one direction or the other.

Understanding this is important. Our movement is not decided by the number of meetings we attend or by how often we read the Bible. Movement depends on the sum of our daily decisions, consciously made or not. This is why we must become sensitive to the leading of the Spirit of God, so that with each step He can guide us in the correct decisions.

Food for Thought

David committed adultery, hid his sin and killed a man. When the Lord says he was a man after God's heart, He is not thinking of particular events in David's life, but of the sum of his life decisions that brought him close to Jehovah.

Plans for Restitution

I will repay you for the years the locusts have eaten—the great locust and the young locust, the other locusts and the locust swarm—my great army that I sent among you. You will have plenty to eat, until you are full, and you will praise the name of the LORD your God, who has worked wonders for you; never again will my people be shamed. Joel 2:25–26

Joel's prophecies came to a people who had suffered devastating loss. In one military campaign after another, different nations had destroyed their cities and taken their cattle, their harvests and their possessions. A series of natural disasters, such as plagues of locusts and periods of intense drought, had also decimated the people's resources.

Today's passage describes God's unmistakable objectives for His people. Every circumstance in our lives is at the service of His eternal purposes. He so orders events that they fulfill a spiritual intent, and His hand is present in all things.

It is important to understand this because in times of disaster we believe that God has forgotten us, or that our situation has somehow gotten out of hand. In the storm on the Sea of Galilee, the disciples woke Jesus up and reproached Him for not caring about their plight. The Lord not only knows what is happening to us, but He Himself has ordered events to produce certain changes in us. He never fails to exercise His absolute sovereignty over the elements, for He is the Creator and can do as He pleases with everything.

The second principle we see is that disasters, adversities and difficulties have a useful "shelf life." In other words, they have not been sent to torment mankind indefinitely. Difficulties have a set period of time. As soon as they have fulfilled their divine objective, they are removed, and God restores what was lost. We can see this principle throughout the Word. When Job's trial ended, God removed his affliction and returned to him twice as much as he had lost (Job 42:10). Joseph, after years of slavery and imprisonment, reached the highest level of government, all the riches of the country at his disposal (Gen. 41:39–43). When Christ's confrontation with the devil in the desert had ended, angels came to minister to Him (Matt. 4:11).

The fulfillment of this principle reveals the tender heart of the Father. His principal desire is to bless and prosper His children. We don't need to beg Him to bless us because He already desires to bless. When He has finished testing us, He restores and multiplies His blessings to us. As the psalmist observes, "His anger lasts only a moment, but his favor lasts a lifetime; weeping may remain for a night, but rejoicing comes in the morning" (Ps. 30:5).

Food for Thought

How do you react to the discipline of God? How do you know when the Lord is trying to discipline you? How can you discover the purpose behind His discipline?

Fullness of the Spirit

Do not get drunk on wine, which leads to debauchery. Instead, be filled with the Spirit.
Ephesians 5:18

Scripture tells us to be filled with the Spirit. Understanding what Paul meant by the fullness of the Spirit is essential to obeying this command.

We can affirm that it is God's desire to fill us with His Spirit. We should have no doubts on this score. We do not need to call out, plead or beg Him to produce an infilling in our lives. Christ reminded His disciples, "If you then, though you are evil, know how to give good gifts to your children, how much more will your Father in heaven give the Holy Spirit to those who ask Him!" (Luke 11:13). The Lord is more interested in our fullness than we are.

At the risk of stating the obvious, we cannot fill a container that is full of something else. If we held a jug of milk and wanted to fill it with juice, we would first have to empty it to create the necessary space. We often ask the Lord for His Spirit without realizing there is no available space in our hearts. We must submit to being emptied of the sinful nature which presently fills us, and the only means for that is the cross. I am not referring to conversion, but about the call to deny ourselves—a central feature of Christ's disciples. Only when we are willing to deny ourselves and take up our cross can God dwell fully in our lives.

Paul states that the fullness of the Spirit can be compared to the intoxication produced by wine. I do not believe he was referring to the mirth that comes with too much drink, though the Spirit does produce joy in our lives. I believe that Paul was referring to the degree of control that wine has over an intoxicated person.

When a person is inebriated, their body no longer responds to commands issued by their mind. They may decide to stand up and walk home. But their legs are no longer under the control of their minds. The wine now "rules" their body. When they attempt to carry out a decision, their body "disobeys" them, as they are under the influence of something stronger than their willpower.

This is like being full of the Spirit. His indwelling presence should produce in us a similar response to that produced by wine. In other words, the power of the Spirit becomes so real that when our flesh suggests a different course of action, we are no longer able to obey, because the One who dwells in us is more powerful than we are.

Food for Thought

"After they prayed, the place where they were meeting was shaken. And they were all filled with the Holy Spirit and spoke the word of God boldly. . . . With great power the apostles continued to testify to the resurrection of the Lord Jesus, and much grace was upon them all" (Acts 4:31, 33).

26 September | The Reward of the Persistent

When he heard that it was Jesus of Nazareth, he began to shout, "Jesus, Son of David, have mercy on me!" Many rebuked him and told him to be quiet, but he shouted all the more, "Son of David, have mercy on me!" Mark 10:47–48

Like anyone who lives in the public places of a city, Bartimaeus knew everything that was going on around him. We don't know exactly when he heard about a certain Jesus of Nazareth, but it is evident he was up to date on the stories people were telling about this "prophet." The event described in this Gospel gives an interesting example of the value of stubbornness in the Kingdom!

The story of Bartimaeus shows that an initial condition of change is dissatisfaction with our present situation. We must desire improvement. Nevertheless, not all dissatisfaction leads to a search for something better. In many people discontent is a way of life and only makes their hearts bitter and resentful. These people say, "I'm not doing well, but that's the way it is." Just like the Israelites in Egypt, they have sunk so deeply into the pit of resignation that there is no room left for hope. But our dissatisfaction, if faced correctly, can actually be a key to spiritual advantage.

Bartimaeus shows us something else. For change to occur, it is necessary to be absolutely, unshakably convinced that Jesus has what we are looking for. I think his situation as a handicapped beggar helped him. He was completely lost in life, deprived of the most basic necessities; he was obliged to depend on others for everything. He didn't have much to lose. But still, Bartimaeus believed through what he had heard that Jesus could resolve his situation. He was willing to seek out what he needed, even if he had to do so at the top of his voice.

Bartimaues gives us one more example. When he began to shout, many scolded him, telling him to keep quiet. If we want change, we must be willing to turn a deaf ear to those who want to discourage us. On too many occasions we have allowed others to intimidate us. At other times, our own fears have stopped us. We have not dared to look silly or to endure embarrassing situations in order to get what we want. We have been too worried about what people will say. Fearful, we have watched from a distance, secretly wishing we could have what God was offering.

Bartimaeus was desperate, and his desperation led him to shout with all his might for Jesus to heal him. Christ heard him and gave him his sight, demonstrating that those who are audacious will be blessed richly in the Kingdom of God.

Food for Thought

How much passion is in your prayers? Are you convinced that you cannot live without the blessing you want? How much humiliation are you willing to bear in order to gain your desire?

A Prophet's Tenacity

"But the house of Israel is not willing to listen to you because they are not willing to listen to me, for the whole house of Israel is hardened and obstinate. But I will make you as unyielding and hardened as they are. I will make your forehead like the hardest stone, harder than flint. Do not be afraid of them or terrified by them, though they are a rebellious house." Ezekiel 3:7–9

God had told the prophet Ezekiel, "Son of man, go now to the house of Israel and speak my words to them" (Ezek. 3:4) But He also warned him that "the house of Israel is not willing to listen to you because they are not willing to listen to me, for the whole house of Israel is hardened and obstinate." The task entrusted to the prophet was clear. What was not clear was its purpose. What was the point of sending someone to speak to a people who were not going to listen to the message? Was this not a waste of time?

One of the biggest challenges for the Lord's servants is to refrain from analyzing whether the mission we have been given is necessary or not. Our call is to obey the instructions of the One who has sent us, even when we don't understand His reasons. In the book of Acts, when God spoke to Ananias and told him to go and visit the prostrate Saul, he replied that the mission was madness (Acts 9:10–15). In other words, not understanding God's intent, he did not want to obey. But God has not called us to analyze His requests—just to carry them out.

It was necessary for Ezekiel to be strong for the task commended to him. It is not easy or pleasant to speak to rebellious people, especially when you know from the outset they will refuse to listen. When we feel intimidated by people with aggressive, violent attitudes, we are tempted to ask the Lord to speak to them Himself; or as Moses did, to suggest sending someone else. God strengthened Ezekiel's heart, showing him that his spirit would be "hardened," in a good sense of the word, so that he would not be overcome by fear. He would be made "like the hardest stone, harder than flint," that the ruthlessness of others would not injure or damage his spirit.

This spiritual strength is indispensable to facing adverse situations we would prefer to avoid. God clothes leaders who are willing to serve Him with these qualities, not only in agreeable situations, but also in those that require boldness and courage. He does not commission His children without equipping them to complete the task before them.

Food for Thought

"Show when you are tempted to hide, and hide when you are tempted to show." (A.B. Bruce) [4]

28 September

He Cannot Be Mocked

Do not be deceived: God cannot be mocked. A man reaps what he sows. The one who sows to please his sinful nature, from that nature will reap destruction; the one who sows to please the Spirit, from the Spirit will reap eternal life. Galatians 6:7–8

The analogy of sowing seed, taken from the agricultural world, loses some of its force for many who live in urban settings. But it provides an excellent illustration of principles governing spiritual growth and is worth consideration. In today's text we can gather at least two truths of great importance.

First, there is an inviolable rule concerning the land: Whatever a person puts into the soil is what will be harvested. No farmer sows wheat expecting to get apples. If wheat is planted, then wheat will be produced. This rule holds true in the spiritual realm. What we sow we will reap. If we sow criticism, condemnation or legalism, we will reap precisely the same.

We should pause at this point to reflect for a moment. As leaders I often feel we are anxious to reap what we have not sown. I ask myself how we can be so naive when we have such a simple, clear law before us. If we don't develop real commitment to our people, how can we expect them to be committed to us? If we, as leaders, don't take time to listen to them and love them, how can we expect them to be a loving, compassionate community? If we don't spend time forming leaders, how can we be surprised when we don't have a single leader in our congregation? We can't expect these results to "magically" appear in our midst. This law governs all aspects of life, and that is why the apostle solemnly warns us, "God cannot be mocked." We mustn't fall into the trap of thinking that the Lord did not see what we sowed, and will therefore give us better fruit than we really deserve.

A second principle to notice is that one never instantly harvests what has been sown. It is important to note this, because it is precisely what leads us to treat lightly the things we do. People accustomed to working the land know that for at least a couple of weeks they will see no results from their work. And when we sow in the flesh, no angel appears to reprimand us, no ray of lightning flashes from the sky as a sign of God's justice. Everything carries on just as it has. This makes us think that what we do matters little. But the farmer sows thinking not of the present, but of the future. Those wise in the Kingdom understand that actions today have consequences tomorrow, and so are careful in the present about how they choose to live.

Food for Thought

"Let us not become weary in doing good, for at the proper time we will reap a harvest if we do not give up" (Gal. 6:9).

A Leader's Heart

Be sure to appoint over you the king the LORD your God chooses. He must be from among your own brothers. Do not place a foreigner over you, one who is not a brother Israelite. The king, moreover, must not acquire great numbers of horses for himself or make the people return to Egypt to get more of them, for the LORD has told you, "You are not to go back that way again." He must not take many wives, or his heart will be led astray. He must not accumulate large amounts of silver and gold. Deuteronomy 17:15–17

Although these words were spoken to Moses almost 4,000 years ago, the concepts they express have not lost their radical nature. A quick look at the text communicates some of the things God considered indispensable for those in positions of authority.

The future king was to be chosen from among the people. This would guarantee that he would really understand the people he would govern. He would know their customs, values, struggles and history. All this would help him avoid the imposition that might unnecessarily provoke the people, as is often typical when an unknown leader takes authority. A leader who comes from another place often implements changes that end up angering a congregation. For anyone in a position of authority, it is fundamental to win the respect and cooperation of the people. Only then will they be willing to follow us in extending the Kingdom.

The king was also to live closely to the people. God did not want him to become too rich, to accumulate many possessions or women. These things would only separate him from the people he would represent. Those who have abundance in their homes easily become hard of heart and insensitive to those in situations of poverty.

Despite this warning, in human history there has never been a king who has not surrounded himself with abundant luxuries. This is why it was so difficult for the spiritual leaders to accept the manner of Christ, the only King actually to have lived among the people. Many leaders take advantage of their position to accumulate scandalous riches, which has done no more than raise a barrier between them and the people they are to be serving. If a leader is to look after the sheep well, he must live in similar circumstances to them.

Finally, God instructed that a king should never meet his needs by joining ranks with other countries, such as Egypt. He should bring the people's needs before the Lord, thus governing them on a purely spiritual basis. In the same way, a leader has been called to a life of absolute dependence on God, seeking from Him whatever is needed. Spiritual work requires a spiritual perspective of authority.

Food for Thought

Compare Ezekiel 34:1–16 with today's text. This brings to light why God condemned Israel's pastors so severely.

Reflections on Unity

As a prisoner for the Lord, then, I urge you to live a life worthy of the calling you have received. . . . Make every effort to keep the unity of the Spirit through the bond of peace.
Ephesians 4:1, 3

No subject concerning Christ's life has received as little attention as unity in the body. It is mostly our failure in this area that that has kept us from convincingly presenting the good news of the gospel to the world. It would be good, therefore, to meditate on some reasons unity is so difficult to practice.

Paul's exhortation does not urge us to work toward unity, but to maintain it. This difference is important, because in the church we frequently hear calls to "work" toward unity. But oneness is a gift from God. We enjoy it because we are associated with a God who lives in perfect unity. But we can, however, destroy this harmony. This is why our efforts should be focused on preserving what the Lord has established.

Much of our difficulty lies in the confusion about what oneness really means. Many of us think it means we should all be the same—we should all think the same way, share the same objectives and work on the same projects. This is not unity, but uniformity. In congregations where uniformity is imposed, the practice of spiritual life is artificial. No one is allowed to disagree or hold a different opinion from that of the pastor, because they would be guilty of creating factions in the body of Christ. In the first church council some of the leaders wanted to impose this false unity (Acts 15:1).

It is this perspective that makes unity so difficult to put into practice. If we believe oneness refers to relationship with only those who think the same way we do, our circle of friends will be small indeed. But unity is not a description of coinciding ideas and concepts; it is rather a commitment. Living in harmony means accepting the call to love and honor all who belong to the house of the Lord, even those entirely different from us. It is based on the conviction that ideas and methods will pass away, but love lasts forever. We breach this unity when we believe that differences with others give us a license to criticize, scorn and condemn.

As leaders our role in this is fundamental. People observe our attitudes. They hear the terms we use when we speak of others. They analyze the way we relate to people who act and think differently from us. Our example will very often be the most important factor in helping them keep the unity of the Spirit. May the Lord grant, above all else, that we are known for the abundance of love in our lives.

Food for Thought

How do you react when faced with differences in others? How tolerant do those who know you consider you? What changes should you make in your life to continue embracing unity?

Paying Attention to Details

You must investigate it thoroughly. Deuteronomy 17:4

One of the mistakes I have most regularly made is being overhasty to judge a situation. I have often had to apologize for my initial conclusions because they were neither correct nor fair.

The Lord knows this is one of the weaknesses of humankind. There are countless examples in history of completely innocent people being condemned unfairly. In some cases people recover their freedom many years later because evidence of their innocence has been uncovered. In many cases, however, the people die and the sentence is irreversible. We simply don't possess the necessary discernment to be fair in every case we evaluate.

This is why the Lord left clear instructions for Moses about how to judge justly when someone brought an accusation against another. These directions indicate that after listening to the complaint firsthand, the person judging was also to examine the problem from other sources. The passage warns us that the viewpoint of a single person is always conditioned by his own position, and this is why a defendant cannot be condemned except on the testimony of two or three people (Deut. 17:6). A judge's best chance of reaching the truth is to consider the testimonies of several.

But we should not base our opinion exclusively on what others say either. God instructed Moses that a judge should "inquire thoroughly" into a case (Deut. 13:14). In other words, the testimony of others alone is not sufficient. The judge should do the work of investigating the accusation, paying attention to those minute details that could ensure a fair outcome. It is in these miniscule details that we frequently find things "not quite" as people told us.

How important for leaders to have the same cautious attitude when called to intervene in conflicting situations in the church! We are complicated beings who twist events to fit our interpretation of things. "The heart," says the prophet Jeremiah, "is deceitful above all things and beyond cure" (Jer. 17:9). We would do well to take our time in making judgments about what we have seen or heard. If we carefully study all the aspects of a situation, we will have the best chance of discovering the truth.

The New Testament tells us that by the Spirit we have been given the gift of discernment. Discernment is the ability to see things that go undetected by our own intelligence. It is important, both in counseling and when intervening in conflicting circumstances, that our ears are tuned to the Spirit. He can reveal to us what cannot be ascertained in any other way.

Food for Thought

"Evil men do not understand justice, but those who seek the LORD understand it fully" (Prov. 28:5).

A Common Mistake

He came to Jesus at night and said, "Rabbi, we know you are a teacher who has come from God. For no one could perform the miraculous signs you are doing if God were not with him."
John 3:2

Nicodemus was evidently unsettled by what he saw in Christ. His fellow Pharisees were constantly looking for ways to discredit Him. Nicodemus, however, managed to speak to Him alone, after taking precautions to remain unseen.

The first thing the Pharisee said reveals one of the most common mistakes of our culture, which is believing that good works are an unquestionable sign of God's presence in a person's life. This is one reason there is such confusion about the veracity of some who work for the Lord. Every week I speak to somebody who tells me that the abundance of "signs" in a certain ministry is clear evidence of the working of the Spirit through their leader.

We should remember that the Enemy also has power to work miracles. When Moses came before Pharaoh and converted his staff into a snake, the court magicians did exactly the same. Christ solemnly warns that on the day of final judgment, people will present themselves before Him saying, "Many will say to me on that day, 'Lord, Lord, did we not prophesy in your name, and in your name drive out demons and perform many miracles?' Then I will tell them plainly, 'I never knew you. Away from me, you evildoers!'" (Matt. 7:22–23).

Despite this warning, in twenty-five years' ministry I have seen the people of God seduced time and again. Countless prophets, healers and miracle workers have paraded through the church. Dazzled by their "credentials," we haven't paused to reflect that many of them have not shown the real sign of a person devoted to Christ—a sign that cannot be imitated or forged. Christ said that the *only* evidence of the work of God is rebirth into a new life through the exclusive action of the Holy Spirit.

It is the sovereign work of the Spirit that produces a renewed heart. This is discernible in completely different attitudes from those of people who live in darkness: "love, joy, peace, patience, kindness, goodness, faithfulness, gentleness and self-control" (Gal. 5:22–23). The Word clearly indicates that those who have been reborn will be known by these fruits.

Food for Thought

Does this imply that all who work miracles are unworthy of our trust? By no means! God has given His people access to **all** ***the manifestations of the Spirit, including the possibility of working miracles, signs and wonders. But we shouldn't look at the manifestations to see if a ministry is genuine, but rather at the life of the person behind this ministry. Those who walk faithfully with the Lord will have a different "look" to their lives; the character of the Messiah will be evident in all they say and do.***

Joy Complete

I have told you this so that my joy may be in you and that your joy may be complete.
John 15:11

The expression "that your joy may be complete" is one which is repeated frequently in the New Testament. John the Baptist, for example, said to his disciples, "The bride belongs to the bridegroom. The friend who attends the bridegroom waits and listens for him, and is full of joy when he hears the bridegroom's voice. That joy is mine, and it is now complete" (John 3:29). When Jesus encouraged His disciples to ask for all they needed, He said, "Until now you have not asked for anything in my name. Ask and you will receive, and your joy will be complete" (John 16:24). Similarly, when He prayed alone to the Father, He said, "I am coming to you now, but I say these things while I am still in the world, so that they may have the full measure of my joy within them" (John 17:13).

Christ's concept of joy seems to have made an impression on the life of His beloved disciple, for John uses expressions very similar to those of the Master. In his first letter he writes, "We write this to make our joy complete" (1 John 1:4). Later he states, "I have much to write to you, but I do not want to use paper and ink. Instead, I hope to visit you and talk with you face to face, so that our joy may be complete" (2 John 1:12)

What component is common to all these expressions? Each assertion of joy involved sharing with others. Delight does not attain its fullest expression until we invite others to participate in the experience. Think of the birth of a child. No parents keep such an event secret, but joyously share the good news with those closest to them. Or think of a trivial event like a goal scored in a soccer game. If you have ever been in a stadium you will have seen how players immediately look around for someone to celebrate with. And not only that, but the fans celebrate with such delight that they hug people they don't even know.

We have been created for fellowship with each other. It was not God's intention for us to experience our most profound moments in isolation, whether happy or sad. It is natural that we seek to share with others those occasions that bring us the greatest joy.

Food for Thought

Could this be the reason many of us don't fully experience the joy of God? We have received abundant expressions of goodness from our Lord, but we are silent. Our silence inhibits the complete expression of joy. Let us imitate Christ. Let us make our joy complete, inviting others to participate in what we have received!

Bargaining with God

Then Jacob made a vow, saying, "If God will be with me and will watch over me on this journey I am taking and will give me food to eat and clothes to wear so that I return safely to my father's house, then the LORD will be my God." Genesis 28:20–21

If we read the stories of the Genesis patriarchs—Abraham, Isaac and Jacob—in a single sitting, we will see plainly that faith is not inherited. Abraham, father of the faith, walked in intimacy with God and received His approval. Although Isaac was a spiritual man, we don't find the same devotion and passion in him that we see in his father. But in Jacob we see the greatest contrast. Jacob struggled all his life, laying his hand on whatever method seemed best suited to secure his wants.

In today's passage Jacob had just received a revelation from God similar to those received by his father and grandfather. God's words manifested His unconditional blessing on Jacob's life. "Your descendants will be like the dust of the earth, and you will spread out to the west and to the east, to the north and to the south. All peoples on earth will be blessed through you and your offspring. I am with you and will watch over you wherever you go, and I will bring you back to this land. I will not leave you until I have done what I have promised you" (Gen. 28:14–15).

The remarkable thing is not the reiteration of this promise, but Jacob's reaction. Normally, a divine manifestation like this would provoke deep worship and a sense of unworthiness in the one who witnessed it. But not in Jacob, whose response astounds us: "You may be my God only under these conditions."

Notice the repetition of the conditional conjunction "if": if You will be with me, if You keep me on the journey, if You give me food, if You give me clothes, if I return in safety. With unbelievable crust Jacob was informing the Lord that he too had his priorities. If his conditions were met, then he would follow God.

Jacob's attitude mirrors our strong affinity to believe we can manage God. We name the conditions, and He must meet our demands. This is why it is difficult to follow the Lord, for He does not negotiate with anyone. To enjoy a relationship with Him, we must submit absolutely to His terms and bow at His feet as Mary did: "'I am the Lord's servant. . . . May it be to me as you have said'" (Luke 1:38). We resist because we fear His control over our lives, which we feel is a great risk. But in the Kingdom it is the only road open to us.

Food for Thought

In what ways do you bargain with God? Do you resist submission to His demands? What are the risks involved in giving way to Him?

Keeping Up Appearances

The chief priests and the whole Sanhedrin were looking for false evidence against Jesus so that they could put him to death. But they did not find any, though many false witnesses came forward. Matthew 26:59–60

Many historians have analyzed, in minute detail, the trial to which the priests and elders subjected Christ. Most agree that the proceedings were no more than a mockery of the legal system established by Israelite society. The council members had already decided previously that whatever the results of the trial, Jesus was to be put to death. Nevertheless, they insisted on putting on a show of acting within the framework of the law.

In doing this the council joins a long list of tyrants, despots and dictators who have worked in a similar fashion. The two most ominous characters of the twentieth century, Hitler and Stalin, both insisted on meticulously following the requirements of law, though there was never any doubt as to the final outcome of their intentions. While sowing panic and horror among the people, they wished to maintain the appearance of legality for the "good" of the people. Evil is perpetuated through masking the wickedness of our actions.

We all have a deep desire to gain the approval of others in what we do. The most common demonstration of this is our inclination to justify ourselves, even when clearly in the wrong.

We must understand this very human tendency. As leaders we don't want to create a bad image of ourselves in the eyes of others. But on the other hand, neither do we want our plans circumvented. This very often leads to complex behavior to attempt the impossible: We seek to impress others with our spirituality while ensuring that our wishes are unquestionably accepted by all.

Consider how easy it is for a leader to convert discussion of a proposal into mere formality. For many leaders inviting others to share their opinion is no more than a matter of form. Everyone else knows they have no freedom to contradict what has already been decided. Or think of the times we have prayed at the end of a long planning meeting, just to put a "varnish" of spirituality on what we have decided. We are not seeking God's will or His input in what we have discussed. All we desire is His blessing on what we have already settled.

This demonstrates our frequent desire to retain control of our lives while hiding from others what we are doing! Intellectually we know this is absurd, but in practice we fall repeatedly into the same patterns of behavior. Change is possible only when we are willing to submit absolutely everything into God's hands. This means running the "risk" of having our plans redirected—from the way we want things to the way He wants.

Food for Thought

"All a man's ways seem innocent to him, but motives are weighed by the LORD" (Prov. 16:2).

6 October | The Works God Prepared for Us

Then Peter invited the men into the house to be his guests. The next day Peter started out with them, and some of the brothers from Joppa went along. The following day he arrived in Caesarea. Cornelius was expecting them and had called together his relatives and close friends. Acts 10:23–24

This is perhaps one of the best illustrations of the text that tells us "we are God's workmanship, created in Christ Jesus to do good works, which God prepared in advance for us to do" (Eph 2:10). The story of Peter and Cornelius demonstrates how the Father, through the Spirit, arranges every detail of a situation to produce an outcome in accordance with His divine will.

God's objective in this plan was that Cornelius and his family would come to know the good news of Christ. The Word tells us that Cornelius was "devout and God-fearing; he gave generously to those in need and prayed to God regularly" (Acts 10:2). There is no doubt that the first action God took was to move the heart of this man to seek Him.

After a time the Lord intervened again, sending an angel to speak to Cornelius. The angel gave him instructions to send for Peter, who would speak to him the way of life. While Cornelius' messengers were on their way, God began the third step. He revealed to Peter in a vision the good works "which God prepared in advance" for him to do.

After a moment's confusion Peter agreed to go. Even as he was expressing his willingness, the men who had been mobilized by the Lord arrived. Peter returned with them to Cornelius' house, where the man, undoubtedly moved by God, had gathered together all his family and neighbors. The preparation was now complete for Peter to present the good news of Jesus Christ to these people.

The outcome is predictable! "While Peter was still speaking these words, the Holy Spirit came on all who heard the message" (Acts 10:44). The details had been meticulously coordinated by the Lord to produce this fruit. And these are just the details we know about; how many others might God have arranged to produce this conversion?

In light of this account, the exaggerated role we assign ourselves within the Kingdom is almost laughable. Too often we think we are the ones making things happen. But in fact, the part we play is exceedingly small. We become weary because we fail to recognize all God is doing; we believe we are working alone. Today's story invites us to relax and open our eyes to see the hand of God in our ministry. Above all, it enjoins us to cease trying to arrange the details for the works He has prepared for us to do.

Food for Thought

The key to participating in this kind of ministry is maintaining absolute sensitivity to the Spirit at all times. Without this sensitivity, we are "flying blind."

Firm in Our Vocation

For if you possess these qualities in increasing measure, they will keep you from being ineffective and unproductive in your knowledge of our Lord Jesus Christ. 2 Peter 1:8

I am always impressed by the terms used in the Word to interpret the eternal truths of God. They are simple, but profoundly illustrative.

Peter uses two terms to communicate conditions we must avoid if we are to be faithful to our call. These words are "ineffective" and "unproductive." It is not necessary to delve much into the original language to understand their meaning, for the significance is evident.

Ineffectiveness is not a lack of activity, but a lack of responsibility in our activities. Ineffective people can be involved in numerous programs, but still fail to be productive or profitable. Their activities are not beneficial. Sadly, this condition describes the lives of many Christians within the church. They are very active, but are of little spiritual value. Their contribution consists mostly in attending an endless succession of meetings supposedly useful in building up our lives. Sometimes these meetings simply encourage passivity, contributing little to real transformation.

Our call is not to this kind of spiritual "idleness" in which our objective is to secure the greatest blessing for our own lives. We have been called to invest in the lives of others. This truth is made clear in what some Bible scholars refer to as the "Magna Carta" of the Bible (Gen. 12:1–3). Here God clearly states His intention to bless us so that we may be a blessing to others. When Christians lose sight of this, they begin to use their time inadequately, causing problems for themselves and others. We should note that most divisions and accusations within the church are brought about by believers who, usually after some years in the faith, are not involved in doing good works.

Peter also tells us we should not become "unproductive." This word refers to an inability to produce new life. This condition too is abnormal in a follower of Christ, for we are called to make disciples of all nations, whatever our work may be. But most Christians, having heard the good news through the loving witness of others, rarely lead anyone to knowledge of the truth. This is not normal, and the apostle exhorts his readers to "be all the more eager" (2 Pet. 1:10).

Our lives can escape these vices only when we keep the purpose of our call in sight. We should progress with a steady step toward this goal. We cannot allow the pull of inaction to carry us off course. The Kingdom belongs to the audacious, those who long to reach the fullness of their call in Christ.

Food for Thought

"Therefore, my brothers, be all the more eager to make your calling and election sure. For if you do these things, you will never fall, and you will receive a rich welcome into the eternal kingdom of our Lord and Savior Jesus Christ" (2 Pet. 1:10).

The Struggle for Life

The thief comes only to steal and kill and destroy; I have come that they may have life, and have it to the full. John 10:10

This passage contrasts the intentions of a good shepherd and a thief. Various interesting observations can be made of their differing objectives.

We should note initially that the thief's strategy is not directed against the good Shepherd, but against the sheep. A common viewpoint within the church is that God and Satan are involved in a great cosmic battle, fighting without relief until the day of the final outcome. This perspective is false, for God is the Creator, and the devil is a created being. The Enemy cannot rise against God any more than an ant can make war on an elephant. Rather, the devil's prey is the people created in the image and likeness of the Creator.

Christ clearly declares the thief's objectives against us. He has not come to distract us momentarily or to make life difficult. Neither does he expect to subdue us. He is an enemy with much more devastating plans than these. He will not rest until he has achieved total destruction of the person in his sights.

Note the progression in his strategy.

First, he steals. When he steals, he takes away the inheritance that belongs to us as beings created in the image and likeness of God: our ability to live on a spiritual plane, to have fellowship and enjoy demonstrations of love, and to experience peace, joy and hope. The absence of these things produces havoc in our own identity and leads to a life plagued with conflict and pain.

In the second stage the thief intends to bring about death; he wants to terminate the life for which God created us as individuals. Even then the thief will not rest, for his third and final objective is our complete and final destruction. We understand this as eternal death, the loss of every vestige of our divine origin.

If we reverse the construction Christ used to describe the thief's purposes, we can affirm that the intention of the Shepherd is to give, revive and build up. That is, His first objective is always to bless. He delights in giving, even to those who don't deserve it. He is a God who does not rest in the search for people to bless, because His very nature is one of unbounded generosity. To the act of blessing He adds the desire to revive His people. God wants us to live fully in every dimension of the life He has given us, physically, emotionally and spiritually. In the long term, however, Christ is in the business of building up a holy people, a kingdom of priests. We are beings with an eternal destiny, and the good Shepherd desires to lead us in that direction.

Food for Thought

Do you live an abundant life? What evidence proves this? How can you experience even greater abundance in Christ?

Renewing the Mind

Do not conform any longer to the pattern of this world, but be transformed by the renewing of your mind. Then you will be able to test and approve what God's will is—his good, pleasing and perfect will. Romans 12:2

A.W. Tozer writes of the mind, "What we think about when we are free to think about what we will—that is what we are or soon will become."[1]

Most of us have no idea how deeply our thoughts affect our lives. But the Scriptures warn us that renewal of the mind is one of the keys to a transformed life. We should, therefore, pay close attention to this matter if we hope for a life that conforms to the parameters of the Word.

Our actions are not spontaneous, even if we do sometimes explain our behavior with the phrase, "I did it without thinking." The truth is that all actions are the result of a thought, even when we are not aware that it was forming in our minds. Jesus highlighted this principle in the Sermon on the Mount when He said God would not judge us by our actions, but by the thoughts that provoked them. This is why the real sin of adultery begins when a person covets his neighbor's wife secretly in his mind. The sin of murder begins when we label a person as stupid or idiotic in our minds. Eventually, if nothing changes, these thoughts will give way to deeds that express what has been developing secretly within.

In today's text the Apostle Paul exhorts us to resist this world. But the fight does not consist of such simple things as avoiding dancing or smoking. The world wants to mold us to the culture that dominates these times. One of the principal means of doing this is through endless messages that "promote" the present perverse system in which we live. Sometimes these methods are easily detectable. In most cases, though, they are hidden subtly in things we consider inoffensive.

This is why believers have an obligation to renew their minds. This can be achieved in two ways. First, we should identify those thoughts not worthy of the Lord and take them captive to the obedience of Christ (2 Cor. 10:5). This means disposing of them. But the mind does not function in a vacuum; the space left by those discarded thoughts must be filled with new ones if we don't want to fall back into sinful thinking. To do this we must occupy our minds with God's truth, meditating on the Word. This nourishes us with thoughts that can produce a transformation of our character.

Food for Thought

"Finally, brothers, whatever is true, whatever is noble, whatever is right, whatever is pure, whatever is lovely, whatever is admirable—if anything is excellent or praiseworthy—think about such things" (Phil. 4:8).

The Value of Memories

Sacrifice as the Passover to the LORD your God an animal from your flock or herd at the place the LORD will choose as a dwelling for his Name. Do not eat it with bread made with yeast, but for seven days eat unleavened bread, the bread of affliction, because you left Egypt in haste—so that all the days of your life you may remember the time of your departure from Egypt. Deuteronomy 16:2–3

Although we often try to erase from our thoughts negative experiences we have had, they can play an important role in our spiritual development. To engage Israel in this practice, the Lord established an annual celebration with the sole purpose of remembering their pilgrimage as God's people.

What exactly were they to remember? First, in the past they had been slaves, with no hope of being freed from their situation. The freedom they now enjoyed had been given; they had not earned it through their efforts or by their own merit. Second, their escape from Egypt was made possible by the powerful intervention of God on their behalf. Their freedom had a price. The Egyptian people suffered numerous calamities so that a hard-hearted Pharaoh would finally give Israel permission to leave. Third, they left Egypt with only the clothes on their backs. They had none of the belongings they now enjoyed in the Promised Land. From absolute poverty God had transformed them into a great and prosperous nation.

Why was it good they should remember these things? It would help them not to take anything for granted. This is a great problem we face each day. We get up in the morning and complain because it is raining, or because we don't like the food on the table, or because we have to go to work. We have forgotten that nothing we have is ours by right; everything comes to us through God's exclusive goodness. Blindness to our true spiritual condition causes ungratefulness, which in turn produces grievances and complaints.

Gratitude not only helps us to remember God, from whose hands comes all that is good; it also brings us delight as we relish each experience, each relationship, every activity we participate in. When we remember that all we have is a gift, we can enjoy it as something undeserved, something which speaks of the loving heart of the Giver.

It is also easy for those serving in the church to forget what the Lord freed us from. We can easily fall into the habit of ungrateful complaining—demanding greater respect or increased privileges—as if we had entered the ministry on our own merit. How good it is to remember daily that we serve only because He has granted us that privilege.

Food for Thought

"Then King David went in and sat before the LORD, and he said: 'Who am I, O Sovereign LORD, and what is my family, that you have brought me this far?'" (2 Sam. 7:18).

God's Kind of Project!

The Lord turned to him and said, "Go in the strength you have and save Israel out of Midian's hand. Am I not sending you?" "But Lord," Gideon asked, "how can I save Israel? My clan is the weakest in Manasseh, and I am the least in my family." Judges 6:14–15

Israel was under occupation by the Midianites. With their powerful army of 135,000 warriors, they had completely overcome the people of God. By way of force they had taken the best of Israel's produce and cattle. The people were understandably demoralized and without hope.

In the midst of this situation, an angel came to Gideon as he was threshing wheat in secret. Without beating around the bush, the Lord shared His unbelievable proposition. He wanted Gideon, an unheard of, poverty-stricken member of the tribe of Manasseh, to rise up and free Israel from the hand of Midian!

If we were to make a list of the qualities Gideon possessed, we wouldn't find much to convince us God had the right person for the job. He probably had no experience in military matters or in leadership. He was the youngest of a poor family, probably accustomed to being passed over by others. If we consider these weaknesses alongside the significance of the mission God was giving him, we would not be blamed for strong reservations about the outcome of such an undertaking. What could this "insignificant character" do in the face of such an enormous challenge?

But this is God's method. He delights in presenting us with assignments that are absolutely impossible for us to carry out. We look at our resources and exclaim, "Nobody can do that!" But God works differently. He proposed that Moses should take two million Israelites who had been living as slaves and possess a land occupied by a host of hostile nations. He asked Joshua to conquer a fortified city by marching and shouting outside its walls! He had Jonah preach the day of reckoning to a people bent on world domination. He expected a group of unlettered fishermen to make disciples of every nation on earth.

It is precisely this feeling of being completely out of our depth that confirms our involvement in divine plans. God never asks us to do what can be achieved in our own strength. He delights in putting us in situations where all our cleverness, our resources and our planning look completely ridiculous.

This is God's method. To participate in God's plans, we need to feel that our own means are completely inadequate. God's assignments can be carried out only with the resources He gives.

Food for Thought

What projects do you have as a leader? What challenges do they present? Would you dare to lay aside your human plans and begin to dream big—not just about the transformation of a few lives, but your city, your nation or even the world? If others laugh at your plans, then you are surely in tune with the Lord.

David's Prayer

O God, you are my God, earnestly I seek you; my soul thirsts for you, my body longs for you, in a dry and weary land where there is no water. I have seen you in the sanctuary and beheld your power and your glory. Psalm 63:1–2

How many generations have been inspired by these beautiful words of David written more than 3,000 years ago! This psalm appeals to us because its phrases capture sentiments we find difficult to express ourselves.

We regularly proclaim our devotion to God through song, prayer and communion with other saints. When life doesn't contain too many setbacks, these words flow easily from our lips. I suspect, however, that our expressions of devotion have more to do with the pleasantness of our circumstances than with true devotion to God.

The moment in which David wrote this psalm was very unlike those we normally face. The psalm's subtitle states it was written when David was in the Desert of Judah. There were only two occasions in which he was found in this desert. The first was when he fled from Saul, seeking refuge in the caves and rocks of the region. The second was when Absalom rose up and usurped the throne. The king had to flee with nothing but the clothes on his back. The Bible tells us David reached the desert covered in dust, exhausted and hungry.

If we stop to meditate on these scenes, we can appreciate the psalm in an entirely new light. Affirming that God is our God differs from David's expression when our worst trial is being hungry for a few hours or getting wet because we forgot our umbrella. Our suffering is generally no more than temporary discomfort. Few of us have had to flee fierce persecution in which our very lives are in danger. We don't know what it feels like to be completely abandoned, without shelter or assistance.

Meditate again on the first phrase of the poem: "O God, you are my God." This declaration is arresting precisely because David had lost everything. Nevertheless, he affirmed that all that really mattered to him was the Lord. Nothing else was of value. His comfort, his security, his future—not even his life was important to him. God was truly his God.

This complete surrender to the Lord in the darkest moments of life is what distinguishes a truly outstanding leader. There are no other gods in such a person's heart. Passion for the Lord eclipses everything else, including the sparkle of ministry.

Food for Thought

What was the secret of David's devotion? He was a man accustomed to seeking communion with God—"I have seen you in the sanctuary and beheld your power and your glory." With time, this discipline changed him until his very being groaned for the glory of the Lord.

Interpreters of Prophecies

October **13**

When King Herod heard this he was disturbed, and all Jerusalem with him. When he had called together all the people's chief priests and teachers of the law, he asked them where the Christ was to be born. "In Bethlehem in Judea," they replied. Matthew 2:3–5

The arrival of the wise men from the east caused a commotion in Jerusalem. They had received a revelation unknown to all the important figures in the city. And their message was really worrying: It proclaimed the birth of a new king for the Jews. Alarmed, King Herod sought an explanation from those who had knowledge of the Scriptures.

The priests and scribes didn't hesitate to provide him immediately with the information he required. They knew Micah's prophesy perfectly, which foretold that the Christ would be born in Bethlehem. They must surely have studied the text in great detail, as is common for those whose spirituality is focused mainly on the intellectual plane. They would have exhaustively considered the various possibilities within the prophet's declaration. It is even possible there were different "schools" of interpretation. Some may have said He would be born in Bethlehem, others that He would develop His ministry in Bethlehem and others that Bethlehem held only symbolic meaning, representing the tribe from which the Messiah would come.

But despite their exact and complete knowledge of the texts referring to the promised One's arrival, none of the specialists knew that He had already appeared!

Today we see renewed interest in biblical prophecies and end times. Multitudes have given themselves to carefully analyzing each text, attempting to uncover details hidden in Scripture. While engrossed in this task they carefully interpret each world event, watching to see if it fulfills any of the texts they know so well. The most daring in this group confidently assert the date for the reconstruction of the temple, the place where the antichrist will show his face, and the exact identity of Gog and Magog.

As with the religious leaders, entire absorption with careful scrutiny of the Bible may spoil their chances of participating in the spiritual events around them. Why? It is inevitable that so much study provides unnecessary stimulation for the imagination, resulting in the development of our own version of final events. The picture we so carefully construct will be the very thing that blurs our vision, hindering us from recognizing events when they do happen. We will be watching for things to occur as we had imagined, discarding anything that doesn't fit this image.

This is why the priests and scribes killed Christ. Their convictions of what the Messiah should look like, supported by many Old Testament texts, kept them from recognizing the true Christ, even as He stood before them.

Food for Thought

It is good to remember that things in the spiritual world are rarely as we perceive them. We have been called to worship the Lord, and this should be our main concern in life.

Faith, Hope and Love

We always thank God for all of you, mentioning you in our prayers. We continually remember before our God and Father your work produced by faith, your labor prompted by love, and your endurance inspired by hope in our Lord Jesus Christ. 1 Thessalonians 1:2–3

This is not the first time these three elements are mentioned together. They are also talked about in Romans, Corinthians, Galatians, Colossians, Hebrews and Peter's first letter. The early church evidently believed that the combination of faith, hope and love was what contributed most toward spiritual maturity. We do well to consider the matter.

In the first place, the apostle mentions their work of faith. It must be said that this is entirely different from faith through works, where it is hoped that works will produce faith. The apostle clearly declares that faith is a gift from God, received by grace. At the same time, biblical faith does *lead* to works. This is difficult for us to understand, having become accustomed to a purely intellectual concept of faith accompanied by a passive spiritual life. Biblical faith is in constant movement—not restless movement, but productive. Faith is active because God is active. To follow Him it is necessary to become involved in the works in which He is involved. In this way the church reveals its convictions through the way it lives.

Second, this congregation demonstrated labor based on love. It is interesting to note that this principle has no common ground with our own concept of love either. In our culture love is mainly a feeling toward others. But in the Thessalonian church, love was a commitment. Believers understood they had been called to love, and it demanded effort on their part. Effort is essential because real love must overcome an incredible diversity of obstacles for its expression. Christ's journey to the cross, His maximum demonstration of love, was filled with complications, adversity and setbacks. The Thessalonian church followed this example, since the expression Paul uses indicates they had labored to the point of exhaustion.

The third grace present in the life of this church was their steadfast hope. Hope most clearly defines the spiritual maturity we seek. In the midst of adversity, conflict and hardship, hope helps us focus on what we seek to obtain in our relationship with Christ. Around us we see the devastation and havoc wrought by sin. In our souls we feel the constant tension caused by the struggle between flesh and spirit. But in all this we don't give up. We hope to lay hold of Christ, to mature and be instruments of transformation in our society through the power of the gospel. If we had no hope, we would surely give up the fight.

Food for Thought

"And now these three remain: faith, hope and love. But the greatest of these is love" (1 Cor. 13:13).

Workers for the Harvest

Ask the Lord of the harvest, therefore, to send out workers into his harvest field.
Matthew 9:38

Raising up new workers is one of the biggest challenges of our pastoral work. The workers who form our team are indispensable for a correct distribution of the workload, so that no one becomes worn out by carrying excessive burdens. In addition, the formation of leaders in our congregations ensures that the work will continue when we are gone. Training workers requires a serious and responsible attitude.

Christ told His disciples, "I tell you, open [or lift up] your eyes and look at the fields! They are ripe for harvest" (John 4:35). This apparently insignificant action—lifting up the eyes—is the first step in training workers. When people walk with their gaze directed at the floor, it is because they are absorbed with themselves, preoccupied with their own world. The world around them does not enter their perspective. They don't see it and are unaware of its existence. On lifting their eyes they will discover a whole world inhabited by individuals like themselves who also experience problems, struggles, difficulties and frustrations. Each person they see has been created for an exclusive relationship with the Father. On seeing them, their spirit should feel the anguish Christ felt when He saw the crowds as sheep without a shepherd.

This new vision also reveals the enormity of the job. Christ pointed His disciples to the fields, not to a small garden. The land stretched out in front of them, waiting to be harvested. It required the help of many hands to complete this task. In the same way, it is good for those serving in the house of the Lord to feel overwhelmed by the immensity of the calling. There are too many workers who are convinced they can accomplish the job alone, without help from anyone. This self-sufficient attitude is counterproductive for the church, since it is totally opposed to the biblical concept of extending the Kingdom. Only a madman would try to harvest an entire field alone.

Recognizing the immensity of the task should not mobilize us to desperate attempts to get the work done—it should bring us to our knees. Jesus told the disciples that their first responsibility was to appeal to the Lord of the harvest. As leaders we have tried to substitute this holy call by provoking the members of our congregations into the fields through guilt. Nevertheless, it is God who must mobilize His people. We would do well to spend less time speaking to the congregation and more time to the Father. There would surely be greater numbers of laborers in His field if we dedicated increased time to prayer!

Food for Thought

"One of those days Jesus went out to a mountainside to pray, and spent the night praying to God. When morning came, he called his disciples to him and chose twelve of them, whom he also designated apostles" (Luke 6:12–13).

The Correct Perspective

Pharaoh said to Joseph, "I had a dream, and no one can interpret it. But I have heard it said of you that when you hear a dream you can interpret it." "I cannot do it," Joseph replied to Pharaoh, "but God will give Pharaoh the answer he desires." Genesis 41:15–16

It is difficult for us to imagine how dramatic and unexpected this event was. Joseph, though he had done nothing to deserve it, languished alone and forgotten in one of Pharaoh's prisons. His position as a slave meant there was little hope of ever being released. Nobody bothered to defend a slave's rights, even less those of a slave condemned by one of the highest court officials.

During his years in jail, Joseph had interpreted the dreams of two fellow-prisoners, the baker and the king's cupbearer. Now suddenly the young Hebrew had been asked to interpret the dreams of Pharaoh himself, the most powerful man on earth. For Joseph, the success of this undertaking could well mean the end of his captivity. The accuracy of the interpretations he had given his prison mates may have given him a certain amount of confidence as he faced this challenge. It would have been so easy for him to say that he had the ability to interpret dreams! What would it have mattered that the gift was not really his? Pharaoh didn't even know who Jehovah was. Why waste time on unnecessary explanations?

It is easy to lay claim to an ability that is entirely God's. We are prone to believe it is our hand that moves things in the church. Leaders appear who tell us they have a special "anointing," and they alone are able to administer it. Their posture reveals how creative we can be when it comes to defending "our" position. We forget that in the spiritual world absolutely nothing happens if God does not ordain it. At the best of times we are no more than fragile vessels in His hands.

Although Joseph's future hung in the balance, he did not hesitate to clarify his situation. He himself could not interpret dreams; this ability belonged to God. In saying so he was also declaring that if God did not give the explanation, then nobody could. God is not manipulated like a machine. He is sovereign and does as He pleases. We can only trust that by His grace He will show Himself, for we have no control over Him. Even if we have interpreted a thousand dreams in the past, the gift continues to belong exclusively to God.

It is terribly important never to lose sight of this truth. We are mere channels for God's working. If we remember this we can be useful tools in His hands.

Food for Thought

"When Peter saw this, he said to them: 'Men of Israel, why does this surprise you? Why do you stare at us as if by our own power or godliness we had made this man walk?'" (Acts 3:12).

Guard the Good Deposit

Guard the good deposit that was entrusted to you—guard it with the help of the Holy Spirit who lives in us. 2 Timothy 1:14

The Apostle Paul had already made this exhortation to Timothy in his first letter. At the end of a long list of instructions concerning his young disciple's life and ministry, he signs off with this warning, "Timothy, guard what has been entrusted to your care" (1 Tim. 6:20). It will be useful for us to reflect on the problem the apostle wanted Timothy to avoid.

The law of entropy, as real as that of gravity, states that with the passing of time everything inevitably enters into a process of deterioration. We could speculate on the reasons for this, although it wouldn't resolve the problem. No doubt the fallen nature of a world under judgment is directly related to this process of declination. But whatever the rationale, the passage of time causes wear and tear. Our bodies gradually lose mobility and agility. Our houses show unmistakable signs of deterioration with flaking paint, leaky roofs and blocked water pipes. The same thing happens with all our everyday items; our televisions, radios, cars and computers wear out and need repair.

The spiritual world is not exempt from this process. Notice the deterioration pointed out by the prophet Isaiah: "See how the faithful city has become a harlot! She once was full of justice; righteousness used to dwell in her—but now murderers! Your silver has become dross, your choice wine is diluted with water" (Isa. 1:21–22). What was at one time glorious can become pathetic and lifeless over the years. You can see this in many churches that have been around for more than a hundred years. Once full of vibrant, sparkling life, today they are relics with only a few tenacious survivors remaining.

Paul was evidently worried about the effects of this process on Timothy's life. By urging him to "guard" what he had, he was indicating that it could be lost. It would not maintain the same vigorous strength forever. If he didn't look after it, it would gradually lose power and become something insignificant.

Yesterday's glory cannot breathe life into the present. It doesn't matter how extraordinary the experiences of the past may have been; the only way to bring life into the present is to enter into contact with the Source of life Himself. In order to guard what we have received, we need to renew our relationship and commitment to the Lord each day. And this is even more crucial for those who are serving as pastors and leaders, because the cost of the "deposit" we have received is considerable. Could this be the reason Christ, in His last days on earth, sought time alone with the Father?

Food for Thought

What are the signs in your own life that you are becoming worn out? What activities can you do in order to bring renewal to your life? How can you prevent further deterioration?

The Presence of the Lord

When the angel of the LORD did not show himself again to Manoah and his wife, Manoah realized that it was the angel of the LORD. "We are doomed to die!" he said to his wife. "We have seen God!" Judges 13:21–22

I never cease to be intrigued by our response to the apparent divine visitations in our weekly gatherings, so different from the reactions of people in Scripture! Manoah's reply is typical of many Bible characters, especially in the Old Testament. Jacob spent an entire night wrestling with the angel of the Lord, marveling when He withdrew because he "saw God face to face, and yet *my life was spared*" (Gen. 32:30). When Gideon realized he had been visited by the angel of the Lord, he said, "'Ah, Sovereign LORD! I have seen the angel of the LORD face to face!' But the LORD said to him, 'Peace! Do not be afraid. *You are not going to die*'" (Judg. 6:22–23). In Revelation the Apostle John, when he beheld the Lord, fell *as dead* at His feet (Rev. 1:17). These are only a few of many Scriptural examples showing dramatic encounters with the living God. In each confrontation those involved were gripped, without exception, by unspeakable terror.

In many meetings I attend these days I hear people entreating God to show His face, visit us with power or send His Spirit upon our gathering. Whenever the music is particularly appealing, the worship leader may declare how "real" God's presence is or how the Spirit is "moving" among us. But despite our confident assertions, I find it hard to ignore that in Scripture every divine visitation awakened a peculiar dread in those present.

What quality do we possess that allows our every experience of God to produce such delight and gratification? We have come to believe that the sum of pleasant sensations we experience in our meetings signals "God's presence in our midst." The fact that we are willing to label these experiences as divine visitations, however, does not in any way add greater depth or meaning to them.

The unpleasant sensation produced by divine visitations in Scripture is not the only characteristic separating us from the biblical accounts. These saints, when God appeared to them, were seized with an indescribable sense of their own smallness. If we look closely, we will also find that not one of them was seeking the experience they were granted. It came without their asking and was rarely granted those who sought it.

Food for Thought

Would it not be more appropriate for us to display a certain amount of caution when attempting to draw close to the living God? Who among us can really understand who He is? Why have our meetings sprouted leaders who so easily identify God's presence in our midst? As for me, I'd rather not give my ignorance too much publicity!

Born of the Spirit

"You should not be surprised at my saying, 'You must be born again.' The wind blows wherever it pleases. You hear its sound, but you cannot tell where it comes from or where it is going. So it is with everyone born of the Spirit." John 3:7–8

As He so often did, Jesus chose simple elements from daily life to illustrate concepts related to the kingdom of God. Nicodemus, however, found His words confusing. The problem was not in the language or in the depth of the concepts. The problem lay elsewhere. They were speaking of two different worlds.

The world in which we live strongly influences the way we view things. Everything in our everyday experience is affected by this perspective. Unaware of our "clouded" vision, we believe that the world and its people are exactly as we see them. To a person who has been beaten and hurt, everyone is a potential aggressor. To those who have been served everything "on a platter," the world exists exclusively for their benefit.

When we try to understand spiritual truths with the perspective we have of this world, we end up as confused and perplexed as Nicodemus. The mind cannot cope with the realities of the spiritual world because they are of an entirely different dimension. They can only be understood through the working of the Spirit, who causes us to see what had previously been a mystery to us. If God does not grant this revelation, then we can analyze and observe until the day we die and still not discern anything.

The new birth reflects more clearly than any facet of the spiritual life the difference between what is spiritual and what is earthly. The process by which a person who is depressive, discouraged, defeated and drowning in a self-centered perspective of life can become full of joy, hope and thoughtfulness is a complete mystery. We don't know how this change comes about or how profound the intervention of the Spirit is. As happens with a gust of wind, we can only perceive a "before and after," and the contrast fills us with wonder.

This has by no means put an end to our attempt to analyze and explain the process of conversion in minute detail. In fact, we have produced thousands of tracts explaining the steps you must take to "welcome Christ into your heart." We have attempted to convert what Jesus Himself called a mystery into a method, nudging the Spirit aside and replacing man as the central character in this sacred event.

Food for Thought

As ministers in His house, it is good to recover a biblical perspective of conversion. In essence it continues to be pure miracle. It bids us invest more time in calling out to the God of signs, miracles and wonders, that He may visit those who walk in darkness. We should not remain silent as to the Good News, but should wait for the evidence that tells us "the wind is blowing."

A Prophetic Voice

He sent back this answer: "Do not think that because you are in the king's house you alone of all the Jews will escape. For if you remain silent at this time, relief and deliverance for the Jews will arise from another place, but you and your father's family will perish. And who knows but that you have come to royal position for such a time as this?"
Esther 4:13–14

The book of Esther contains the amazing story of Mordecai's intervention to save God's people from a great disaster—one similar to that of Hitler's horrific dictatorship. By means of a royal decree, a powerful man in the palace tried to exterminate the Jews completely and confiscate all their goods. In today's text we find an important example of the prophetic voice that should exist in the face of injustice in this present evil time.

We should note that Mordecai believed deeply that nobody would escape this persecution, including Queen Esther, the king's favorite. He understood that the evil behind this kind of plan is such that those responsible will not rest until they have achieved complete obliteration of the people. He warned the queen that no place was safe, not even the dwelling of the king's palace.

We see a marked contrast between Mordecai's response then and the church's attempts today to win the respect of society so that it may co-exist in peace with others. In many nations I have known people who believe we are called to seek laws from ungodly men that would bring great benefits to the institution of the church. But the history of God's people shows that commitment to the Lord brings persecution from the world.

Mordecai also understood that Queen Esther had a prophetic responsibility in the unjust situation taking place. She was called to raise her voice to denounce that which offends God's good and righteous laws. On many occasions the church has taken a passive role when faced with inequity, worried more about ensuring the evil will not affect its own people. But our mission is to lead people to repentance by means of a message as clear as that of John the Baptist. Mordecai believed that the position occupied by the queen had been granted her in order to fulfill this purpose.

Finally, Mordecai was strongly convinced that if Esther had not performed this duty, God would have raised up other voices, for the Lord will not remain silent in the face of evil. In fact, the history of God's people provides us with abundant examples of this. When those who were to speak out failed to do so, the Lord used others, shaming those who had kept silent.

Food for Thought

It should gladden our hearts to know that the Lord has such a strong commitment to proclaiming His truth. He will certainly not remain silent, even if He must use stones to say what He wants to say!

Knowing His Will

As he walked along, he saw Levi son of Alphaeus sitting at the tax collector's booth. "Follow me," Jesus told him, and Levi got up and followed him. Mark 2:14

We should be eager to know God's will, because we wish to please Him in all we do. Sometimes when faced with important decisions, my whole life comes to a standstill as I endeavor to discern the Lord's will for that particular situation. I also confess to having read a great variety of books and articles offering advice on how to discover God's will. Over the past few years, however, a new perspective on this subject has been developing in my mind and spirit.

When I look through Scripture, I don't see many scenarios in which people earnestly sought to learn the Lord's will. Of course, there are incidents, especially in David's life, in which it was necessary to make an urgent decision. This was the case when he and his men had to know if they should pursue the raiders who had destroyed Ziklag (1 Sam. 30). On this occasion David asked for the ephod in order to learn the will of God. But these examples seem to be the exception rather than the rule.

The pattern throughout the Bible is otherwise. As with Levi, we read of people going about their everyday business. They were not seeking God's will, nor did they seem particularly interested in it. They were simply living in the circumstances in which they had been placed. In the midst of their indifference, God burst upon the scene with revelation that changed their lives. The list of such people is long: Abraham, Moses, Gideon, David, Zechariah, Mary, Elizabeth, Joseph, Peter, Ananias and even the Apostle Paul. In every case a divine manifestation changed their lives.

This leads to a second observation: The revelation of God's will implies an interruption of whatever these people had been doing. They were not the same after the divine visitation; they did not return to their prior activities. The course of their lives was dramatically changed, and they were led along an entirely different path. Of course, many of them didn't accept this change until they had first argued intensely with the Lord. What He showed them did not fit into the plans they had for their lives.

Food for Thought

These observations enable me to outline an idea without presuming to introduce a "theology" on the subject. The Bible doesn't seem to present us overtly with the need for "seeking" God's will. It would seem it invites us to walk in the light we have, and let God bring course corrections as we go about our business. I suspect the reason we often don't know His will is because what we really want is His approval of what we have already chosen. To know His will we must be willing to let Him interrupt our lives dramatically and impose His plans over and above our own.

From Crisis to Crisis

We always carry around in our body the death of Jesus, so that the life of Jesus may also be revealed in our body. 2 Corinthians 4:10

A veteran pastor of many years' experience in ministry shared the following observation: "A leader lives in a permanent state of crisis. He may be emerging from one or in the middle of one or just going into one, but he is always in crisis." When I reflect on almost thirty years of ministerial experience, I realize how accurate this observation is. I have spent a great deal of time over the years facing difficulties of the most varied intensity and nature. I am certain, having heard testimony from many colleagues, that my experience is not unique. The experience of great biblical figures adds further weight to the persuasion that a leader is always involved in crisis.

It becomes essential, then, to learn to deal with crises if we want to avoid the devastation of our spiritual resources. An important step is to recognize that it is normal for a leader to undergo crises. The Apostle Paul indicates that he bears the signs of Christ's death permanently in his body. Without identifying specific experiences, we know he refers to the ongoing struggle between life and death. A crisis would not be one if it did not affect those attitudes and reactions that should be submitted to God's sovereign rule. Even though the trouble may have originated in an event outside us, its deepest expression is always felt in the inner self. The clearest example of this is Jesus in Gethsemane.

Crises, however, frequently assault us with unusual strength because we cannot reconcile their presence with God's purposes for our life. "How can this be happening to us?" we exclaim, as if it was something abnormal. This lack of acceptance sometimes produces more pain than the trial itself.

It would be a great help to keep the second part of Paul's declaration in mind. Our experience of death allows the life of Christ to be expressed within us. So we can consider a crisis the most appropriate means for allowing God's power to be fully manifest in our lives. If we recognize that in our natural state "there is no one righteous, not even one; there is no one who understands, no one who seeks God" (Rom. 3:10–11), we can see that crisis is the most efficient way to produce holy dependence in us. In times of crisis, a leader has two paths from which to choose: the path of discouragement which leads to giving up or the path to the throne of grace where the Lord can grant the help we need. There is no doubt that a crisis experience is disagreeable, but it can be of immeasurable value to a leader's life.

Food for Thought

"Dear friends, do not be surprised at the painful trial you are suffering, as though something strange were happening to you" (1 Pet. 4:12).

Life in Black and White

They sent their disciples to him along with the Herodians. "Teacher," they said, "we know you are a man of integrity and that you teach the way of God in accordance with the truth. You aren't swayed by men, because you pay no attention to who they are. Tell us then, what is your opinion? Is it right to pay taxes to Caesar or not?"
Matthew 22:16–17

Christ immediately discerned the intentions of these men's hearts. In His reply we see that their charming words did not impress Him for an instant. "But Jesus, knowing their evil intent, said, 'You hypocrites, why are you trying to trap me?'" (Matt. 22:18).

What mindset led the Herodians to formulate their question this way? Their words expose an extremely simplistic perspective on life. They believed problems had no more than two possible solutions. In the matter they presented to Jesus, there was no room for complexities or even gray areas.

The Herodians' posture is very similar to that of most people. This perspective is due partly to our desire to reduce complexities to manageable parameters. But undoubtedly, it is also due to an attitude of arrogance that leads us to believe that the world around us can be understood by beings as insignificant as ourselves.

Leaders can easily give way to the temptation of this perspective. We smoothly say, "All human problems have only one origin," or "With these three steps we will achieve growth in the church," or "For disciples the matter is very simple; either they are committed or they aren't." This posture always leads to condemnation and severity. We have no time for people who do not possess the same "clarity" we do. We are impatient when they doubt, hesitate or fall along the way. Our ministry ends up being caustic and tedious.

But when we stop for a moment, we realize the absurdity of this stance. Not even our own lives are that simple! We are a mixture of right and wrong, hits and misses, holiness and sin, truth and lies. Those we are leading are just as complex as we are. Sometimes our investments in their lives are in perfect harmony with the Spirit, but at other times, the people grow in spite of our bungling attempts to serve them! Who among us can confidently make statements about God and the way He works? Instead, we should embrace Jesus' statement about the Spirit being like the wind. We have no idea of its source or destination; we are only granted the ability to see the movement of the branches.

Food for Thought

This highlights, once again, that most precious legacy of the gospel: the grace of God. Grace sustains, consoles and guides those who feel overwhelmed by the mysteries of life. It is an infinitely more gratifying experience than that offered by our tidy theories about life. Grace invites us to rest, because there is One who understands everything. It is enough simply to know that.

Gathered in His Name

"Again, I tell you that if two of you on earth agree about anything you ask for, it will be done for you by my Father in heaven. For where two or three come together in my name, there am I with them." Matthew 18:19–20

I must confess, quite frankly, that this verse makes me uncomfortable. It contains declarations that don't fit my interpretation of the gospel or what I have seen in the church.

Look at this incredible statement: "If two of you on earth agree about anything you ask for, it will be done for you by my Father in heaven." Could Christ possibly mean that the Father will act according to our agreements on earth? This is what He seems to say! But how can that be possible? Can it be true that the Father will do what we ask?

Our initial reaction is to qualify or alter the meaning of the words. Our arguments, however, will not eliminate them or remove our discomfort. This "power" of having the heavens align with our petitions has been granted to us.

But the manifestation of this truth among us is rare. Why? It depends on two or three coming to an agreement. Such a simple statement, but so difficult to bring about! Our tireless commitment to ourselves rears its head and proves a significant obstacle. We want to own our ideas, to think them up and control them, to be central in everything. These are the very attitudes that impede agreement, for accordance is possible only when we die to ourselves.

And what can we say about the second part of the verse? In so many places I have heard it proclaimed that Christ is present because two or three are gathered. Can it be so simple? Two or three Christians meet together physically and the Lord is automatically present? What happens when those two or three don't even speak together, except on Sundays? How can Christ be present among those whose only agreement is a common prayer, as if that could guarantee unity in the Spirit?

The condition for Christ's presence among us is not that we are two or three or that we are gathered in one place. It is rather that we meet in His name. The three who are present must recognize that joint submission to His name is necessary. Further, our meeting is not the sum of my submission plus that of the others. As a community we bow at His feet and, inevitably, at one another's feet! Only when we are willing to confer the same honor on those with us will it be possible for Christ to accompany us.

Food for Thought

The reality pointed out by Christ is so interesting! "There am I with them." He does not identify with any individual or give preference to one above another. He is among them. He is the God of a community of faith, equally accessible to all, equally desirous of blessing each one.

Only for the Daring!

October 25

"Lord, if it's you," Peter replied, "tell me to come to you on the water." "Come," he said.
Matthew 14:28–29

I have heard dozens of messages on this passage and have used it myself in more than one sermon. Most of these talks expose a too common tendency to focus on Peter's mistake. In this case, we use the adventure to illustrate the importance of keeping our eyes on Jesus so we don't fail in our undertakings. We mustn't look at the waves as Peter did. This is true, of course, but along the way we miss the fullness of the disciple's experience.

The teaching of one friend, an excellent expositor of the Word, led me to contemplate this passage from another perspective. Peter provides a very good example of how to start something new. Overflowing with enthusiasm, we tend to launch into a project without previous deliberation. On our way we offer up a prayer asking God's blessing, even though we have already decided to continue. Peter himself, when he denied Christ, paid the penalty for proceeding in this way.

In this incident Peter desired to do what his friend Jesus was doing. Despite this, he did not just jump out of the boat. "Lord, if it's You, tell me to come to You on the water." This is the correct way to proceed in any plans we are considering. We should stop to ask the Lord if He is authorizing the venture, even when the circumstances seem to indicate that we have a unique opportunity.

This is especially important for those leading diverse ministries. It is tremendously easy to give in to the temptation of planning things for God, believing that all we do in His name automatically has His blessing. Our ways are not His ways, though. The discipline of stopping and seeking approval from on High is most crucial for effective ministry.

Second, I would like to draw your attention to the boldness of Peter's request. He did not want to miss this chance. When he heard the invitation, he set out to walk on the waves. What an extraordinary experience!

It is true that he ended up sinking, but he didn't miss the chance to experience something out of this world. The other disciples stayed in the security of the boat. In a way this scene represents the church. Most of us prefer the security of the boat, from where we heap criticism on those who try something new. A few, bold in the faith, prefer the adventure of following Christ no matter where He may decide to go!

Imagine the disciples as the years went by. The majority perhaps would tell others: "We once knew a man who walked on the water." But only Peter could say, "Once, when I was young, I walked on the water!"

Food for Thought

***"One man with courage constitutes a majority." (Andrew Jackson)*[2]**

26 October

A Divided Heart

So Ahab sent word throughout all Israel and assembled the prophets on Mount Carmel. Elijah went before the people and said, "How long will you waver between two opinions? If the LORD is God, follow him; but if Baal is God, follow him." But the people said nothing. 1 Kings 18:20–21

When Elijah confronted the people on Mount Carmel, the Israelites already had a long history of prostitution with the gods of the earth. Before challenging the prophets of Baal, however, Elijah spoke to the people with strong words. Although it was the leaders who had led God's people along a profligate path, nobody could hide behind that fact. Elijah's question showed that in the end, everyone present was responsible for their own sin.

The root of the Israelites' situation can be found in the word "waver." The dictionary of synonyms offers us a list of similar terms: vacillate, fluctuate, oscillate, hesitate, dither. All of these give a clear idea of the state the people were in. They had no definite direction—they were not committed to anything. They did not have the unshakeable conviction of those who know where they stand.

This wavering has a particular effect on those who belong to God. Unbelievers are totally given over to the way of darkness. Only occasionally do their consciences give them pangs of remorse. Most of the time they advance with confidence in the direction everybody around them is going. They follow the way of the majority and have no reason to question whether or not it is best.

But indecision is most unfortunate in the lives of God's children. They are neither one thing nor another. Having tasted a sample of the life of God, they have decided to return to the way they had once renounced. They can't manage, however, to forget their close communion with Jehovah, so the old lifestyle does not produce the satisfaction it once did. They don't enjoy full communion with the Father, because their hearts are contaminated with the many worries typical of those who walk in darkness.

The best description of this unfortunate state was made by Solomon, a king whose heart was never entirely given over to God. He tried to walk both ways at the same time. His conclusions are related in the book of Ecclesiastes in which he declares time and again, "Everything is meaningless" (Eccles. 1:2)

Elijah exhorts the people to a position of complete surrender, whether for one side or the other. Vacillation paralyzes us and fills us with doubt and fear. When we decide on a certain path, it is good not to question the decision further, so we can advance with a firm, confident step in the chosen direction.

Food for Thought

"That man should not think he will receive anything from the Lord; he is a double-minded man, unstable in all he does" (James 1:7–8).

A Fireproof Commitment

Shadrach, Meshach and Abednego replied to the king, "O Nebuchadnezzar, we do not need to defend ourselves before you in this matter. If we are thrown into the blazing furnace, the God we serve is able to save us from it, and he will rescue us from your hand, O king. But even if he does not, we want you to know, O king, that we will not serve your gods or worship the image of gold you have set up." Daniel 3:16–18

How easy it is to read this story comfortably seated in our homes, knowing before hand how it will end! Our Hollywood-style perspective leads us to believe that all stories should end in this same spectacular way when we declare our faithfulness to God. But then we remember Stephen and John the Baptist, or John Hus, Dietrich Bonhoeffer and Watchman Nee, to mention just a few of many who paid for their faith with their lives.

Nevertheless, the three bold characters in today's text model an important lesson on the stance we should take in times of persecution. Our persecution need not be as dramatic as that of Shadrach, Meshach and Abednego, for we daily face the same pressures they did, but in different ways. We shouldn't doubt for one moment that the same evil forces are seeking to mold us to the image of this world. It could be through pressure not to pay taxes, to cheat in an exam, to join in some dishonest project at work or to give way to predominant philosophies concerning the family.

The three Israelites used two arguments to respond to Nebuchadnezzar. The first was based on a radical conviction that God would determine their future, not the Babylonian king. This is the posture Christ adopted when Pilate tried to convince Him of the authority he had over Him. But Jesus answered him, "You would have no power over me if it were not given to you from above" (John 19:11). In the hour of trial, they did not doubt that their circumstances were out of the Lord's control. They knew that even before the most atrocious evil, there is a sovereign God without whose approval nobody can act, not even the most wicked.

These brave men clung to a second conviction, that God's children are called to a life of unconditional obedience. When their personal welfare was at risk, they didn't hesitate to choose loyalty to the Lord. They would not allow their obedience to be conditioned by circumstances or people. By maintaining such a stance, they created an opportunity to see the most incredible demonstration of grace. In this case they came out of the fire unhurt. In the case of Stephen, as he was dying he saw the final destiny of his faithfulness: the arms of the One he had been unwilling to deny.

Food for Thought

The last word in all of human history belongs to Him in whose hands life itself is hidden.

28 October

The Effectiveness of Love

There is no fear in love. But perfect love drives out fear, because fear has to do with punishment. The man who fears is not made perfect in love. 1 John 4:18

As adults it is easy to recognize inappropriate ways we were disciplined during our childhood. Too often the discipline imposed by parents on their children is inflicted in anger, resulting in exaggerated punishment instead of correction and restoration. Because of this the children obey mainly out of fear. This may be a relatively effective method of motivation in childhood; but as people grow they should go through a maturing process that leads to obedience resulting from their own desires, not from those imposed on them.

Today's text explains the importance of this proper motivation in the children of God. Obedience through fear does free a person from punishment, but it lacks the necessary power to produce serious transformation in a person's life.

It is important to recognize the difference between these motivations. In too many congregations people are intimidated by threats disguised as spirituality, so that they obey the desires of those leading the ministry. In large sectors of the congregation, this will produce sufficient fear to guarantee submission to the leadership. A minority will resist this kind of pressure, will question the leader's intentions and in time will leave the congregation. The atmosphere of fear in the congregation will lead the group to refer to those who left as "rebels."

Our principal call is not to ensure the congregation's loyalty to us or to the institution to which we belong. We have been called to participate in the ministry of transformation, which is the priority of the Spirit of God. We work to present everybody "perfect in Christ" (Col. 1:28). But it is impossible to bring this about if the only means we use are intimidation and punishment. These were the preferred instruments of the Pharisees, and the entire nation of Israel gave testimony to how ineffective these methods were in changing peoples' lives. Only a handful of fanatics could really fulfill the endless list of requirements in order to be "acceptable" before God.

Note how effective love was in Christ's ministry. It achieved the dramatic transformation of a hardened materialist like Zacchaeus. It produced brokenness in a prostitute, scorned and condemned, who fell to kiss His feet at a public dinner. It softened the heart of a woman who had committed adultery. Love is the most powerful instrument on the face of the earth. It should be the chosen means of all those serving in ministry.

Food for Thought

A friend's mother used to say, "It is easier to trap flies with honey than with vinegar." How true that is!

The Other Half of the Gospel

If you confess with your mouth, "Jesus is Lord," and believe in your heart that God raised him from the dead, you will be saved. For it is with your heart that you believe and are justified, and it is with your mouth that you confess and are saved. Romans 10:9–10

It is interesting to meditate on the conditions for salvation that Paul stated. There is a marked difference from the "formula" we often use for people to "invite Jesus into their hearts." In most of our gospel presentations, we emphasize the fact that Christ died for our sins, paying the price of our redemption on the cross. There is clear and abundant evidence in the Bible for this; we don't need to quote references to justify this truth. But I want to point out that the work of the cross is only half the gospel. The other half is centered on the fact that Christ was raised from the dead and is seated at the Father's right hand, where He reigns today.

When our concept of the gospel is based exclusively on the cross, we end up relating to a Jesus stuck in time. The event that freed us from sin happened two thousand years ago. It is easy to feel separated from the figure who walked the lands of Palestine and to view Him as a wise teacher who illuminates from history our steps today. We cannot escape the sensation that we are alone in life, each seeking spiritual victory in our own way.

Note the contrast today's verse presents us with. Paul says that to be saved, two things are necessary. First, we must confess with our mouths that Jesus is Lord. It is interesting that this declaration must be verbal and audible. In the apostle's world, declaring someone as Lord implied recognizing them as masters. A master was not simply a manager, director or guide, but had absolute rights over the life of the other. The master could use the person's time and belongings in any way desired. Since it goes without saying that a dead man cannot be Lord over anyone, this confession was centered on the living Christ.

The second condition for salvation referred to believing from the heart "that God raised him from the dead." Note once again the emphasis on events following Christ's death. Believing He was raised from the dead leads automatically to the conclusion that He is alive today! And this is the true hope of those who are in Christ. "It is no longer I who live, but Christ lives in me" (Gal. 2:20), declared the apostle. The Christian life consists in discovering how the risen Christ works in me, here in my world in the twenty-first century.

Food for Thought

***"Easter is to our faith what water is to the ocean, what stone is to the mountain, what blood is to the body." (Raymond Lindquist)*[3]**

30 October | Working Out Our Salvation

Therefore, my dear friends, as you have always obeyed—not only in my presence, but now much more in my absence—continue to work out your salvation with fear and trembling, for it is God who works in you to will and to act according to his good purpose.
Philippians 2:12–13

The phrase used by the Apostle Paul in this text, "work out your salvation," catches us off guard. In the modern church we are used to thinking of salvation as a particular event, a moment in our earthly pilgrimage.

The fact is that this is not the only text in the New Testament to present salvation as a process. The Apostle Peter declares that we should, like newborn babies, desire pure spiritual milk so that we can grow up in our salvation (1 Pet. 2:2). Paul explains that "if, when we were God's enemies, we were reconciled to him through the death of his Son, how much more, having been reconciled, shall we be saved through his life!" (Rom. 5:10). He also states that salvation is only possible if we "hold firmly to the word I preached" (1 Cor. 15:2).

The idea that one single moment can define our spiritual status forever appeals to our modern perspective of life. This thinking is a product of what A.W. Tozer calls "instant Christianity." For those who believe in this kind of salvation, it is just like any other deal we make. If we are buying a house, arranging for a new telephone line, enrolling a child in the birth register, all we have to do is fill out the necessary forms. Once done, we don't need to go back over it several times, for the deal has been completed.

Unfortunately, we are not talking here about one more of life's chores. When we speak of salvation we refer to the reality of another Kingdom with essentially different dimensions than this world. Believing a person can be saved simply because they "accept" Christ at a certain moment, even as they continue to live their own way, reveals the depth of our spiritual naivety.

Paul exhorts us to work out our salvation in fear and trembling—the reason being that God produces in us the desire to will and to act. In other words, the apostle points out that the transformation of our being is not our work, but the product of divine intervention in our lives. As such, it is similar to receiving a gift. The One who has given the gift expects us to use it well, doing something with what we have been given. Salvation is not an event, but rather a call to a certain lifestyle. We are expected to align our lives with this change of style and live according to God's principles.

Food for Thought

"How shall we escape if we ignore such a great salvation? This salvation, which was first announced by the Lord, was confirmed to us by those who heard him" (Heb. 2:3).

A Bad Choice

The king answered the people harshly. Rejecting the advice given him by the elders, he followed the advice of the young men and said, "My father made your yoke heavy; I will make it even heavier. My father scourged you with whips; I will scourge you with scorpions." 1 Kings 12:13–14

Anybody who takes responsibility for a position new to them does well to seek guidance. This is practically the only right thing Rehoboam did when his father Solomon died. Before deciding how he would proceed as king, he sought advice from close advisors. The elders, familiar with Solomon's excesses, recommended greater compassion and kindness. The young men, perhaps conceited merely because they had been consulted, recommended "the iron fist in the gloved hand."

The disparity between the two postures illustrates the distance between the generations. Young people, caught up with their dreams and idealism, frequently believe they can discover a way that nobody else has tried. They scorn the experience of others because they suppose their own proposal has never been tested. They even believe in the impossible, wanting a world of peace, a land without pollution and a society ruled by love. Their proposals all suffer from the same weakness: They have not been tested in the crucible of life and are therefore no more than innocent dreams.

On the other hand we have the elders. They have traveled through a good many years. Life has dealt them tough blows. They have suffered setbacks, obstacles, misfortunes and injustice, and have been obliged to accept that life did not turn out with the simplicity and malleability they had hoped. They have enough experience to give an intelligent opinion without having to study the details of each case intricately.

In today's passage the elders recommended nothing revolutionary or extraordinary. They suggested the way of meekness, consideration and simplicity. The ideas of the young men seemed more daring and appeared to guarantee impressive short-term results. Unfortunately, Rehoboam chose this second option. The result was irreparable damage to relationships with the northern tribes. Discontent eventually produced an insurmountable division in the nation of Israel.

We live in an age when people with experience are treated with less respect every day. The elderly are looked on with pity rather than admiration. Their opinions are considered old fashioned. But the Word encourages us to treasure the elderly, offering them the respect they deserve for having traveled much further in life than we have. This doesn't mean we are obliged to follow all their advice, but the wise person will listen carefully to what they have to say. Their perspective is sure to enrich ours and on occasion will save us from unnecessary mistakes.

Food for Thought

What place do the elderly have in your congregation? What kind of dialogue do you have with them? In what way are they honored?

Every Day I Will Praise You

I will exalt you, my God the King; I will praise your name for ever and ever. Every day I will praise you and extol your name for ever and ever. Psalm 145:1–2

We don't know when David composed this psalm. But we know that the commitment expressed in the first two verses summarized his attitude through the whole of life. The practice of this spiritual discipline is one way the simple shepherd attained such a high level of intimacy with God. His insistent decision to proclaim God's greatness wherever he went nourished his devotion to the Most High.

We would do well to meditate on what these verses express. They contain a vow, the expression of a commitment that would guide the psalmist's behavior in the future. This pact he made is similar to what we declare when we enter into the bond of matrimony. We promise to love our spouse at all times, whatever happens. Whoever has gone some distance in the experience of marriage knows how difficult this is to do.

Our spirituality is also based on a vow. This is what keeps it alive and vibrant throughout our lives. A vow is a promise to keep firm in a posture or conviction. There are no clauses or conditions concerning its fulfillment. It looks to the future and establishes guidelines for behavior that will remain constant at all times, whatever life contains.

What the future will bring is something no one can know. But we can predict with a certain degree of accuracy that whatever comes will contain a mixture of good and bad, happiness and sadness, victories and defeats, abundance and scarcity. Every human being is exposed to these fluctuating conditions of living in a fallen world.

David's life was filled with all kinds of difficulties. He faced Saul's tenacious persecution. He had to deal with solitude and desertion. He lived with the serious consequences of the sin of adultery. He drank the bitter cup of betrayal at the hands of his own son. But in the midst of this long list of afflictions, he always remained firm in his commitment to praising and blessing the name of God.

What a marked contrast we see in our culture, so ruled by feelings! We blindly believe in the importance of being "genuine," which really means doing things when we "feel" like doing them. And so we praise and worship only when our feelings give us permission to do so. David shows us the importance of subjecting our feelings to our will, practicing the discipline of the spiritual life even when our whole being rebels against the idea. Consistent practice in times of adversity may produce the richest spiritual harvest in our lives.

Food for Thought

How important are feelings to you? In what ways do they hinder or enhance your spiritual life? What can you do so your feelings play a bigger part in your expressions of devotion to God?

Our "Search" for God

My heart says of you, "Seek his face!" Your face, LORD, I will seek. Psalm 27:8

In this verse the psalmist shares important information on how spiritual life is made visible in us. One of the scars sin has left in humanity is a belief that we are the focal point of all that happens around us. Our self-centered perspective causes us to magnify our own importance. It is difficult for us to imagine life without our involvement or to understand that the world turns independently of us.

This hinders our spiritual development, for we insist on believing we are the "engine" that propels our devotion. Our distorted view places us in a position belonging to the Lord, and for this reason we invest a great deal of time and energy attempting things that are not our responsibility. We are convinced that closeness to God depends on our efforts; but when we find ourselves without sufficient discipline to sustain a deep, long-term relationship, we become discouraged. "I am seeking God," we say, "but I never manage to develop a significant relationship with Him." We condemn ourselves for our lack of devotion and make endless promises to start over. But our poor behavior continues. Reaching God seems so difficult!

The psalmist, who did not understand the workings of the Spirit as we do, heard a message in his heart to "seek his face." This is nothing but the voice of God, for the words are expressed in the form of a divine invitation. Having perceived this message, the psalmist goes on to enjoy a meeting with the Lord. Note how simple the process is, how easy it is to "find" Him in this fashion. The simplicity is due precisely to the fact that it is God Himself seeking us, long before we have worked out a plan to reach Him!

So what does a relationship with God consist of? What dynamics govern these spiritual encounters? We must discard our own techniques and methods for developing a relationship with Him. We do not power the relationship, He does. We have to relax and allow Him to persuade us with His invitations. For this to happen we need to quiet the racket that is part of our everyday existence. The Father longs for relationship with us and seeks in a thousand ways to speak to us what the psalmist heard: "Seek my face."

If we can understand that He always insists on drawing close to us, we will realize that our effort is unnecessary. We don't have to look for Him, because He has already drawn close to us. With this attitude of inner quiet, we can begin to hear His tender invitations and can answer, "Your face, LORD, I will seek."

Food for Thought

We have not been called to find God, but to let ourselves be found by Him.

3 November

Lack of Knowledge

"My people are destroyed from lack of knowledge. Because you have rejected knowledge, I also reject you as my priests; because you have ignored the law of your God, I also will ignore your children." Hosea 4:6

Through the prophets the Lord told Israel His reasons for rejecting them as a people and sending them into exile. We find one of these explanations in today's text, which is certainly not the only time God points out the wrongs of His people.

It is profitable to reflect on this, because the church today displays the same worrying propensity to disregard a solid, life-changing knowledge of the Word. A preaching style has become popular in which speakers share their personal concepts of Christianity. These sermons are sometimes adorned with one or two verses from the Word, but in general Scripture is included only to make the message more respectable.

People who lack knowledge are vulnerable to seduction by whatever prevalent philosophy crops up around them. This condition is described by Paul when he refers to the danger of becoming infants, "tossed back and forth by the waves, and blown here and there by every wind of teaching and by the cunning and craftiness of men in their deceitful scheming" (Eph. 4:14–15). This attitude is observable in many congregations, the leaders chasing every fad that comes their way. These assemblies are easily seduced by the eloquence of men and do not possess the tools to evaluate whether the message is God's revealed truth or not.

The responsibility for this neglect lies squarely with those called to disciple the saints, namely, leaders. The prophet Hosea declared that the priests had "rejected" knowledge. This evinces a deeper problem: an attitude of scorn for the Word. This dislike for Scripture may originate in the desire to ingratiate oneself with the congregation, speaking words to accommodate our culture's widely-held ideas. We see the Word as antiquated and old-fashioned, and strive for a message more appropriate to the times in which we live.

I suspect that this boredom with Scripture is due mainly to the commitment it takes to become people of the Word. Pastors must commit to diligent study of the text in order to discern the particular message God has for His people. This arduous effort is avoided by leaders who simply choose to speak about their favorite subjects.

People need the undiluted Word of God. Only the Word brings light to our lives and guides our steps.

This is the only means of true spiritual transformation and of living a life pleasing to God.

Food for Thought

Our job as leaders is not to entertain people, but to shape them in the image of Christ. This can be accomplished only by the Word of God.

Hope

Hope deferred makes the heart sick, but a longing fulfilled is a tree of life. Proverbs 13:12

Hope is something so interwoven with our everyday existence that we are practically unaware of its influence on us. Nevertheless, it fulfills an important role in our lives.

Hope looks to a future situation or reality that promises to be better than the present. As life brings its fair share of setbacks and difficulties, hope helps offset the natural inclination to discouragement and disillusionment that results from our negative experiences.

Hope may be directed toward relatively unimportant matters such as the weather, our food or a series on television. But it also focuses on much weightier matters such as our work situation, reconciliation with an estranged family member or improvement in relating to our nearest and dearest. In all of these, our hearts reach out to future situations that we hope will one day become reality.

For this reason the author of Proverbs describes a fulfilled longing as a "tree of life." It produces a feeling of well-being in us that compares to the benefits a fertile tree brings to a piece of ground. It not only beautifies the land, but also gives shade and fruit to its owner, making it a true blessing.

If hope is important to those who walk in darkness, it is much more so for those touched by grace. The New Testament identifies hope as a fundamental component of a full experience in Christ. The Apostle Paul considered it so important that he specifically prayed "that the eyes of your heart may be enlightened in order that you may know the hope to which he has called you, the riches of his glorious inheritance in the saints" (Eph. 1:18). He thought that without a real understanding of hope, the church was in danger of building on an unstable foundation, one more closely related to this world than to the kingdom of God. In fact, misunderstanding the real nature of our hope in Christ has led the church to translate the realization of dreams into surface things such as the acquiring of pews, sound equipment and buildings.

It is important that leaders understand the important role of hope in their own lives. It is an instrument through which the Spirit transforms those called to minister.

We should also note how burdensome life becomes when hope is delayed indefinitely. For many congregations the pastors' promises are no more than empty words. At first the people hold to these words and dream about the future. But as time passes resignation creeps in, and indifference takes hold of their souls. Once this happens it is very difficult to motivate people again.

Food for Thought

"Praise be to the God and Father of our Lord Jesus Christ! In his great mercy he has given us new birth into a living hope through the resurrection of Jesus Christ from the dead" (1 Pet. 1:3).

5 November

Too Comfortable

As they were walking along the road, a man said to him, "I will follow you wherever you go." Jesus replied, "Foxes have holes and birds of the air have nests, but the Son of Man has no place to lay his head." Luke 9:57–58

This encounter between Jesus and an aspiring disciple has many interesting aspects. Our first impression is that the man's proposal was more than generous: "I will follow you wherever you go!" He was speaking of unconditional surrender, wanting to throw in his lot with Christ no matter what might come. This is similar to vows we often make at church meetings, offering the Lord our unconditional loyalty and commitment.

Jesus' response surprises us because it doesn't seem to relate to the man's declaration. We can understand His meaning, however, when we remember that the Lord is not impressed by our words. He knows that we frequently make statements having little connection with the content of our hearts. Commitment to the Lord is found not in words, but in deeds.

This man, seemingly so committed, had a serious problem immediately recognizable to Christ. He desired to be close to Jesus as long as it didn't imply any kind of discomfort or involve personal unpleasantness. But the Lord had already indicated that anyone who wanted to follow Him must be willing to endure the privations He did. These might include such sacrifices as having no home to return to or bed to rest in.

In Mediaeval times the monastic movement understood this call to mean a denial of all comforts and so subjected their bodies to all kinds of affliction. Bernard of Clairvaux, founder of an important order, almost lost his life as a result of harsh treatment of his body.

Such practices have little value aside from demonstrating our ineffectiveness in subjecting the flesh to Christ. The Lord was not calling His disciples to punish their bodies with harsh discipline, but to be willing to relinquish the right to personal comfort in order to follow Him.

Christ's response extends to us. Personal comfort is tremendously important in today's culture. We only have to attempt a fast to realize how weak we are in the slightest deprivation. The Lord may ask us to follow Him as He moves among people who smell badly, or who don't have roomy houses or warm beds to offer us. If we want to accompany Him, we must be willing to sacrifice these amenities. Eagerness to secure our own well-being may become a serious obstacle to intimate relationship with Him.

Food for Thought

How can we become aware of the importance personal comfort has in our lives? What elements in our lives are unnecessary? What can we do to live in greater subjection to Christ?

Conflicting Calendars

He said to another man, "Follow me." But the man replied, "Lord, first let me go and bury my father." Jesus said to him, "Let the dead bury their own dead, but you go and proclaim the kingdom of God." Luke 9:59–60

In one of three encounters related in Luke's ninth chapter, we meet a man whose behavior is like many of ours. He didn't offer himself as a disciple of Christ; instead, he was called. It is worth noticing, incidentally, that there are no volunteers in the Kingdom—only those who are chosen.

Jesus' summons to this individual is the one He gave to dozens of people: "Follow Me." This simple phrase captures the essence of discipleship. We are not called to join a religion, attend a series of meetings or express agreement with Christian doctrine. We are invited to accompany Christ as He visits places and touches people. The disciple does not decide where to go, or how, or when. The only decision given the follower is to step out and walk with the Lord.

The man in today's passage wanted to follow the Lord, but he requested time to deal with family matters first. As an aside, he was not asking permission literally to bury his father; he was using a common phrase of that day which meant to care for one's parents until they died. Once they no longer required his assistance, he would be free to follow Christ.

In today's vernacular the man might have said, "Lord, I'd love to follow You, but first I have some things to take care of." In sharing the gospel I have often heard, "It sounds great, but first let me enjoy life a little."

In this response we find a major obstacle to following Christ: our desire to choose "when." It is not that we are disobedient; on the contrary, we intend to do exactly what the Lord asks. But we suppose we can do it when it is most convenient to us.

This is the same as disobeying. The clearest example of this can be found in Israel's lamentable decision not to enter the Promised Land because of ten spies' negative report. When the Lord advised them that they would spend forty years in the desert for their disobedience, they changed their minds and decided to conquer the land after all. But the Lord was no longer with them. The time for obedience had come and gone, and they suffered a humiliating defeat (Num. 14:40–45).

It is important to point out that there is nothing wrong with looking after our parents. Many things that keep us from complete surrender are not bad in themselves; they may be highly commendable. But anything that comes between Christ and His disciple must be cast aside.

Food for Thought

"Anyone who loves his father or mother more than me is not worthy of me; anyone who loves his son or daughter more than me is not worthy of me" (Matt. 10:37).

7 November

Inconvenient Relationships

Still another said, "I will follow you, Lord; but first let me go back and say good-by to my family." Luke 9:61

In today's text we meet a third individual interested in following Christ. We have already noted that the Kingdom does not accept volunteers, although our attitude often seems to indicate that it was we who chose God. The New Testament makes it plain that those who walk with Christ have been drawn by His mercy.

This man wanted to join the company of Christ's permanent followers. Perhaps he expected the Lord would be impressed by his self-sacrifice. Whatever his motivation, he imposed a condition on his commitment: He desired first to say goodbye to his family. Any such stipulation is inappropriate to a life of complete submission to the Lord.

There is much to be said for the courtesy of bidding farewell to relatives before embarking on an adventure. But Christ perceived that the man's desire was rooted in unhealthy emotional ties. Perhaps his family would try to convince him to stay home. Perhaps they would busy him with other activities that would delay him. The fact is that these people represented a threat to making an unwavering decision to follow Christ.

As on so many other occasions, Jesus used an everyday image to help the man understand the danger. Who among his listeners had not seen someone plowing with a team of oxen? The heavy plough would require the animals' full strength to turn over the earth, but would also need the ploughman's complete concentration to dig straight furrows. No farmer could plow properly if continually looking back to see the results of the work.

The message is clear. Following Christ demands a commitment that will not give way to distractions. We should be paying full attention to His leading, to His words and to all He wants to address in our lives. This will be difficult if we are distracted by matters unrelated to the Kingdom. If as disciples of Christ we remain attuned to other interests, the Lord will know the same frustration we do when we attempt to speak to a child engrossed in a favorite toy. Many activities and passions in our daily lives may serve to divert our devotion to Christ.

Food for Thought

For those of us in discipleship ministries, it is very important to have clear objectives! There are so many activities within the church that are mere distractions. Efficient workers never lose sight of their call to the transformation of lives. All they do should be directed toward the fulfillment of this goal.

Wisdom from on High

Who is wise and understanding among you? Let him show it by his good life, by deeds done in the humility that comes from wisdom. James 3:13

All of us, especially those in leadership, should meditate on the question James poses. The apostle does not ask on a whim. Throughout the chapter he describes the damage caused by wrong use of the tongue. He declares directly, "The tongue also is a fire, a world of evil among the parts of the body. It corrupts the whole person, sets the whole course of his life on fire, and is itself set on fire by hell" (James 3:6). His question is obviously a continuing development of this theme.

The world in which James lived had been greatly influenced by Greek culture—a culture not much different from our own. This society elevated knowledge to such a level that it was considered of highest value. Great orators, through elaborate expositions, dazzled audiences with their understanding of complex concepts and were the most revered members of Hellenic society. The Greeks judged wisdom to be found in the enlightened speeches of great philosophers.

Is it not so with us? Only on rare occasions do we choose people to teach in our seminaries and institutes based on their proven experience. Our rule, almost without exception, is to seek men and women who possess great intellectual knowledge of the subject to be taught. In the church we have frequently witnessed heated discussions among people attempting to define the direction of a program or the procedures for a particular situation. We erroneously believe that our eloquent arguments are an indication of true wisdom.

James points out that this so-called wisdom does not matter in the Kingdom. In the spiritual realm entirely different principles are followed, openly contradicting the values so treasured by humanity. Biblical wisdom is found in how we live, not in what we say. Godly wisdom is not ornamented with elaborate words and arguments, but is clothed in meekness. We could even say it is expressed through the use of *few* words!

Such was Abraham's wisdom when he climbed the mountain to offer Isaac in sacrifice. When his son questioned him, he did not offer articulate explanations. He simply said, "God himself will provide the lamb" (Gen. 22:8). Another example is found in Moses. When faced with the rebellion of Korah's sons, he fell on his face and said nothing (Num. 16:4). The depth of these men's meekness indicates they had reached the highest levels of spiritual understanding in which they possessed a correct perspective of their own lack of importance. For the gaining of this maturity, our words should be few.

Food for Thought

How important it is for a leader to possess these qualities! Our actions will speak louder than a thousand words, and our attitudes will point to the Lord as clearly as if verbally sharing the truth. To be clothed with true wisdom is to be clothed with Christ.

An Absurdity

"Woe to him who quarrels with his Maker, to him who is but a potsherd among the potsherds on the ground. Does the clay say to the potter, 'What are you making?' Does your work say, 'He has no hands'? Woe to him who says to his father, 'What have you begotten?' or to his mother, 'What have you brought to birth?'"
Isaiah 45:9–10

When one of my sons was very small, he suggested we should buy something highly expensive. "Son, we don't have enough money to buy that," I told him. He looked at me, surprised that I hadn't thought of the obvious solution. "But Daddy," he replied, "we just have to go to the bank and ask them for the money we need!" His innocent proposal amused me. He knew that the bank had money, and lots of it. What he couldn't understand were the complex mechanisms involved in defining whether a person may or may not have access to credit. Neither was he old enough for me to explain it to him.

It is easy to make mistakes when we dare to speak of matters we know little or nothing about. Perhaps you have encountered those who, regardless of the subject, always have something to say. These individuals, far from impressing with their information, are irritating; it is usually obvious that they have no understanding of the subject. Nevertheless, they let no opportunity pass to flaunt their ignorance.

This is the kind of absurd scene presented by the prophet Isaiah. Imagine any of these situations: A brick argues with a builder about where it should be placed; a nail argues with a carpenter about the furniture in which it is used; the salt argues with the cook about its necessity in the food. Sounds ridiculous, doesn't it? Even the idea of these objects speaking seems absurd. How can the clay tell the potter the best use for it? How can a newborn baby argue with its mother about the timing for coming into the world?

But though we recognize these scenes as ludicrous, we do not consider it ridiculous to question God's acts. "I don't understand how He has allowed this to happen!" we exclaim, perplexed. "If God loves me," we argue, "why does He not intervene?" Even if we don't ask these questions, we often feel we can confidently explain what He is doing—as if we were experts in the subject. The distance separating us from God is the same as that between the clay and the potter. The clay understands nothing of what the artisan is doing. And so it is with us. It is best that we remain silent in the presence of our Creator!

Food for Thought

"Some have wandered away from these and turned to meaningless talk. They want to be teachers of the law, but they do not know what they are talking about or what they so confidently affirm" (1 Tim. 1:6–7).

Exaggerated Caution

November **10**

Whoever watches the wind will not plant; whoever looks at the clouds will not reap.
Ecclesiastes 11:4

Some of us have inherited a tendency toward perfectionism. Perfectionists cannot accept things that don't transpire according to their expectations. When these expectations have to do with pleasing others, there are demands involved that are practically impossible to meet. By seeking perfection—that state where things can't be improved upon—the person wastes valuable time and effort. Not only this, but sometimes their work is ruined because their requirements delay it unnecessarily; when they finish, the original need for the project no longer exists!

Solomon may not have been considering perfectionism when he wrote this verse. Nevertheless, his wisdom has a practical edge appropriate to beginning a new project. There is an established time for sowing seed, and every farmer knows it well. If we sow in spring, we will not get the same results as if we sowed in winter. Each crop has its own season, and within that period there is little room for flexibility. The farmer may delay for a week or two, but a longer deferment will ruin the opportunity for a harvest. God has created nature with its own cycles, and they wait for no one.

Despite this, some farmers may wait for the "perfect" moment to plant their seeds. They carefully observe the wind and measure the clouds, calculating the rain's arrival and hoping their seeds will germinate quickly. King Solomon warns that whoever invests too much time in such planning will miss the opportunity to sow and, therefore, to reap as well. For a people who lived off the land, this would be an absolute catastrophe.

This principle is valid for us on a spiritual level. It is true that in ministry we must demonstrate a reasonable level of caution—I have witnessed many projects that were set up hastily and produced few results because their structure was not sound. But on the other hand, believing that everything must be just right to begin a new task is even more dangerous. In the Kingdom it is unusual for everything to be exactly in place when a work is initiated. This is what the adventure of walking in faith is all about. We progress in situations that are not perfect with the conviction that we have received orders from our Lord to start. As they say in my part of the world, "Don't hang around too long or you'll miss the train!"

Food for Thought

"I am convinced the great tragedy is not sins that we commit, but the life we fail to live" (Erwin McManus) [1]

Steadiness of Purpose

As the time approached for him to be taken up to heaven, Jesus resolutely set out for Jerusalem. Luke 9:51

Today's verse gives an interesting perspective on Jesus' ministry. The Son of God revealed that during His earthly pilgrimage, His only interest was to fulfill the work God had planned for Him. "My food . . . is to do the will of him who sent me and to finish his work . . . I have come down from heaven not to do my will but to do the will of him who sent me" (John 4:34, 6:38). He clearly understood His mission, which included the call to offer His life on the cross for those He loved.

The text illustrates God's method for our service. This is important, for even if leaders know the work to which they are called, they can make mistakes in its implementation. Such was the case with Moses, who at the age of forty had the same objective God set before him at eighty: the liberation of Israel from the Egyptian yoke. But Moses made the grave mistake of believing that the end justified the means, and the result was forty years' delay for the fulfillment of this mission.

First, then, we notice Christ understood a time had been established by the sovereign God for the implementation of His plan. Our responsibility as leaders is to discern the appropriate moment to initiate a project. When the Spirit dissuaded Paul from going to Asia (Acts 16:7–10), this did not indicate that He lacked interest in the Asian people receiving the good news. Rather, it was the perfect time for intervention in Macedonia, and the apostle was encouraged to join the work of the Spirit there. In the same way, Jesus perceived the timing in which He was to go to Jerusalem. He had previously said to His brothers, "You go to the Feast. I am not yet going up to this Feast, because for me the right time has not yet come" (John 7:8).

Second, we see that Jesus "resolutely set out for Jerusalem." This phrase indicates something much more deliberate than walking along toward the great city. Jesus understood that He was entering the most difficult stage of His pilgrimage in which He would face not only growing opposition, but also His own fears of the cross. To advance with a firm step toward the Father's will, He needed to steady His spirit and ignore all that might distract Him from this commitment. Although aware of the great difficulties ahead, He would not allow them to affect the fulfillment of His mission. This steadiness of purpose is fundamental for any leader, for surely a multitude of obstacles will be faced along the way.

Food for Thought

"Be strong and very courageous. Be careful to obey all the law my servant Moses gave you; do not turn from it to the right or to the left, that you may be successful wherever you go" (Josh. 1:7).

An Unshakeable Conviction

Though he slay me, yet will I hope in him; I will surely defend my ways to his face. Indeed, this will turn out for my deliverance, for no godless man would dare come before him!
Job 13:15–16

Job's statement reveals one reason the Lord says of him, "There is no one on earth like him; he is blameless and upright, a man who fears God and shuns evil" (Job 1:8). Here we see the foundation for a life of greatness in God's Kingdom.

Job makes this confession after a prolonged exchange with three friends who had come to offer comfort: Eliphaz the Temanite, Bildad the Shuhite and Zophar the Naamathite (Job 2:11). They had kept quiet for seven days, but then felt they had sufficient authority to explain to Job the reason for his calamities. With the same conviction some leaders maintain today, these three believed Job's suffering was directly related to hidden sin. "Those who walk in integrity," they said, "do not suffer troubles." We need not examine the error of this posture. Suffice it to say that even the Son of God Himself went through the purifying fire of suffering (Heb. 5:8).

Some translations of this verse are unfair to Job, portraying him as saying, "Even if God takes my life, I won't change my opinion." But this incorrect rendering fails to reflect his humble, God-fearing spirit.

Job didn't understand why this misfortune had come upon him and his family. It is difficult for us to comprehend, as well, even though we are granted access to the incredible conversation between God and Satan in the first chapter. We know God wanted to demonstrate something, but if we look at the situation with human eyes, it seems that the Lord's attitude is cruel. This is where we differ from Job. He believed God was righteous and just, even when acting in a completely incomprehensible fashion.

The book of Job reveals the deep confusion the patriarch experienced. But in the midst of the maelstrom, there was one certainty: "Even if I lose my life, I know God will not act unjustly toward me; He is good, and He rewards those who wait on Him." This unmovable conviction, pleasing to our heavenly Father, forms the foundation of a life of faith. On this earth we will pass through much anguish, some of it extremely difficult to understand or explain. But something we should never relinquish is the conviction that God is good. Even when all evidence seems to indicate otherwise, we know He will never act unjustly, and evil will never be found in Him.

Food for Thought

When this conviction becomes the bedrock of our faith, we can face life with courage. Will we experience suffering? Of course we will! But we won't suffer the torment and anguish of those who believe God has abandoned them. Even through tears we can say, "The Lord is upright; he is my Rock, and there is no wickedness in him" (Ps. 92:15).

Limitations

Elisha sent a messenger to say to him, "Go, wash yourself seven times in the Jordan, and your flesh will be restored and you will be cleansed." But Naaman went away angry and said, "I thought that he would surely come out to me and stand and call on the name of the LORD his God, wave his hand over the spot and cure me of my leprosy. Are not Abana and Pharpar, the rivers of Damascus, better than any of the waters of Israel? Couldn't I wash in them and be cleansed?" So he turned and went off in a rage. 2 Kings 5:10–12

Naaman's reception by Elisha should not escape our notice. The commander was used to being paid homage, for he held an important position in the court of his king. He normally received the most deferential and servile respect wherever he went. We shouldn't be surprised that he considered himself more important than he was. In this respect he is no different from us; we are easily intoxicated with a sense of our own importance.

Without doubt, God's dealings with those He is drawing to Himself include humbling experiences. When Naaman arrived at Elisha's house, the great prophet did not even welcome him in person; he sent out a servant with a message for the great lord. Naaman felt insulted by such behavior, but it was this wounded dignity that was the biggest obstacle to his healing. He himself reveals the reason for his anger: "I thought the prophet would . . ." That is, Naaman had already decided how God might intervene in his life. Like many of us, once he had formed his expectations, he was incapable of accepting God's provision in any other way.

When we anticipate God's movements, we automatically discard other possibilities and become trapped by our expectations. But the Lord is so creative and unpredictable that we can never foresee His plan. Knowing that His ability to intervene is as unlimited as the sky itself, we should keep our spirits open, willing to be surprised by the extraordinary and unexpected manifestations of His care for us.

Naaman's second problem is that he found the prophet's proposal ridiculous. If Naaman's healing could be had by bathing, then there were plenty of better rivers in his own country. If he had known they would propose such an absurd plan, he could have saved himself the long journey! But it is precisely at this point that people with the most privileged minds stumble: They believe that God's plans have to fit their own logic. If we measure everything with this criterion, however, we will discover that the vast majority of the Lord's proposals seem incoherent, quite frankly—as God's people have witnessed time after time throughout their history. Those who desire to walk with Him must be willing to accept some apparently irrational requests!

Food for Thought

"I know not the way God leads me, but well do I know my guide." (Martin Luther) [2]

A Teachable Spirit

I will instruct you and teach you in the way you should go; I will counsel you and watch over you. Do not be like the horse or the mule, which have no understanding but must be controlled by bit and bridle or they will not come to you. Psalm 32:8–9

This psalm is one of three that offers a deeper perspective on the effects of sin in our lives (see also Psalms 36 and 51). In this text especially, the psalmist celebrates the relief found after the moment of confession and urges, "let everyone who is godly pray to you while you may be found" (Ps. 32:6).

The problem of sin requires that we daily practice the discipline of confession. It is the only way we can walk in holiness, for we daily offend God in many ways. But the psalmist includes in his text a word received from the Lord. In it God reveals what we could call a preventative path, one to keep us from falling into sin so frequently.

What solution does our Father suggest? It is to be a people willing to learn "the way you should go." Sin is often the result of our ignorance of God's designs. But the Lord wants to guide us in the way that is pleasing in His eyes. Like a father who teaches his child to walk, the Lord is committed to "watch over" us. In other words, He will closely observe our path. In every circumstance in which we might fall, the Lord will provide instruction to overcome the difficulty. In a sense, this is a picture of the same tender care Christ prophesied respecting the ministry of the Spirit (John 14, 16).

But the Lord also knows the stubborn, obstinate heart of man. He knows that many of our sins are not due to ignorance, but rather our rebellious nature. The Lord uses this illustration to explain the posture we must avoid: "Do not be like the horse or the mule, which have no understanding but must be controlled by bit and bridle or they will not come to you." The stubbornness of the mule and the horse's spirited nature clearly exemplify common human attitudes, even as we desire to walk with God. We prefer to go our own way rather than follow the Lord's; we believe more in our own wisdom than in His. Nevertheless, He commands us to resist the tendency to rebellion, or it might be necessary to control us with "bit and bridle." Since this stubborn posture is natural for us, we must be on the lookout for its manifestation in our lives. Each time it appears we should quiet our spirit and seek the guidance of our good Father. Only in this way can we be taught by Him.

Food for Thought

"The way of a fool seems right to him, but a wise man listens to advice" (Prov. 12:15).

15 November — The Weight of Influence

If a ruler listens to lies, all his officials become wicked. Proverbs 29:12

The principle put forth in this proverb is simple, but vital to remember: People end up being like their leader. When leaders are corrupt, their people will become corrupt. Conversely, when leaders are upright, their people will display justice. Why does this happen? Because those who are close to a leader "soak up" the convictions they see lived before them. This transference of lifestyle is so intangible that we realize it only when we detect traces of the leader's attitudes in the followers. This is why one author defines influence as "the power that affects people, things, or events without any deliberate effort on anyone's part."[3]

This concept is central to being good stewards of our influence on others. We do not directly control this process, but we can contribute to it, having positive input in peoples' lives. The secret of influence lies in a leader's character; this will greatly determine the quality of a person's effect in the lives of others.

This principle is true in every area in which someone has authority to lead. It can be a group as small as a family, or it can be a huge institution in which the influence of a "corporate culture" is often mentioned. In each case the result is the same: The attributes of the person in charge will determine the traits of those who carry out the venture.

The church is equally subject to this principle. A congregation reflects the characteristics of its pastor. This is why I insist that efforts directed at changing a congregation are generally ineffective. When a change comes about in the pastor, the congregation will begin to change naturally. If the pastor loves prayer, the congregation will not need to be repeatedly told to develop a prayer life. They will become infected with the same spirit shown them.

We can also say that the reverse is true. When a pastor is corrupt, the team of coworkers will be too. It is not even necessary that they know about the pastor's corruption; they will pick it up automatically. In one congregation I knew, the senior pastor lived in an adulterous relationship for decades. Nobody knew about it, but time and again sexual scandals by the elders and deacons were uncovered. The congregation had a particular problem in this area. The pastor's lack of morals had unquestionably been "caught" by those working with him.

Food for Thought

The responsibility is upon us as leaders to conduct lives of holiness and commitment. This is the best gift we can give our congregations. We will be able to influence them far more greatly than if we implement the most proven church programs available today.

A Mere Sixty Words

So they took the bull given them and prepared it. Then they called on the name of Baal from morning till noon. "O Baal, answer us!" they shouted. But there was no response; no one answered. And they danced around the altar they had made. 1 Kings 18:26

The conflict between Elijah and the prophets of Baal is one of the most daring adventures recorded in Scripture. As the scene unfolds toward a dramatic climax, we are filled with admiration for this man who stood alone against the forces of evil. And what a great ending! The hero in us longs to be involved in adventures like this, boldly advancing the Kingdom in one battle after another.

One of the keys to this victory is found in Elijah's prayer. It stands in stark contrast to the desperate pleas of Baal's prophets. We know, of course, that their prayers were destined to fail because they were offered to an inexistent god. They could have cried out for a week without receiving an answer, because no one was listening. Nevertheless, the way they prayed gives evidence of their religious convictions—convictions that sometimes creep into our own beliefs.

They started praying early in the morning and continued calling until midday. Their passion did not waver despite receiving no answer. They continued to pray passionately through the afternoon, spurred on by Elijah's insolent remarks. What moved them to continue so fervently? If their god had not responded after one hour, why should he respond after eight? I am convinced they believed that the sheer volume of their words would actually secure an answer.

Jesus warned His disciples that they should avoid "babbling like pagans, for they think they will be heard because of their many words" (Matt. 6:7). But it is hard for us to break away from our habitually wordy prayers. Short requests that go straight to the point make us uncomfortable. They seem to lack spirituality, so we feel obliged to add phrases that speak of our devotion or the worthiness of our petition. We end up trying to impress God with eloquence or with well-rounded arguments.

How did Elijah pray after the prophets' elaborate show? His prayer contained only sixty words! But when he finished, "the fire of the LORD fell and burned up the sacrifice, the wood, the stones and the soil, and also licked up the water in the trench" (1 Kings 18:38). His prayer was not effective simply because he prayed to the right God, but also because he knew the confrontation had been initiated by the Lord Himself. He didn't waste precious time informing God what he was doing or trying to convince the Lord to prove Himself. He simply asked Him to answer, and God responded. In this the prophet offers an excellent model of effective prayer!

Food for Thought

"I tell you the truth, unless you change and become like little children, you will never enter the kingdom of heaven" (Matt. 18:3).

17 November | Today, If You Hear His Voice…

But encourage one another daily, as long as it is called Today, so that none of you may be hardened by sin's deceitfulness. We have come to share in Christ if we hold firmly till the end the confidence we had at first. As has just been said: "Today, if you hear his voice, do not harden your hearts as you did in the rebellion." Hebrews 3:13–15

The expression "hard hearted" is used in the Word to describe those who have little or no sensitivity to spiritual matters. If this condition remains unchanged, it is impossible for the Lord to deal with such a person, for their very hardness blocks spiritual input. Furthermore, the harsh, hostile behavior it produces in them impedes relationships.

It is easy for a hardened person to become convinced that their condition is an insurmountable obstacle to a significant relationship with God. They believe they are trapped in a situation they cannot change, so they feel it is unfair to expect them to give what they cannot. Today's text, however, reveals that the hardening of a heart is a conscious process.

It is ironic that the hardening begins precisely with the very thing that could bring spiritual life: the revelation of God's will. God gives all of us an opportunity to align our lives with His truth. No one can argue that they are victims of circumstances beyond their control, since even when we were dead in our sin, the Lord had already initiated reconciliation. Because of His missionary heart, He always takes the initiative in approaching us, inviting us into intimacy with Him. Each of us frequently hears His voice as He whispers this invitation.

However, as the author of Hebrews declares, hearing the Lord's voice may produce a wrong reaction in us because of "sin's deceitfulness." We believe we have authority to question, argue and contradict His Word to us. We think we can plan an alternative to God's will and can evaluate our options. Seduced by our own astute philosophy, we choose to act according to our own criteria. At this moment the hardening of our heart distances us from God. He has spoken and invited us to walk with Him. We listen to His proposal and acknowledge that we understand, but even so we choose to follow our own will.

If we recognize this process, we can avoid it. The wise person will fight it energetically as Paul did: "We demolish arguments and every pretension that sets itself up against the knowledge of God, and we take captive every thought to make it obedient to Christ" (2 Cor. 10:5). We must understand that the key to intimacy with God is surrendering our will completely to Him. We cannot afford to consider whether or not we like what He asks. We must choose obedience, which will in turn soften our hearts.

Food for Thought

"No man is conquered until his heart is conquered." (George Barlow) [4]

The Hope of Those Who Fear God

For who is God besides the L*ORD? And who is the Rock except our God? It is God who arms me with strength and makes my way perfect.* Psalm 18:31–32

Many of us grew up hearing messages on the importance of discovering God's will for our lives. The conviction that motivates this belief is that if we discover the Father's will, we can lead a successful life. In my role as counselor, I have met people who literally live in a state of paralysis for fear they might make a wrong choice. They suppose there is only one path for their lives, and there is no chance of obtaining the Lord's blessing outside this plan.

With the passing of time, I have grown skeptical about this concept. The margin for error is so great that failure is almost certain for most of us. Only a fortunate few will discover the path "laid out for them." The rest of us are destined to a life of mediocrity because—so the explanation goes—we have not discovered God's true will for our lives.

The psalmist offers a much broader view of this subject. He tells us that Jehovah is the One who makes our way perfect. I like the words chosen by some Spanish versions: "He makes my way straight." The idea it conveys is that the Lord arranges our path, wherever we are. The man or woman who fears God can be sure that He will go before them, straightening the way, even when they are not sure of the direction.

This principle does not apply to everyone, but only to those who with all their hearts want what is right in the eyes of the Most High. Was this not Joseph's experience? I don't think he knew which way he was to go, or that he had much choice in the matter. Nevertheless, the Word affirms that the hand of God was with Joseph, and He prospered him in all he did (Gen. 39:3, 21).

Rather than discovering a plan specially set up for us, it would seem that the Lord would desire us to live lives that honor Him, in whatever sphere we find ourselves. This refers more to what we do than to who we are. The hand of God will be upon the life of those people who long to live in holiness, whether in school, at home or at work. As a result of this longing, all they do will be blessed and, I would dare to say, even their mistakes will be redeemed by the Lord.

The conviction that God was making his way straight understandably led the psalmist to break into songs of worship and praise. Those who know that the Most High is guiding their lives possess a level of confidence and peace that goes far beyond words.

Food for Thought

"God's will is not an itinerary, but an attitude." (Andrew Dhuse) [5]

19 November | Learning by Serving

"After the death of Moses the servant of the Lord, *the* Lord *said to Joshua son of Nun, Moses' aide: . . . Get ready to cross the Jordan River."* Joshua 1:1–2

These verses, as those of many opening books of the Bible, can easily be overlooked as merely an introduction to the main text. But these few words present the appropriate model for a new leader's formation, a process that must be undertaken by anyone who will eventually have responsibility among the people of God.

The author describes Moses as the servant of the Lord, although this wasn't always true of the great liberator of Israel. For much of his life, Moses didn't access this privilege. It was not that God wouldn't give it to him; rather, Moses first needed to undergo that process in which he would die to himself. Without this experience of death, he could never have become "the Lord's servant." This title presupposes that those who bear it are entirely at the service of the Most High, with no agenda of their own.

The text also describes Joshua as Moses' aide. For at least forty years this man had been serving Moses. This doesn't mean that Joshua had not been serving the Lord, but the way he did so was by waiting on Moses. During these years his life had been at the disposal of Israel's leader. Like his mentor, Joshua did not have a personal agenda; instead, he gave his resources and gifts for Moses' use. His goal was to be useful for every need, and Scripture seems to indicate that Joshua ministered with singular happiness and surrender.

Such service is a good school of formation for a young person. Wise leaders should commit to bringing people into their lives who will learn alongside them. According to the book of Numbers, various young people served Moses this way (Num. 11:28). These young people placed themselves at the service of the leader, and Moses made them participants in much of the work God entrusted to him. He used real-life circumstances to form in them abilities and attitudes which would ultimately equip them to assume greater responsibility among the people of God.

Today we think this slow and prolonged formation process is unnecessary. We are more interested in hurrying the work than in investing deeply in the lives of our assistants. But poorly-formed workers end up doing a great deal of damage in the house of God. What we gain in time, we lose in quality. Wise leaders know that this slow work is one of the best investments they can make in the future of the church. It is not a small thing to have formed a Joshua or a Timothy. Those trained in this way represent a new generation of leaders who will carry on after we have finished our race.

Food for Thought

Lessons learned while serving someone else provide the best preparation for the ministry to which one will eventually be called.

Repentance of the Heart

"Even now," declares the LORD, "return to me with all your heart, with fasting and weeping and mourning." Rend your heart and not your garments. Return to the LORD your God, for he is gracious and compassionate, slow to anger and abounding in love, and he relents from sending calamity. Joel 2:12–13

We're always in danger of being taken over by religiosity, so attractive to human beings. This false spirituality offers a calm conscience in exchange for practices that, in theory, satisfy the Lord's demands. But the Word indicates that we are called to an intimate relationship with God. We can't cultivate significant friendship with anyone in the confines of a few routine exercises. Deep relationships are the result of work and dedication springing from a commitment fostered in the heart.

The prophet Joel speaks to this when he conveys to Israel a message from God: "Rend your heart and not your garments." The only repentance that counts spiritually is that which transforms our hard hearts and produces in us brokenness regarding sin. It is accompanied, as today's text indicates, by fasting, weeping and mourning. These are the manifestations of true interior anguish.

Anyone with even a minimal understanding of spiritual things knows well that we cannot produce real repentance. It results only from the sovereign action of God. This is what happened to Isaiah when he saw the Lord seated in His holy temple (Isa. 6) and to Peter when he bowed at the feet of Jesus, proclaiming his unworthy condition (Luke 5:8). Only the Lord can generate genuine spiritual repentance (2 Tim. 2:25). So what is our responsibility, since we are unable to produce the interior brokenness God desires?

In the first place, we should reject all trivial perspectives of repentance. Sometimes in our prayers we make such declarations as, "Lord, please forgive whatever sin I've committed against You." Such general expressions have no value. Sin is too serious to be enclosed in a single phrase.

Second, if we know that repentance is an act of the Spirit of God, we must create the moments during the day in which we can hear God's revelation leading us to repentance. That is, we have to permit the Spirit to examine our hearts and bring to light those matters that offend the Lord. Only by asking for discernment will we prove how much the Lord longs to cleanse us. And He will not delay in responding to our request.

Third, we should know that genuine repentance is accompanied by external signs that can't be fabricated: brokenness, mourning and tears. These signs can help us differentiate between repentance that is superficial and that which comes from the deepest part of our heart. Let us seek such closeness to the Lord that He produces in us sensitive and humble hearts.

Food for Thought

"Repentance involves much more than asking God for forgiveness." (Anonymous)

Antidote to Division

On the contrary, those parts of the body that seem to be weaker are indispensable, and the parts that we think are less honorable we treat with special honor. 1 Corinthians 12:22

Every congregation has at least two or three people we would describe as "weak." They never quite fit into the body, their inappropriate behavior or insensitive remarks causing them to stand out. The rest of us coexist with them, moved by a mix of tolerance and pity. After all, haven't we been called to compassion?

Yet even while we live with them, Paul's declaration confuses us. What is this? The weaker members of the body are the most necessary? We are accustomed to valuing people according to the contribution they make to us. Using this measure, these "little brothers and sisters" definitely don't appear most necessary! On the contrary, we consider them least important. We feel that the ones really necessary for the functioning of the body are people like the pastor, the elders or the deacons.

But we are looking at the apostle's declaration from the wrong perspective. As long as we try to understand it in light of others' benefit to us, it doesn't make sense. But Paul wasn't thinking of what these problematical brothers and sisters give to us, but rather what we can give to them. Consider how the passage continues: "The parts that we think are less honorable we treat with special honor. And the parts that are unpresentable are treated with special modesty, while our presentable parts need no special treatment" (1 Cor. 12:23–24). Observe carefully descriptions such as "clothe" and "protect." We are the ones who must do these things, and we do them precisely with these weaker members.

This is our Creator's sovereign design. "God has combined the members of the body and has given greater honor to the parts that lacked it, so that there should be no division in the body, but that its parts should have equal concern for each other" (1 Cor. 12:24–25). The Lord, guided by His marvelous wisdom, knows that the only way to teach genuine love and compassion is to place in our midst a person who needs them. Just as we extend care toward delicate or injured parts of our physical body, God also desires that we cultivate attitudes of tenderness toward those who possess less spiritual maturity. These people are necessary for us, since through them we cultivate patience and goodness.

As a leader you can set an example of this for your congregation. Don't always prioritize people who stimulate you or sit well with you. Dedicate time and effort to those who seem least deserving. When you live with this perspective, you illustrate God's love for humanity, since He drew near to us despite our profound unworthiness.

Food for Thought

Division is the result of preferring some people over others. The presence of the weak among us obligates us to consider all, not just a few.

A Question of Balance

"Two things I ask of you, O LORD; do not refuse me before I die: Keep falsehood and lies far from me; give me neither poverty nor riches, but give me only my daily bread. Otherwise, I may have too much and disown you and say, 'Who is the LORD?' Or I may become poor and steal, and so dishonor the name of my God."
Proverbs 30:7–9

I don't think I've ever heard anyone pray this way. Neither can I remember an occasion on which I myself have offered this kind of petition. Nonetheless, the appeal contained in this prayer offers penetrating insight into human nature well worth considering.

The person who prayed this recognized the inherent danger in extremes, not only concerning money, but in any aspect of life. Many spiritual principles become effective only when practiced in tension with other truths. Grace must be balanced with discipline. Faith must be combined with deeds. Pure worship requires a right fusion of spirit and truth. Work necessitates rest. The strength of youth must be compensated by the wisdom of age. Each element finds its best expression when accompanied by an apparent opposite that "completes" it, to use a biblical term.

The author of today's text chose to pinpoint the dangers that come from economic extremes. Most of us wouldn't argue that grinding poverty can drive people to desperation, easily leading them to commit the kind of sin mentioned, namely, stealing from others to feed one's own family. In fact, this has become one of the scourges of Latin America. In many of our big cities, street violence is on the increase, and people live in constant fear of being held up at gunpoint. The author asks to be freed from the desperation that could lead to violence.

It's probably harder for most of us to recognize the dangers of abundance. In our age the quest for financial affluence has become a driving force in most peoples' lives, as much a part of our culture as eating or sleeping. The church, always susceptible to the influence of its environment, has developed its own particular brand of "spiritually acceptable" prosperity, and many have unhesitatingly embraced it. The proverb we are looking at delivers a clear warning: Those who possess much can easily forget the God who blessed them with wealth! We need only look at the spiritual resistance in the world's most prosperous countries to understand how true this observation is.

So what should we aim for? We should seek a life in which all things are given balanced proportion.

Food for Thought

"I know what it is to be in need, and I know what it is to have plenty. I have learned the secret of being content in any and every situation, whether well fed or hungry, whether living in plenty or in want. I can do everything through him who gives me strength" (Phil. 4:12–13).

Attaining Steadfastness

But when he asks, he must believe and not doubt, because he who doubts is like a wave of the sea, blown and tossed by the wind. That man should not think he will receive anything from the Lord; he is a double-minded man, unstable in all he does. James 1:6–8

I never cease to wonder at the amazing analogies employed in the Word as teaching tools. It has been said that an illustration is worth a thousand words, and it is true. To show how profoundly a disciple's life is affected by doubts, James points to the waves of the sea. Anybody who has stood on the seashore can easily understand the principle taught here.

Think for a moment about the waves. They contain tremendous power, and when "blown and tossed by the wind" can cause terrible destruction. But even with their amazing power, the ocean waves do not have any direction or willpower of their own. They are simply a visible demonstration of the strength of the winds and the tides. They do not choose their direction, but are propelled by a force greater than themselves. So it is with those disciples filled with doubts. They lose their way and begin to fall under the influence of the prevailing philosophies in our midst. Just like the waves, when the devil himself adds fuel to these philosophies, people who grow deceived can become real instruments of destruction.

In order to remove all question as to the illustration, James specifically describes the person who doubts: "He is a double-minded man, unstable in all he does." We have here a description of the troubling symptoms in so many believers of our day. Double-minded people are those who exhibit more than one kind of behavior. One day they believe one thing; the next day another. Their convictions change as quickly as the weather, and this leads to instability and inconsistency. They don't persevere in anything, because they so easily abandon the convictions basic to perseverance.

These doubts do not originate with the plan of God for our lives, even though the Lord's instructions rarely seem straightforward to us. The real problem lies in our misperception of the person of God. We can easily attribute to Him the same imperfection that afflicts men, and therefore we doubt His trustworthiness. Does He really know what He is doing? Has He considered all the options? Has He taken my particular circumstances into account? Life seems so complicated to us that we struggle to believe He can easily dissolve the tangled webs that cause us so much trouble.

Food for Thought

Faith distinguishes the visibility of this world from the kingdom of God. It reserves our submission for the Most High and gives it to no other. It resists the comings and goings typical of humanity. It believes, because in the Kingdom unbelief and doubt are abnormal.

A Covenant between Friends

After David had finished talking with Saul, Jonathan became one in spirit with David, and he loved him as himself. From that day Saul kept David with him and did not let him return to his father's house. And Jonathan made a covenant with David because he loved him as himself. 1 Samuel 18:1–3

Jonathan and David provide one of the best examples of friendship anywhere in Scripture. Although they spent much of their lives apart, the Word reveals the strength of the commitment that existed between them. It gives a good model of the kind of relationships to which we should aspire.

Today's text tells us that "Jonathan became one in spirit with David." We can assume the two young warriors had many things in common, so they would have felt a natural desire to develop a meaningful friendship. However, the phrase "became one in spirit" indicates that something happened in Jonathan's heart that took him beyond the typical attachment of two individuals having similar personalities. True friendship comes from spiritual affinity between people; the bonds that join them are rooted in the most profound areas of the heart. This spiritual tie is able to withstand life's most severe blows as well as the inevitable wear and tear that comes with the passing of time.

This kind of union in friendship can only be produced by the Lord. But on the human side, it is only given to those whose hearts are willing to go beyond superficial relationships. Where there is an obsession with one's own life or an interest in using another for one's own benefit, a devoted relationship cannot exist. Those who enter this dimension of friendship deeply value others and are interested in discovering the beauty God has placed in those around us.

The fact that a relationship begins on a spiritual plane does not guarantee, however, that this friendship will last forever. This is where the maturity of these two men is evident, for they decided to seal their bond of friendship with a covenant.

A covenant is a commitment that frees us from the fluctuations of feelings, a promise to care for and nourish a relationship in both good and bad times. It allows two people to deliberately develop a friendship by growing together as a result of specific choices. In this way those involved can intentionally contribute instead of hoping it will just happen naturally. Anyone who takes on this kind of commitment harvests the most precious fruit available to human relationships.

Food for Thought

With whom do you share this kind of relationship? What steps do you take to build it up? What spiritual aspects do you share together?

25 November | Looking After Our Own

Saul told his son Jonathan and all the attendants to kill David. But Jonathan was very fond of David and warned him, "My father Saul is looking for a chance to kill you. Be on your guard tomorrow morning; go into hiding and stay there."
1 Samuel 19:1–2

We don't know the strange processes of King Saul's mind that caused him to order the death of his most popular official: the man who had saved Israel's honor by defeating Goliath. But we do know that sin produces terrible disfigurement, sowing jealousy, envy and hatred in our hearts and leading us to hurt even those we most love. An order from Israel's king was not a meaningless command from a deluded madman; Saul was an implacable foe who would do whatever it took to eliminate David. As long as he remained within the king's reach, the young shepherd's days were numbered.

We should not forget, either, that anyone who helped David would run the risk of the same punishment—even the king's own son. Scripture relates the hair-raising incident in which Saul tried to strike Jonathan down with a spear because he had defended his friend (1 Sam. 20:30–33). Jonathan was aware of the real danger when he warned David of his father's intentions. Nevertheless, he did not hesitate to warn him.

This is one of the distinguishing characteristics of a true friend. We are given not only the gift of enjoying the affection of our closest friends, but also the responsibility of protecting their well-being. When we see them at risk for any reason, it is our responsibility—our obligation—to draw near and speak to those we love.

This is a difficult step for two reasons. First, when we see the danger in a situation, we often believe our friend will realize it as well. The danger could be in the development of an unhealthy relationship, in spending too much time on some activity or in looking at pornography on the Internet. It really doesn't matter; any such situation could put someone's spiritual life in danger and endanger relationships with close friends. We must remember that what seems clear to us is rarely so for the one involved. This is why God has called us to be brothers and sisters willing to speak out when necessary.

The second reason we hesitate is for fear of the consequences. Perhaps we are concerned about the other's reaction or are afraid of losing the friendship. Perhaps we think we will be criticized for getting involved or that we are exaggerating the danger. But this fear often causes us to keep quiet when we need to speak. A good friend knows that love demands our care for the other's well-being. When we see someone in danger, we should act. Their future may depend upon it.

Food for Thought

"A friend is someone who shows up when everyone else disappears." (Anonymous)

Spiritual Leadership

O L*ORD*, *you deceived me, and I was deceived; you overpowered me and prevailed. I am ridiculed all day long; everyone mocks me.* Jeremiah 20:7

The twentieth chapter of Jeremiah reveals one of the lowest points in the prophet's life. He had not been surprised by sin, nor had he made a wrong decision. Rather, he had fallen into a period of depression, and with all his heart he wanted a decisive end to the torment caused by ministry. This kind of dejection is common among the leaders of God's people; anyone in this position is bound to feel the desire to quit at least once along the way.

Jeremiah's words show an interesting viewpoint on the origins of biblical leadership: The effective leader rarely wishes to have such a position. On the contrary, most of those called to leadership in the Scriptures resisted God's call. They would have preferred to be somewhere else, doing something different than what God proposed. Moses argued with Jehovah at length, trying to convince Him that he was the wrong man for the job. Gideon delayed in accepting the challenge from the angel of the Lord, carrying out various tests to make sure the word was indeed for him. David was completely absorbed in looking after sheep when Samuel anointed him king. And Jeremiah was overpowered by the Lord. He did not give in easily, but the Lord was stronger than he was, and eventually he relented. These men arrived at places of leadership despite their most strenuous objections.

Their experience is distinctly different from that of leadership motivated by personal ambition. How often have we heard restless, dissatisfied individuals unhappily complaining in a congregation because they were meant for "greater things"? The course of their ministry is marked by an interminable string of complaints about the opportunities supposedly denied them. But leaders who achieve highly effective ministries would often prefer to be elsewhere.

This truth became clear to me a few years ago when I encountered a congregation that had lost their pastor. A good group of elders had been developed, but when they began to work on appointing a new leader, it led to a real battle. The ambitious spirit of most of the men eventually neutralized their ministries and led the church into a serious crisis. The interesting thing is that the only elder who did not want the post was the very one the church desired as their pastor!

This is God's way. Those willing are not considered, and those not willing are called. This is the Lord's efficient method of ensuring that ministry is not propelled by His children's pretention, but by the recognition of His call.

Food for Thought

"A true leader is the one who does not care to lead, but who has felt under the obligation to take on the role of leader due to the pressure of the Spirit and the urgency of the situation." (A.W. Tozer)[6]

Spiritual Ambition

And Saul's son Jonathan went to David at Horesh and helped him find strength in God. "Don't be afraid," he said. "My father Saul will not lay a hand on you. You will be king over Israel, and I will be second to you. Even my father Saul knows this." The two of them made a covenant before the L*ORD. Then Jonathan went home, but David remained at Horesh.* 1 Samuel 23:16–18

This passage presents a beautiful picture of God's intention for friendship, developed as it was through the spiritual principles that should guide those who love God. To properly understand the depth of Jonathan's words, we should observe the context in which they were spoken.

We can't be sure how much time had passed since Saul's distaste for David had developed. The young shepherd was no longer living in the king's palace as he had after his victory over Goliath. Saul's envy had turned to open hostility, and eventually David had fled from the king's presence.

The injustice of the situation attracted other persecuted people who quickly joined him, and they formed a band of about four hundred men. The chronicler tells us that at this time "David stayed in the desert strongholds and in the hills of the Desert of Ziph. Day after day Saul searched for him, but God did not give David into his hands" (1 Sam. 23:14).

At this point, when David's future seemed so uncertain, Jonathan came to offer support to the friend with whom he could no longer be seen publicly. Samuel tells us that Jonathan "helped him find strength in God." This is precisely how someone sensitive to the Spirit's guidance is used to encourage another.

What are the ingredients that go into ministering spiritually to a friend? First, we must be willing to come alongside the afflicted person at the correct moment. Second, we should be ready to say something if the Lord so indicates. Third, we need sensitivity to say what God would have us communicate, not simply to state the first thing that comes to mind. This is where we often fail to be true instruments in the Lord's hands. We try to comfort with words that are purely human, and we also speak them at the wrong moment.

Notice the content of Jonathan's words of encouragement. They reveal the spiritual maturity of a man whose original destiny had been to inherit his father's throne. But now he understood that God had raised up another, and he was willing to submit to that leadership as a follower. Few men manage to give up a promising future so magnanimously. It is even harder to show support toward the one replacing them. But the purest expression of love is to wish for the betterment of those we care for more than for our own.

Food for Thought

"In friendship there is one soul in two bodies." (Richard Sibbes)[7]

Disciplined Listening

He who answers before listening—that is his folly and his shame. Proverbs 18:13

Every leader should be well versed in the art of conversation, since through this medium we develop relationships with those we serve. Without thoughtful dialogue it is difficult to get to know people well, to understand their struggles and their dreams. If we fail in this responsibility, ministry will inevitably lose its focus, and we will be distracted by things of little value for those we are trying to serve.

If we want to develop helpful discourse, we must learn to listen to others. I often hear people complain that we live in a time in which everyone wants to talk, but nobody wants to listen. Listening shows people we want to make room in our relationships to know their hearts, not just do all the talking ourselves.

The author of Proverbs states two characteristics of a person who rushes to talk before another has finished speaking their thoughts: folly and shame. Why refer to the simple act of interrupting with such severity? First, interrupting reveals a lack of appreciation for others. It actually communicates that what we have to say is much more important than what they want to share. Our own information seems so important that we feel compelled to cut them short.

Second, if we don't let others finish their words, we won't fully understand what they wanted to express. If we don't possess the information to correctly evaluate their comments, we won't be able to offer an intelligent response. Thus, we will end up dominating the conversation. In doing this we often believe we know what the other person is going to tell us. We then declare, "I knew what you were going to say," as if we possessed some special ability to read their thoughts before they opened their mouths. Other times we try to hurry the conversation along by completing their phrases for them. But most often our endings are completely different from what the other person wanted to convey.

To maintain silence and to wait is much more effective. This isn't simply refraining from interrupting; we must also resist the temptation to cogitate a premature response while "listening." When we give our whole selves to careful attention, our questions are often answered as we listen. Not only this, but we also begin to perceive the heart of the person talking; we understand the intention of their words. This is after all the most important information we can receive, since it will enable us to speak, at the right moment, to their heart and not only to their words. This was how the Master from Galilee worked and is one reason His words so deeply penetrated His listeners' hearts.

Food for Thought

What do you tend to talk about with others? How do you show your interest in what they are sharing? How can you resist the temptation to interrupt?

29 November

Gathered in Vain

Saul and the Israelites assembled and camped in the Valley of Elah and drew up their battle line to meet the Philistines. The Philistines occupied one hill and the Israelites another, with the valley between them. 1 Samuel 17:2–3

This passage describes the preliminary setting of David's victory over Goliath. As we know, this confrontation was only one of a long list of conflicts between these two nations. In this incident we find the Israelites paralyzed with fear. For forty interminable days the giant came out twice daily, in the morning and in the afternoon, to present his challenge to Saul's army, but not a single man was willing to face the Philistine. The Israelites were assembled for battle, but they were doing no fighting.

Battles are not won by gathering together. Calling out the warriors is necessary preparation for the confrontation of an enemy, but if the soldiers don't engage the adversary, their coming together is of little use. Even if an army has superior strength over the enemy, the battle can be won only after determining to enter the fray.

This picture of the Israelites—filled with indecision and alarm at the moment strength and decisiveness were most required—is a good illustration of the church when it has lost its way. We have always struggled with a tendency to make the meeting an end in itself, when in reality the purpose of gathering is to prepare the troops for battle. In countless congregations the members' commitment involves nothing but the monotonous habit of gathering and dispersing—a practice that does not in the least intimidate the Enemy. When the church gets caught up in this cycle, its enemies laugh and mock because it fulfills no meaningful mission in the world to which it has been called.

The reason for the church's existence is to be salt and light on the earth. We are here to "declare the praises of him who called you out of darkness into his wonderful light" (1 Pet. 2:9). This is the continuation of God's original purpose in creating a people for Himself. The blessing He bestowed on His people was to result in blessing for the world, that all nations on earth will be blessed (Gen. 12:2–3).

As leaders it is essential to maintain our hold on this reality. Our function is not to provide a never-ending succession of meetings to keep the church busy. We are "to prepare God's people for works of service, so that the body of Christ may be built up" (Eph. 4:12). To keep people in a perpetual state of self-absorption works against the very purpose for which they were called into discipleship. The church, operating with the right dynamics, meets together so it may go out to conquer new enemy territory. This is its vocation, and not even the gates of hell can prevail against it!

Food for Thought

"The Church exists by mission as a fire exists by burning." (Emil Brunner) [8]

Practicing What We Preach

You, then, who teach others, do you not teach yourself? You who preach against stealing, do you steal? You who say that people should not commit adultery, do you commit adultery? You who abhor idols, do you rob temples? Romans 2:21–22

The way of a leader will always contain painful, anxious situations we would prefer to avoid. These may include such bitter experiences as opposition, abandonment or betrayal. All of these afflicted the One who went before us as He showed the way. A mature leader has come to understand that this is part of the call, and accepts it as the price of exercising influence in others' lives.

There is a condition referred to by the Apostle Paul, however, that is even more weighty and difficult for a leader to bear. It is the anguish felt by those who proclaim truths to which they themselves do not adhere. Even though Paul was speaking to the Jews, this passage can apply to those of us responsible for training God's people. "Now you, if you call yourself a Jew; if you rely on the law and brag about your relationship to God; if you know his will and approve of what is superior because you are instructed by the law; if you are convinced that you are a guide for the blind, a light for those who are in the dark, an instructor of the foolish, a teacher of infants, because you have in the law the embodiment of knowledge and truth—you, then, who teach others, do you not teach yourself?" (Rom. 2:17–21).

It is precisely our better understanding of the Word that can make us believe we are more spiritual than we really are. We can easily trust that our greater perception of God's truth, along with the role we are given of discipling believers, is essentially the same as living the truths we call others to live. But our ability as communicators cannot extinguish the insistent testimony of our own spirit when it tells us we are not where God wants us to be. Leaders who retain a degree of spiritual sensitivity will not be able to endure such a dichotomy for very long.

Does this mean we cannot speak or teach about subjects we have not experienced? Not at all! We need not get divorced to be able to speak with authority on the subject of divorce! But we should know that our authority is directly related to our commitment to live what we attempt to teach. We will have a better response from others when our behavior and attitudes back the message we preach than we will through eloquent words or depth of biblical knowledge.

Food for Thought

"The law of the teacher, simply stated, is this: If you stop growing today, you stop teaching tomorrow." (Howard Hendricks)[9]

The Armor Bearer

One day Jonathan son of Saul said to the young man bearing his armor, "Come, let's go over to the Philistines outpost on the other side." But he did not tell his father. 1 Samuel 14:1

If you have never read the fourteenth chapter of First Samuel, don't miss the opportunity to do so today. It narrates an amazing adventure, the kind of exploit given those who dare to march forward by faith for God's glory. The chapter has two visible actors: Jonathan and his bearer of arms. The unseen main role is reserved as always for the Lord of hosts.

The Philistines had assembled against Israel and were camped at Micmash. Saul was already showing signs of the worrying tendency that would eventually end his reign, namely, the absence of clear leadership in times of crisis. The Philistine monopoly on the manufacture of swords had left Israel without necessary weapons. The king's six hundred men were soon gripped by the same irresolution their monarch displayed. In the midst of this extremity, Jonathan seized the initiative and decided to attack on his own, taking with him one of the only two swords the Israelites possessed.

Jonathan's courage is well-recorded in Scripture. But we are given absolutely no information as to the identity of the armor bearer who fought beside him. This man remains anonymous, though his feat is recorded alongside those of Israel's great warriors. He will no doubt receive a wonderful reward when he stands before the throne of grace.

Despite this warrior's unknown status, I want to highlight his role in the victory given to Israel in this skirmish. No doubt the attendant was young and inexperienced in battle. For this very reason he had been assigned the task of bearing arms for seasoned warriors. Despite his limited responsibilities he had a vital task, for he freed Jonathan from the encumbrance of carrying his unwieldy amour into battle.

Every leader requires a faithful "armor bearer" in order to achieve great victories for the Lord. Such workers have no personal ambition and are willing to serve with humility. They understand that allegiance in their task will eventually bring them assignments of greater weight and significance.

Indeed, it was the servant's unconditional faithfulness that allowed him to fully participate in the victory Jonathan obtained. "Jonathan climbed up, using his hands and feet, with his armor bearer right behind him. In that first attack Jonathan and his armor bearer killed some twenty men in an area of about half an acre" (1 Sam. 14:13–14).

Wise leaders will value the contribution of their "armor bearers" and be willing to share their victories with them. A leader should be mindful that one day, by God's grace, these servants may be the ones waging battle with the Enemy. The investment made in them today is crucial to the character they will possess tomorrow.

Food for Thought

"There is no limit to the good a man can do if he doesn't care who gets the credit." (Anonymous)

Selling Out to the Enemy

Those Hebrews who had previously been with the Philistines and had gone up with them to their camp went over to the Israelites who were with Saul and Jonathan.
1 Samuel 14:21

Chapter fourteen in the first book of Samuel records an extraordinary feat on the part of Jonathan. He fought the Philistines accompanied only by his armor bearer, and the Lord rewarded his courage with such an incredible victory that it mobilized the indecisive Saul and his troops. The young warrior's deed set in motion a series of events, one of them being that the Israelites who had gone over to the enemy decided to return to their compatriots.

But why had these men been collaborating with the Philistines? How could they have joined ranks with those who were a constant source of torment for God's people? To understand their decision, we have to realize that Israel was in desperate straits. The Philistines who had risen up to attack them had a cartel over weapons production. Only two of the six hundred Israelite men—the king and his son—had swords. How could they take on the well-equipped Philistine army? Some of the Hebrews, seeing they would surely lose, decided to throw in their lot with the enemy. They wanted at all costs to avoid being on the losing side.

Their decision reveals the depth of our desire to be counted among the winners in life. Success almost always goes hand in hand with the respect and recognition of those around us. Having grown up in a fallen world, our intense longing to be accepted by others leads us to seek this approval. The problem is that we can forget to measure the cost of obtaining this endorsement, even to the point of "selling our birthright for a bowl of stew" (Gen. 25:29–34).

As leaders we must guard against the desire to please others. We are sometimes so desperate for prosperous ventures, congregational growth or good program attendance that we lay our hands on any method to attain it. Without realizing it we begin to negotiate the principles the Lord has set for a profitable ministry. We may even go as far as transferring to the Enemy side, incorporating techniques, philosophies and principles that ensure acclaim in the world. In this sense many pastors behave more like executive managers than shepherds. However, we have been called to stand firm in the principles of the Kingdom. Our lot is cast with Jesus Christ, and we must not back down or return to our former life, even if it seems the Enemy has surrounded us. God's truths are simply not negotiable! He will sustain the lives of those who remain faithful, even when the majority has sold out to the Enemy. We will still be on the winning team!

Food for Thought

"Blessed is the man who makes the LORD his trust, who does not look to the proud, to those who turn aside to false gods" (Ps. 40:4).

3 December

Blessed in All Things!

But the man who looks intently into the perfect law that gives freedom, and continues to do this, not forgetting what he has heard, but doing it—he will be blessed in what he does.
James 1:25

The Apostle James, the eminently practical writer of the New Testament, gives some key points to keep us from being what the New American Standard Bible calls "forgetful hearers" of the Word. This phrase succinctly describes our tendency to forget those things that will help direct our steps. Our forgetfulness could be as silly as arriving in a room and not remembering why we went there or something much more complex, caused by a terrible disease such as Alzheimer's. To all effects the results are the same, since one becomes disoriented and confused about what to do next.

James similarly describes the person who does not retain the Word of God. These individuals rejoice in proclaiming the Word, but do not make any use of it in their personal lives. As happened when the Israelites collected an excess of manna in the desert, the Word "rots" and is soon forgotten.

This condition is common today, even with our unprecedented access to God's Word. But we should not despair, for James tells us how to be blessed in *all* we do. The person who lives by the Word has been promised blessings, and blessings in abundance!

This should not be confused with having a problem-free life, which is the interpretation our present culture might give this text. God promises to sustain those who live according to His designs, though they may experience extremely difficult situations. We should also be careful to note that the blessing is for those who practice the Word of God—not those who hear, study or memorize it. There is an enormous difference between these intellectual exercises and the process of adjusting our thoughts and actions to the eternal principles laid down by the Word.

What instruction does James then give us? First, we should look "intently" at the perfect law. This requires concentration, something not possible with a superficial reading of the text. Such focus will come from a conviction that the Word's most precious treasures are within reach for those willing to seek them through the Spirit's revealing work. It is a willingness to go beyond what is easily observable on the surface, digging into the depths of Scripture.

Second, James exhorts us to do this continually, becoming effective doers. Learning to live by the Word is the result of a process. We must constantly return to Scripture and transfer its treasures to our hearts. A slow and steady transformation will take place, making us people to whom the Lord is eager to show Himself (John 14:21).

Food for Thought

Perseverance is necessary, because neither the flesh nor the world will help us in our desire to live in the light. Victory belongs to those who do not easily give up on what they have proposed.

Totally Inadequate

Against all hope, Abraham in hope believed and so became the father of many nations, just as it had been said to him, "So shall your offspring be." Without weakening in his faith, he faced the fact that his body was as good as dead—since he was about a hundred years old—and that Sarah's womb was also dead. Romans 4:18–19

It is difficult for us to understand the real dimensions of the trials suffered by great heroes of the faith. This is partly due to our habitual weakness in understanding the adversity of others. But it doesn't help that we know how the stories end, making the outcomes look much simpler than they really were.

Today's text helps us recognize the patriarch's struggle. The Lord had promised him a son, announcing that he would eventually become the father of many nations. But Abraham's body was in a state of deterioration. Those of us who have entered the second stage of our lives don't need anyone to remind us of this natural progression; we need only look in the mirror to see the evidence of passing time. As if this were not enough, we feel daily the physical limitations that come with age. We get short of breath more easily, must be careful not to overstrain ourselves and have more difficulty climbing stairs. Some foods no longer agree with us as they did years ago, when we could eat whatever and as much as we liked. The small print in newspapers or magazines reminds us that our eyes no longer focus as they used to. The years have left their mark on us.

This is why, when promised a son, Abraham could not help considering his limitations in helping to accomplish this happy event. It was not just age that worried him, but that their endless attempts for Sarah to conceive had always ended in frustration. Perhaps the Lord's proposal even seemed to contain a measure of cruelty.

We should remember that the Lord most frequently works in this way. He delights in choosing men and women who have no qualifications whatsoever to recommend them. Many think the Lord has made a serious mistake in selecting them. How, for example, could He choose someone who stammered for such a delicate diplomatic task as negotiating with Pharaoh?

There is no mistake in the call, my friend. It is our very weaknesses that have enabled you and me to be called by our God. Because of them we are obliged to depend entirely on His grace. Inadequacies, though they produce fear and doubt in us, are the best qualifications for success in God's plans. We should imitate Abraham's faith, for he did not take his personal limitations into account, but believed against all hope. And it was credited to him as righteousness.

Food for Thought

How do you react when you feel unprepared for a task? How can you convert your weaknesses into steps toward progress?

5 December

The Privilege of Giving

And now, brothers, we want you to know about the grace that God has given the Macedonian churches. Out of the most severe trial, their overflowing joy and their extreme poverty welled up in rich generosity. For I testify that they gave as much as they were able, and even beyond their ability. Entirely on their own, they urgently pleaded with us for the privilege of sharing in this service to the saints. 2 Corinthians 8:1–4

Perhaps nothing reveals our commitment to Christ as accurately as our attitude toward money. Many serious Christians demonstrate real ignorance in managing their resources as citizens of the kingdom of heaven. Even though we exhort our congregation with the text "God loves a cheerful giver" (2 Cor. 9:7), we can fail to recognize the dynamics of giving born by the initiative of the Spirit.

It is good for us to note that the Macedonian church's giving was done through the grace of God. It is important to highlight this truth because giving does not come naturally to man. On the contrary, the natural man thinks only of his own needs. Even after Christ has broken this selfish tendency within us, we still require abundant grace to open our hearts and our wallets, and to act with generosity toward others.

The Macedonian church, presented in the New Testament as a model of generosity, was going through a time of severe difficulties. This was probably the result of church persecution throughout the length and breadth of the empire, which grew increasingly violent over time. Those of us who have been through deep grief know how easy it is to allow our sorrow to blind us to others' needs. But their affliction did not distract this congregation from their duty.

This church also gave while in a situation of "extreme poverty." In this we notice a difference from our own tendencies, since in times of financial trouble one of the first things we discontinue is our offerings. The Macedonians knew that the best way to combat the bitterness and uneasiness that come with poverty was to be absolutely generous. In this way they ensured that money would not control their happiness or be their source of security.

The full expression of their selflessness is revealed in that "they urgently pleaded with us for the privilege of sharing in this service." What a tremendous example! Nobody had to impel them to give. Rather, they felt that they would miss a blessing if they didn't share their resources with others. This is definitely a conviction born of the Spirit, since we naturally struggle with the idea that to give is to lose. They understood that giving was a means of great gain.

Food for Thought

"One man gives freely, yet gains even more; another withholds unduly, but comes to poverty" (Prov. 11:24).

Believing with the Heart

But what does it say? "The word is near you; it is in your mouth and in your heart," that is, the word of faith we are proclaiming: That if you confess with your mouth, "Jesus is Lord," and believe in your heart that God raised him from the dead, you will be saved. For it is with your heart that you believe and are justified, and it is with your mouth that you confess and are saved. Romans 10:8–10

To better understand how we work as human beings, it is useful to identify the components that form who we are. People consist of body, mind, soul and spirit (sometimes expressed as the heart), and a complete person has achieved healthy development in each area. In our times people live increasingly fragmented lives, revealing imbalance in areas essential to wholeness.

When we consider humanity today, there is no doubt that the area receiving the greatest stimulation is the mind. The formal education process, almost exclusively related to the intellect, takes up at least a third of a person's life. We also live in days in which a dramatic explosion in our access to data has occurred. Richard Swenson has observed that a typical newspaper from any large city today contains more information than a person living in the seventeenth century acquired in an entire lifetime.[1]

Amazingly, this avalanche of intelligence has not produced healthier or more evenly-balanced individuals. On the contrary, the distance separating mental health from emotional and spiritual soundness is even greater than before. The disparity in the development of these human facets has reached alarming levels, so that many people display mature mental processes, but childlike reactions at an emotional and spiritual level.

This poses a genuine obstacle for those seeking greater depth in the spiritual dimension of their lives. The principal language in the kingdom of heaven is spiritual, but this is the aspect of our lives to which we have paid least attention.

In today's text, however, Paul states that the act of believing occurs mainly in the heart. Faith is a spiritual conviction that will challenge the intellectual structures we typically use to analyze and understand our lives. The mind works with confidence in the setting peculiar to this present culture, but in matters of the spirit it must be content with a secondary role. It is not that the mind has no function in the spiritual world; but it is absolutely limited in its capacity to apprehend the mysteries of God. An individual who is mature in Christ has not reached their level of growth by grasping God's plans logically, but by reaping the fruits of a meaningful relationship with the Lord.

Food for Thought

The spiritual conviction that motivates disciples' lives is directly related to their closeness to God. Where there is greater intimacy, there is also greater certainty that the way shown by the Spirit is correct.

7 December

Well-used Gifts

We have different gifts, according to the grace given us. If a man's gift is prophesying, let him use it in proportion to his faith. If it is serving, let him serve; if it is teaching, let him teach; if it is encouraging, let him encourage; if it is contributing to the needs of others, let him give generously; if it is leadership, let him govern diligently; if it is showing mercy, let him do it cheerfully. Romans 12:6–8

In the final stages of His earthly ministry, the Lord shared the parable of the talents with His disciples. In this story (Matt. 25:14–30) He made it very clear that after He physically departed, He expected them to make good use of their God-given talents. The results He desired would not be the same for each of them, but proportional to the gifting they had received. But all of them would be rewarded for wise administration of the King's resources.

In today's text Paul shares a similar idea. Each member of Christ's body has received gifts. None of us had any say in what we were assigned, but God gave to each of us according to His wisdom and the needs of the church (1 Cor. 12:11). The Father knows us perfectly; He gives talents that will complement our personality and our individual background.

The apostle wanted the Roman church to understand that they were responsible to add to what they had received. They were to use their gifts in a way pleasing to God. In other words, God's gifts will achieve maximum effectiveness when accompanied by a correct attitude: Prophecy should be accompanied by faith, service by acts of encouragement, administration by a compassionate and generous spirit, etc.

This is significant because it is easy for leaders to fuel their ministries by the strength of their own talents. A good example of this is Solomon, who had asked God for wisdom to govern the people. The Lord was pleased with his petition and granted what he asked (1 Kings 3:10–15). Nevertheless, the king departed from the way of his father David. He took women for himself from other nations, in open opposition to the Law. He invested an enormous amount of resources in building a luxurious palace for himself. The wisdom he had received ceased to be useful, and he ended up writing a depressing message in the book of Ecclesiastes about the "vanity" of his pursuits.

All leaders are responsible for making good use of God's gifts to them. To the gift one should add the effort, discipline and practice that will guarantee its maximum potential. In this way leaders can ensure all the support and blessing of God in the ministry entrusted to them.

Food for Thought

What gifts have you received from God? What steps have you taken to develop their use? What can you do to further this development?

Offering Hope to the Lost

Jesus straightened up and asked her, "Woman, where are they? Has no one condemned you?" "No one, sir," she said. "Then neither do I condemn you," Jesus declared.
John 8:10–11

When the religious leaders in Jerusalem caught a woman in adultery, they saw it as the perfect opportunity to trap Jesus. The Lord, however, surprised them with a completely unexpected response: "If any one of you is without sin, let him be the first to throw a stone at her" (John 8:7). Suddenly, all eyes were focused on the accusers. They clearly had no interest in the woman except to use her as a tool for their evil intentions. To Jesus, however, she was exactly the kind of person He had come to rescue from the clutches of sin. Despite the shameless way in which these men were using her, none of them felt confident enough to throw the first stone, and they slowly began to withdraw.

What is involved in condemning someone? Condemnation is the final step in a process of judgment. It comes after a lengthy procedure to establish whether or not a person is guilty in a given situation. When all the evidence is in, a jury will deliver its verdict and, for those who are found guilty, the judge will pass sentence. The moment someone is condemned they lose all hope of overturning the ruling.

Christ was indicating that in the Kingdom, only those free from sin have the right to condemn others. It is not only the Pharisees and the teachers of the law who are excluded from casting judgment. We too suffer from the same ailment which led the woman to commit adultery: a heart that is desperately corrupt.

But this condition did not affect the Son of Man. He would have done nothing wrong in passing sentence on the woman, for He was without sin. Nevertheless, He told the Pharisees: "You judge by human standards; I pass judgment on no one" (John 8:15). He had not come to condemn the world, but to save it (John 12:47).

It is in this statement that we find the clearest definition of compassion. Jesus abhors the sin that affects us all, but desperately loves those who are trapped in it. He insists on drawing close to sinners because He believes that as long as there is breath in a person, there is hope for salvation. Condemnation is reserved for those who have already passed from this life.

As leaders we truly need this perspective. We cannot offer salvation to people if we believe they are beyond hope. Yet the gospel teaches us that no matter how low a person has fallen, there is always the possibility they may turn from sin to embrace the redeeming hope of the cross.

Food for Thought

"If God should have no more mercy on us than we have charity one to another, what would become of us?" (Thomas Fuller)[2]

9 December

Danger of Intoxication

The crucible for silver and the furnace for gold, but man is tested by the praise he receives.
Proverbs 27:21

The process of purifying precious metals is not very complex and was known in biblical times. A metal in its natural state of mineral formations is submitted to an intense heating process. The torridity causes the impure elements to separate, thus leaving the iron, silver or gold in isolation.

The illustration used by the author of Proverbs helps us understand the similar process of purification in human beings. It is very easy to trust in our own ability to accurately evaluate our heart. But Scripture reminds us, "Who can say, 'I have kept my heart pure, I am clean and without sin'?" (Prov. 20:9). The very wording of the question indicates that nobody can respond in the affirmative. It is virtually impossible to purify our heart, especially when it comes to matters of pride and humility.

Today's text provides a more trustworthy message. A good way to tell what kind of person we are is to measure our reaction to praise. As in trials of great intensity, acclaim often brings to light the motivations and attitudes hidden in the deepest recesses of our lives.

There are two possible responses to praise that should worry us. The first is when people become puffed up with importance and believe their achievements result from their own effort and intelligence. This is a dangerous road because it becomes easy to forget that everything we have and are comes from the Father's generous goodness toward us. As John the Baptist pointed out, "a man can receive only what is given him from heaven" (John 3:27). Jesus reminded us of this truth when He told the parable of the servant who had served his master faithfully, not only in the fields, but also in the home. Was his master to thank him for what he had done? The Lord's answer was clear, "So you also, when you have done everything you were told to do, should say, 'We are unworthy servants; we have only done our duty" (Luke 17:10).

The other reaction we should guard against is being excessively "humble," refusing to recognize that we played a part at all in a project's success. I suspect this attitude also displays a distorted sense of pride, since the lack of willingness to receive compliments is a form of arrogance. True humility knows how to give, but also knows how to receive.

So we should acknowledge the compliment we have been paid and then hand it over to our Father with as little fuss as possible. The best way to manage praise is not to give it too much importance.

Food for Thought

"The proud hate pride . . . in others!" (Benjamin Franklin)[3]

The Anti-Leader

He would get up early and stand by the side of the road leading to the city gate. Whenever anyone came with a complaint to be placed before the king for a decision, Absalom would call out to him, "What town are you from?" He would answer, "Your servant is from one of the tribes of Israel." Then Absalom would say to him, "Look, your claims are valid and proper, but there is no representative of the king to hear you." And Absalom would add, "If only I were appointed judge in the land! Then everyone who has a complaint or case could come to me and I would see that he gets justice." 2 Samuel 15:2–4

The strategy followed by Absalom gives insight into how someone can work astutely to undermine a leader. Absalom did not confront David directly, but began to subtly influence the hearts of those who supported the king. This procedure is no more than an imitation of how the devil himself works; he maneuvers in such a way that people don't realize they are turning their backs on the Father's will. David's son positioned himself at the city gates and feigned a real interest in the lives of those who came to see the king.

It has to be pointed out that he would have failed in this ploy if David had been taking good care of his people. Over the years, however, the king had grown distant and had neglected the vital work of shepherding to which he had been called. The peoples' dissatisfaction and frustration provided fertile ground for Absalom to sow seeds of discord.

It is difficult to steal the heart of someone who feels loved and cared for. When pastors begin losing people, it is often an indication they are not adequately seeing to the needs of their followers. As a wise teacher of mine once said, "It is difficult to steal well-fed sheep!" In other words, sheep who begin looking for other fields in which to feed are not obtaining adequate nutrition from their own.

So what strategy should we employ with anti-leaders, those like Absalom who are unhappy with the headship recognized by the group? These situations are not resolved through aggression toward such a person. Rather, we must make the necessary adjustments in our shepherding to ensure the congregation is well cared for.

This does not imply that you and I must have perfect ministries. But the principal aim of our work should be to share the love and grace of Christ with those we serve. If they feel loved and valued by their pastor, it is very unlikely they will heed the proposals of someone who wants to lead them in another direction.

Food for Thought

How do you show your love for the people you serve? What aspects of your ministry should you improve on so as to give them better care? Who shares with you the burden of caring for the congregation's needs?

11 December | Paying the Price

From this time many of his disciples turned back and no longer followed him. "You do not want to leave too, do you?" Jesus asked the Twelve. John 6:66–67

One characteristic marking the enormous difference between Jesus' leadership style and that which has become popular today is in the method of proclaiming God's truth. Without meaning to deliberately offend, Jesus was not afraid to talk about the most radical aspects of the Kingdom. We, however, live in times in which it is considered fundamental not to scare people away with postures considered too severe. As such, we have tended toward a gospel consisting of a long list of benefits that demand little or nothing of the disciple in terms of surrender.

In the Gospels we find various incidents in which the teachings of Christ were considered an affront to His hearers. Even the disciples worried about this, sometimes pointing out to the Lord the reaction He had provoked as if expecting Him to retract His words (Matt. 15:12). Today's passage captures a moment in which Jesus' teaching was too much for His listeners. From this time, the evangelist tells us, many of His followers "turned back and no longer followed him."

Jesus was not concerned. He did not run after them to make amends, seeking their return at all costs. He knew that without a radical decision to follow Him despite the cost, they would surely have a lukewarm spiritual experience. Far from being distressed, Jesus turned to the Twelve and confronted them as well: "You do not want to leave too, do you?"

Christ's reaction seems a little strange to our postmodern mindset, but it has a reason. Those who would follow Him should be aware not only of the cost, but also that they must show their willingness to pay it. If they cannot do this, they will continually lean on others to sustain them.

This principle contains an important lesson for our own ministries. In our eagerness to form disciples in a responsible way, we can end up making all the effort ourselves, seeking to ensure the commitment of those we are training through unconditional surrender on *our* part! In my pastoral experience, results from this kind of investment rarely last. Sooner or later those we are discipling must decide for themselves how they will proceed, whatever that decision may be.

Peter answered on behalf of the disciples, "Lord, to whom shall we go? You have the words of eternal life. We believe and know that you are the Holy One of God" (John 6:68–69) He knew that the life ahead of them would have many difficulties. But he was also sure that to leave Jesus was to lose everything. Embracing this truth, they decided to pay the price of following the Messiah.

Food for Thought

What is your leadership style? How much sacrifice do you make for the people you are investing in? How much sacrifice do they make to obtain their training?

The Purity of Our Eyes

"I made a covenant with my eyes not to look lustfully at a girl." Job 31:1

What an interesting phrase Job uses to describe his desire for purity! The patriarch, at some moment in his life, consciously determined to guard his eyes so they wouldn't be instruments of iniquity. Although his era didn't offer the sexually charged visual landscape that literally overwhelms our view today, he still recognized the danger in looking at something inappropriate.

If we know that sin is really targeting our spirits, it might seem unnecessary to discipline the physical body—in this case our eyes—to avoid wickedness. But Job understood that the eyes are windows; through them enter images that will affect our hearts.

If we consider for a moment how a human being functions, we will understand the importance of this concept. Shopkeepers invest a great deal of time and money in dressing up their windows, since an attractive front will win customers. In a shop selling magazines, we can easily see how carefully the covers of each publication have been produced. In fact, studies show that the cover is a decisive factor in the sale of a magazine. Similarly, we can recognize the effort invested in attractive design of cars, electrical appliances or tourist brochures. All these appeal to our profound appreciation of beauty, which comes through the eyes.

As a shop window attracts a person to further action, so our eyes can be the means of fostering sin in our hearts. We are surrounded by seductive images appealing to base desires that are offensive to God. The psalmist observes of the fallen that "their eye bulges from fatness; the imaginations of their heart run riot" (Ps. 73:7, NASB). In other words, they lay their hands on whatever their eyes desire without measuring the consequences of their actions.

The Bible bids us discipline our sight to keep it within the parameters established by God for a life of purity. David prays, "Turn away my eyes from looking at vanity" (Ps. 119:37, NASB). The author of Proverbs encourages us along a similar line: "Let your eyes look straight ahead, fix your gaze directly before you" (Prov. 4:25). In the New Testament the Apostle John identifies the desire of our eyes as one of the great dangers for God's children. "Do not love the world or anything in the world," he warns. "For everything in the world—the cravings of sinful man, the lust of his eyes and the boasting of what he has and does—comes not from the Father but from the world" (1 John 2:15–16).

Food for Thought

Sight is one of the most precious gifts we have received from God. It is up to us to use it in a way that contributes to our edification. Through iron discipline we can learn to delight in what is good and to avoid what is evil.

13 December — Sins of Omission

Anyone, then, who knows the good he ought to do and doesn't do it, sins. James 4:17

Within the church much emphasis has been placed on the care a disciple must take not to sin. The concept generally refers to avoiding behavior and activities that the Bible specifically catalogs as sinful. In this way, then, God's people try not to participate in things that could damage or destroy their relationship with the Lord such as lying, cheating, bribing or illicit relationships.

Avoiding these sins can lull us into a false sense of security, causing us to feel safe because we practice none of the obvious behaviors associated with wickedness. The Apostle James, however, takes the concept of a sinless life to a deeper level. He tells us that to live a life acceptable before the Father, it is not enough only to avoid evil, though this is an important part of our commitment. To live our spiritual life to the full, we must also be willing to become involved in what we know is good. In other words, our life cannot be lived purely on a defensive posture. The Lord calls us to take the initiative and deliberately engage in doing what is right.

Understanding this truth can free us from a life of comfort in which our main objective is simply to avoid the wrong path. The Lord calls us to be actively involved in promoting good and extending the Kingdom. This means that our faith impels us to imitate our Father's commitment. When He saw the condition we were in, He made the decision to do something about it. We should behave in the same way. On seeing people around us trapped by sin and evil, we should put our own interests to one side and work actively in seeking to help our neighbor.

James wants us to understand that *not* doing what we know is right is just as condemnable as doing wrong. Think, for example, of the parable of the Good Samaritan. For many of us, the attitude of the priest and the Levite as they passed by the wounded man was one of negligence. In light of the principle presented by James, however, their noncommittal attitude was actually sin; they knew what they should do, but didn't want to do it.

This has serious implications for those in the body of Christ. The church should always be an active, visible force in the society in which we have been placed. It fulfills this function when it is willing to take the initiative and carry out those things it knows are good. God calls us as leaders to constantly encourage our congregations to take their place within God's vision among their neighbors, their workmates, their friends and all those who cross their paths each day.

Food for Thought

"Every man is guilty of all the good he didn't do." (Voltaire) [4]

Participants in His Triumph

But thanks be to God, who always leads us in triumphal procession in Christ and through us spreads everywhere the fragrance of the knowledge of him. For we are to God the aroma of Christ among those who are being saved and those who are perishing. To the one we are the smell of death; to the other, the fragrance of life. And who is equal to such a task?
2 Corinthians 2:14–16

Like Christ, the Apostle Paul often used real-life images to illustrate eternal truths. If we are not familiar with the analogy in today's passage, we may miss much of the richness in the text.

This illustration was taken from a practice common to the endless military campaigns of the invincible Roman army. Any inhabitant of the Imperial capital would have had the opportunity to witness one of these events, and others would have heard of these memorable spectacles. Paul is speaking of the triumphal parade of the Roman generals, returning home after defeating an enemy of the vast empire.

When they had put down a rebellion—as in the fatal Jewish uprising in the year 70 AD —or completed an invasion of foreign lands, the victorious army would return to Rome, entering the great city with a jubilant cavalcade. The exhibition displaying the fruits of the campaign was witnessed by multitudes.

The incredible procession was accompanied by all the pomp and ceremony typical of life in Rome. At the head went the priests, who served the various gods of the empire. They carried incense that released fragrant perfume the length of the parade route. Behind them marched the victorious army, cheered on by the crowds. The soldiers were followed by the defeated warriors, arriving in chains to be sold as slaves or converted into gladiators. The procession was brought up with the chariot of the general who had led the victorious troops.

All those marching could smell the priest's perfume, but it held different meaning for each one. For the Roman troops it was a sweet reminder of victory and the promise of reward to come. For the conquered army, however, the same fragrance signaled despair for many who would soon die under deplorable circumstances.

In the same way, Christ spreads the perfume of His victory to all humanity. His church is the vessel through which this aroma is diffused. Some will associate the sweet fragrance with all that Christ offers those who receive His invitation of discipleship. But to others the foolishness of the cross will mean the foretelling of their spiritual death.

Whatever message Christ's aroma brings, we are witnesses to our Lord's triumph. We radiate the perfume of holiness when we live the life of Christ. We will enable others to see the Messiah in our words, gestures, attitudes and good deeds.

Food for Thought

Christ's triumphal procession is not reserved for the future, but a visible reality wherever the church advances in victory over darkness.

Intimacy

"I tell you the truth, the Son can do nothing by himself; he can do only what he sees his Father doing, because whatever the Father does the Son also does. For the Father loves the Son and shows him all he does. Yes, to your amazement he will show him even greater things than these." John 5:19–20

This text from John's Gospel explains clearly why Jesus' ministry was so successful. It also tells us why, when facing the cross, Christ declared that He had completed the task commended to Him—which is not the same as saying He had done all He could do. The secret of having completed His ministry successfully is found in the absolute unity He maintained with the Father.

We see first of all that the Son did not make plans of His own accord, but was about the business of His heavenly Father. This is absolutely fundamental for anyone in ministry. Of course, the easiest approach is to set up an enterprise for the Father and simply ask Him to bless it. But the ventures that really advance are those that coincide fully with what the Father is doing in the place He has put us. The truth is that we are not able on our own to discern the intentions or thoughts of our heavenly Father. Without His revelation we are essentially working in the dark. Knowledge of His will, therefore, is essential to building a ministry that enjoys God's full support.

The text tells us how Jesus achieved this knowledge. Because of the bond of love uniting them, the Father revealed His plans to His Son. In other words, the quality of the relationship they enjoyed led the Father to naturally include His Son in the intimacies of His heart. The Father's love was based on the life of absolute submission Jesus lived.

How does this affect our own ministries? We cannot progress successfully if we are not standing firm in God's will. To have this foundation, we must know the Father's heart. He shares this knowledge only with those who give Him their unconditional love and commitment. So the revelation of His desire is not so much the fruit of seeking Him in prayer—though this is part of our relationship with Him—as the result of intimacy between two beings who love each other.

What should bring overwhelming joy to our hearts as leaders is that this intimacy is available to all who will have it. Jesus said to His disciples, "Whoever has my commands and obeys them, he is the one who loves me. He who loves me will be loved by my Father, and I too will love him and show myself to him" (John 14:21).

Food for Thought

"I no longer call you servants, because a servant does not know his master's business. Instead, I have called you friends, for everything that I learned from my Father I have made known to you" (John 15:15).

Ambassadors for Christ

All this is from God, who reconciled us to himself through Christ and gave us the ministry of reconciliation: that God was reconciling the world to himself in Christ, not counting men's sins against them. And he has committed to us the message of reconciliation. We are therefore Christ's ambassadors, as though God were making his appeal through us. We implore you on Christ's behalf: Be reconciled to God. 2 Corinthians 5:18–20

Today's text clearly defines our identity and the task we have been given by the grace of God. The Apostle Paul declares that as ambassadors for Christ, we have a mission similar to the Son's in serving a lost world. As ambassadors, our basic role is to represent to a third party the person who sends us. This not only includes making known and defending the interests of those we represent, but behaving in a way that proclaims their dignity and solemnity.

This is common knowledge, but it is worth repeating that our main objective is not to work for ourselves, but for Him who has sent us. All our efforts are for Christ. So are our achievements. Our decisions should be ones He would make. The image we present, the language we use and the way we perform determine the way others will see the Lord. However, it is easy to lose our way in ministry and begin to believe we are working for the congregation, denomination or organization we represent. It is even easier for leaders to start promoting their own image and interests, using their achievements for the good of their own goals. To avoid this danger, we should stop from time to time to recover an accurate perspective. We are no more than representatives of the One we serve.

What is the principal task to which we have been called? Paul declares it is a work of reconciliation, an attempt to recover a relationship between two opposing parties. It assumes first that one of the people involved wants to recover fellowship with the other, which is absolutely true on the Lord's part. "But because of his great love for us, God, who is rich in mercy, made us alive with Christ even when we were dead in transgressions" (Eph. 2:4–5). But perhaps the other party shows no interest in reconciliation. It is even possible they are unaware the relationship has been broken.

This is where the patient, gentle diplomacy of an ambassador comes in. It enables the messenger to approach the estranged party and begin the process of drawing that person close to the One represented. At the same time, the emissary should keep the Master informed and seek His guidance for successfully concluding the business at hand. This requires discretion, kindness and perseverance. We cannot come back empty-handed, for the One who sent us waits eagerly for the recovery of yet another relationship.

Food for Thought

"The clearest evidence of love is its willingness to suffer for those it loves." (Anonymous)

17 December

Beyond Failure

But Peter and John replied, "Judge for yourselves whether it is right in God's sight to obey you rather than God. For we cannot help speaking about what we have seen and heard."
Acts 4:19–20

If we take a moment to review Peter's denial in Matthew 26, it will be difficult for us, in light of today's text, to believe we are reading about the same person. The circumstances are nearly the same. In both incidents the apostle was confronted and had the opportunity to confess he was a follower of Christ. In the first scene Peter was fearful, terrified of opening his mouth and affirming he was one of Jesus' disciples. He opted for a lie—not once, but three times. He denied, with the vehemence of those who are cornered, that he had ever spent time with the Man from Galilee.

But Peter's transformation, as demonstrated in Acts, was absolute. Far from feeling intimidated by the Sanhedrin's threats, he confronted them boldly and proclaimed that he had no intention whatsoever of following the silent path he had once so defensively embraced. How do we explain such a radical change in the apostle?

I believe we will find the answer in the dramatic encounter he had with the risen Jesus at the Sea of Galilee. Peter had tasted the bitter consequences of his denial. Devastation and heavy disillusionment had overwhelmed his soul. He must have believed that his dreams of being part of Jesus' mission were now shattered. The enormity of his fall, however, prepared the ground for his amazing recovery. This meeting with Jesus unlocked the potential which had earlier led the Father to include the fisherman among the Twelve.

The Lord gave Peter precise instructions during that visit: "Shepherd my sheep." That is, he was to dedicate himself to the work to which he had been called. This extraordinary commission is difficult for us to take in, because we are used to evaluating someone's work on the strength of their achievements. I can say without fear of erring that in many congregations someone who had failed as Peter did would certainly be expelled from ministry—probably permanently. But on the shores of the Sea of Galilee, Christ revealed one of the greatest truths of the gospel: Our failures do not condition God's plans. What sustains the Lord's plans for our lives is not our own faithfulness, but the faithfulness of the One who has called us. In a very real way Jesus is saying to the disillusioned disciple, "Get up! I still believe in you."

It is only when we discover the extraordinary depth of God's grace that we can fulfill our true potential in Christ. Nobody seems to understand this better than those who have experienced heart-rending failure. This is why the most intrepid members of the church are often those who have been rescued from the worst situations.

Food for Thought

"It's incredible how strong we become when we understand how weak we are!" (François Fénelon) [5]

When it is Wise to Flee

One day he went into the house to attend to his duties, and none of the household servants was inside. She caught him by his cloak and said, "Come to bed with me!" But he left his cloak in her hand and ran out of the house. Genesis 39:11–12

A concept firmly rooted in our culture is that running away is for cowards, for those who cannot handle life's real challenges. According to this criterion, those who flee cannot succeed, for victory belongs to those who advance against all odds. We often transfer this philosophy to ministry, developing a posture of obstinate perseverance in all we do. However, as Joseph's story illustrates, at times this is a recipe for disaster.

Some could object that Joseph landed in jail as a result of his decision to flee. But his heart was being prepared for the immense responsibilities God would give him in a few years' time. In the short term flight looked like defeat, but in the long run his decision set the foundation for a life of great consequence in the kingdom of God.

What led Joseph to run away? First, his strongest commitment was to God's honor. His refusal to dishonor Jehovah also extended to honoring Potiphar, who had entrusted him with everything in his household. At his master's wife's insistent insinuations, Joseph had declared, "With me in charge . . . my master does not concern himself with anything in the house; everything he owns he has entrusted to my care. No one is greater in this house than I am. My master has withheld nothing from me except you, because you are his wife. How then could I do such a wicked thing and sin against God?" (Gen. 39:8–9).

But then Joseph found himself alone with Potiphar's wife, an extremely dangerous situation for any man who wants to maintain purity of heart. Not satisfied with harassing him with her perverse invitations, she threw caution to the wind and tried to take him by force. Joseph knew that in a few short moments he would not have the discipline or clarity to stand firm in his posture. He did not try to maintain his strength in the midst of a situation that appealed to the sensuality of the flesh. Faced with such danger, he decided to flee.

This is the key to his decision. Joseph recognized his limitations and knew only too well through which door the Enemy could enter. Wise leaders know there are situations in which they cannot control themselves sufficiently to maintain the holiness of their vocation. They prefer to completely sidestep the fight, knowing they are not up to it. The decision to avoid conflict requires greater courage and valor than believing we can triumph where others better than us have fallen.

Food for Thought

"Flee the evil desires of youth, and pursue righteousness, faith, love and peace, along with those who call on the Lord out of a pure heart" (2 Tim. 2:22).

19 December — Corrupt Pastors

Be shepherds of God's flock that is under your care, serving as overseers—not because you must, but because you are willing, as God wants you to be; not greedy for money, but eager to serve; not lording it over those entrusted to you, but being examples to the flock.
1 Peter 5:2–3

The basic meaning of the term "corrupt" refers to something that has lost its original state of purity. In this sense today's text clearly identifies the ways a pastor's call can become adulterated. This happens when a leadership style is adopted that completely contradicts Jesus' unique model of a pastor.

Peter urges that the work of a pastor is to nourish the flock, a task that should be carried out with tenderness through one's own free choice. In other words, pastors should never feel they are working under a sense of obligation, but rather purely and exclusively through the personal conviction born of a heavenly call. Those who shepherd because they feel bound will carry out their work without the love and affection which should proceed from the heart. When this happens, pastoring becomes a job in which the only goal is to fulfill one's duties. Under these circumstances we will never give of our best.

It is just as harmful for pastors to serve because of the benefits they can reap in their own lives. Although Peter writes of economic benefits, we need not limit ourselves exclusively to this aspect. Pastoring can also lend itself to building up a reputation, earning people's affection and recognition, or gaining access to certain privileges. All these distract from the essential purpose, which is to look after the interests of the people.

Peter also warns against what has become a curse of our times: pastors who become lords of their congregations. These pastors believe that the sheep belong to them, that their people can do nothing without first receiving their authorization. This model seriously deviates from the figure of shepherding known in Israel, since the sheep being watched rarely belonged to the shepherd. The shepherd usually worked for others who, because of their advantageous economic position, could afford to hire someone to do the work for them.

In the same way, pastors who work in the Kingdom are not master of those they lead. Instead, they look after and nourish people for the One who has bought them with His own blood. They would not dream for a moment of setting themselves up as their "lord"—a title reserved only for the Son of God. This is why the ministry of such pastors is characterized by grace and mercy; they know each person has the same freedom of choice granted to them. They love each individual deeply, but do not impose themselves on anyone. The need to control and restrict the people's freedom is the clearest indication of a miserly, fearful love.

Food for Thought

"Duty makes us do things well, but love makes us do things beautifully." (Phillips Brooks)[6]

The Party Must Go On

Jesus replied: "A certain man was preparing a great banquet and invited many guests."
Luke 14:16

This is one of the many stories Jesus used to illustrate Kingdom principles. Like all good illustrations, it is short and simple, making the lesson more easily recorded in the listeners' hearts. If you don't remember the details, I would like to suggest taking a few moments to read the complete parable.

The story contains various interesting details. First, notice the man decided on his own to have the feast. We don't know his motives, but we do know his desire to hold a banquet was very strong. Our God feels the same way. I believe we can never fully understand why He decided to create humanity, but the Word gives some indications that His main desire was to share with us the overflow of profound joy the Father, Son and Holy Spirit experience together. It gives our Lord incomparable pleasure to share this relationship with His creatures. He delights in blessing our lives.

Second, we should note the excuses made by the friends and invited guests. Each one had legitimate reasons for not attending the dinner, related to their lives and particular responsibilities. This highlights the grave danger we face each day as Jesus' disciples: that of allowing life's details to so absorb us that we cease to share in the adventure offered by the Son.

The clearest example of this can be seen in Martha (Luke 10:41). There was nothing wrong with her desire to serve, except that she didn't recognize when to lay aside her housework to enjoy a moment of intimacy with Jesus. In the same way, we can be so engrossed in our many projects that we consider Christ's invitation an unwelcome interruption instead of an opportunity to enter another dimension of life.

If we had been organizing this feast, we would likely have canceled it when faced with our guests' refusals to attend. How can one hold a feast if those invited reject the invitation? But this man didn't consider that option even for a moment. He simply decided to extend his invitation to other people. And here we come to the most interesting point of the story: God will go ahead with His banquet whether we decide to join Him or not. He will not be denied the pleasure of holding His feast, with or without our presence. This clearly reveals that none of us is the center of the story—we are not so indispensable that our absence leads to cancellation. Our Lord is the Beginning and the End of everything, the only One without whom the celebration will be stopped. The responsibility lies with us, therefore, to accept His invitation and enter into the celebration of our great God.

Food for Thought

"Holy delight and joy is the great antidote to despair and is a wellspring of genuine gratitude." (Dallas Willard)[7]

21 December Minister and Be Ministered To

I long to see you so that I may impart to you some spiritual gift to make you strong—that is, that you and I may be mutually encouraged by each other's faith. Romans 1:11–12

For a long time Paul had desired to visit the Christians in Rome. It was inevitable that the apostle, having contributed so much to the expansion of the Kingdom, should fix his eyes on the capital of the vast Roman Empire.

As in every place he visited, Paul wished to minister the Word in Rome and encourage his brothers in the faith. Those who have a true pastoral heart cannot avoid exercising their ministry wherever they find themselves, for shepherding is not a job, but the manifestation of a calling. For this reason the apostle wished to establish the believers in the Roman capital, imparting some spiritual gift. By this phrase we understand that he wanted to build up the church so it would reach its full potential in Jesus Christ. This included helping them receive and use the gifts the Lord had granted His people.

It is interesting to notice, however, that Paul did not wish to visit Rome only to minister to them; he also longed to receive all they had to give him. In this desire we find a wise understanding of the dynamics of the church. Paul knew that all of us are to edify one another to produce growth.

This receptivity to being served by others is a most unusual attitude to find in leaders. It is very easy for pastors to think that they are the ones who encourage the church and that their only function within the body is to lead and minister to others. When this perspective is strongly entrenched, it is very difficult for such leaders to relax in the presence of others, to take off their "pastor's hat" and behave as just one more member of the body. Some pastors even take this attitude into their homes and treat their spouse and children as members of the congregation.

The danger of this posture is in believing that within the congregation there is no one who can really minister to us. And so our dealings with them become a one-way street. We always give, and they always receive. Yet the Apostle Paul, despite enjoying a prestige and a high profile unequalled in the first century church, had a humble heart that was willing to receive from the church whatever they could offer him on behalf of God. These kinds of leaders most inspire their followers, because they do not present themselves as perfect, but rather as also undergoing a process of formation. Far from decreasing their authority, this attitude magnifies the virtues they possess.

Food for Thought

"The eye cannot say to the hand, 'I don't need you!' And the head cannot say to the feet, 'I don't need you!' On the contrary, those parts of the body that seem to be weaker are indispensable" (1 Cor. 12:21).

The Sin of Sodom

December 22

"'As surely as I live, declares the Sovereign LORD, your sister Sodom and her daughters never did what you and your daughters have done. Now this was the sin of your sister Sodom: She and her daughters were arrogant, overfed and unconcerned; they did not help the poor and needy.'" Ezekiel 16:48–49

It is helpful to read the commentaries of Bible authors on historical Scriptural events. They often add something to our perspective that we don't find in the original report. Psalm 78, for example, provides a commentary on Israel's departure from Egypt and their forty years' passage through the desert. Similarly, in today's text we find an interesting commentary on the destruction of Sodom which complements the original Genesis account.

If I asked a believer why God destroyed the cities of Sodom and Gomorrah, I am sure I would receive a typical reply: The Lord obliterated these cities because of their serious moral deterioration, with sexual practices still detestable today.

It is true that this decadence was the visible problem, but the prophet Ezekiel doesn't even mention it. I think the reason is clear: The hateful practices they had fallen into were not the *cause* of the trouble, but the *symptom*. In other words, a life of unbridled pleasure was the result of other, more serious failings mentioned in Ezekiel's passage. The prophet identifies four aspects of the citizens' lives that provide interesting clues to the essence of their sin.

First, he says they were "overfed." By this we understand that God had blessed them richly with material goods; they experienced prosperity as the fruit of their work. Their second and third steps toward trouble were attitudes common to those who have much: They became "arrogant" and "unconcerned." Arrogance comes from believing that our blessings were obtained by our own astuteness and personal sagacity; our affluence leaves us no room to recognize the generous provision of the Most High. Being unconcerned, or idle, is a result of having so many riches that we don't need to work for our daily bread. With time to burn, we inevitably look for ways to fill the empty space in our lives that would normally be filled with work. The combination of too much time and too much money never led anyone to a more significant life.

These attitudes resulted in a fourth aspect of self-focus. Sodom did not follow the plan of God for those He has materially blessed, which is to bless others. The inhabitants of Sodom did not take care of the afflicted or the poor. And so their real problem was discovered: They had not wisely managed the good things they had received from the Lord. Having refused to invest in others, they turned toward a life of absolute selfishness.

Food for Thought

God never blesses us exclusively for our own well-being. What we receive is always given with community in mind and should serve to bless the lives of many. This is the essence of our call.

23 December — The Valley of Tears

Blessed are those whose strength is in you, who have set their hearts on pilgrimage. As they pass through the Valley of Baca, they make it a place of springs; the autumn rains also cover it with pools. They go from strength to strength, till each appears before God in Zion.
Psalm 84:5–7

How refreshing it is to come to the Psalms and read of the struggles, victories and defeats of those who have walked faith's road ahead of us! They especially bless us because they capture the most complex human emotions, those we sometimes struggle to identify. These "songs of the soul" offer us the assurance that many others have experienced the trials we face today.

The psalmist describes the advantage for those who have made Jehovah their strength. These people have the same difficulties as anyone else. They experience adversity, injustice, oppression and personal trials. The secret of their success is not in their circumstances, but in their advanced level of spiritual development. The measure of their inner fullness is such that they can see life through completely different eyes than other people. Not only do they successfully overcome predicaments that would disconcert and discourage most, but they also manage to bring transformation to their situations.

The Valley of Baca mentioned by the psalmist is a place of tribulation and anguish in which life is threatened by drought. Nevertheless, those who have made the Lord their strength, who have set their hearts on pilgrimage, pass through this place of death and bring blessing with them. Where no hope exists, they bring good news. Where there is sadness, they impart joy. Where there is damnation, they offer blessing.

This is nothing but the manifestation of God's work in these peoples' lives. The Lord blesses those who trust Him, converting them into instruments of blessing for others—thus completing the circle of life. This is why the psalmist can declare confidently that such people will go from strength to strength, even in the worst circumstances. The victory they experience daily is the demonstration of a reality in the deepest recesses of their hearts. There is no situation that can change this.

What does the psalmist mean when he writes of these people having their strength in the Lord? The phrase "who have set their hearts on pilgrimage" gives a good clue. These courageous people delight in Jehovah's law and follow only the road He has set before them. They do not spend their lives asking God to bless their own plans and interests, but at each step seek to act by specific instructions received from on High. They have a healthy mistrust of their own wisdom. They know that even when a choice seems obvious, they should always seek the face of God.

Food for Thought

"But those who hope in the LORD will renew their strength. They will soar on wings like eagles; they will run and not grow weary, they will walk and not be faint" (Isa. 40:31).

Not Difficult At All!

Now what I am commanding you today is not too difficult for you or beyond your reach . . . No, the word is very near you; it is in your mouth and in your heart so you may obey it.
Deuteronomy 30:11, 14

If we go into any Christian bookshop, we will find a great many books dealing with every conceivable aspect of the spiritual life. Many of them offer "recipes" that guarantee the Lord's blessing in our lives. With this abundance of material, one might think that a lack of understanding on the part of God's children has brought about this proliferation of books. Compare this mountain of information with the simple message of today's text. What an incredible difference, right? It would even seem that at times so much literature distracts us from the simplicity of the Divine plan.

Do not misunderstand. I don't mean that these books are not useful or that the authors' work is in vain. I myself am a fan of good books and always manage to maintain the discipline of reading profitable literature. But the abundance of written resources should not make us think that the spiritual life is an extremely complicated matter. Rather, the requirement for living in Christ is very simple and can be summed up in one single word: obedience.

Think about what God was saying to the people who had been forty years in the desert: "What I am commanding you today is not too difficult for you or beyond your reach." It was easily accessible to all who wanted to please Jehovah. Their problems had not come from the complexity of the Word. On the contrary, the message only appeared complicated as it got tangled up in pedantic explanations by supposed interpreters of the Law. Their difficulties, rather, lay in the obstinate resistance of the human spirit to take orders from others.

The Lord was telling the people that the Word would always be with them, in their mouths and in their hearts. In other words, through the Spirit they would be able to store in their souls all the truth they needed for living holy lives. Notice this was spoken to a people who had no books or Bibles. The absence of the written word could not impede a life of obedience. No one would ever be able to fain ignorance, since the Lord Himself would make sure the Word was always close to each of them.

The passage reveals once again how incredibly generous our God's heart is. He is much more interested in our holiness than any of us are. To this end He has made ample provision for us, placing the Word within reach of all who love the truth. Furthermore, to this generation He has given the help of the Spirit, who reminds us at each step of our heavenly Father's commandments. How can we fail to lead a life of victory?!

Food for Thought

"One act of obedience is better than a hundred sermons." (Dietrich Bonhoeffer)[8]

25 December | The Hope of the "Forgotten"

So Pharaoh sent for Joseph, and he was quickly brought from the dungeon. When he had shaved and changed his clothes, he came before Pharaoh. Pharaoh said to Joseph, "I had a dream, and no one can interpret it. But I have heard it said of you that when you hear a dream you can interpret it." Genesis 41:14–15

During the years God has granted me in counseling ministry, I have often come across frustrated workers, especially among the young. Each story, though possessing details unique to the individual, has similar overtones. "I would like to develop my ministry within the church, but the leaders don't give me any support at all." From the person's perspective, their access to ministry is blocked by those who for some reason are hindering its progress.

If this seems true, I would like to ask a question: What chance did Joseph have of progressing toward any meaningful personal plans, languishing in an Egyptian jail as an insignificant slave? Let's discard immediately the notion that he could improve his situation through any effort on his part. Prisoners had no chance of bettering their lot once found behind bars. The help Joseph needed had to come from outside—but who was going to bother about a Hebrew slave condemned by such a powerful figure as Potiphar? Joseph had literally ceased to exist for the rest of the world!

Perhaps you realize how utterly helpless Joseph's situation was. Our options in life may look like this when we imagine that, no matter what direction we move, our way seems obstructed. Unlike Joseph, however, we easily focus on those apparently responsible for our frustration. In our hearts we begin to harbor anger and resentment against them. We feel that if it were not for their meanness, we could surely be in a much better situation.

Let me plainly express the principle today's text points to: The one who opens and closes doors of opportunity is the Lord! No one can stop Him when He has decided to place one of His children in a position of responsibility, whether in the church or in our work. We could be languishing in a jail, forgotten by the world; but when the Lord fixes His eye on us, nobody can hold us back. Don't make the mistake of believing that anyone on the face of this earth possesses the power to stand in your way. Only the Lord creates the opportunities we need to advance to the fullness of His plans.

So what should our attitude be? We should not attack those who don't have authority to order our lives. They have the same limitations we do. We have been called to wait on God's timing, for that moment when Pharaoh's messenger arrives to bring us before princes and governors. Meanwhile, let us imitate Joseph. Let us be model "prisoners" wherever we are today.

Food for Thought

When God stops, nobody can move Him. When God moves, nobody can stop Him.

The Road to Purity

How can a young man keep his way pure? By living according to your word. Psalm 119:9

The question asked by the psalmist is of no little importance because, first of all, purity is a fundamental aspect of the spiritual life. The Apostle Peter writes to God's people, saying: "As obedient children, do not conform to the evil desires you had when you lived in ignorance. But just as he who called you is holy, so be holy in all you do; for it is written: 'Be holy, because I am holy'" (1 Pet. 1:14–16). This is one of the greatest challenges for the church, which should in turn impact a profoundly impure world.

David's question is important for another reason. He wishes to discover precisely how a *young* person can maintain a pure walk. This does not mean the older generation is exempt from this responsibility. However, it is of particular importance that the young discover the secret of purity, because they are in a stage of life when temptations hold an especially seductive power. Young people have not yet acquired the maturity or wisdom to discern the outcome of the many alluring proposals offered by the world. The answer in the psalm is short, simple and absolutely to the point. What they have to do is *keep* the word.

I would like to consider for a moment what this answer does not include. David is not saying that purity is achieved by means of memorizing Bible texts, although this discipline certainly brings great blessing. He is not indicating that purity can be obtained through the diligent study of Scripture. Neither do we gain purity by listening to sound biblical preaching. All these activities can doubtless help the task proposed by the psalmist, but none of them can take its place.

I believe it is important to stress this because it is very easy to grow confused, believing that these Bible-based activities are practically the same thing as the path indicated by the psalmist. However, David's reply is very clear. Purity is a result of *keeping* the Word. And what exactly does this mean? Fulfill, obey, follow, practice, execute, live, do, exercise—I think the implication is clear. Purity can only be achieved when we determine that all our actions, at every moment, every day will be directed by the Lord's eternal designs.

Notice that purity is not realized through an elaborate strategy to avoid evil. In too many congregations the focus of the Christian life is a long list of sins to avoid. David indicates that we become pure by walking in the truth—a much healthier, attractive posture for us. When we live rightly, the wrong is automatically excluded from our lives. It is well worth keeping His Word!

Food for Thought

What Word is the Lord speaking into your life at this time? What steps are you taking to keep it? What results have you seen?

27 December The "Gospel" of Aggression

When the disciples James and John saw this, they asked, "Lord, do you want us to call fire down from heaven to destroy them?" But Jesus turned and rebuked them. Luke 9:54–55

Human beings have never been renowned for their capacity to tolerate those with views different from their own. Intolerance can degenerate into discrimination at school, work or society in general. When taken to its most despicable extreme, it can bring about murder, rioting and war. These things reveal how far we have fallen from the generous spirit of God our Creator. However much we deplore these attitudes, we should not be surprised by them.

We should be surprised, however, when intolerance becomes rooted in the church—the visible representative of the Father's grace extended to a fallen world. On His way to Jerusalem, Jesus had sent some of His disciples ahead to prepare a place in the villages they would pass through. In one of these, a Samaritan village, He was denied hospitality. The hostile reception Jesus received from these people provoked the disciples' irate reaction.

The disciples did appeal to a biblical precedent in the rash proposal they made to the Lord. But they did not understand that the spirit with which Elijah had confronted the prophets of Baal was completely different from the one they were demonstrating now. On that occasion the prophet had faced a group of religious leaders who were spreading idolatry throughout an entire nation. But in this case the Samaritans concerned were simply unwilling to welcome Christ. This trivial episode awoke the surprising request for revenge in the disciples.

Jesus pointed out that they had no idea who they were serving, for they were clearly out of line with the Son of God, who had not come to bring condemnation, but life. This is the essence of the gospel, which we have not always managed to grasp correctly. If we remember how much patience the Lord showed us before we accepted His invitation to join His family, it would help us be more merciful to others. Conversion is more a process than a moment, and the method by which people are most drawn is love.

It is precisely lack of love that often keeps unbelievers from being convinced by what we say. They sense that if they do not accept the gospel, they will receive condemnation from us. They understand that it is not a pure love that motivates us, and so we do not succeed in touching their hearts. But their initial rejection could be a precious God-given opportunity for us to persevere in this work of love. It will certainly surprise them when we continue to love, whether or not they believe in the good news we announce. Perhaps this, more than our eloquence, will eventually lead them to reconciliation with the Lord.

Food for Thought

"He who demands mercy and shows none ruins the bridge over which he himself must pass." (Thomas Adams) [9]

A Healthy Perspective

Now while he was in Jerusalem at the Passover Feast, many people saw the miraculous signs he was doing and believed in his name. But Jesus would not entrust himself to them, for he knew all men. He did not need man's testimony about man, for he knew what was in a man. John 2:23–25

How easy it is for us to get carried away by peoples' enthusiasm at a given moment. When we see people respond with fervor to the proclamation of the Word, making vows of submission and renewed commitment, a kind of general fervor takes hold of the church. We declare that God has visited us or that an amazing move of the Spirit has taken place in our midst. This is perhaps why it has become common for preachers to lead people into showing their approval of the message through public manifestations.

People also responded enthusiastically to Jesus' ministry. The evangelist tells us that many believed when they saw the signs He performed. Nevertheless, John clarifies what Jesus' attitude was to these responses, which were based on passing emotions: The Son of God did not trust them. That is, He was not impressed by the vows they made at that moment, nor did He give much importance to the crowd's response. What was the reason for this lack of trust? "He did not need man's testimony about man, for he knew what was in a man."

This phrase offers an explanation as to why Christ's behavior so often contradicts what we would have done in a similar situation. Jesus knew that the rebelliousness rooted in man's heart would not give way in a moment's religious fervor. Only the prolonged, intense working of the Spirit can achieve genuine transformation, thus making room for the Father's grace. In this sense, therefore, one does not advance spiritually in sudden leaps and bounds, but in a daily walk which is sustained by patience and perseverance.

It is important that those of us who have pastoral responsibility in God's house do not encourage these kinds of expressions. I don't mean to say we can never call people to publicly demonstrate their faith and spiritual conviction. It is good occasionally for the members of a congregation to have opportunity to give public testimony of their spiritual convictions. The problem develops when this becomes a ritual in every meeting, for we are encouraging people to believe that these are the moments in which the most important spiritual experiences occur. In reality, the major changes in our lives unfold when we put the Word into practice within the framework of our daily lives. When God's people do not correctly understand this, they become addicted to attending meetings. It is our responsibility to help them see a balanced perspective on walking in newness of life.

Food for Thought

"God is more concerned with the state of peoples' hearts than with their feelings." (A.W. Tozer)[10]

Living in Isolation

An unfriendly man pursues selfish ends; he defies all sound judgment. Proverbs 18:1

The book of Proverbs offers abundant words of wisdom and good advice to those who seek to walk according to the Lord's precepts. Today we see one of the many pearls of wisdom available to God's people.

The Spanish Good News Version translates this verse: "People who do not get along with others are interested only in themselves; they will disagree with what everyone else knows is right." The language is simple and direct, offering a precise description of behavior we see around us all the time. But we run a risk in reading this text. We can be so busy identifying the people described by this verse that we neglect personal reflection on the subject, which would be much more useful to us.

It is obvious that people who isolate themselves are interested only in their own needs. To develop a compassionate, generous heart, it is absolutely necessary to be in contact with others. However, isolation is a natural tendency in those who have been affected by sin. The first thing Adam and Eve did after sinning was to hide from each other and from their Creator. Even when surrounded by people, we can insulate ourselves from others. Think about a believer who avoids contact with sinners, or a congregation that stays away from other church groups, or even those within a congregation who only fellowship with those like them. The fact is that it is not necessary for people to deliberately isolate themselves, since it is a normal result of our heart's natural tendencies.

The danger is in believing that we do not have this problem. Nevertheless, the author of Proverbs gives an interesting clue for evaluating whether or not we are avoiding meaningful contact with others.

We are told that a secluded person "defies all sound judgment." This reaction should not surprise us, since those who live away from others do not enjoy the wisdom or breadth of vision that can only come from human interaction. For such people, the advice of others inevitably causes conflict with their own interests, so they will always react inappropriately. They do not realize that this very reaction can provide revelation on the state of their own heart.

Food for Thought

How do you react when given advice? Do you receive it happily? Do you get tangled up in arguments and explanations to justify your behavior? Your reaction may be the best demonstration of whether you are living in isolation or are developing meaningful relationships. After being in ministry for some time, it is easy for leaders to start believing that they are the only ones who know how things should be done. But wise leaders will always be open not only to listening, but also to accepting advice from those in their circle of friends.

Unhindered Prayers

Husbands, in the same way be considerate as you live with your wives, and treat them with respect as the weaker partner and as heirs with you of the gracious gift of life, so that nothing will hinder your prayers. 1 Peter 3:7

This verse in Peter's first epistle gives the most trustworthy proof that spiritual life cannot be divorced from daily living. Although many Christians live two totally different lives—inside and outside the church—to the Lord it is only one life. When disciples' experiences in the so-called "secular world" contradict the statements of truth they make when with the congregation, their relationship with God is seriously affected.

The particular example chosen by the apostle addresses married life, the sphere in which a person's spiritual commitment can best be measured. It is easy to "love" somebody we see only a few hours each week, but it is a real challenge to show love and compassion to those not easily impressed by our words. This is why God calls the couple to reserve the best investment of their spiritual life for the home, since there they will see the truest expression of commitment to Christ.

This is valuable for learning to love; but it is also important because it affects our relationship with the Lord. Speaking to husbands, Peter indicates that they should live wisely with their wives in a "considerate" way. This demands that men make an effort to enter their wives' world, resisting the common tendency of relating to their wives as if they were men. When they begin to understand life from their wife's perspective, they can truly begin to love.

The process of drawing close with this understanding attitude will guarantee unhindered access to the Lord in prayer. What does the apostle mean by this? He is writing of prayer that flows naturally before the Father, guided and energized by the Spirit. All effective prayer has its origin in the person of God Himself, so that to pray without hindrance means to know the Father's guidance and the burdens on His heart. Only those who are putting their natural selfishness aside can enjoy this freedom, and this kind of prayer is affected by the daily reality of matrimony.

This principle can be applied to other spheres of life. People who pray with bitterness in their heart cannot enjoy a full spiritual life. Disciples who try to relate to the Lord while continuing in disobedience to a particular word from Him can certainly not enter freely into His presence. It is fundamental for every child of God, and especially those who shepherd His flock, to draw no distinction between what happens in the spiritual sphere of our lives and the world of our everyday activities. The best school for prayer is precisely those ordinary moments that are a part of each day.

Food for Thought

What is your everyday life like? What attitudes can those around you see? What does this display about the way you practice your spirituality?

31 December

Getting Our Feet Wet!

So when the people broke camp to cross the Jordan, the priests carrying the ark of the covenant went ahead of them. Now the Jordan is at flood stage all during harvest. Yet as soon as the priests who carried the ark reached the Jordan and their feet touched the water's edge, the water from upstream stopped flowing. It piled up in a heap a great distance away.
Joshua 3:14–16

The people accompanying Joshua on the adventure to conquer the Promised Land were not the ones who had so severely tested Moses' patience during forty years in the desert. That earlier generation, according to the Lord's own testimony, was a perverse generation completely lacking in faith (Num. 14:26–35). This new group had learned, perhaps the hard way, the importance of obeying Jehovah's commands. Nevertheless, the challenge set before them by the Lord had real elements of risk, as do all adventures of faith even today. God had instructed Joshua that the priests were to take the Ark and begin to cross the river. The Lord had told him that the river would open before them, allowing the entire nation to cross. But the priests would have to step into the water and get their feet wet before the miracle would occur.

I would like to freeze the scene at the exact moment the waters splashed around their ankles. This is the instant immediately preceding God's intervention, when we are most susceptible to abandoning the venture we have begun. It is precisely then that doubts crowd our mind and fear fills our hearts. God has promised to part the waters, but we are already in the river and nothing has happened. If we continue, we will have to start swimming. Have we correctly interpreted His word to us? And perhaps we have never encountered a similar experience that can strengthen us now. Of those present at the river, only Joshua and Caleb had ever seen waters part to allow the chosen people through.

We all love the end of the story, when the people have reached the other side of the river. We want to be among those who joyfully celebrate the intervention of the Most High. But very few are willing to get their feet wet; few will gamble on the Lord's "crazy" plans when the element of risk is at its highest.

This stage in the adventure is the most uncomfortable. God's people are in danger of looking like fools. However, this is where the difference should be seen in those who are committed. They will not hesitate to move forward to what God has set before them. Armed with the same courage as Joshua, they will pay no attention to fearful voices. They know in whom they have put their trust. The challenging moment will pass, and they will be counted among those who celebrate the victory of the Lord.

Food for Thought

"Courage does not mean the absence of fear, but the adequate management of fear." (Anonymous)

Endnotes

January

1. Richard Foster, *Prayer* (San Francisco: Harper Collins, 1992), p. 9.
2. Thomas Goodwin in John Blanchard, ed., *Gathered Gold* (Durham, UK: Evangelical Press, 1984), p. 202.
3. Christian Schwarz, *Natural Church Development* (Carol Stream, IL: Church Smart Resources, 1996), pp. 46–47.
4. Samuel Wilberforce in John Blanchard, ed., *More Gathered Gold* (Hertfordshire, UK: Evangelical Press, 1986), p. 158.
5. Howard Hendricks, *The Seven Laws of the Teacher* (Atlanta: Walk Thru the Bible Ministries, 1987), p. 27.
6. Norman Grubb, *The Deep Things of God* (Fort Washington, PA: Christian Literature Crusade, 1958), ch. 2.
7. Henri Nouwen, *The Life of the Beloved* (New York: Crossroad, 1995), p. 67.
8. Larry Crabb, *Finding God* (Grand Rapids: Zondervan, 1993), p. 29.

February

1. Foster, *Prayer*, p. 191.
2. Gordon MacDonald, *Ordering Your Private World* (Nashville: Oliver Nelson Books, 1985), p. 76.
3. Matthew Henry in Blanchard, ed., *More Gathered Gold*, p. 204.
4. Cyril Powell, *Secrets of Answered Prayer* (New York: Thomas Y. Crowell Company, 1958), p. 72.
5. D.L. Moody, source unknown.
6. Hendricks, *The Seven Laws of the Teacher*, p. 98.
7. Thomas Kelly, *A Testament of Devotion* (New York: Harper and Brothers, 1941), pp. 29–30.
8. Donald Barnhouse in Blanchard, ed., *Gathered Gold*, p. 294.
9. Gordon MacDonald, source unknown.
10. Dick Eastman, *No Easy Road* (Grand Rapids: Baker, 1983), p. 100.
11. W.E. Sangster in Blanchard, ed., *Gathered Gold*, p. 225.
12. Dwight L. Moody in Charles Swindoll, "Moses: God's Man for a Crisis" (taped sermon). Published in booklet form by W Publishing Group, Nashville, 1986.
13. Oscar Wilde in "Annabelle's Quotation Guide." http://www.annabelle.net/topicsauthor.php?firstname=Oscar&lastname=Wilde (Accessed August 15, 2008).
14. Henry in Blanchard, ed., *Gathered Gold*, p. 134.

March

1. Martin Luther in Blanchard, ed., *Gathered Gold*, p. 138.
2. Augustine, source unknown.
3. Charles Swindoll, *Strengthening Your Grip* (Nashville: Thomas Nelson, 2003).
4. Henry in Blanchard, ed., *More Gathered Gold*, p. 338.
5. David Sarnoff in Blanchard, ed., *More Gathered Gold*, p. 221.
6. Source unknown.
7. Augustine, source unknown.
8. Dr. J. Robert Clinton, source unknown.
9. Oswald Chambers in Blanchard, ed., *Gathered Gold*, p. 286.
10. Paul Moody in Blanchard, ed., *More Gathered Gold*, p. 292.
11. Robert Murray M'Cheyne in Blanchard, ed., *Gathered Gold*, p. 155.
12. Phillips Brooks in Blanchard, ed., *More Gathered Gold*, p. 158.
13. Hendricks, *The Seven Laws of the Teacher*, p. 62.
14. D.L. Moody in Blanchard, ed., *More Gathered Gold*, p. 193.
15. Richard Foster, *Celebration of Discipline* (San Francisco: Harper and Row, 1978), p. 164.

April

1. Kelly, *A Testament of Devotion*, p. 39.
2. John A. James in Blanchard, ed., *More Gathered Gold*, p. 293.
3. Augustine in Foster, *Prayer*, p. 1.
4. Foster, *Prayer*, p. 1.
5. Ignacio Larrañaga, *Encuentro* (Santiago de Chile: Ediciones San Pablo, 1994), p. 19.
6. Crabb, *Finding God*, p. 172.
7. Henry Smith in Blanchard, ed., *More Gathered Gold*, p. 297.
8. William Plumer in Blanchard, ed., *Gathered Gold*, p. 111.
9. Henry and Richard Blackaby, *Spiritual Leadership* (Nashville: Broadman and Holman, 2001), p. 42.
10. Dallas Willard, *The Spirit of the Disciplines* (San Francisco: Harper and Row, 1988), p. 179.
11. Dietrich Bonhoeffer, source unknown.
12. A.W. Tozer in Blanchard, ed., *More Gathered Gold*, p. 49.

May

1. Charles Hodge in Blanchard, ed., *Gathered Gold*, p. 130.
2. Jim Kouzes and Barry Posner in Blackaby and Blackaby, *Spiritual Leadership*, p. 104.
3. Henry in Blanchard, ed., *More Gathered Gold*, p. 251.
4. Elisabeth Elliot in Blanchard, ed., *Gathered Gold*, p. 94.
5. Foster, *Prayer*, pp. 19–20.

June

1. Colin Brown, ed., *The New International Dictionary of New Testament Theology*, Vol. II (Grand Rapids: Zondervan, 1977), p. 115.
2. Thomas Chisholm, "Great is Thy Faithfulness" (hymn), 1923.
3. Statement commonly known as "John Wesley's Rule," source disputed.
4. Augustus Strong in Blanchard, ed., *Gathered Gold*, p. 134.
5. J.C. Ryle in Blanchard, ed., *More Gathered Gold*, p. 276.
6. Augustine in Ignacio Larrañaga, *Muéstrame tu Rostro* (Mexico City: Librería Parroquial, 1996), p. 114.
7. J.A. Motyer in Blanchard, ed., Gathered Gold, p. 219.
8. Charles H. Spurgeon in Blanchard, ed., *Gathered Gold*, p. 144.

July

1. Walter Hendricksen, *Disciples Are Made Not Born* (Victor Books: Wheaton, 1974).
2. Juan Carlos Ortiz in Blanchard, ed., *Gathered Gold*, p. 68.
3. Hendricks, *The Seven Laws of the Teacher*, p. 104.
4. Bruce Wilkinson, *The Seven Laws of the Learner*, Course Notebook (Atlanta: Walk Thru the Bible Ministries, 1988), p. 28.
5. Moody in Blanchard, ed., *Gathered Gold*, p. 19.
6. John Wesley in Blanchard, ed., *Gathered Gold*, p. 16.
7. Augustine in Blanchard, ed., *Gathered Gold*, p. 121.
8. Vance Havner in Blanchard, ed., *More Gathered Gold*, p. 76.
9. Thomas Manton in Blanchard, ed., *More Gathered Gold*, p. 202.
10. Watchman Nee, source unknown.
11. Augustine in Blanchard, ed., *Gathered Gold*, p. 95.

August

1. Foster, *Celebration of Discipline*, p. 30.
2. Henry Blackaby, *Spiritual Leadership*, p. 30.
3. Calvin Miller, *Leadership* (Colorado Springs: Navpress, 1987), p. 78.
4. Foster, *Celebration of Discipline*, p. 98.
5. Booklet on New Testament gifts by British theologian, source unknown.
6. Billy Graham, in Blanchard, ed., *Gathered Gold*, p. 83.

September

1. Thomas Watson, in Blanchard, ed., *More Gathered Gold*, p. 297.
2. Blaise Pascal in Blanchard, ed., *More Gathered Gold*, p. 258.
3. Foster, *Celebration of Discipline*, p. 86.
4. Alexander Balmain Bruce in Blanchard, ed., *More Gathered Gold*, p. 160.

October

1. A.W. Tozer, *The Best of A.W. Tozer* (Harrisburg: Christian Publications, 1978), p. 43.
2. Andrew Jackson in Blanchard, ed., *Gathered Gold*, p. 62.
3. Raymond Lindquist in Blanchard, ed., *More Gathered Gold*, p. 269.

November

1. Erwin Raphael McManus, *Seizing Your Divine Moment* (Nashville: Thomas Nelson Publishers, 2002), p. 34.
2. Luther in Blanchard, ed., *Gathered Gold*, p. 135.
3. J. Oswald Sanders, *Spiritual Leadership* (Chicago: Moody Publishers, 1994).
4. George Barlow in Blanchard, ed., *More Gathered Gold*, p. 138.
5. Andrew Dhuse in Blanchard, ed., *Gathered Gold*, p. 333.
6. Tozer, *The Best of A.W. Tozer*, p. 74.
7. Richard Sibbes in Blanchard, ed., *More Gathered Gold*, p. 107.
8. Emil Brunner in Blanchard, ed., *Gathered Gold*, p. 36.
9. Hendricks, *The Seven Laws of the Teacher*, p. 27.

December

1. Richard Swenson, M.D., *Margin* (Colorado Springs: Navpress, 1992), p. 85.
2. Thomas Fuller in Blanchard, ed., *More Gathered Gold*, p. 204.
3. Benjamin Franklin in Blanchard, ed., *Gathered Gold*, p. 247.
4. Voltaire in Blanchard, ed., *More Gathered Gold*, p. 301.
5. François Fénelon, source unknown.
6. Brooks in Blanchard, ed., *Gathered Gold*, p. 189.
7. Willard, *The Spirit of the Disciplines* (San Francisco: Harper and Row, 1988), p. 179.
8. Dietrich Bonhoeffer in Blanchard, ed., *Gathered Gold*, p. 209.
9. Thomas Adams in Blanchard, ed., *Gathered Gold*, p. 202.
10. Tozer in Blanchard, ed., *More Gathered Gold*, p. 139.

This book was produced by CLC Publications. We hope it has been life-changing and has given you a fresh experience of God through the work of the Holy Spirit. CLC Publications is an outreach of CLC Ministries International, a global literature mission with work in over 50 countries. If you would like to know more about us or are interested in opportunities to serve with a faith mission, we invite you to contact us at:

CLC Ministries International
P.O. Box 1449
Fort Washington, PA 19034

Phone: (215) 542-1242
E-mail: orders@clcpublications.com
Website: www.clcpublications.com

A TABLE IN THE WILDERNESS

Rich daily devotional thoughts from Watchman Nee

When God spreads for us a table in the wilderness, when five loaves provide food for five thousand and leave twelve baskets of fragments, that is blessing! Blessing is fruit out of all relation to what we are. It comes when God works completely beyond our understanding, for His name's sake.

These meditations, drawn from the author's widely varied ministry in China and beyond, share insightful meditations on the glories of Christ. They will draw you to a fresh response to God's all-sufficient grace shown us in the gift of His Son.

Trade Paper ISBN 978-0-87508-699-3

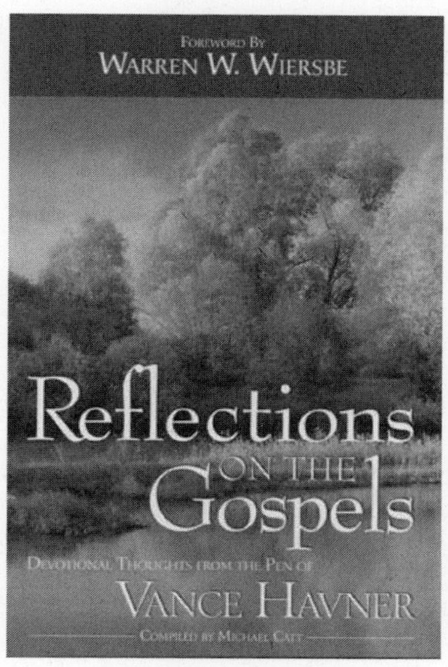

REFLECTIONS ON THE GOSPELS

Vance Havner

Rescued by Michael Catt from a collection of newspaper columns and compiled for the first time in book form, this wonderful volume gives a unique insight into God's Word through the eyes of this great preacher.

Useful as a personal devotional or as a study tool, this book provides an enlightening and inspiring opportunity to spend a few moments with a New Testament prophet.

Trade paper ISBN 978-0-87508-783-3